Kare Kano

his and her circumstances

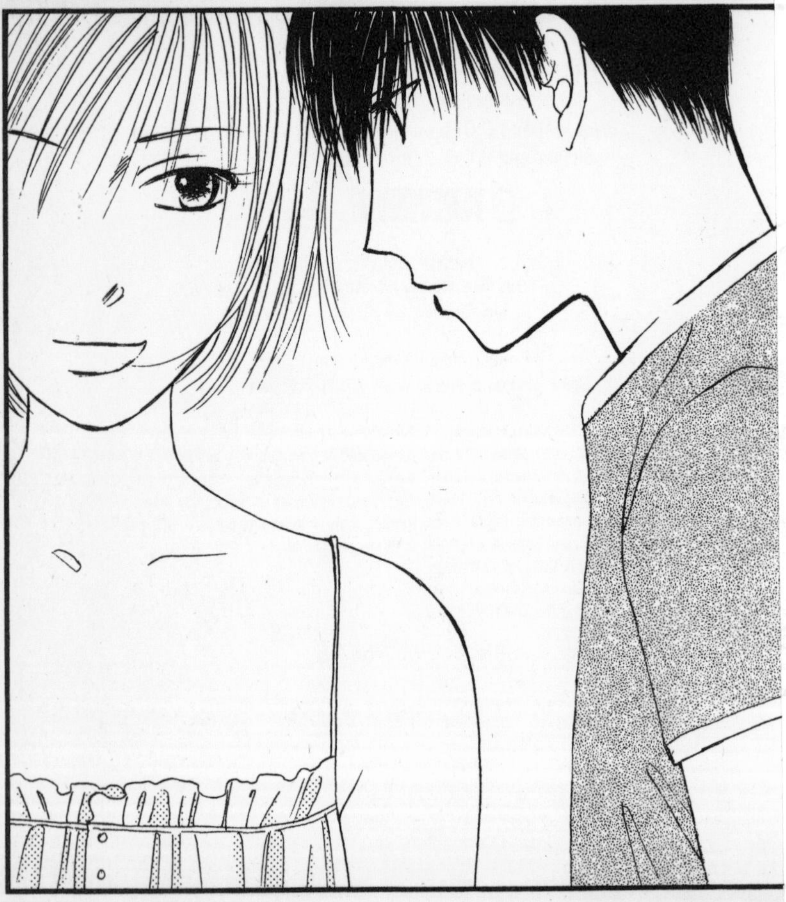

Kare Kano Vol. 13
Created by Masami Tsuda

Translation - Michelle Kobayashi
Additional Translation - Chrissy Schilling
Retouch and Lettering - Vicente Rivera, Jr.
Graphic Designer - Vicente Rivera, Jr.
Cover Design - Gary Shum

Editor - Carol Fox
Digital Imaging Manager - Chris Buford
Pre-Press Manager - Antonio DePietro
Production Managers - Jennifer Miller and Mutsumi Miyazaki
Art Director - Matt Alford
Managing Editor - Jill Freshney
VP of Production - Ron Klamert
President and C.O.O. - John Parker
Publisher and C.E.O. - Stuart Levy

A  Manga

TOKYOPOP Inc.
5900 Wilshire Blvd. Suite 2000
Los Angeles, CA 90036

E-mail: info@TOKYOPOP.com
Come visit us online at www.TOKYOPOP.com

KARESHI KANOJO NO JIJOU All rights reserved. No portion of this book may be
by Masami Tsuda © 2001 Masami Tsuda. reproduced or transmitted in any form or by any means
All rights reserved. First published in Japan in without written permission from the copyright holders.
2002 by HAKUSENSHA, INC., Tokyo This manga is a work of fiction. Any resemblance to
English language translation rights in the actual events or locales or persons, living or dead, is
United States of America and Canada arranged entirely coincidental.
with HAKUSENSHA, INC., Tokyo through
Tuttle-Mori Agency Inc., Tokyo
English text copyright © 2005 TOKYOPOP Inc.

ISBN: 1-59532-587-5

First TOKYOPOP printing: January 2005
10 9 8 7 6 5 4 3 2 1
Printed in the USA

kare kano

his and her circumstances

volume thirteen

by Masami Tsuda

Fic
T
Tsu

NORTH BAY
JUL 26 2010
NORTH BAY
DISCARDED
PUBLIC LIBRARY

HAMBURG // LONDON // LOS ANGELES // TOKYO

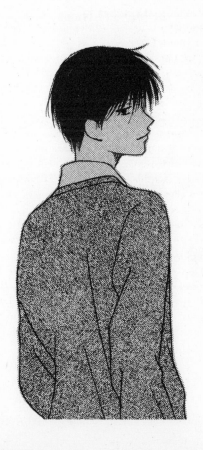

KARE KANO: THE STORY SO FAR

Yukino Miyazawa is the perfect student: kind, athletic and smart. But she's not all she seems. She is really the self-professed "queen of vanity," and her only goal in life is winning the praise and admiration of everyone around her. Therefore, she makes it her business to always look and act perfect during school hours. At home, however, she lets her guard down and lets her true self show.

When Yukino enters high school, she finally meets her match: Soichiro Arima, a handsome, popular, ultra-intelligent guy. Once he steals the top seat in class away from her, Yukino sees him as a bitter rival. Over time, her anger turns to amazement, when she discovers she and Soichiro have more in common than she ever imagined. As their love blossoms, they promise to stop pretending to be perfect and just be true to themselves.

But they have plenty of obstacles in their way. First, Hideaki, the school's token pretty boy, tries to come between them. Then Yukino and Soichiro's grades drop because they've been spending so much time together, and their teacher pressures them to break up. Once that's resolved, two more speed bumps are encountered on their road to romance. Maho, a jealous classmate, is convinced that Yukino is deceiving everyone and vows to turn everyone against her. Then an old friend of Soichiro's from junior high tries to steal Soichiro's affections. Somehow, Yukino and Soichiro's love manages to persevere—even after Soichiro spends the summer away at a kendo tournament. In fact, it makes their romance that much stronger, although Soichiro is dealing with some personal issues.

And now, love is in the air at Hokuei High School! Tsubaki and Tonami have fallen for each other, Maho recently confessed her feelings for Takashi, and Kazuma just proposed to his stepsister Tsubasa! Meanwhile, Yukino and Soichiro are still deeply in love. But graduation will soon be upon them all—and with it will come very serious choices...

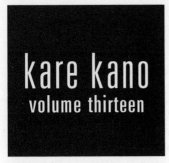

kare kano
volume thirteen

TABLE OF CONTENTS

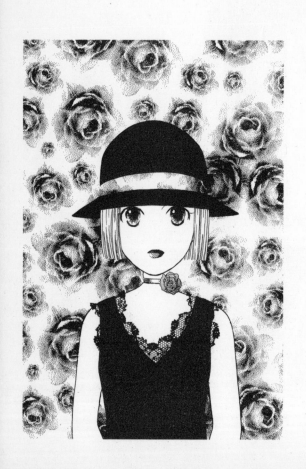

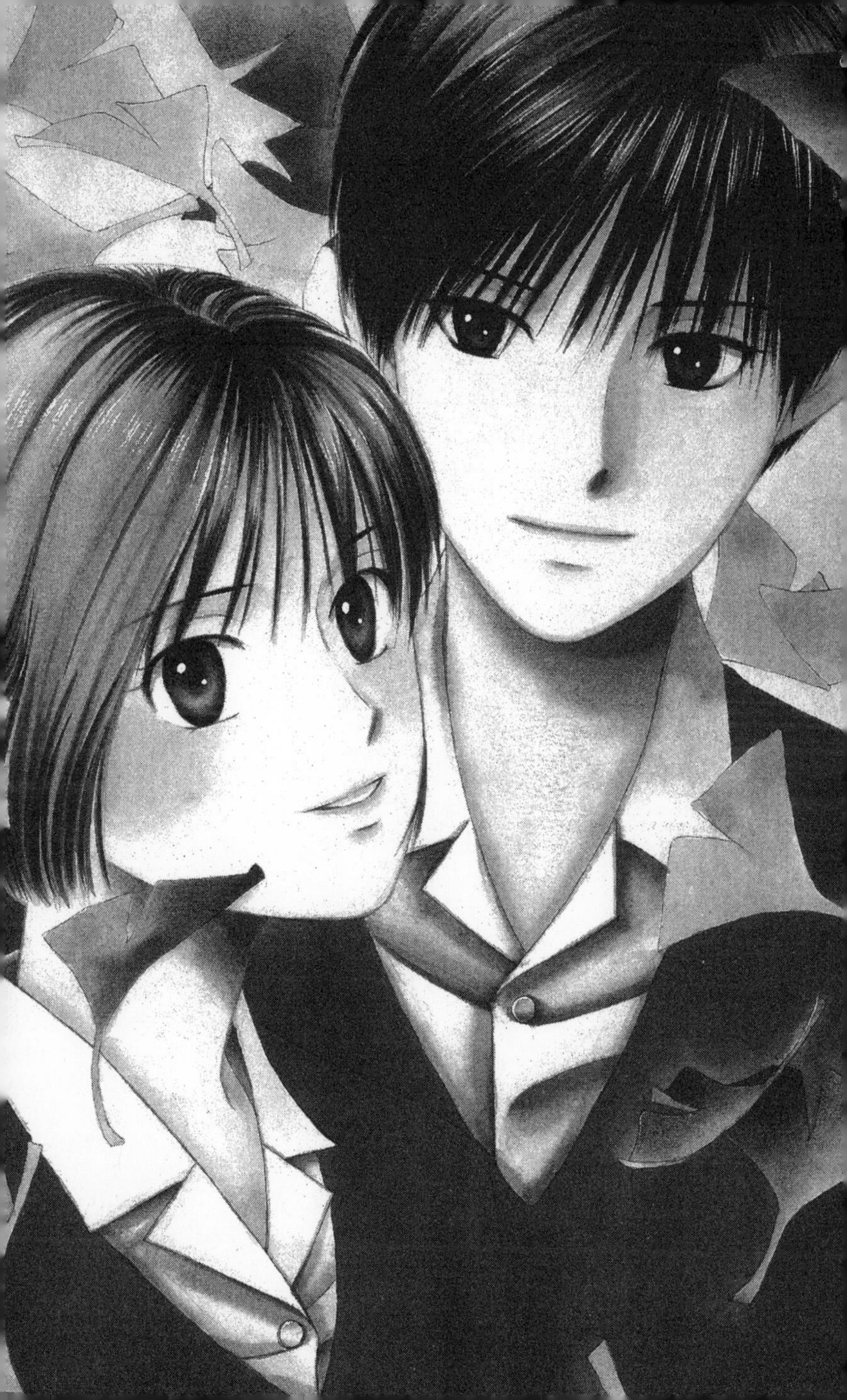

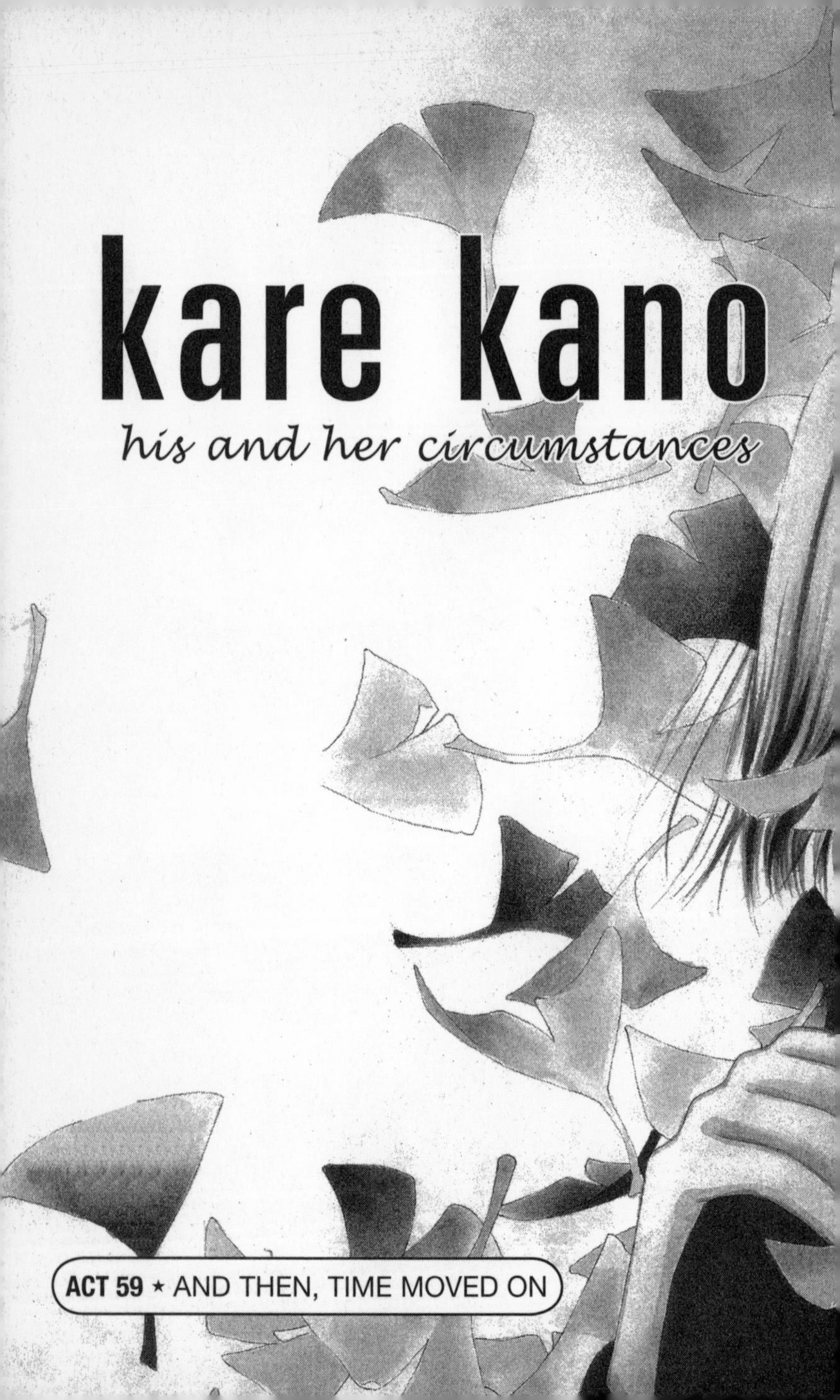
kare kano
his and her circumstances
ACT 59 ★ AND THEN, TIME MOVED ON

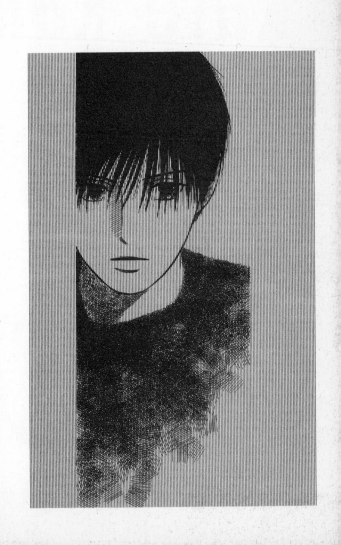

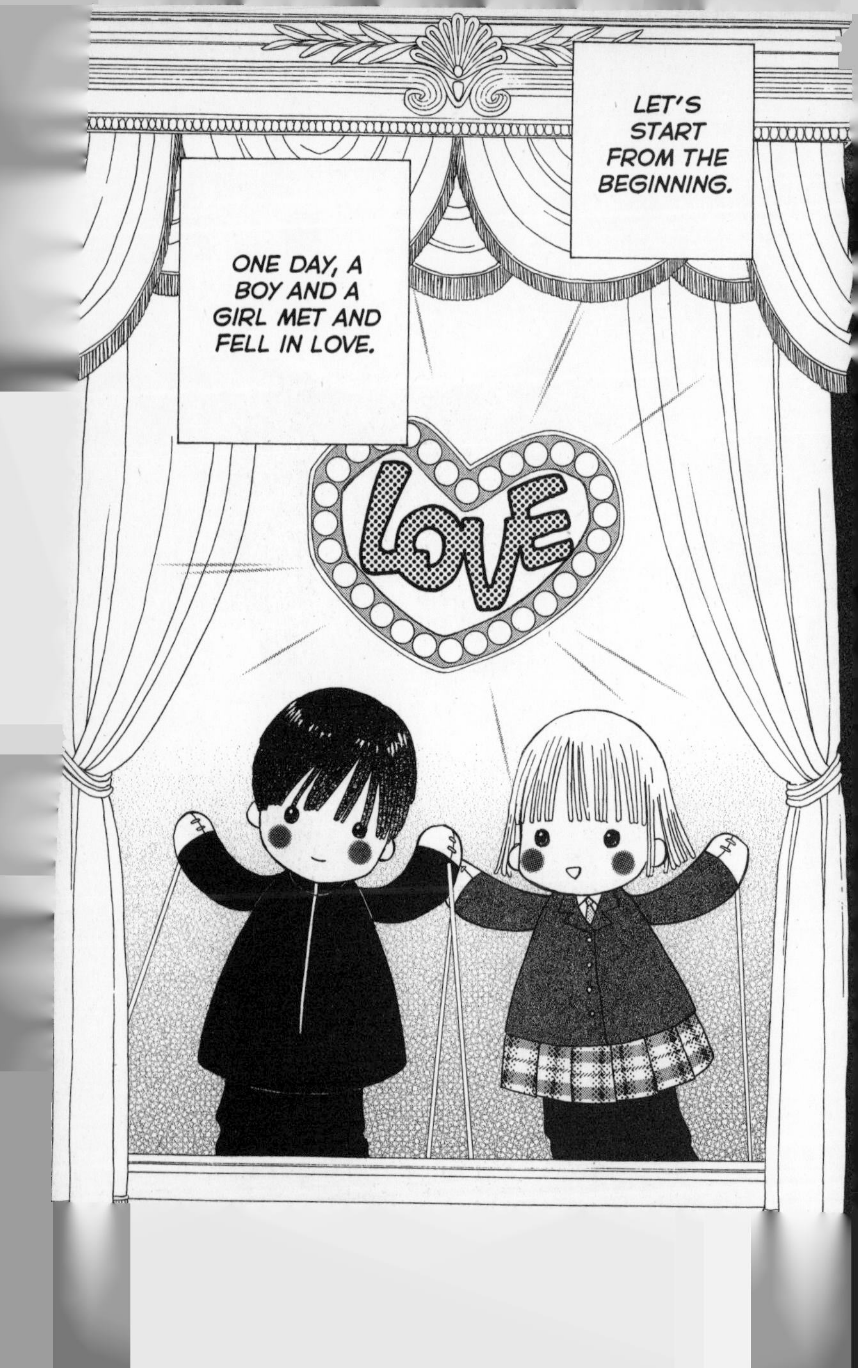
LET'S START FROM THE BEGINNING.
ONE DAY, A BOY AND A GIRL MET AND FELL IN LOVE.
LOVE

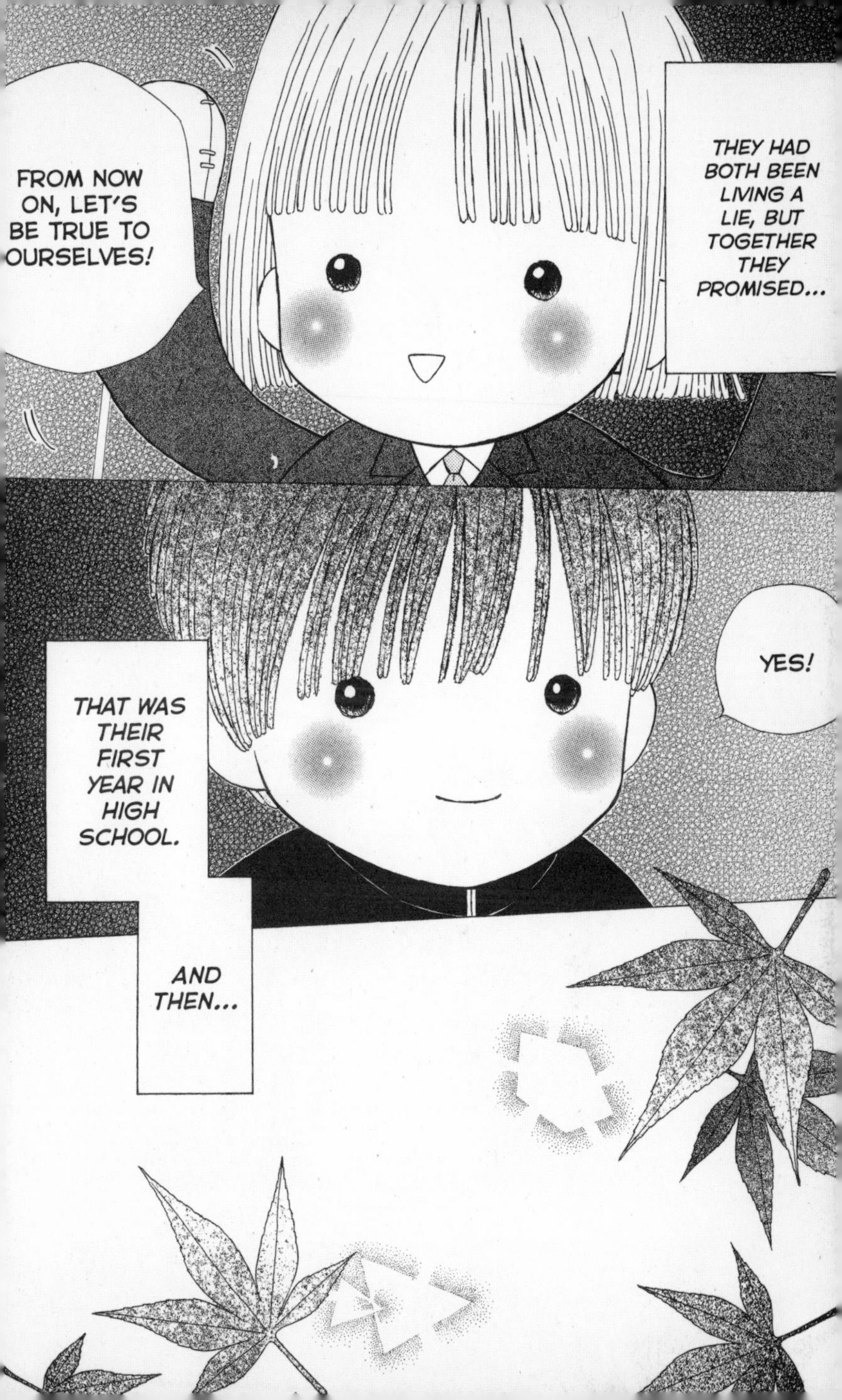
THEY HAD BOTH BEEN LIVING A LIE, BUT TOGETHER THEY PROMISED...
FROM NOW ON, LET'S BE TRUE TO OURSELVES!
YES!
THAT WAS THEIR FIRST YEAR IN HIGH SCHOOL.
AND THEN...

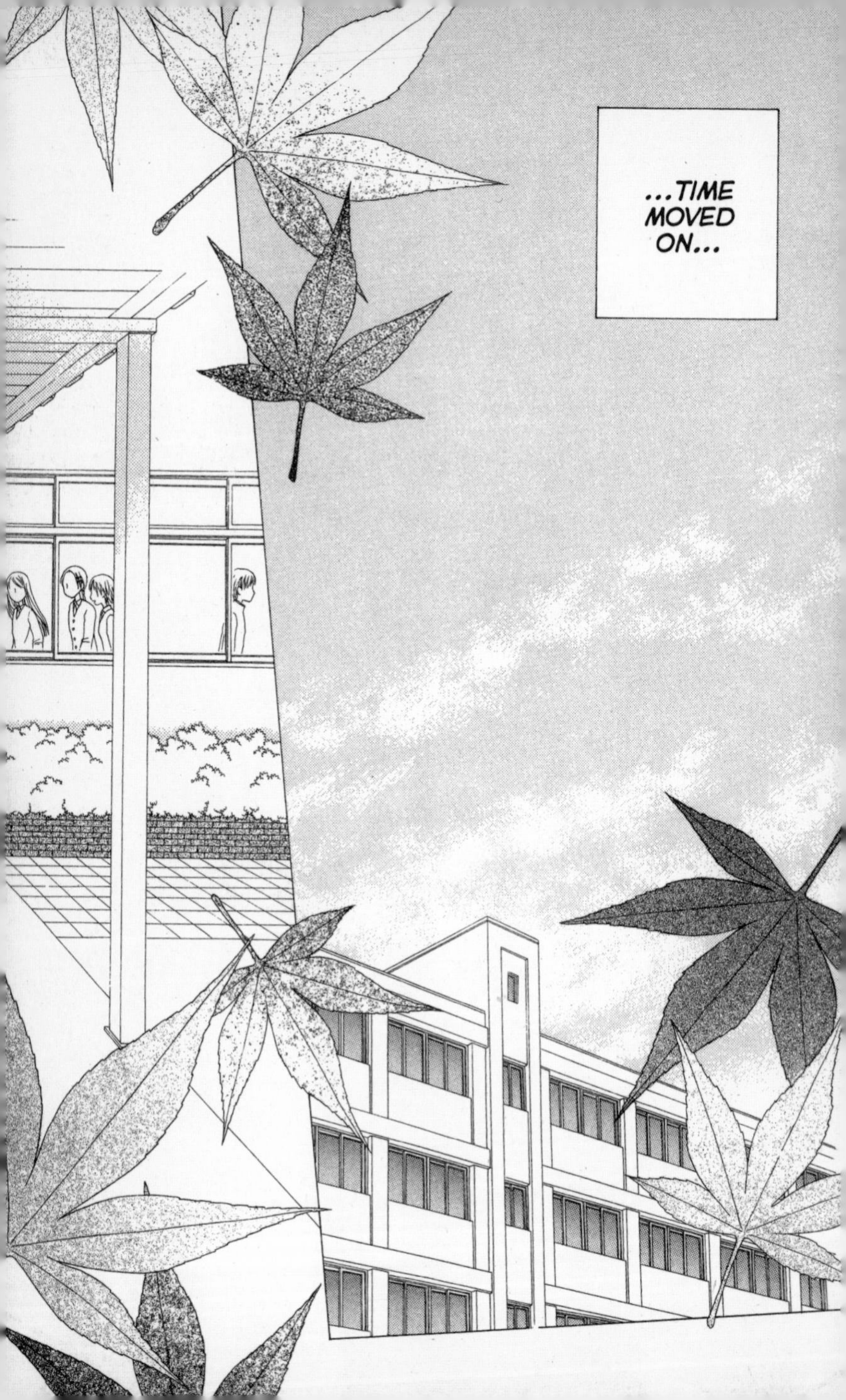
...TIME MOVED ON...

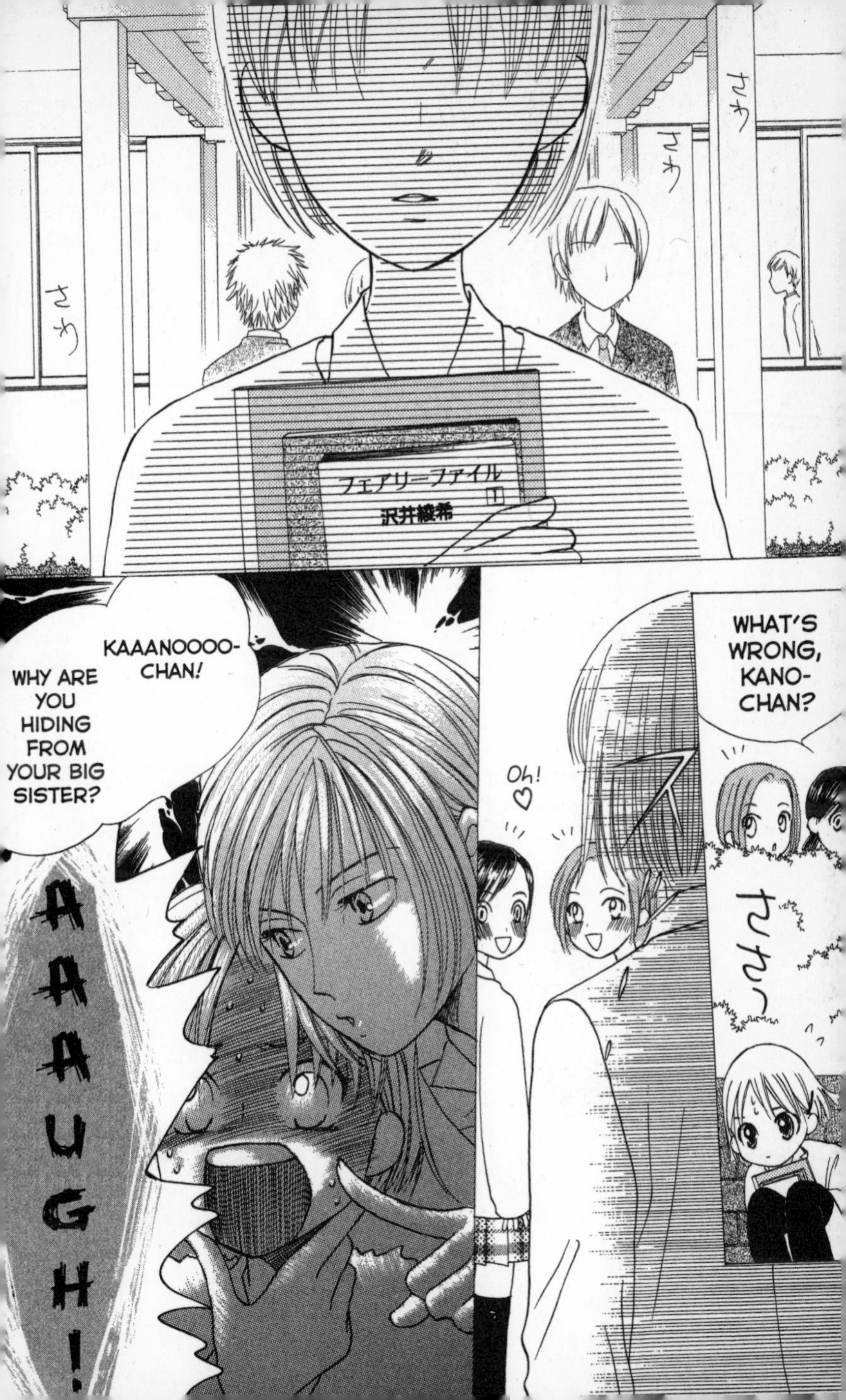
さわ
さわ
さわ
フェアリーファイル 1
沢井綾希
WHAT'S WRONG, KANO-CHAN?
Oh!
さわ
KAAANOOOO-CHAN!
WHY ARE YOU HIDING FROM YOUR BIG SISTER?
AAAAUGH!

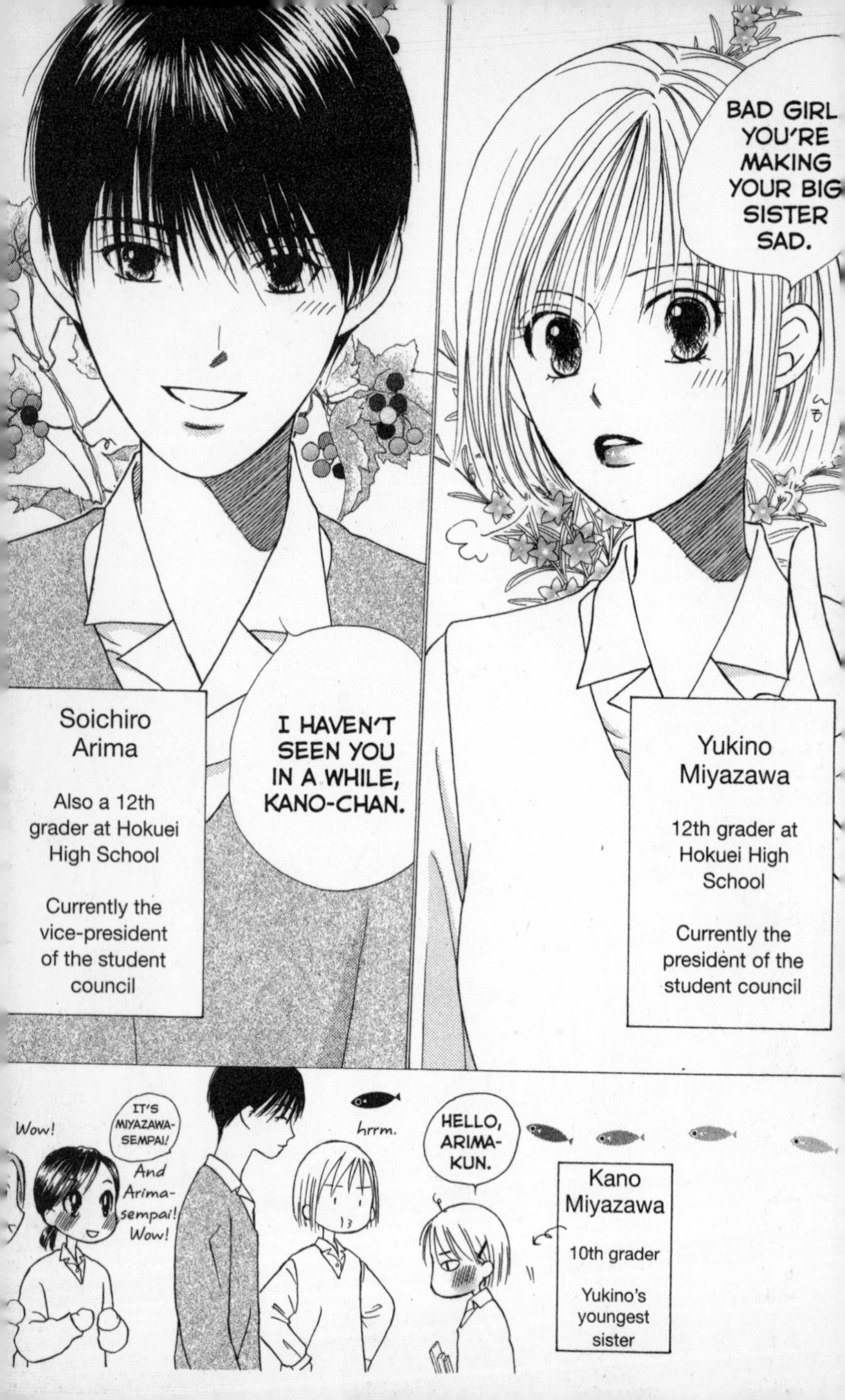
BAD GIRL YOU'RE MAKING YOUR BIG SISTER SAD.
Yukino Miyazawa
12th grader at Hokuei High School
Currently the president of the student council
I HAVEN'T SEEN YOU IN A WHILE, KANO-CHAN.
Soichiro Arima
Also a 12th grader at Hokuei High School
Currently the vice-president of the student council
Kano Miyazawa
10th grader
Yukino's youngest sister
HELLO, ARIMA-KUN.
hrrm.
IT'S MIYAZAWA-SEMPAI!
And Arima-sempai! Wow!
Wow!

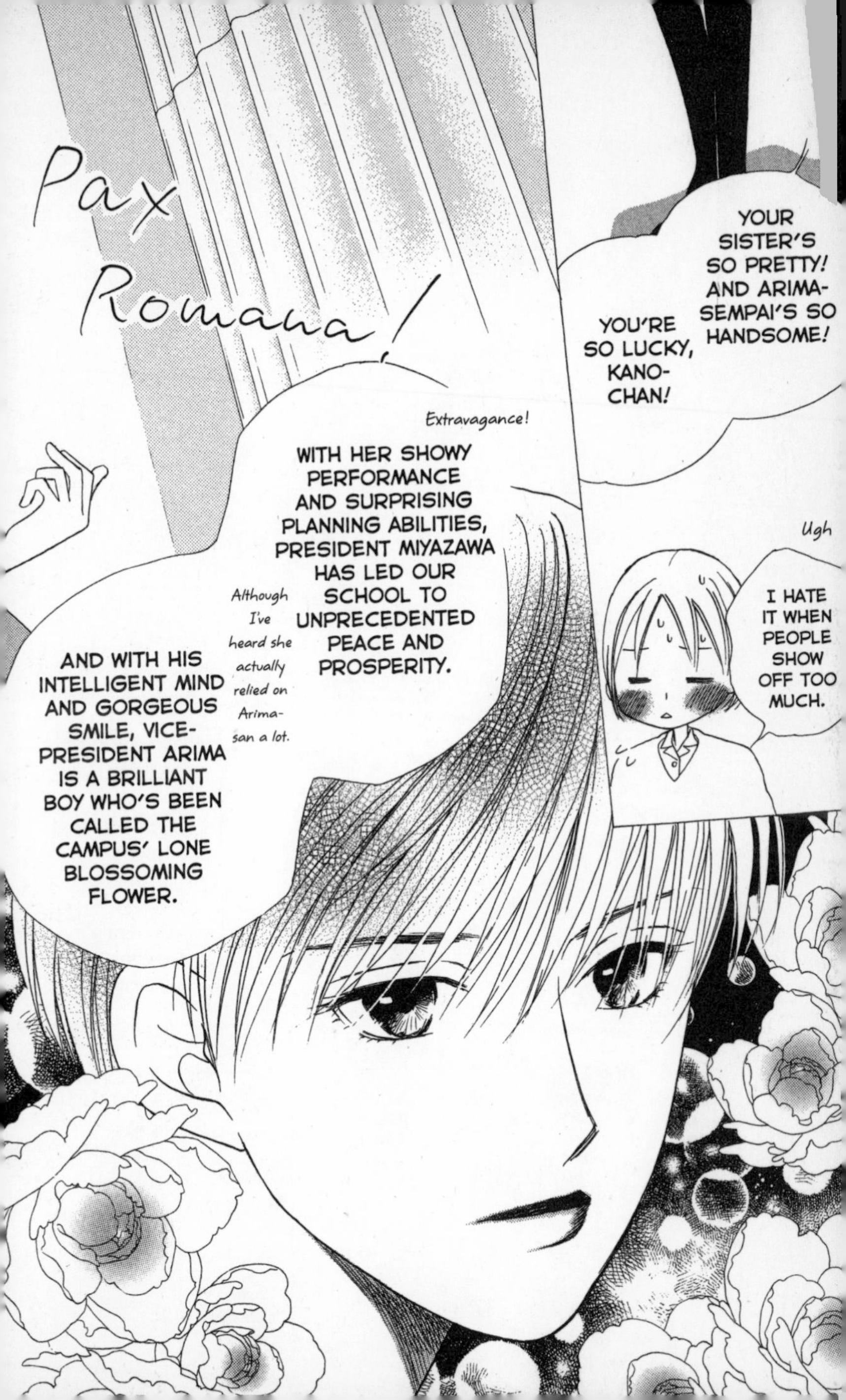
YOUR SISTER'S SO PRETTY! AND ARIMA-SEMPAI'S SO HANDSOME!
YOU'RE SO LUCKY, KANO-CHAN!
Ugh
I HATE IT WHEN PEOPLE SHOW OFF TOO MUCH.
Pax Romana!
Extravagance!
WITH HER SHOWY PERFORMANCE AND SURPRISING PLANNING ABILITIES, PRESIDENT MIYAZAWA HAS LED OUR SCHOOL TO UNPRECEDENTED PEACE AND PROSPERITY.
Although I've heard she actually relied on Arima-san a lot.
AND WITH HIS INTELLIGENT MIND AND GORGEOUS SMILE, VICE-PRESIDENT ARIMA IS A BRILLIANT BOY WHO'S BEEN CALLED THE CAMPUS' LONE BLOSSOMING FLOWER.

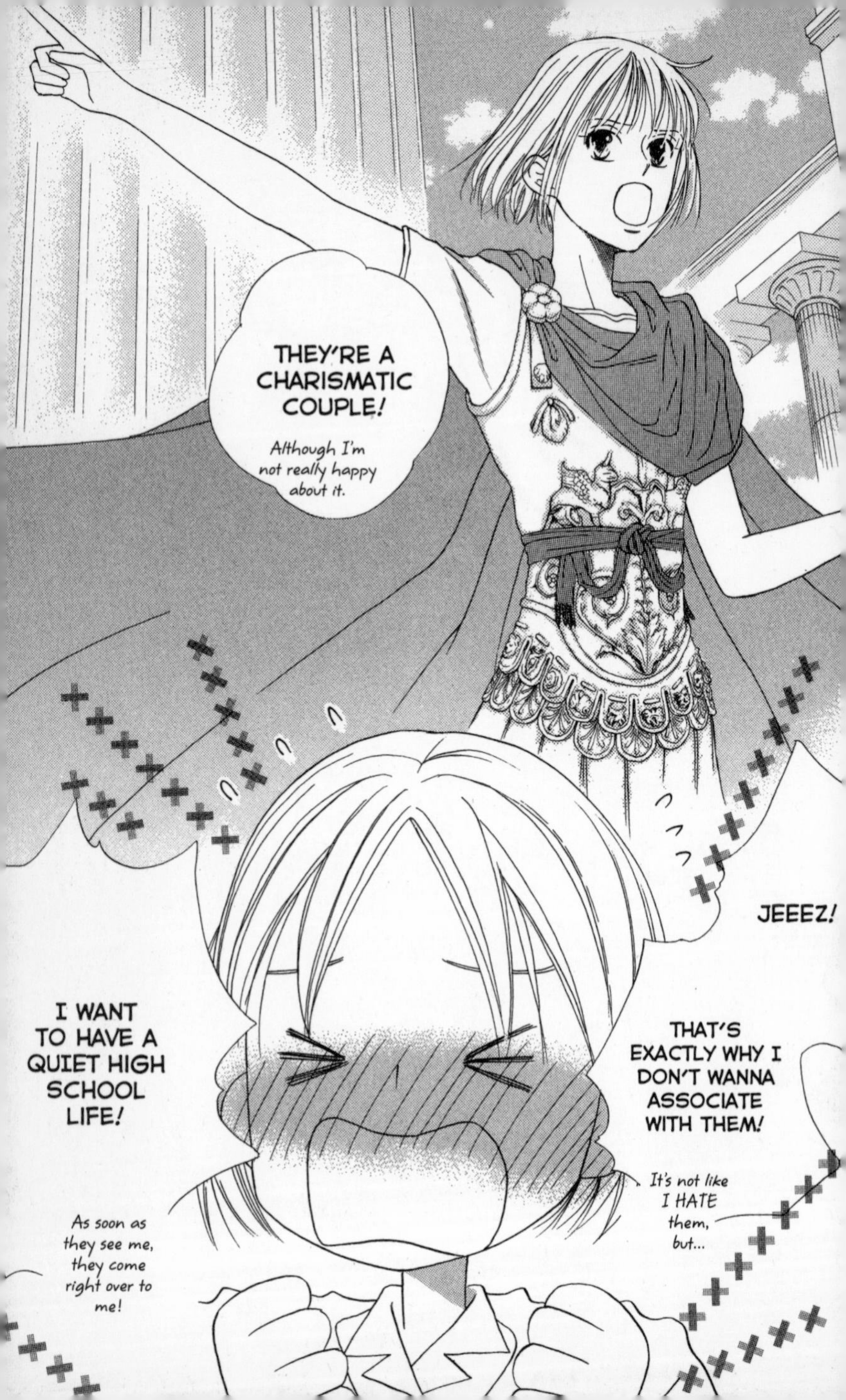
THEY'RE A CHARISMATIC COUPLE!
Although I'm not really happy about it.
JEEEZ!
THAT'S EXACTLY WHY I DON'T WANNA ASSOCIATE WITH THEM!
It's not like I HATE them, but...
I WANT TO HAVE A QUIET HIGH SCHOOL LIFE!
As soon as they see me, they come right over to me!

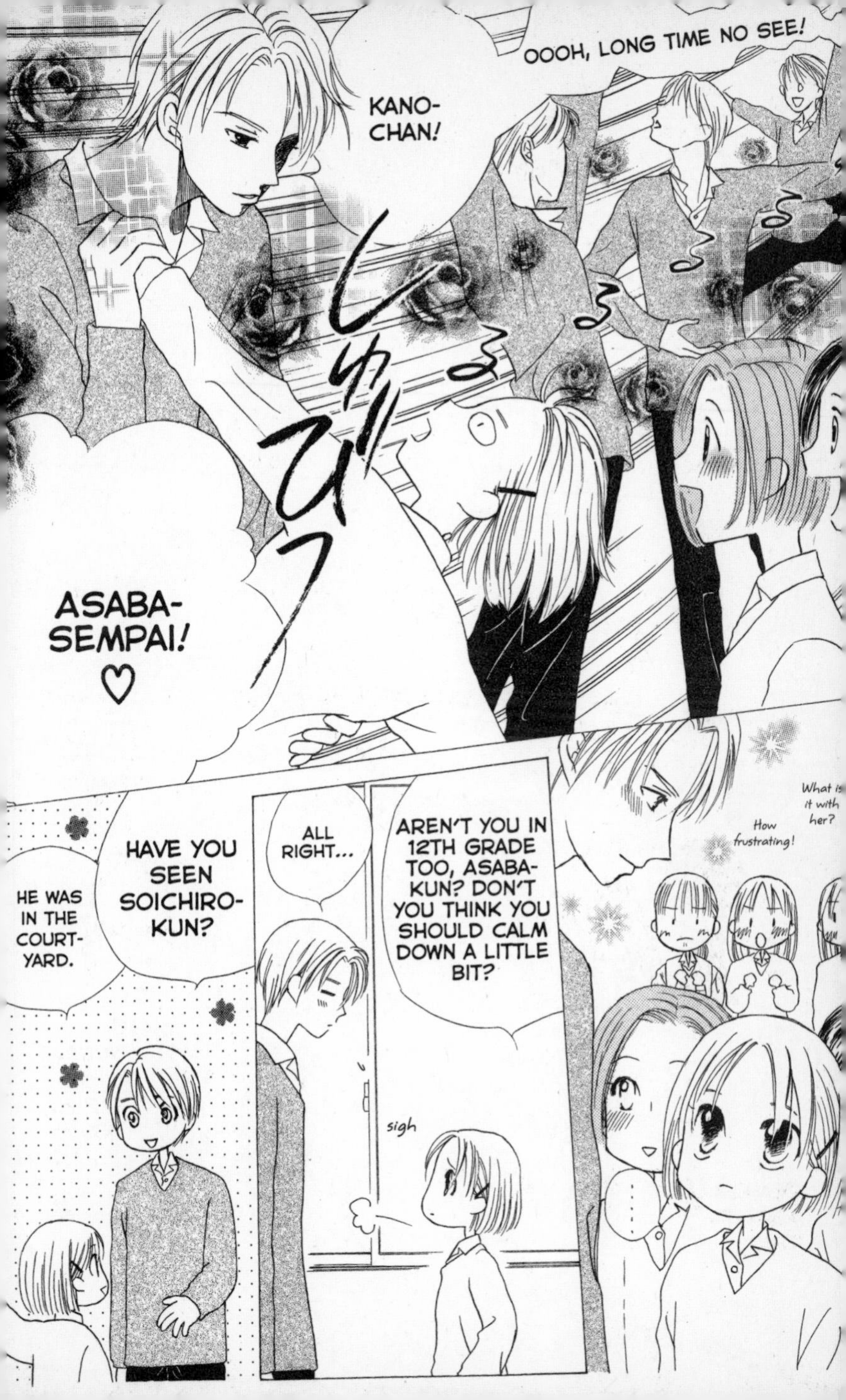
OOOH, LONG TIME NO SEE!
KANO-CHAN!
ASABA-SEMPAI! ♡
What is it with her?
How frustrating!
AREN'T YOU IN 12TH GRADE TOO, ASABA-KUN? DON'T YOU THINK YOU SHOULD CALM DOWN A LITTLE BIT?
ALL RIGHT...
sigh
HAVE YOU SEEN SOICHIRO-KUN?
HE WAS IN THE COURT-YARD.

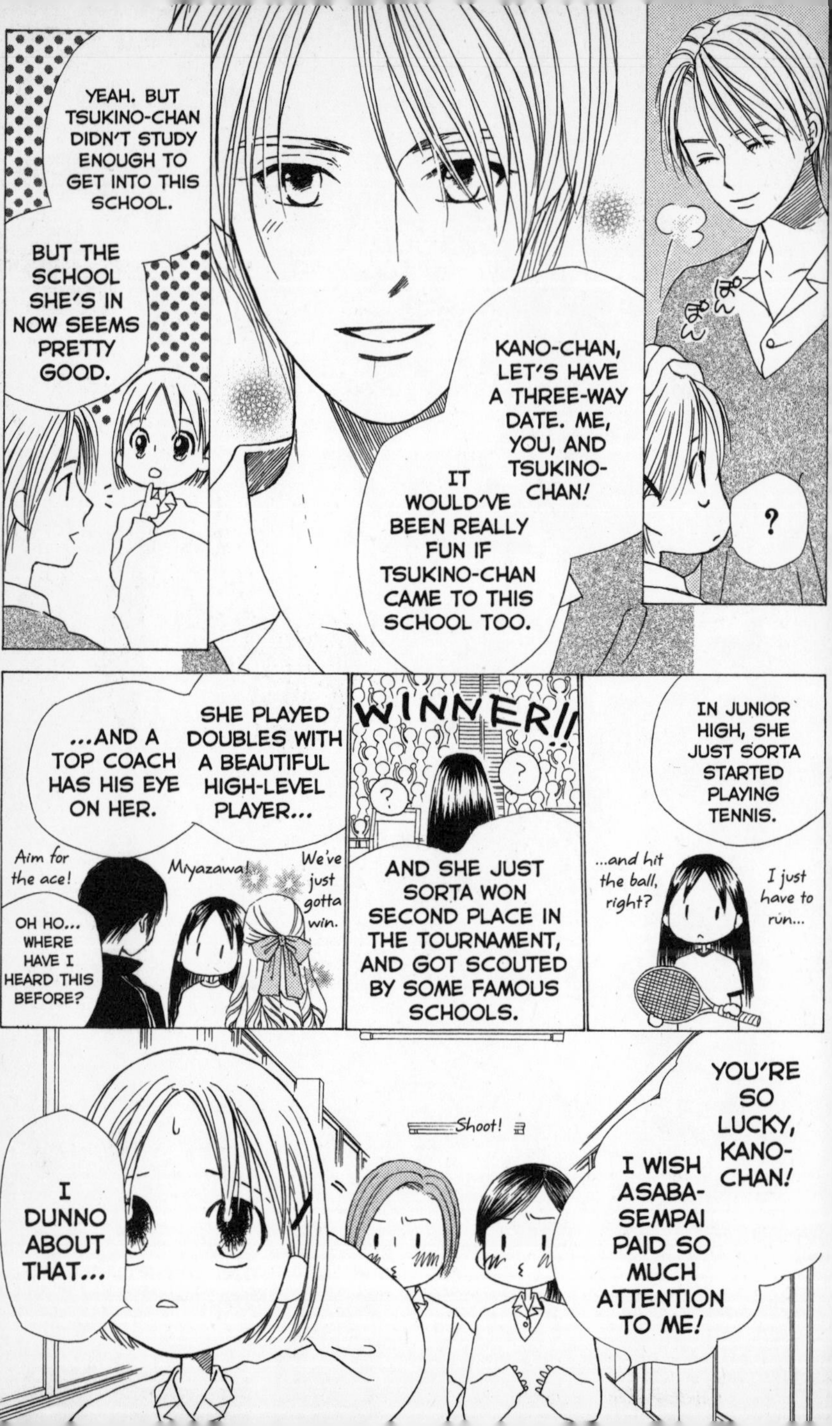
ぽん
ぽん
?
KANO-CHAN, LET'S HAVE A THREE-WAY DATE. ME, YOU, AND TSUKINO-CHAN!
IT WOULD'VE BEEN REALLY FUN IF TSUKINO-CHAN CAME TO THIS SCHOOL TOO.
YEAH. BUT TSUKINO-CHAN DIDN'T STUDY ENOUGH TO GET INTO THIS SCHOOL.
BUT THE SCHOOL SHE'S IN NOW SEEMS PRETTY GOOD.
IN JUNIOR HIGH, SHE JUST SORTA STARTED PLAYING TENNIS.
I just have to run...
...and hit the ball, right?
WINNER!!
?
?
AND SHE JUST SORTA WON SECOND PLACE IN THE TOURNAMENT, AND GOT SCOUTED BY SOME FAMOUS SCHOOLS.
SHE PLAYED DOUBLES WITH A BEAUTIFUL HIGH-LEVEL PLAYER...
...AND A TOP COACH HAS HIS EYE ON HER.
We've just gotta win.
Miyazawa!
Aim for the ace!
OH HO... WHERE HAVE I HEARD THIS BEFORE?
YOU'RE SO LUCKY, KANO-CHAN!
I WISH ASABA-SEMPAI PAID SO MUCH ATTENTION TO ME!
Shoot!
I DUNNO ABOUT THAT...

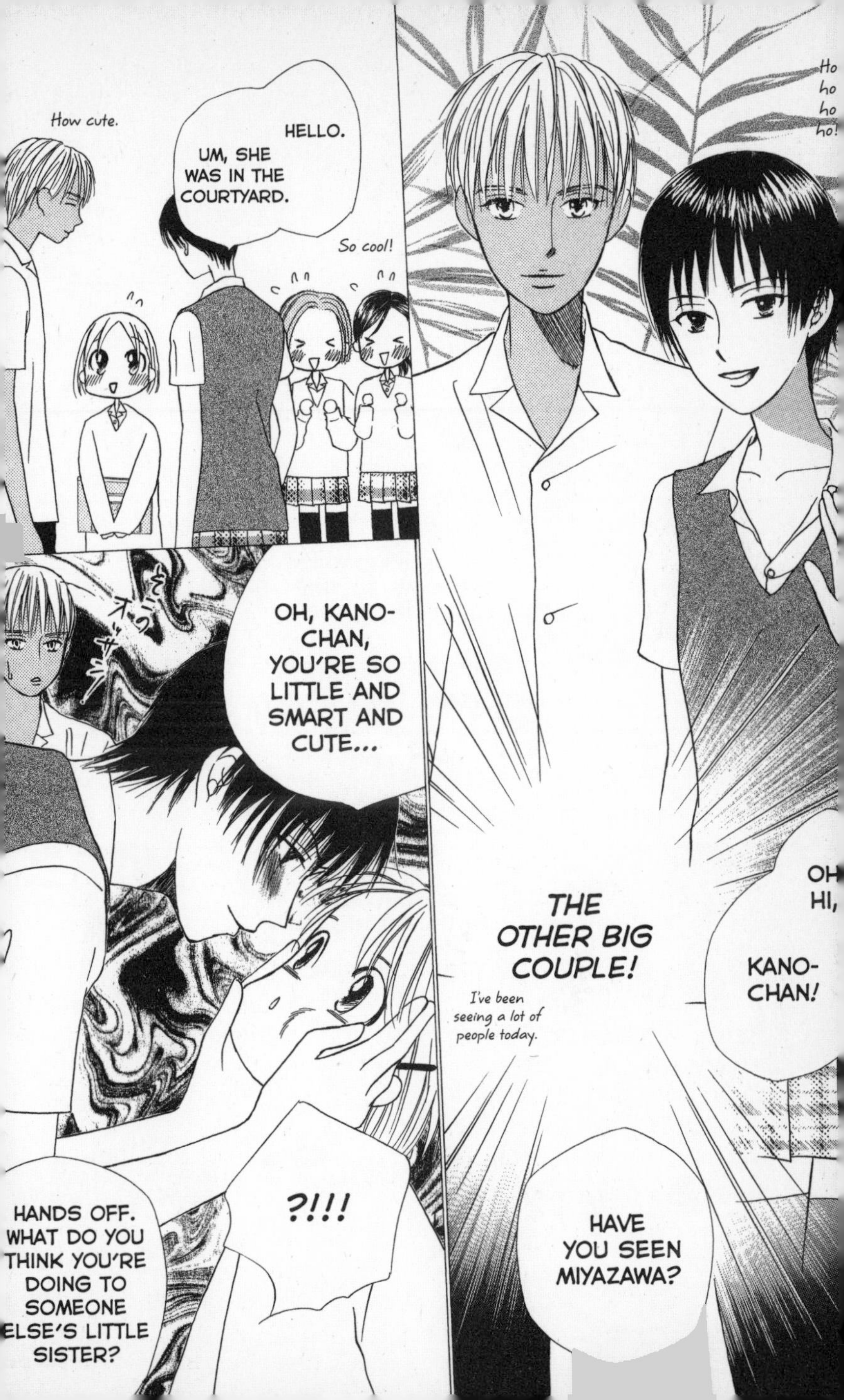
Ho ho ho ho!
OH HI, KANO-CHAN!
THE OTHER BIG COUPLE!
I've been seeing a lot of people today.
HAVE YOU SEEN MIYAZAWA?
HELLO.
UM, SHE WAS IN THE COURTYARD.
So cool!
How cute.
OH, KANO-CHAN, YOU'RE SO LITTLE AND SMART AND CUTE...
?!!!
HANDS OFF. WHAT DO YOU THINK YOU'RE DOING TO SOMEONE ELSE'S LITTLE SISTER?

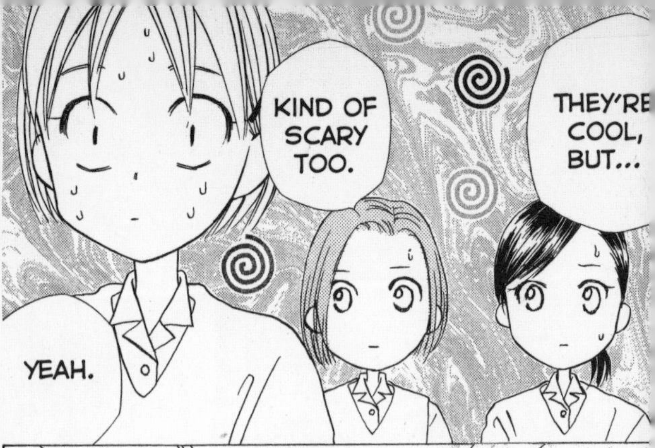
THEY'RE COOL, BUT...
KIND OF SCARY TOO.
YEAH.
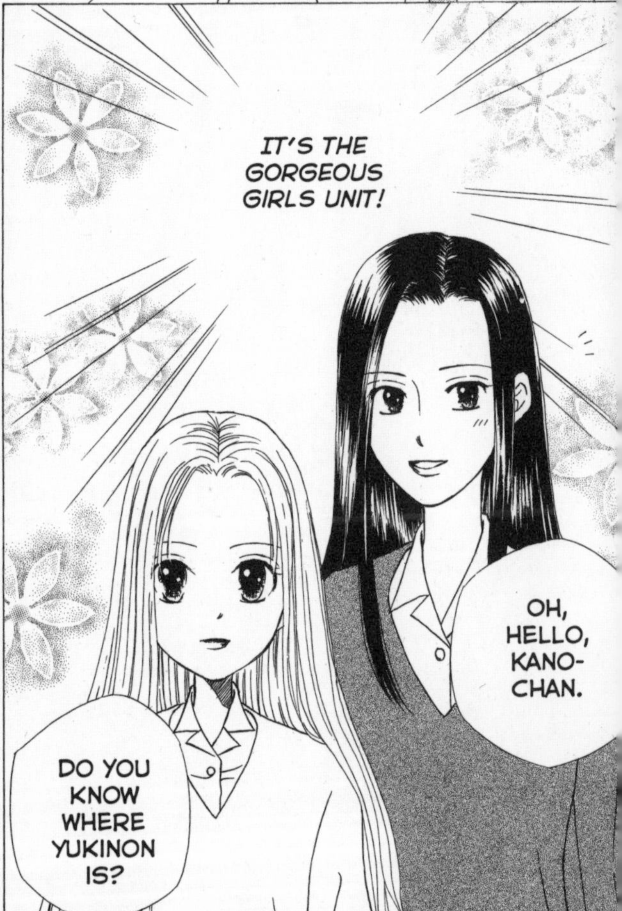
IT'S THE GORGEOUS GIRLS UNIT!
OH, HELLO, KANO-CHAN.
DO YOU KNOW WHERE YUKINON IS?

1

Hello. Welcome to Volume 13 of Kare Kano.

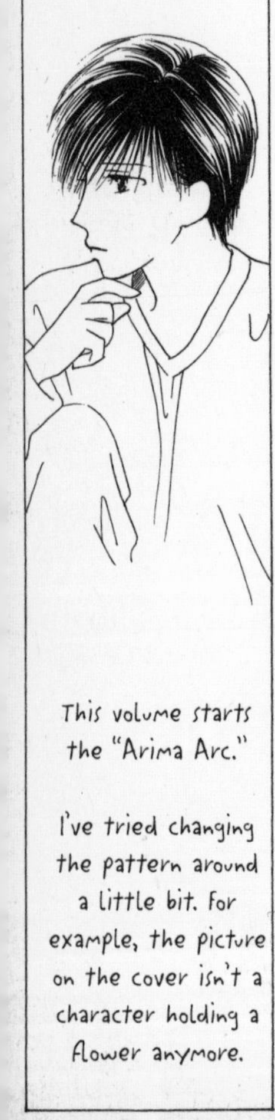

This volume starts the "Arima Arc."

I've tried changing the pattern around a little bit. For example, the picture on the cover isn't a character holding a flower anymore.

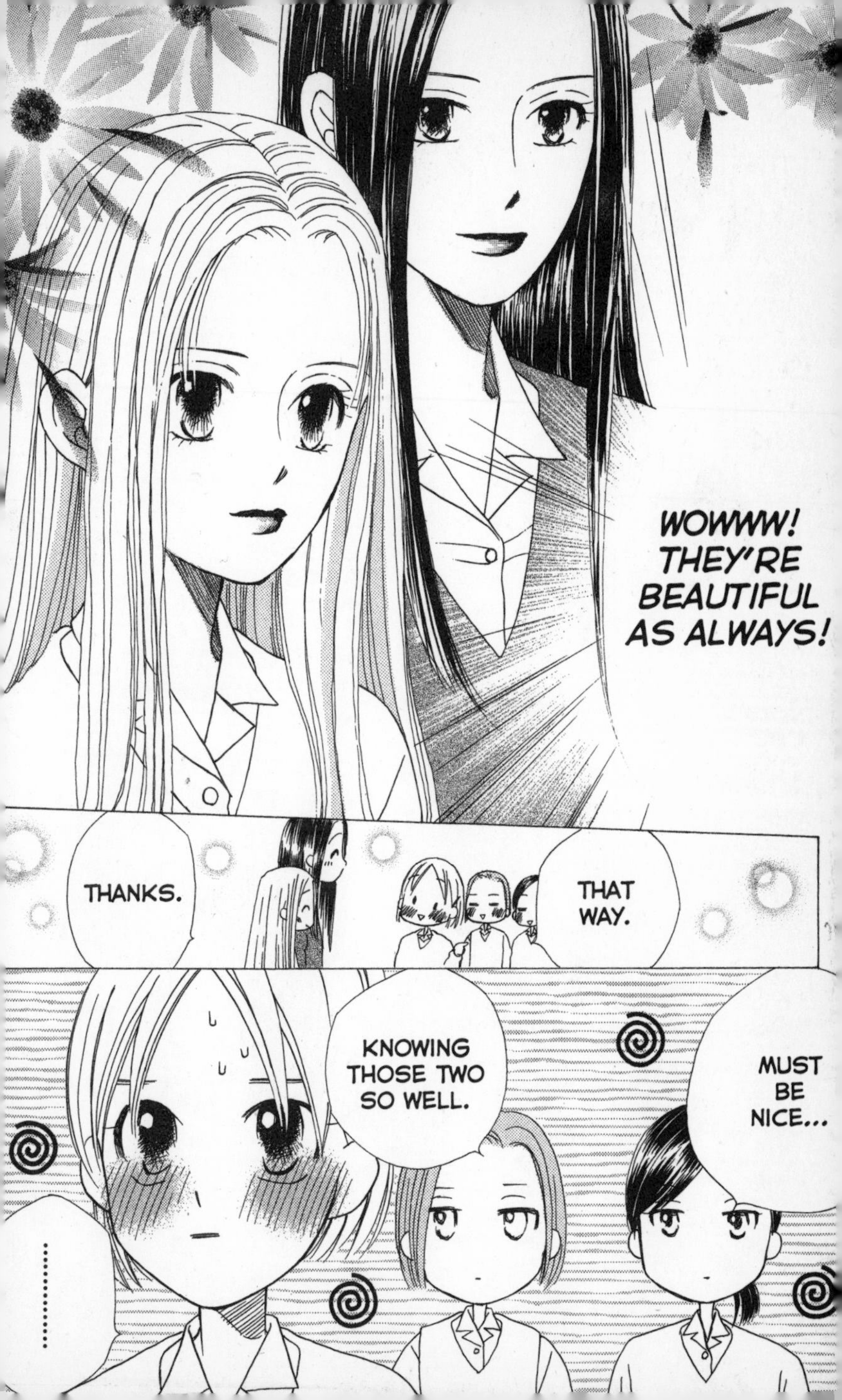
WOWWW! THEY'RE BEAUTIFUL AS ALWAYS!
THAT WAY.
THANKS.
MUST BE NICE...
KNOWING THOSE TWO SO WELL.
....

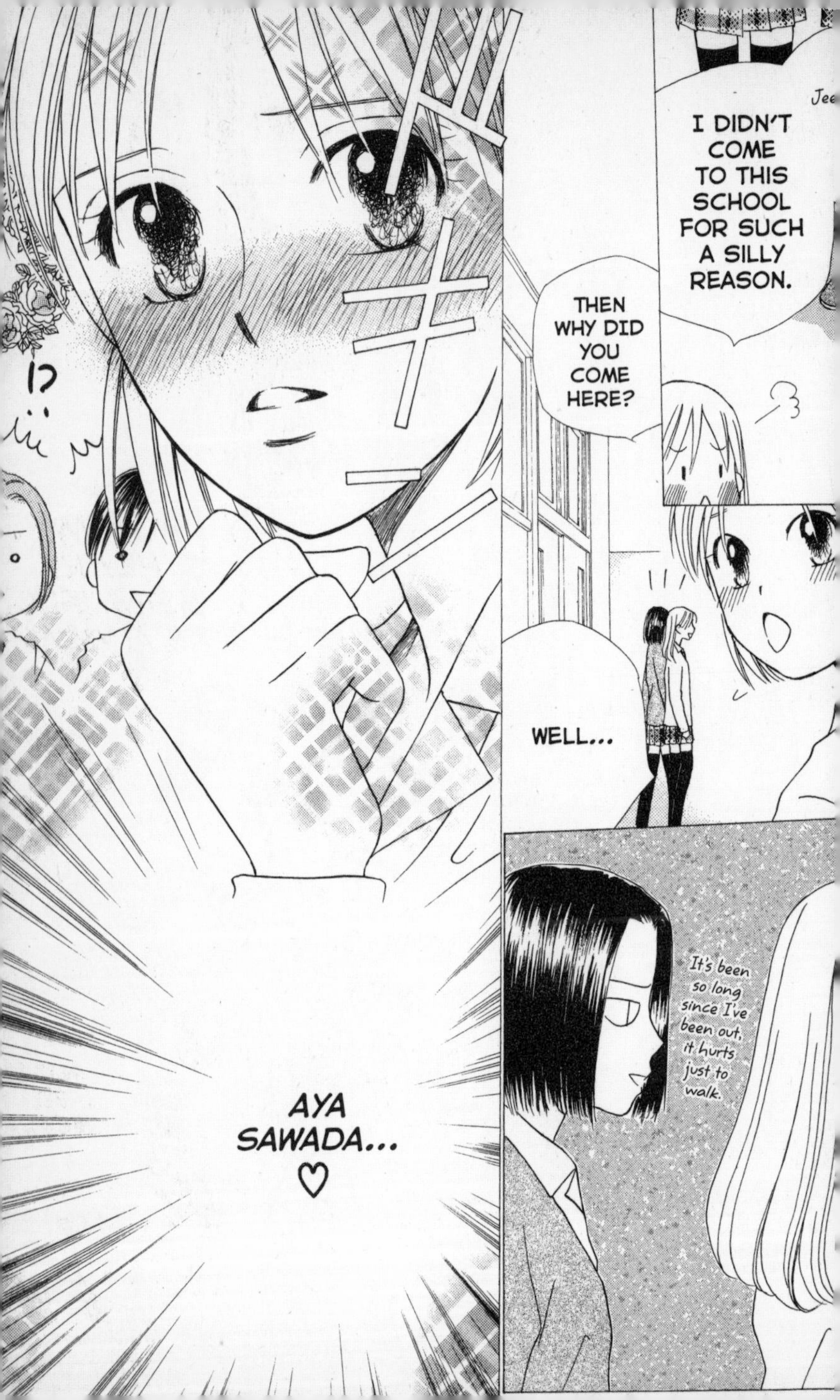
Jee
I DIDN'T COME TO THIS SCHOOL FOR SUCH A SILLY REASON.
THEN WHY DID YOU COME HERE?
WELL...
It's been so long since I've been out, it hurts just to walk.
AYA SAWADA... ♡

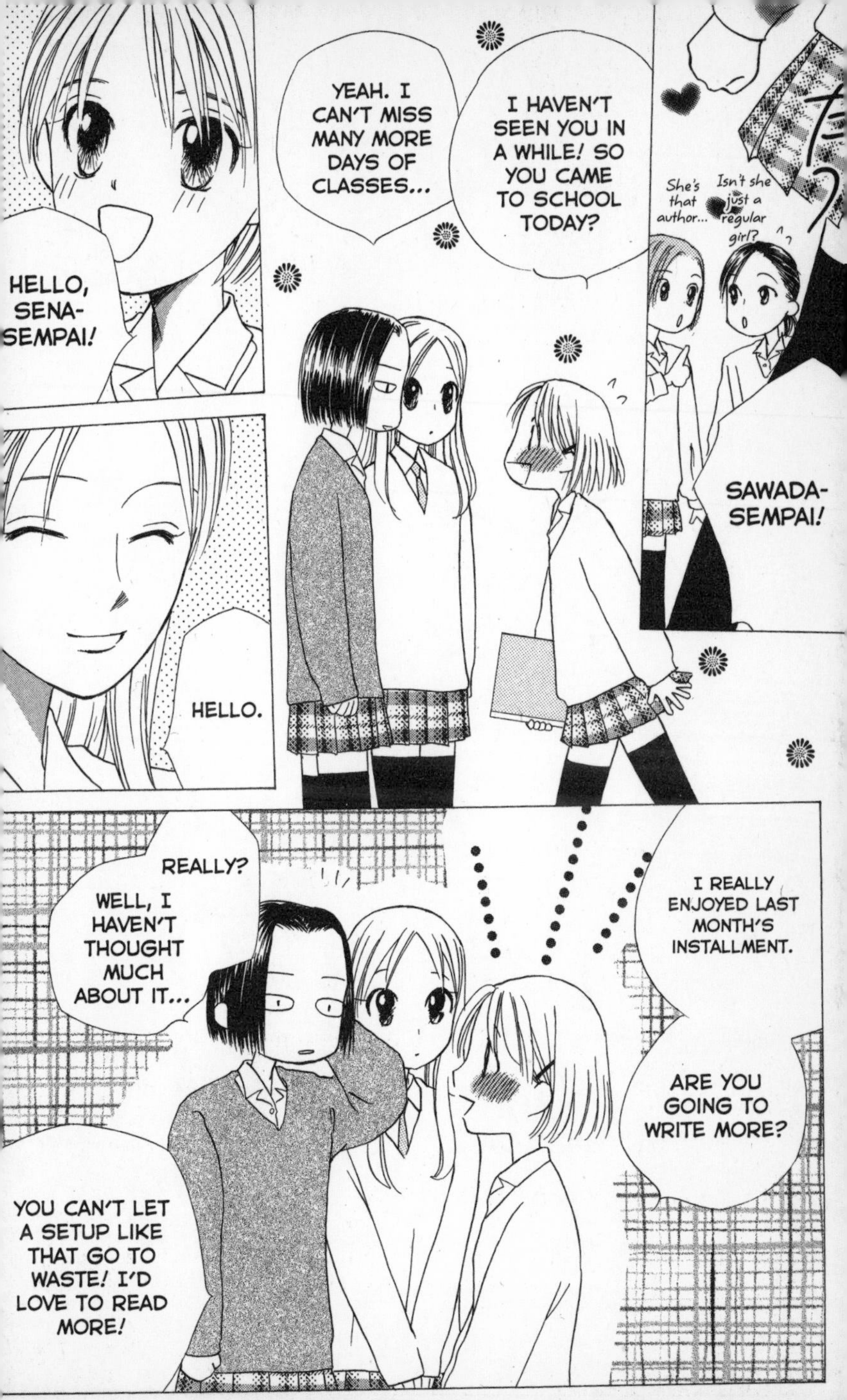
Isn't she just a regular girl?
She's that author...
SAWADA-SEMPAI!
I HAVEN'T SEEN YOU IN A WHILE! SO YOU CAME TO SCHOOL TODAY?
YEAH. I CAN'T MISS MANY MORE DAYS OF CLASSES...
HELLO, SENA-SEMPAI!
HELLO.
I REALLY ENJOYED LAST MONTH'S INSTALLMENT.
ARE YOU GOING TO WRITE MORE?
REALLY?
WELL, I HAVEN'T THOUGHT MUCH ABOUT IT...
YOU CAN'T LET A SETUP LIKE THAT GO TO WASTE! I'D LOVE TO READ MORE!

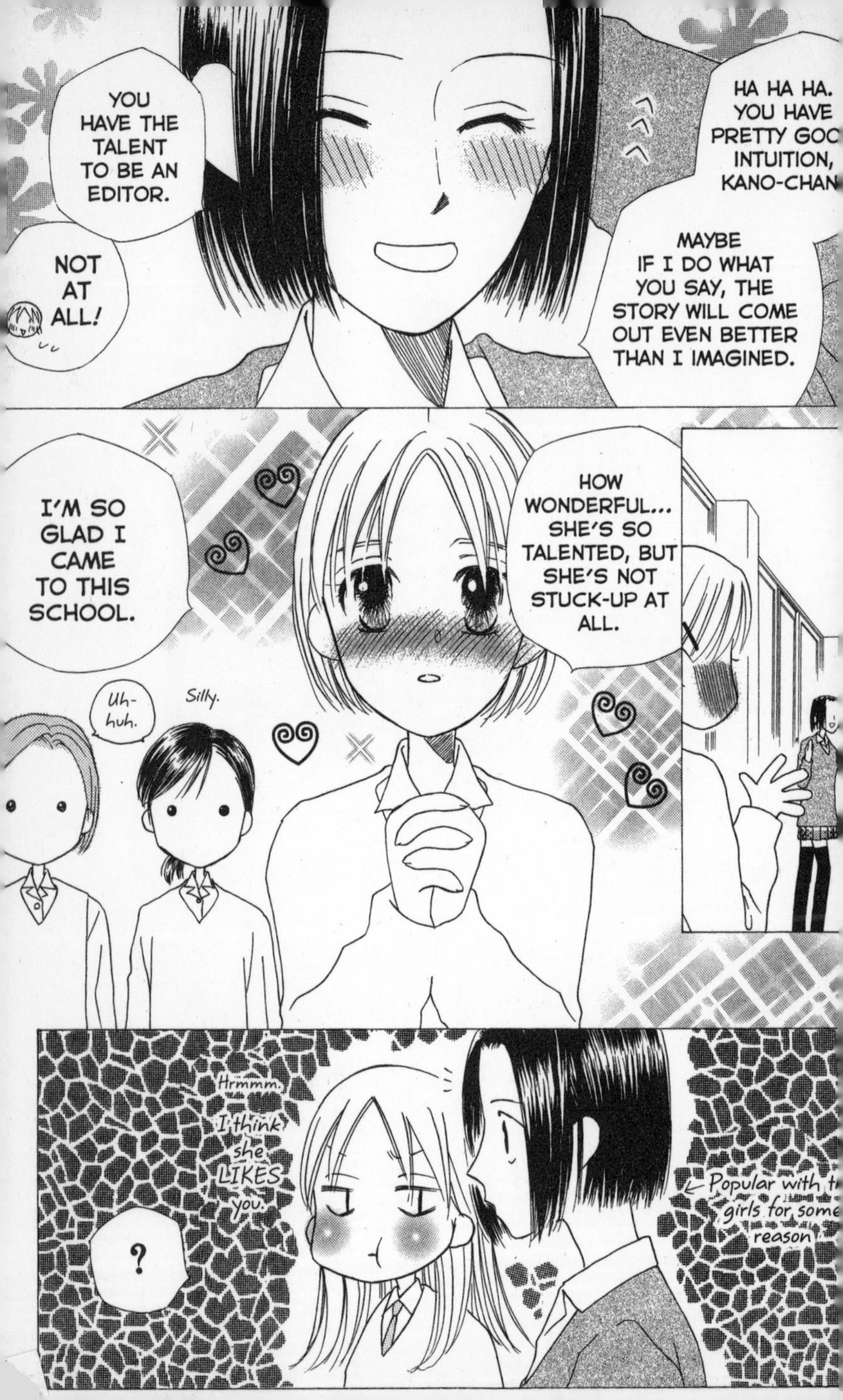
HA HA HA. YOU HAVE PRETTY GOO INTUITION, KANO-CHAN
MAYBE IF I DO WHAT YOU SAY, THE STORY WILL COME OUT EVEN BETTER THAN I IMAGINED.
YOU HAVE THE TALENT TO BE AN EDITOR.
NOT AT ALL!
HOW WONDERFUL... SHE'S SO TALENTED, BUT SHE'S NOT STUCK-UP AT ALL.
I'M SO GLAD I CAME TO THIS SCHOOL.
Silly.
Uh-huh.
Popular with t girls for some reason
Hrmmm. I think she LIKES you.
?

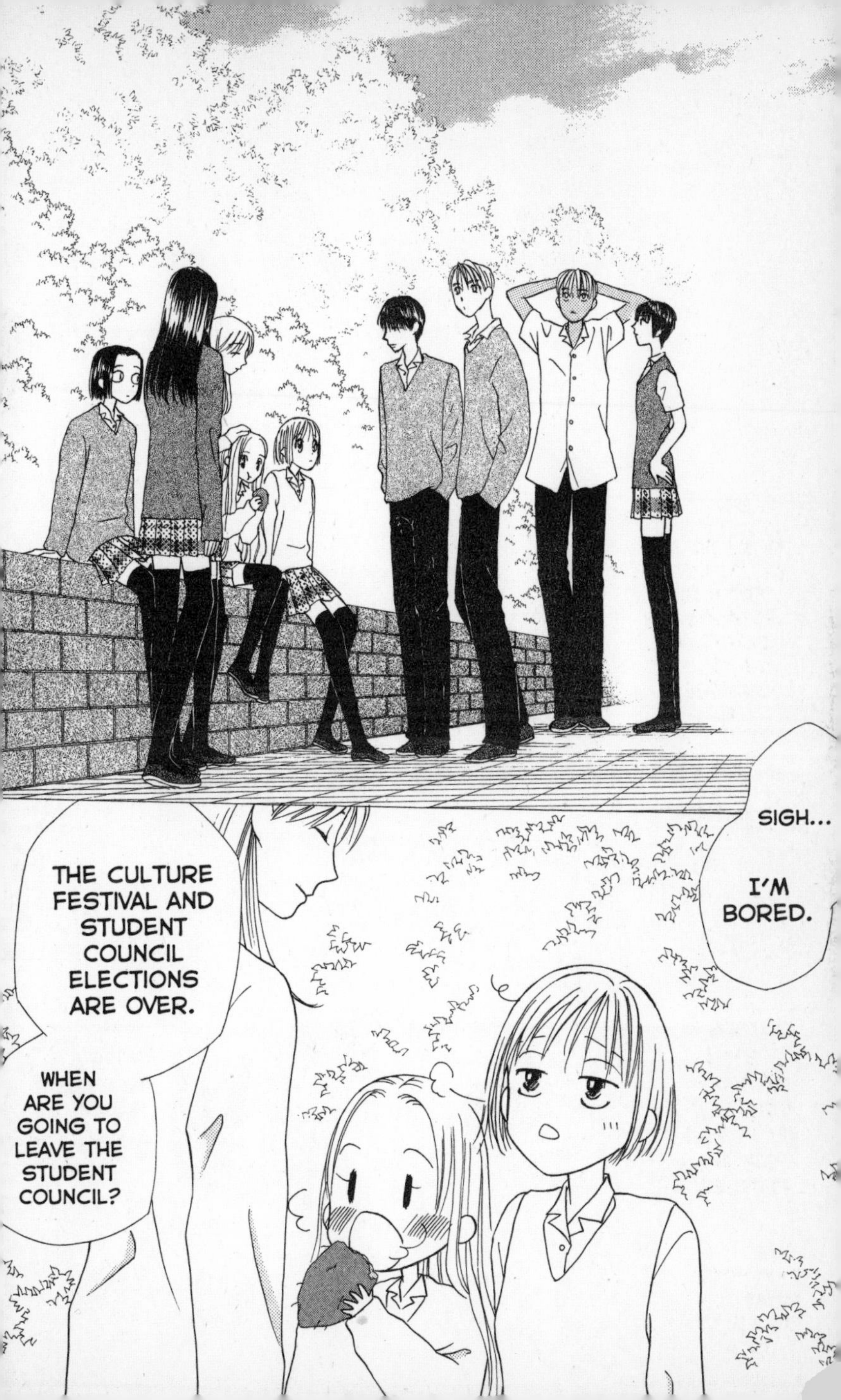
SIGH... I'M BORED.
THE CULTURE FESTIVAL AND STUDENT COUNCIL ELECTIONS ARE OVER.
WHEN ARE YOU GOING TO LEAVE THE STUDENT COUNCIL?

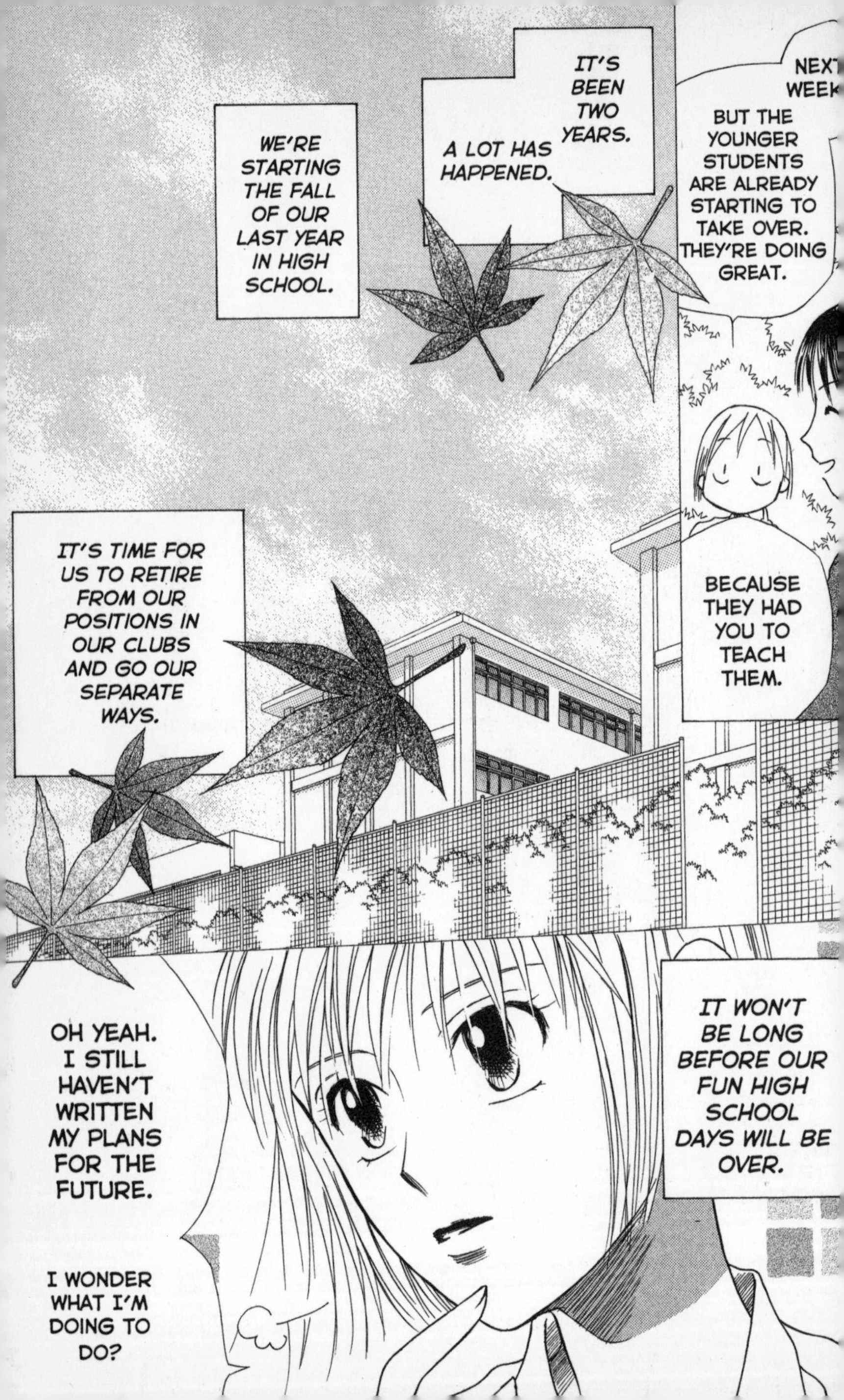
NEXT WEEK
BUT THE YOUNGER STUDENTS ARE ALREADY STARTING TO TAKE OVER. THEY'RE DOING GREAT.
BECAUSE THEY HAD YOU TO TEACH THEM.
IT'S BEEN TWO YEARS.
A LOT HAS HAPPENED.
WE'RE STARTING THE FALL OF OUR LAST YEAR IN HIGH SCHOOL.
IT'S TIME FOR US TO RETIRE FROM OUR POSITIONS IN OUR CLUBS AND GO OUR SEPARATE WAYS.
IT WON'T BE LONG BEFORE OUR FUN HIGH SCHOOL DAYS WILL BE OVER.
OH YEAH. I STILL HAVEN'T WRITTEN MY PLANS FOR THE FUTURE.
I WONDER WHAT I'M DOING TO DO?

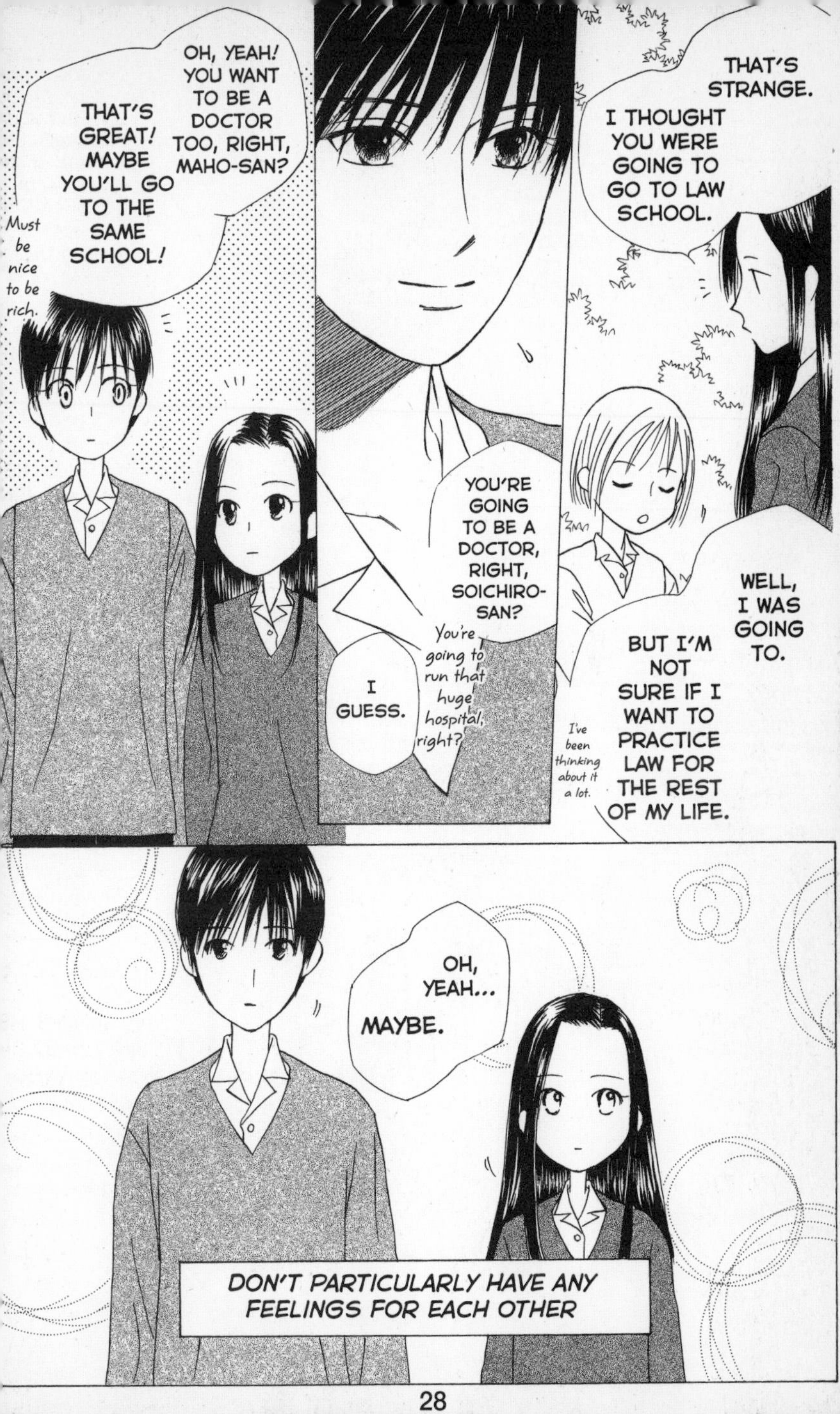

THAT'S STRANGE.
I THOUGHT YOU WERE GOING TO GO TO LAW SCHOOL.
WELL, I WAS GOING TO.
BUT I'M NOT SURE IF I WANT TO PRACTICE LAW FOR THE REST OF MY LIFE.
I've been thinking about it a lot.
YOU'RE GOING TO BE A DOCTOR, RIGHT, SOICHIRO-SAN?
You're going to run that huge hospital, right?
I GUESS.
OH, YEAH! YOU WANT TO BE A DOCTOR TOO, RIGHT, MAHO-SAN?
THAT'S GREAT! MAYBE YOU'LL GO TO THE SAME SCHOOL!
Must be nice to be rich.
OH, YEAH... MAYBE.
DON'T PARTICULARLY HAVE ANY FEELINGS FOR EACH OTHER

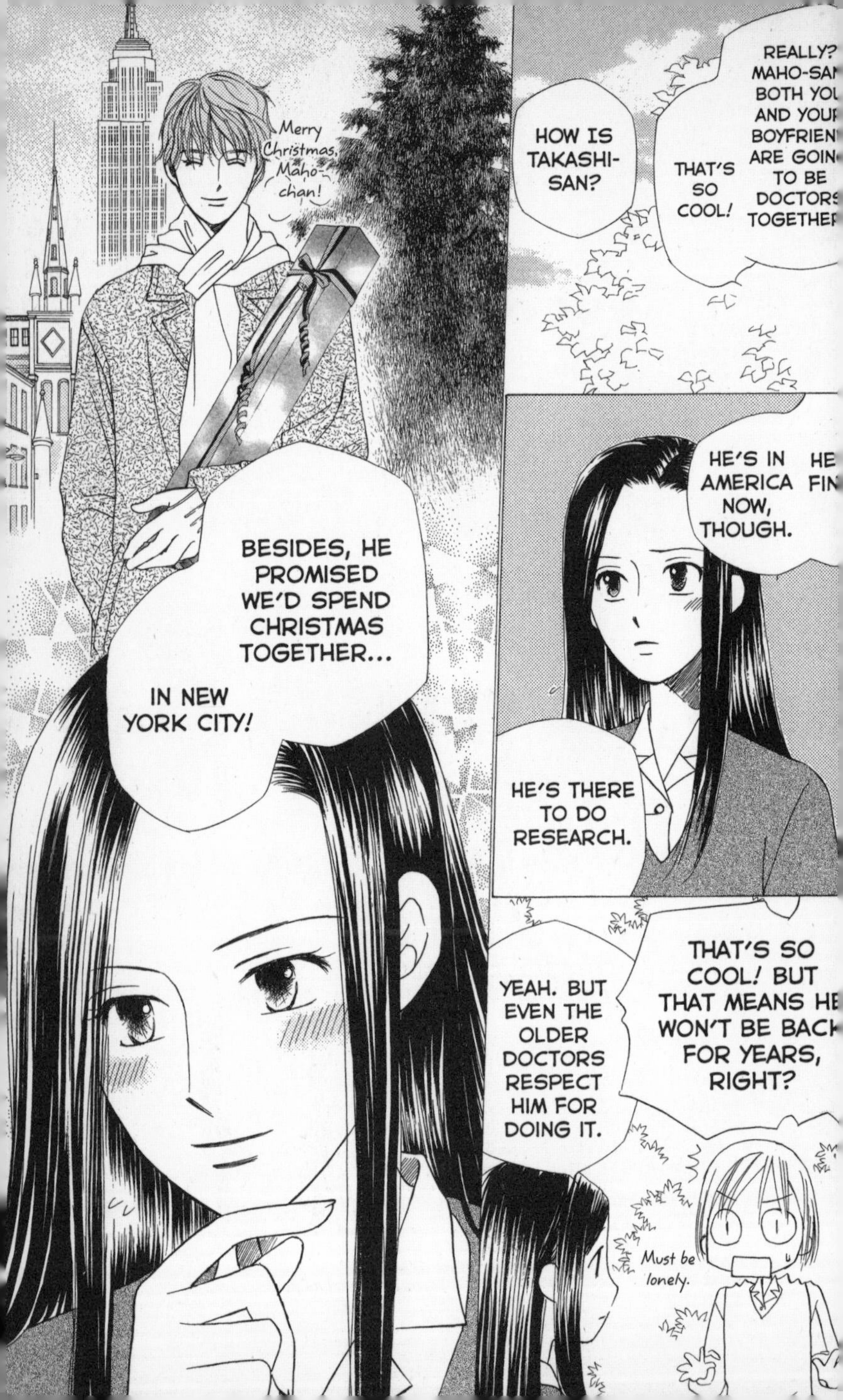
REALLY? MAHO-SAN BOTH YOU AND YOUR BOYFRIEN ARE GOIN TO BE DOCTORS TOGETHER
THAT'S SO COOL!
HOW IS TAKASHI-SAN?
HE FIN
HE'S IN AMERICA NOW, THOUGH.
HE'S THERE TO DO RESEARCH.
THAT'S SO COOL! BUT THAT MEANS HE WON'T BE BACK FOR YEARS, RIGHT?
YEAH. BUT EVEN THE OLDER DOCTORS RESPECT HIM FOR DOING IT.
Must be lonely.
Merry Christmas, Maho-chan!
BESIDES, HE PROMISED WE'D SPEND CHRISTMAS TOGETHER...
IN NEW YORK CITY!

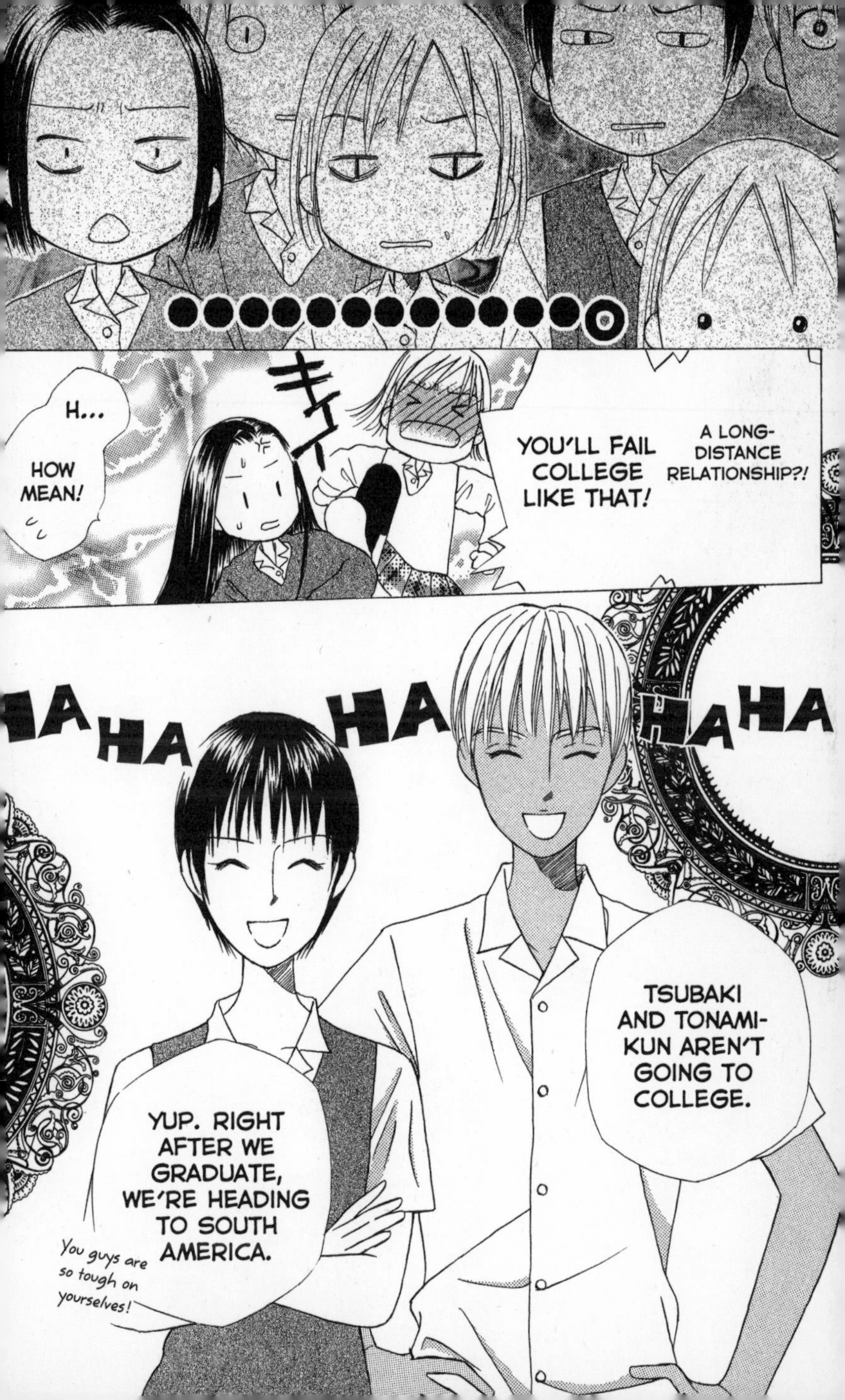
A LONG-DISTANCE RELATIONSHIP?!
YOU'LL FAIL COLLEGE LIKE THAT!
H...
HOW MEAN!
HAHA
HA
HAHA
TSUBAKI AND TONAMI-KUN AREN'T GOING TO COLLEGE.
YUP. RIGHT AFTER WE GRADUATE, WE'RE HEADING TO SOUTH AMERICA.
You guys are so tough on yourselves!

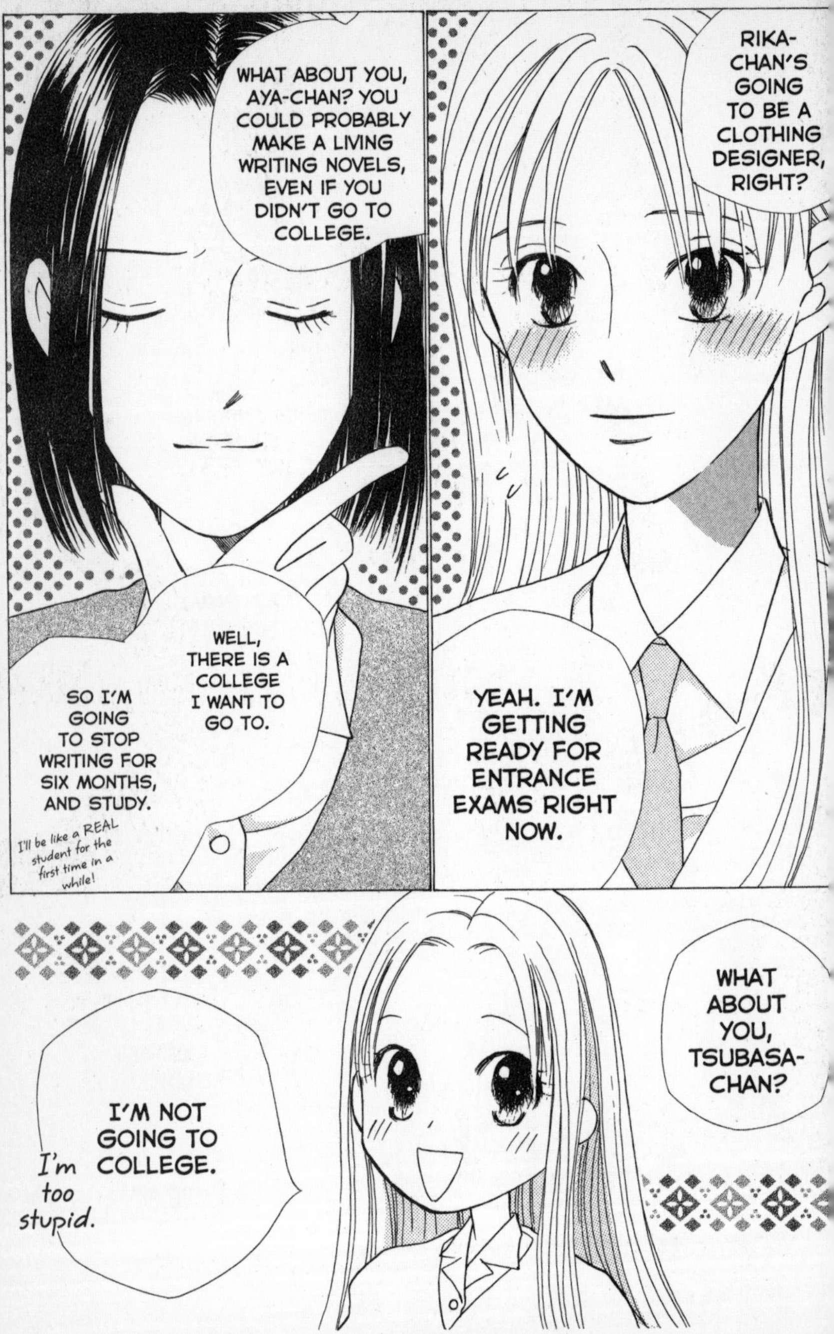
RIKA-CHAN'S GOING TO BE A CLOTHING DESIGNER, RIGHT?
YEAH. I'M GETTING READY FOR ENTRANCE EXAMS RIGHT NOW.
WHAT ABOUT YOU, AYA-CHAN? YOU COULD PROBABLY MAKE A LIVING WRITING NOVELS, EVEN IF YOU DIDN'T GO TO COLLEGE.
WELL, THERE IS A COLLEGE I WANT TO GO TO.
SO I'M GOING TO STOP WRITING FOR SIX MONTHS, AND STUDY.
I'll be like a REAL student for the first time in a while!
WHAT ABOUT YOU, TSUBASA-CHAN?
I'M NOT GOING TO COLLEGE.
I'm too stupid.

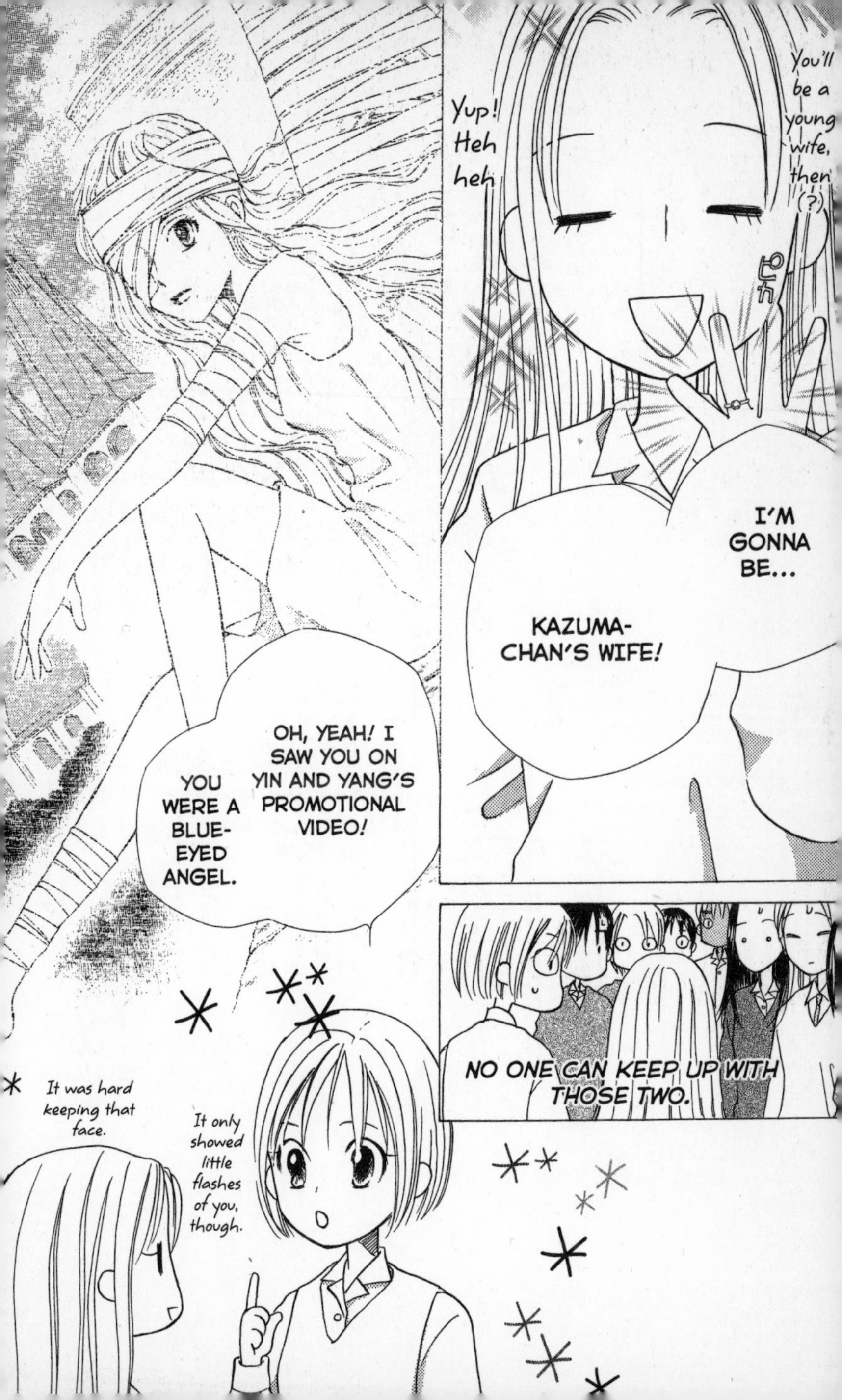

You'll be a young wife, then (?)
Yup! Heh heh
I'M GONNA BE...
KAZUMA-CHAN'S WIFE!
NO ONE CAN KEEP UP WITH THOSE TWO.
OH, YEAH! I SAW YOU ON YIN AND YANG'S PROMOTIONAL VIDEO!
YOU WERE A BLUE-EYED ANGEL.
It only showed little flashes of you, though.
* It was hard keeping that face.

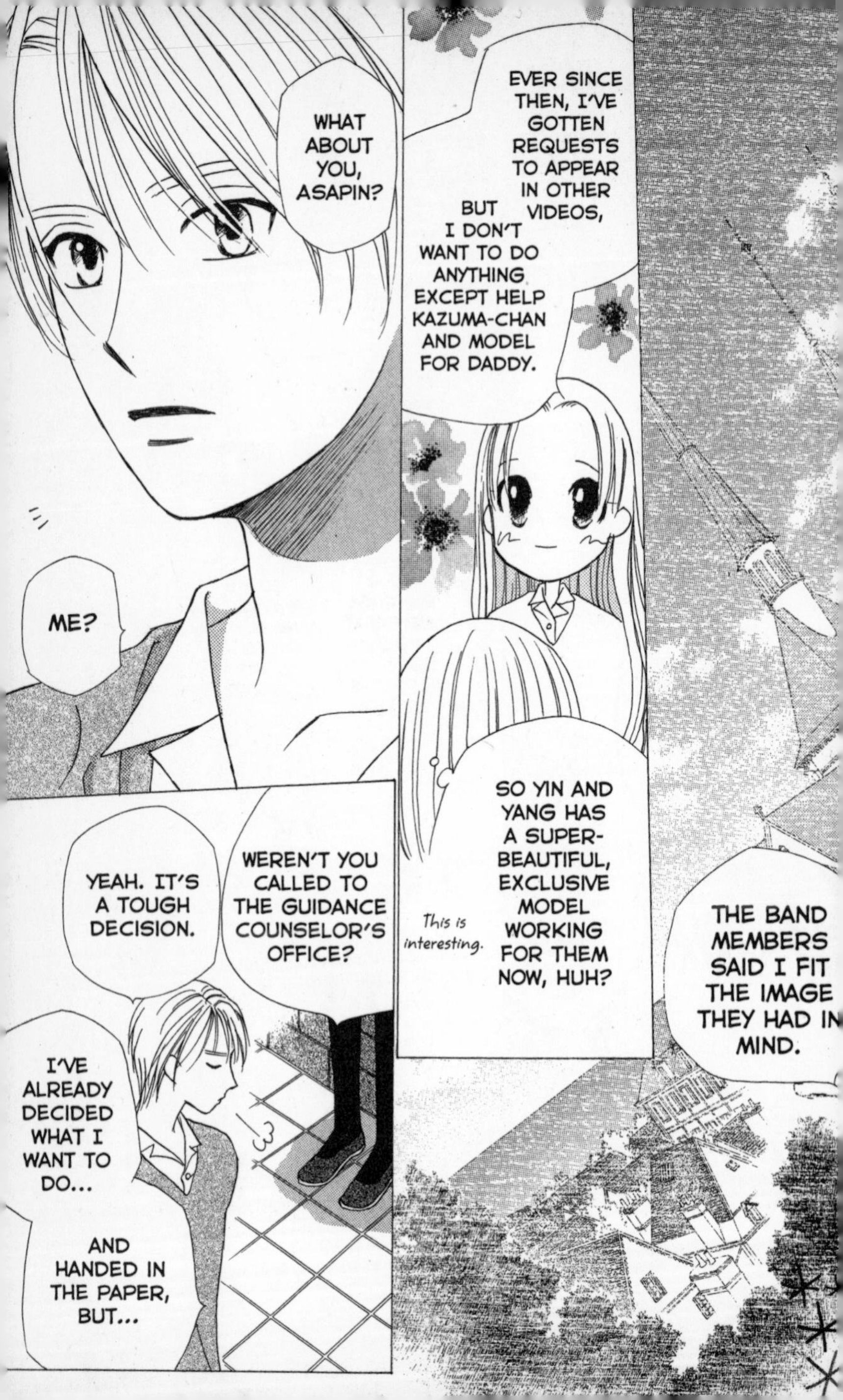
SO YIN AND YANG HAS A SUPER-BEAUTIFUL, EXCLUSIVE MODEL WORKING FOR THEM NOW, HUH?
This is interesting.
THE BAND MEMBERS SAID I FIT THE IMAGE THEY HAD IN MIND.
EVER SINCE THEN, I'VE GOTTEN REQUESTS TO APPEAR IN OTHER VIDEOS,
BUT I DON'T WANT TO DO ANYTHING EXCEPT HELP KAZUMA-CHAN AND MODEL FOR DADDY.
WHAT ABOUT YOU, ASAPIN?
ME?
WEREN'T YOU CALLED TO THE GUIDANCE COUNSELOR'S OFFICE?
YEAH. IT'S A TOUGH DECISION.
I'VE ALREADY DECIDED WHAT I WANT TO DO...
AND HANDED IN THE PAPER, BUT...

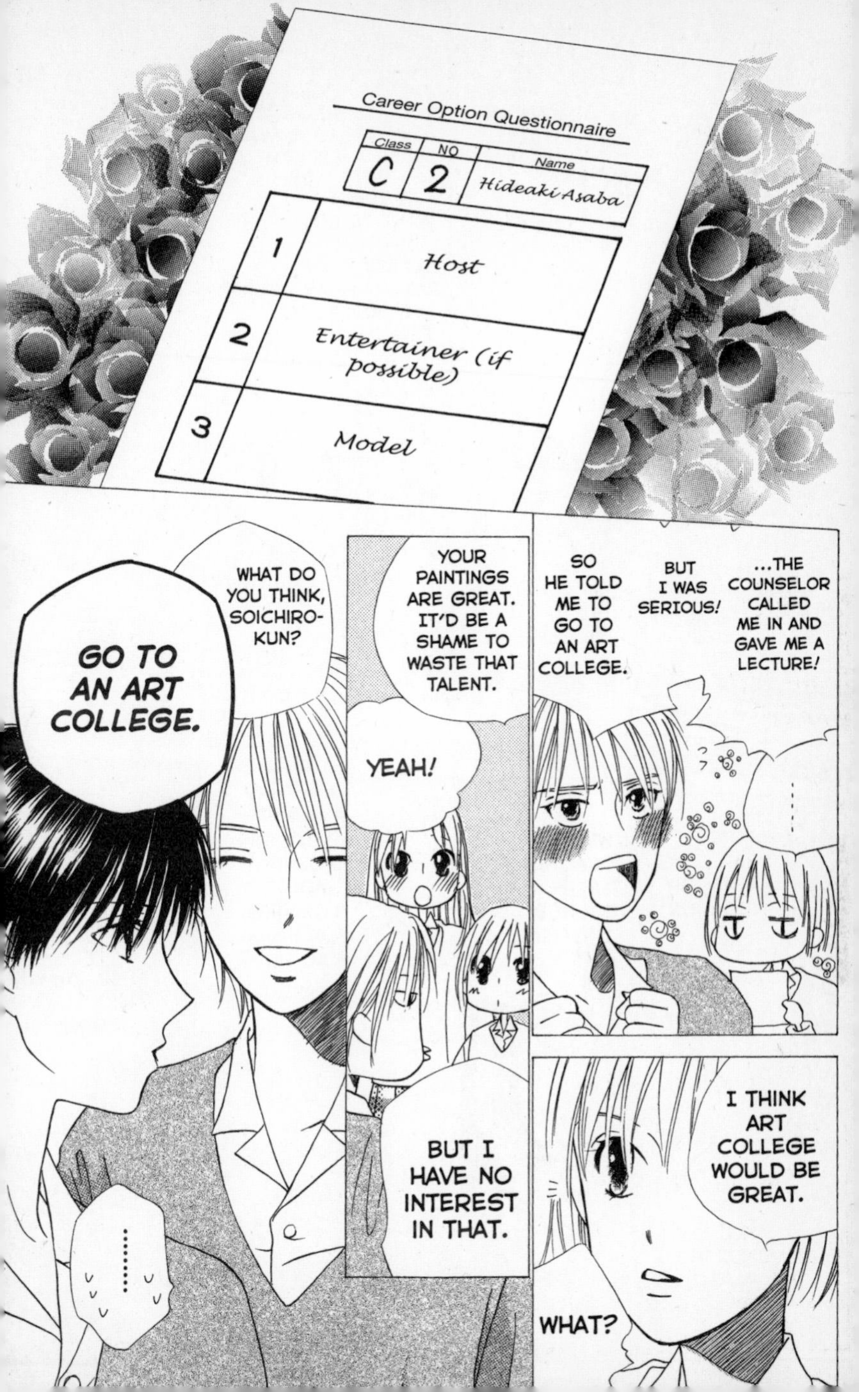
Career Option Questionnaire
Class C
NO 2
Name Hideaki Asaba
1 Host
2 Entertainer (if possible)
3 Model
...THE COUNSELOR CALLED ME IN AND GAVE ME A LECTURE!
BUT I WAS SERIOUS!
SO HE TOLD ME TO GO TO AN ART COLLEGE.
.....
I THINK ART COLLEGE WOULD BE GREAT.
WHAT?
YOUR PAINTINGS ARE GREAT. IT'D BE A SHAME TO WASTE THAT TALENT.
YEAH!
BUT I HAVE NO INTEREST IN THAT.
WHAT DO YOU THINK, SOICHIRO-KUN?
GO TO AN ART COLLEGE.
......

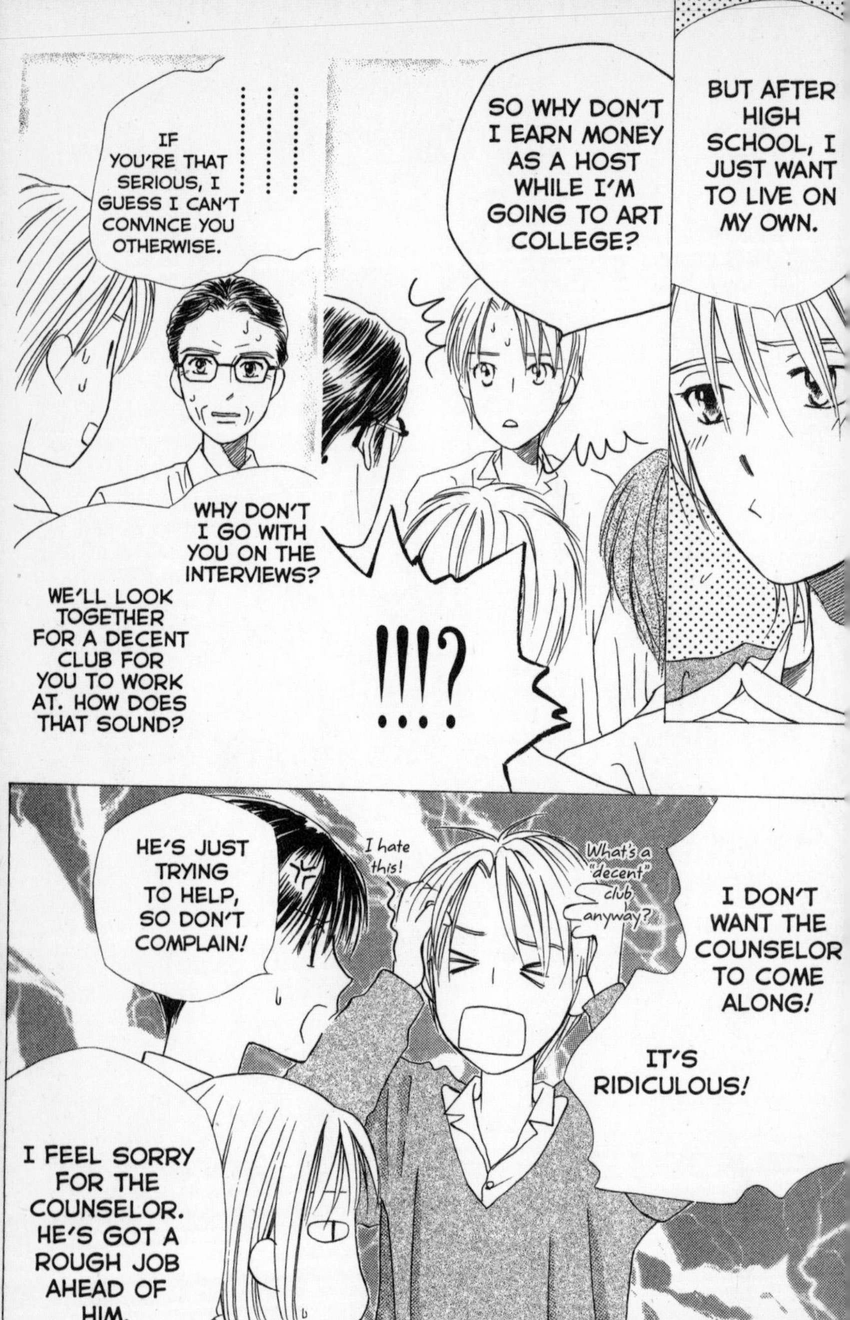
BUT AFTER HIGH SCHOOL, I JUST WANT TO LIVE ON MY OWN.
SO WHY DON'T I EARN MONEY AS A HOST WHILE I'M GOING TO ART COLLEGE?
IF YOU'RE THAT SERIOUS, I GUESS I CAN'T CONVINCE YOU OTHERWISE.
WHY DON'T I GO WITH YOU ON THE INTERVIEWS?
WE'LL LOOK TOGETHER FOR A DECENT CLUB FOR YOU TO WORK AT. HOW DOES THAT SOUND?
!!!?
I DON'T WANT THE COUNSELOR TO COME ALONG!
IT'S RIDICULOUS!
What's a "decent" club anyway?
I hate this!
HE'S JUST TRYING TO HELP, SO DON'T COMPLAIN!
I FEEL SORRY FOR THE COUNSELOR. HE'S GOT A ROUGH JOB AHEAD OF HIM.

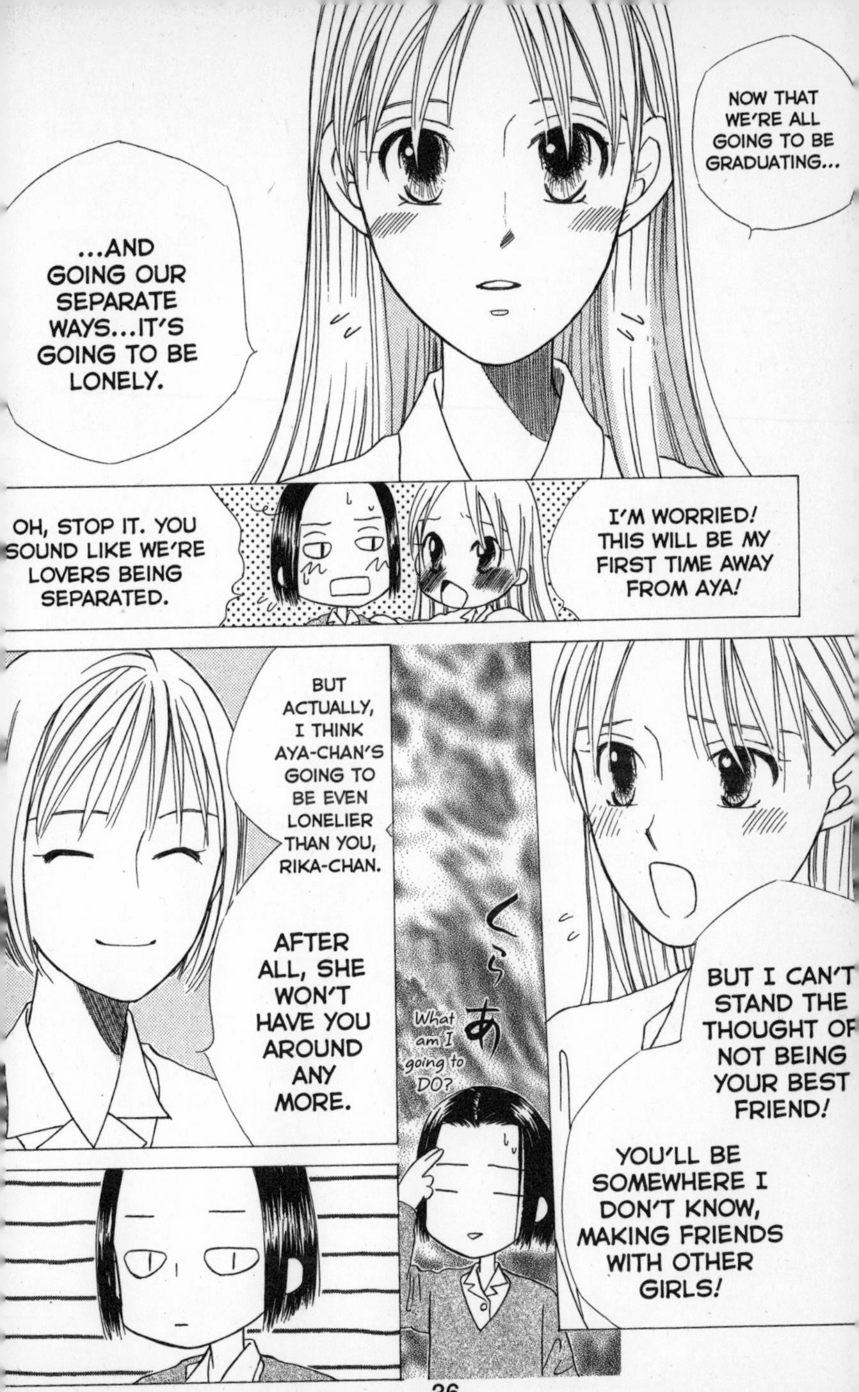
NOW THAT WE'RE ALL GOING TO BE GRADUATING...
...AND GOING OUR SEPARATE WAYS...IT'S GOING TO BE LONELY.
I'M WORRIED! THIS WILL BE MY FIRST TIME AWAY FROM AYA!
OH, STOP IT. YOU SOUND LIKE WE'RE LOVERS BEING SEPARATED.
BUT I CAN'T STAND THE THOUGHT OF NOT BEING YOUR BEST FRIEND!
YOU'LL BE SOMEWHERE I DON'T KNOW, MAKING FRIENDS WITH OTHER GIRLS!
くらあ
What am I going to DO?
BUT ACTUALLY, I THINK AYA-CHAN'S GOING TO BE EVEN LONELIER THAN YOU, RIKA-CHAN.
AFTER ALL, SHE WON'T HAVE YOU AROUND ANY MORE.

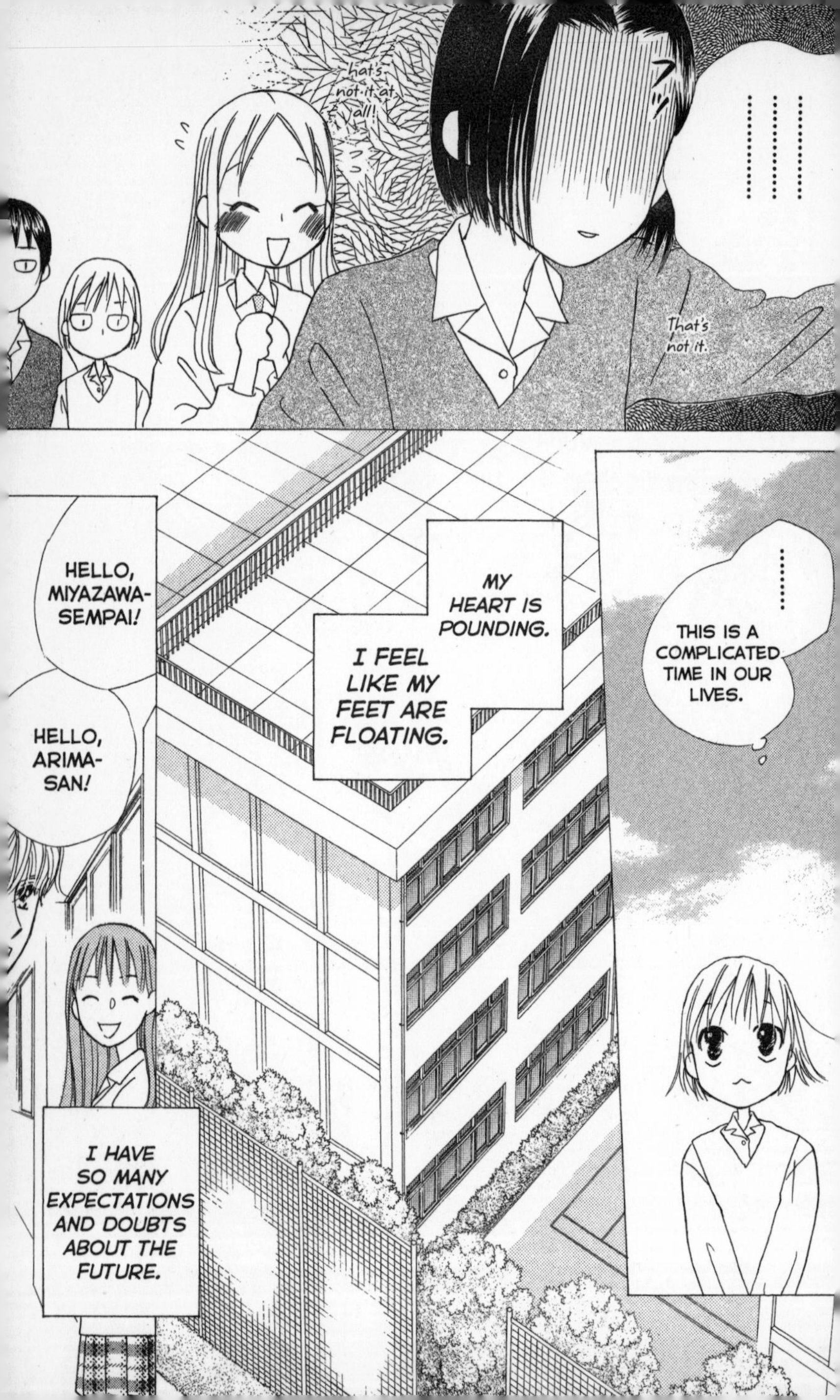

......
......
......
That's not it.
hat's not it at all!
......
THIS IS A COMPLICATED TIME IN OUR LIVES.
MY HEART IS POUNDING.
I FEEL LIKE MY FEET ARE FLOATING.
HELLO, MIYAZAWA-SEMPAI!
HELLO, ARIMA-SAN!
I HAVE SO MANY EXPECTATIONS AND DOUBTS ABOUT THE FUTURE.

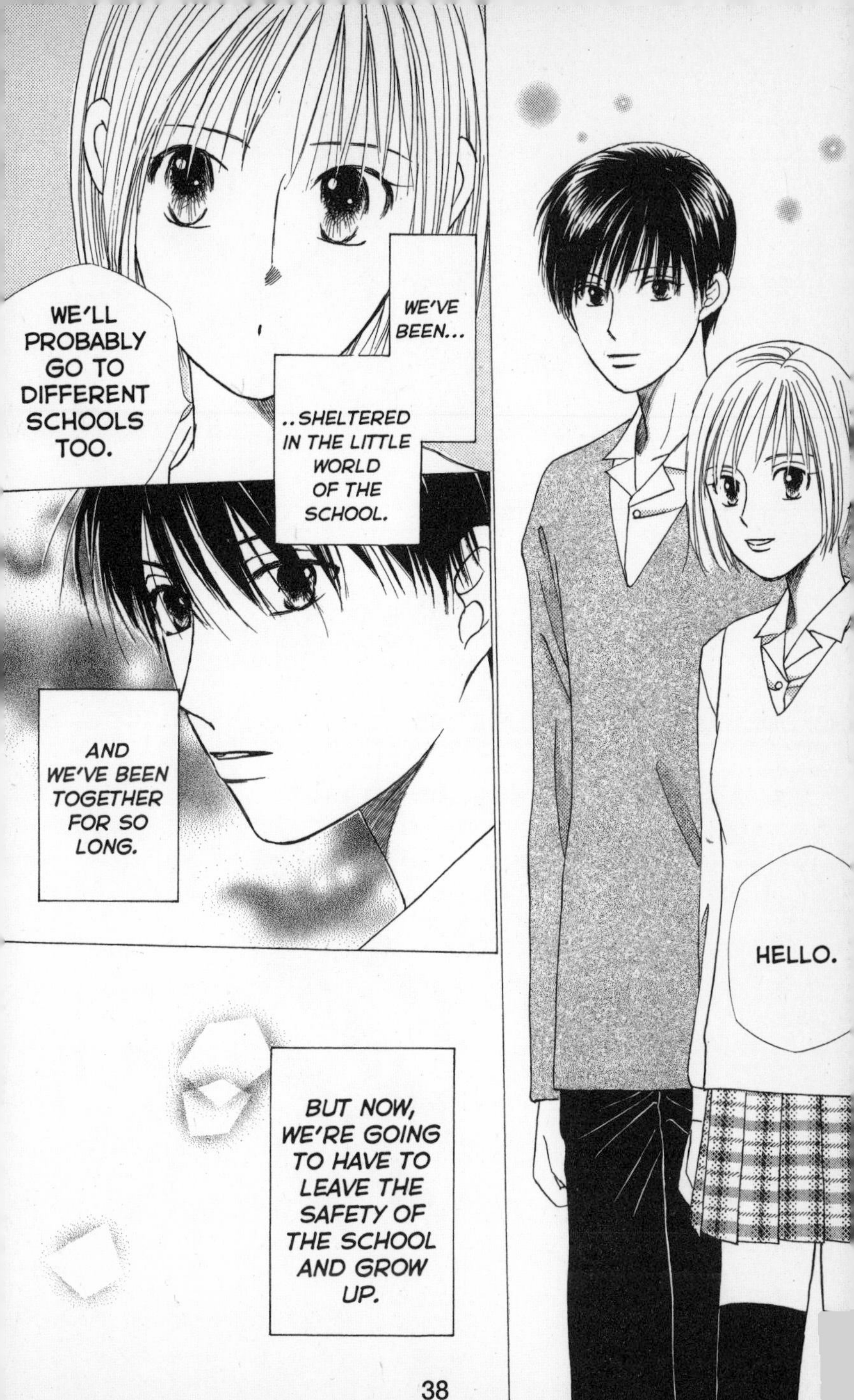
HELLO.
WE'LL PROBABLY GO TO DIFFERENT SCHOOLS TOO.
WE'VE BEEN...
..SHELTERED IN THE LITTLE WORLD OF THE SCHOOL.
AND WE'VE BEEN TOGETHER FOR SO LONG.
BUT NOW, WE'RE GOING TO HAVE TO LEAVE THE SAFETY OF THE SCHOOL AND GROW UP.

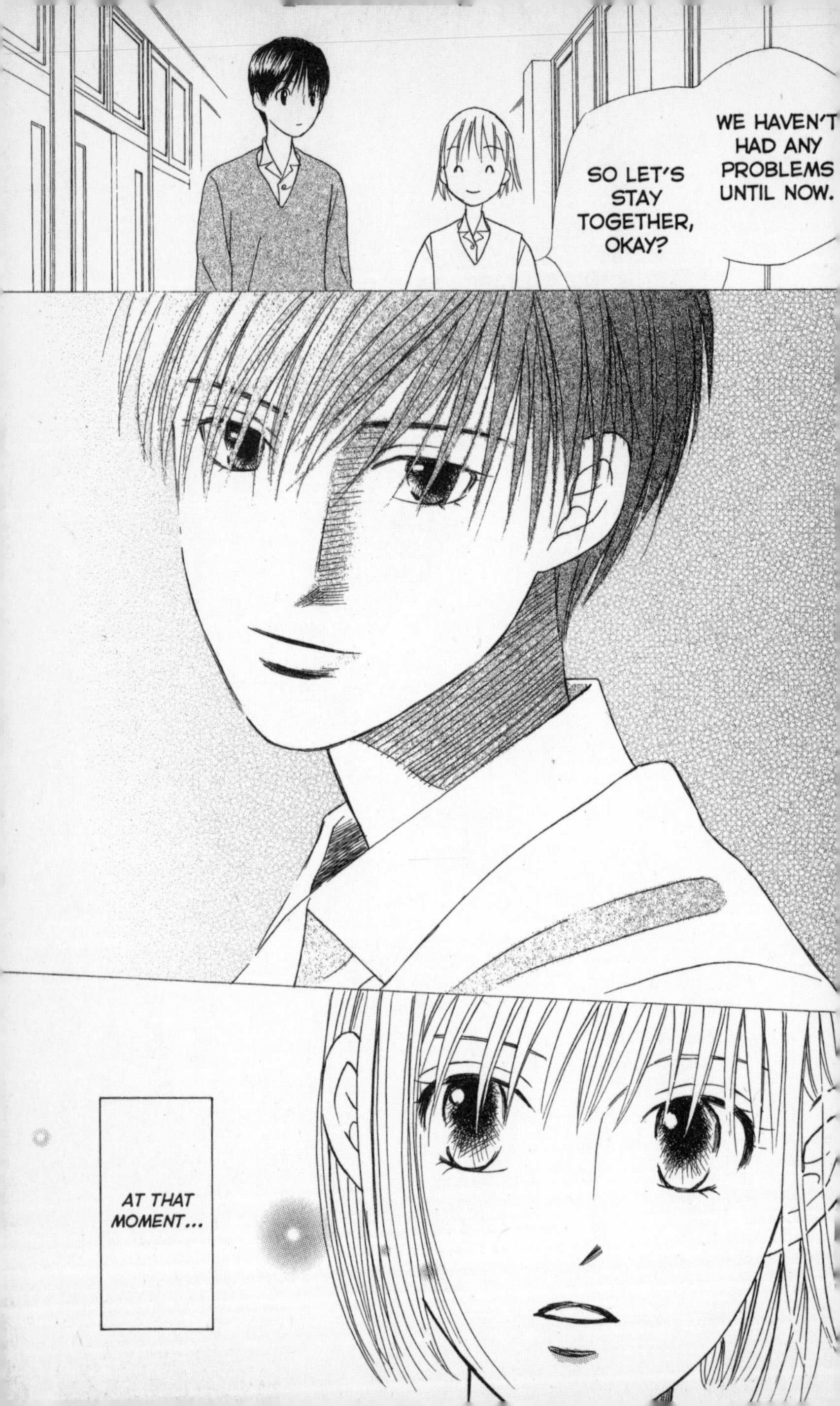
WE HAVEN'T HAD ANY PROBLEMS UNTIL NOW.
SO LET'S STAY TOGETHER, OKAY?
AT THAT MOMENT...

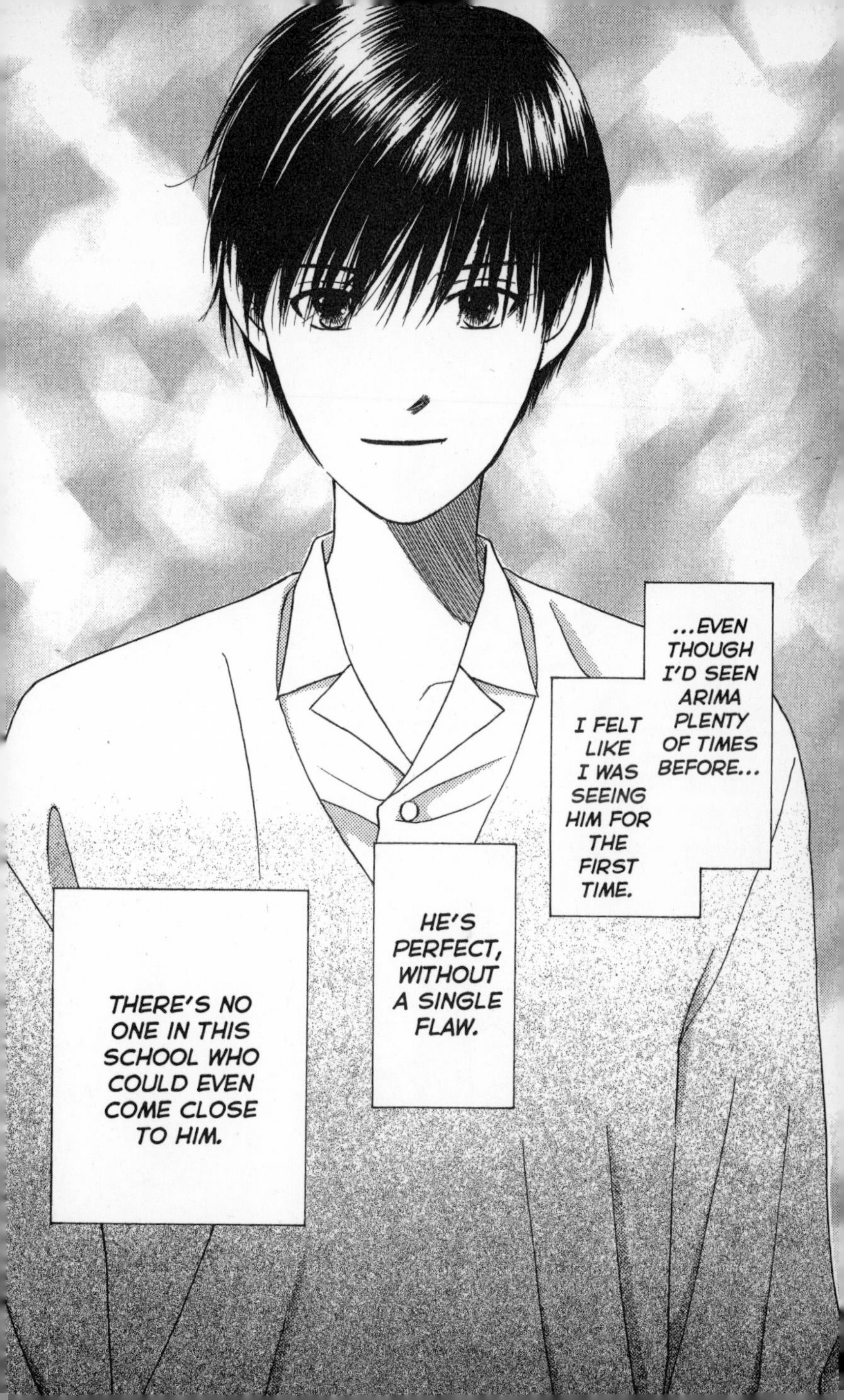
...EVEN THOUGH I'D SEEN ARIMA PLENTY OF TIMES BEFORE...
I FELT LIKE I WAS SEEING HIM FOR THE FIRST TIME.
HE'S PERFECT, WITHOUT A SINGLE FLAW.
THERE'S NO ONE IN THIS SCHOOL WHO COULD EVEN COME CLOSE TO HIM.

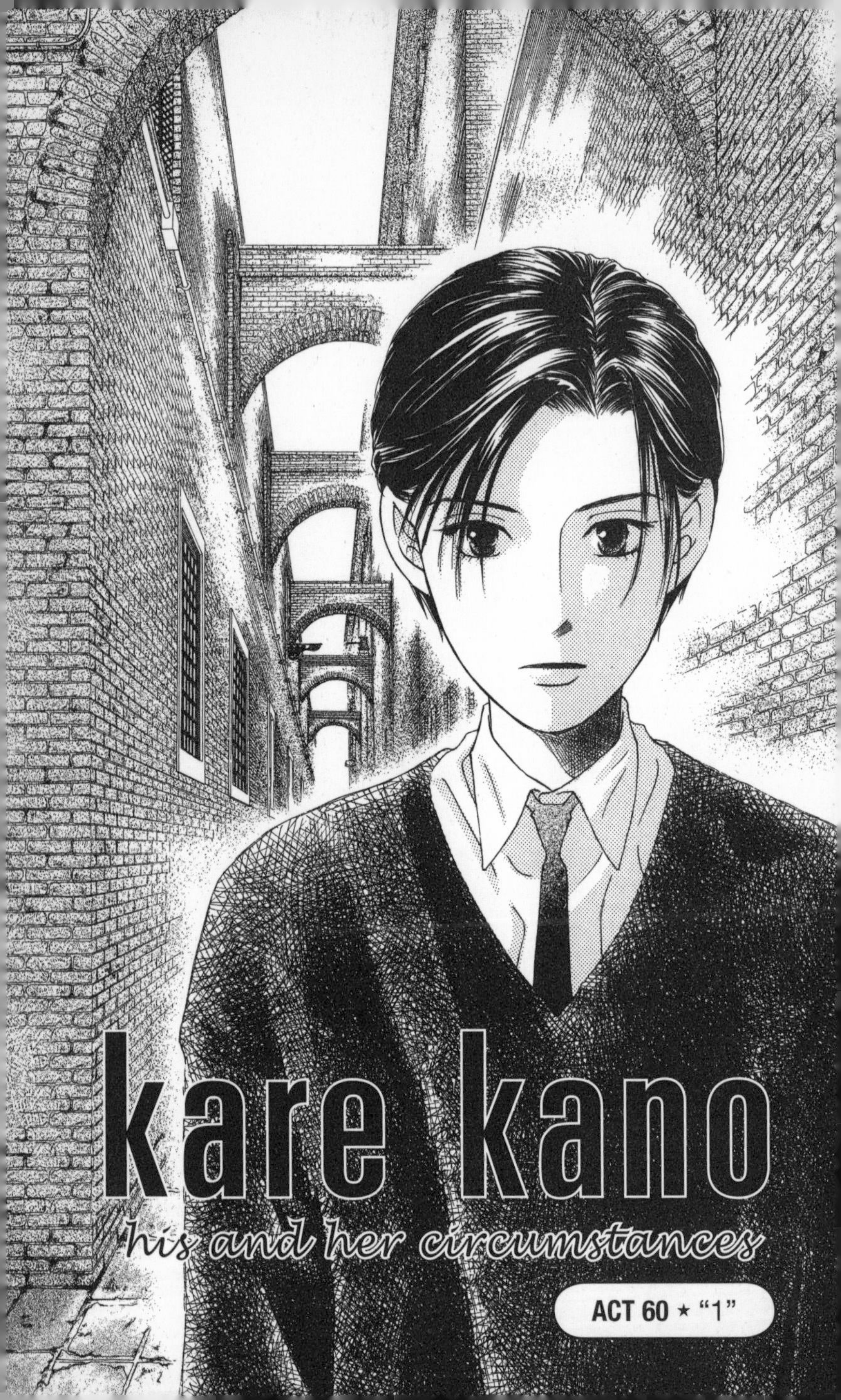

kare kano
his and her circumstances
ACT 60 ★ "1"

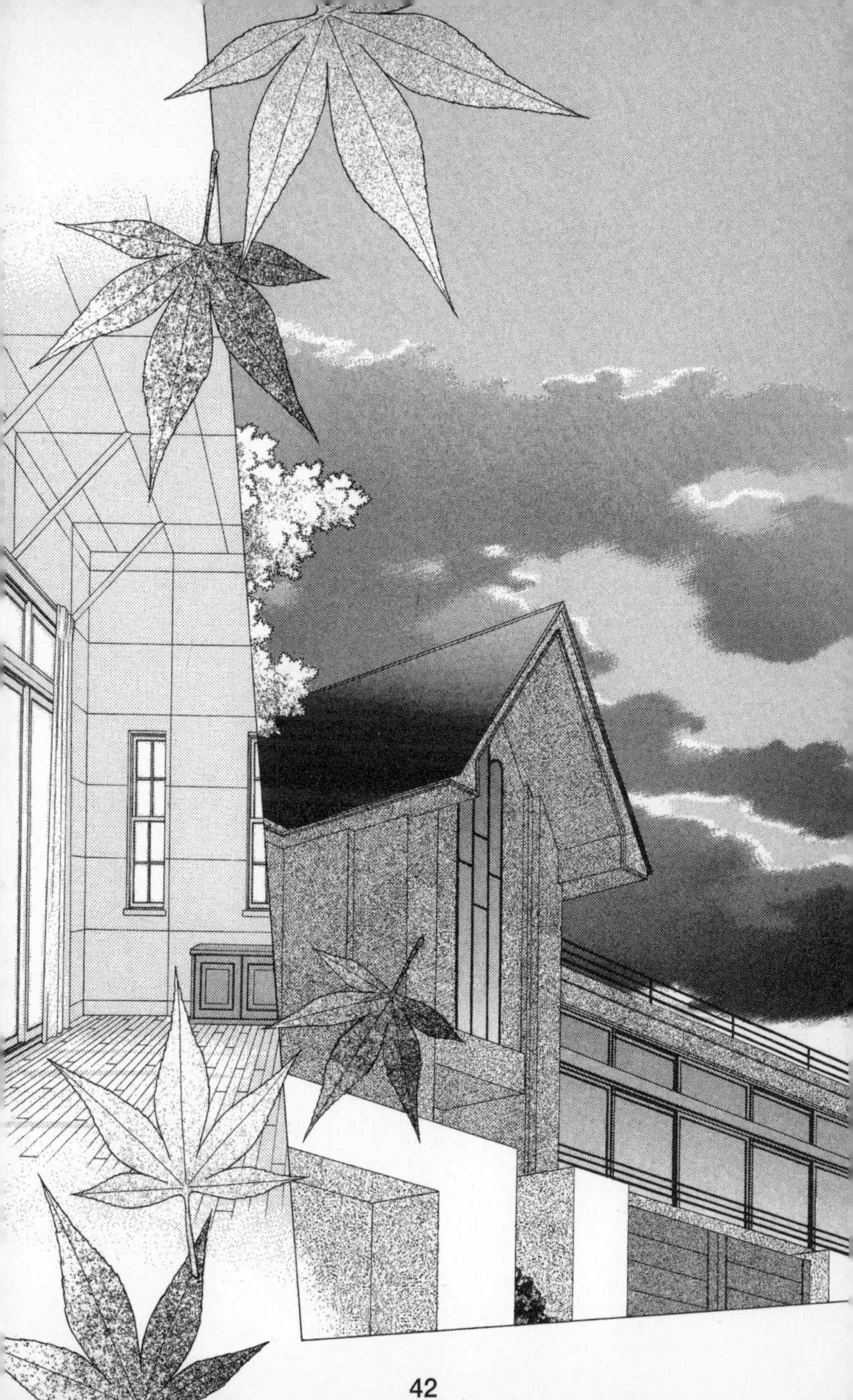

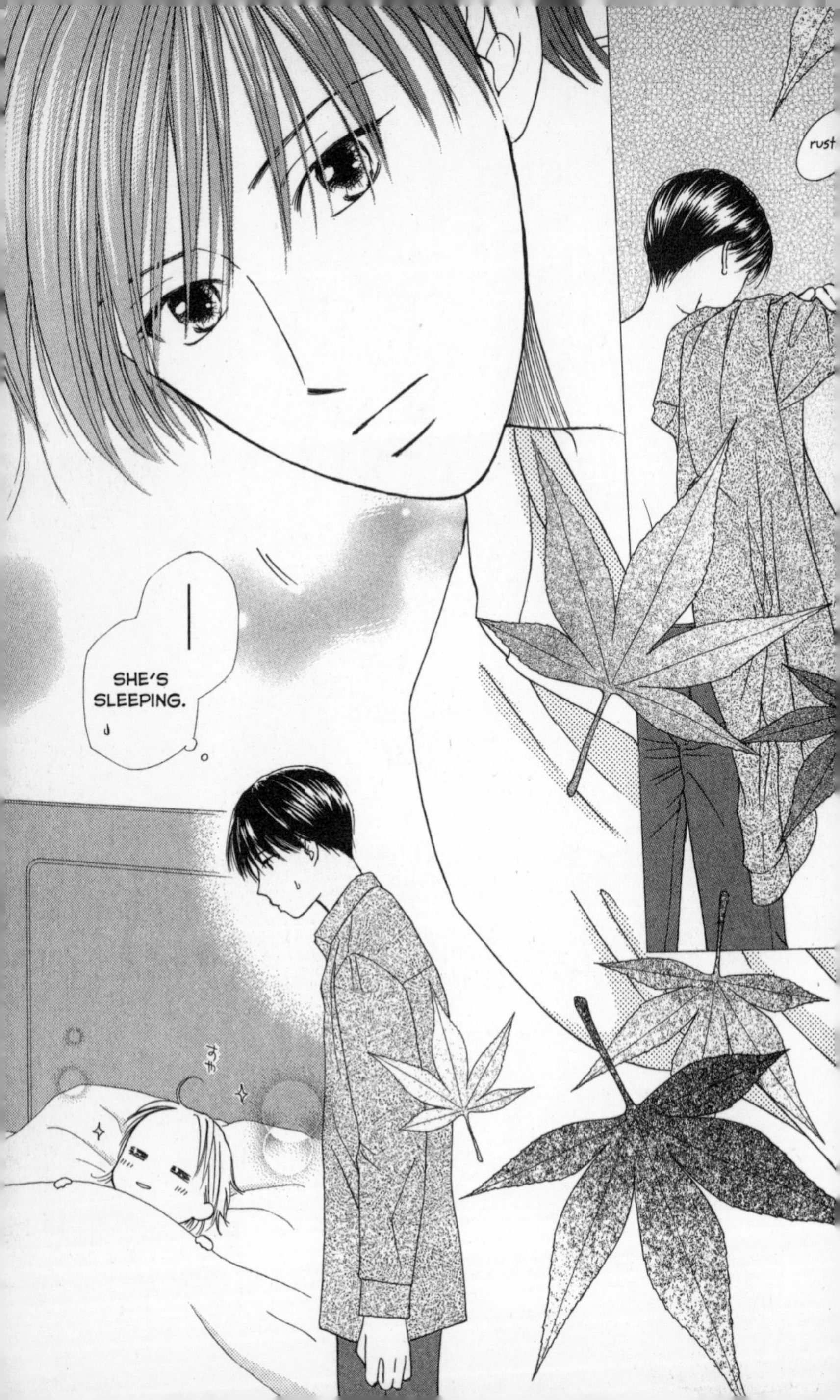
rust
— SHE'S SLEEPING.

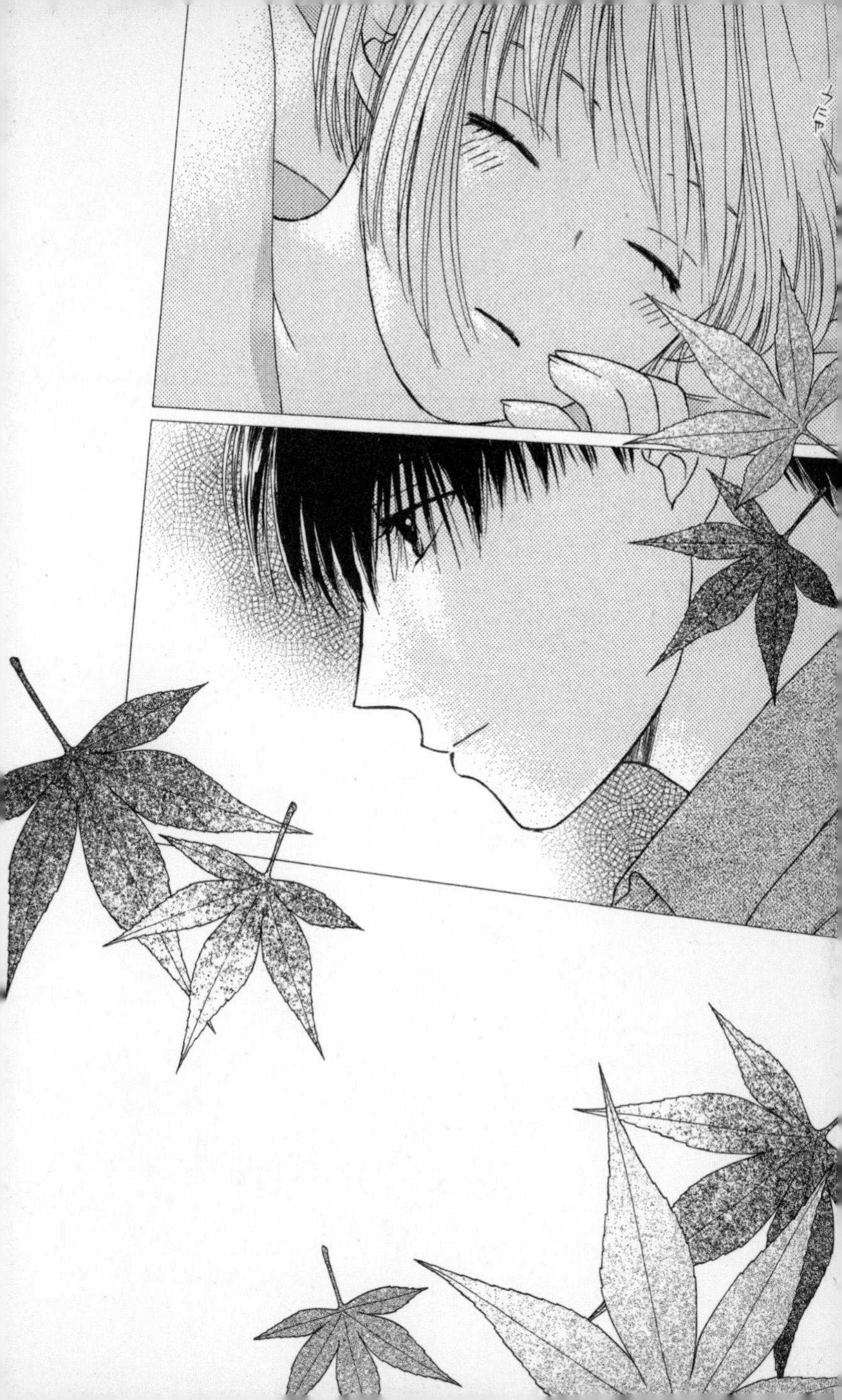
ナニャ

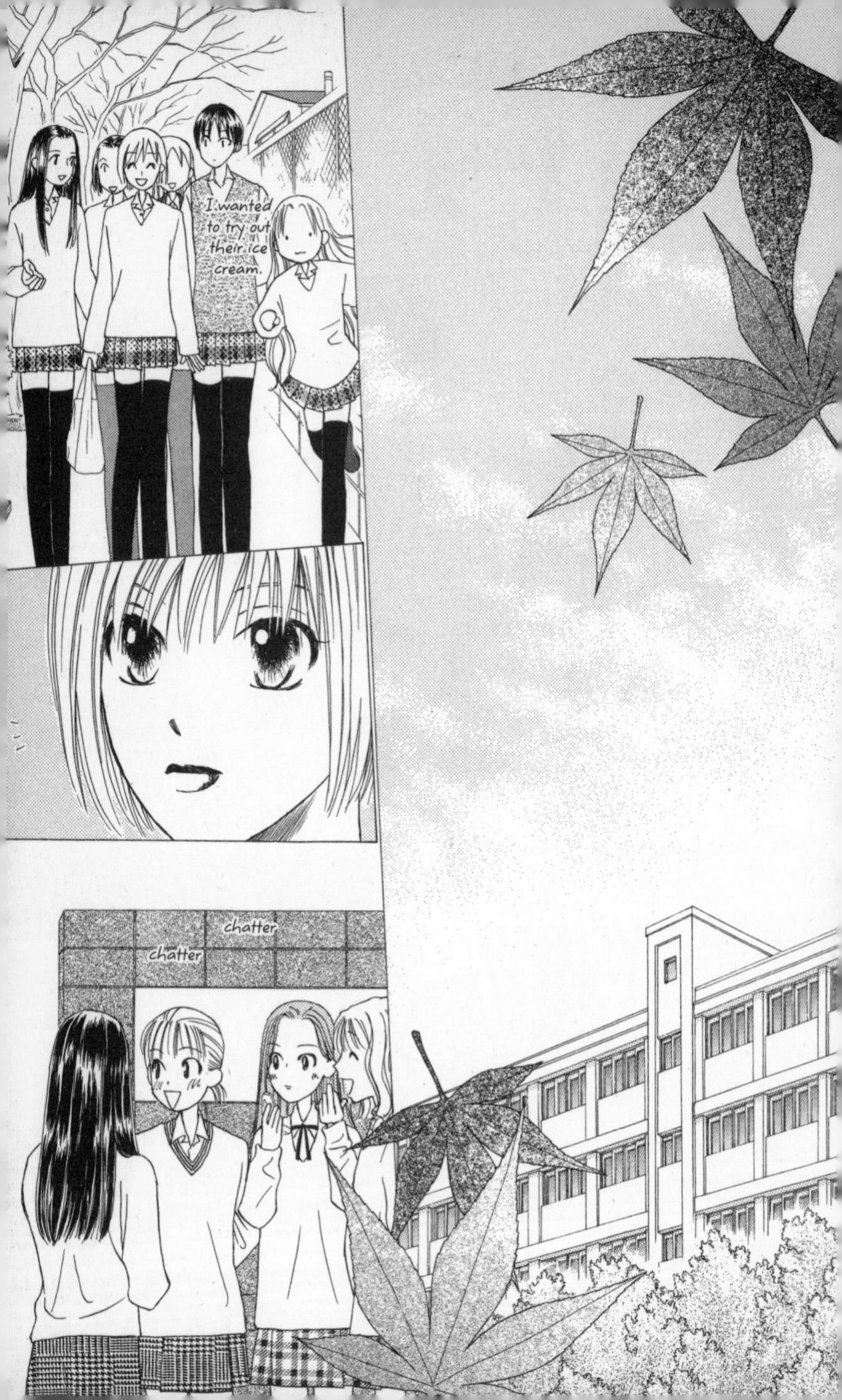
I wanted to try out their ice cream.
chatter
chatter

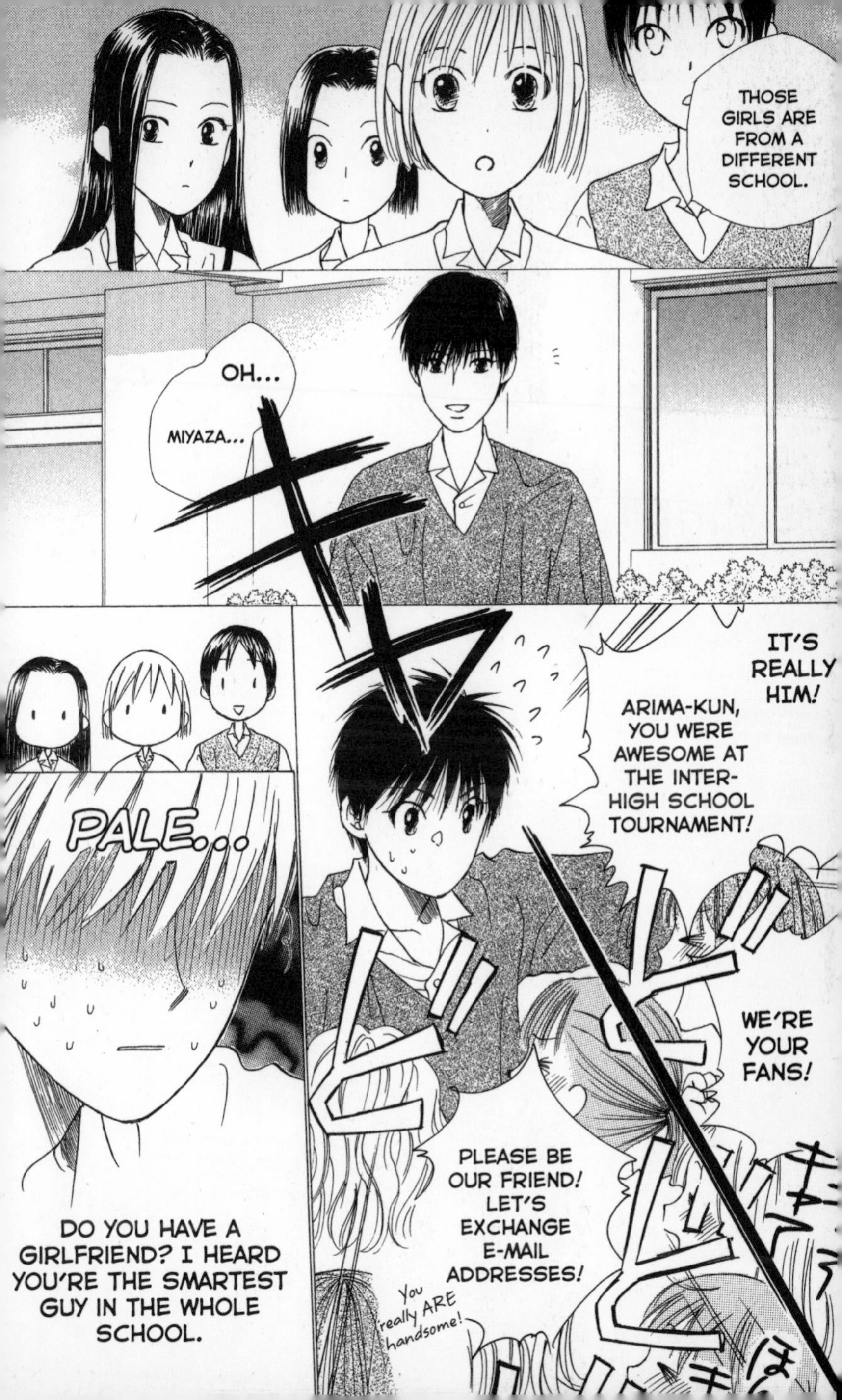
THOSE GIRLS ARE FROM A DIFFERENT SCHOOL.
OH...
MIYAZA...
IT'S REALLY HIM!
ARIMA-KUN, YOU WERE AWESOME AT THE INTER-HIGH SCHOOL TOURNAMENT!
WE'RE YOUR FANS!
PLEASE BE OUR FRIEND! LET'S EXCHANGE E-MAIL ADDRESSES!
You really ARE handsome!
PALE...
DO YOU HAVE A GIRLFRIEND? I HEARD YOU'RE THE SMARTEST GUY IN THE WHOLE SCHOOL.

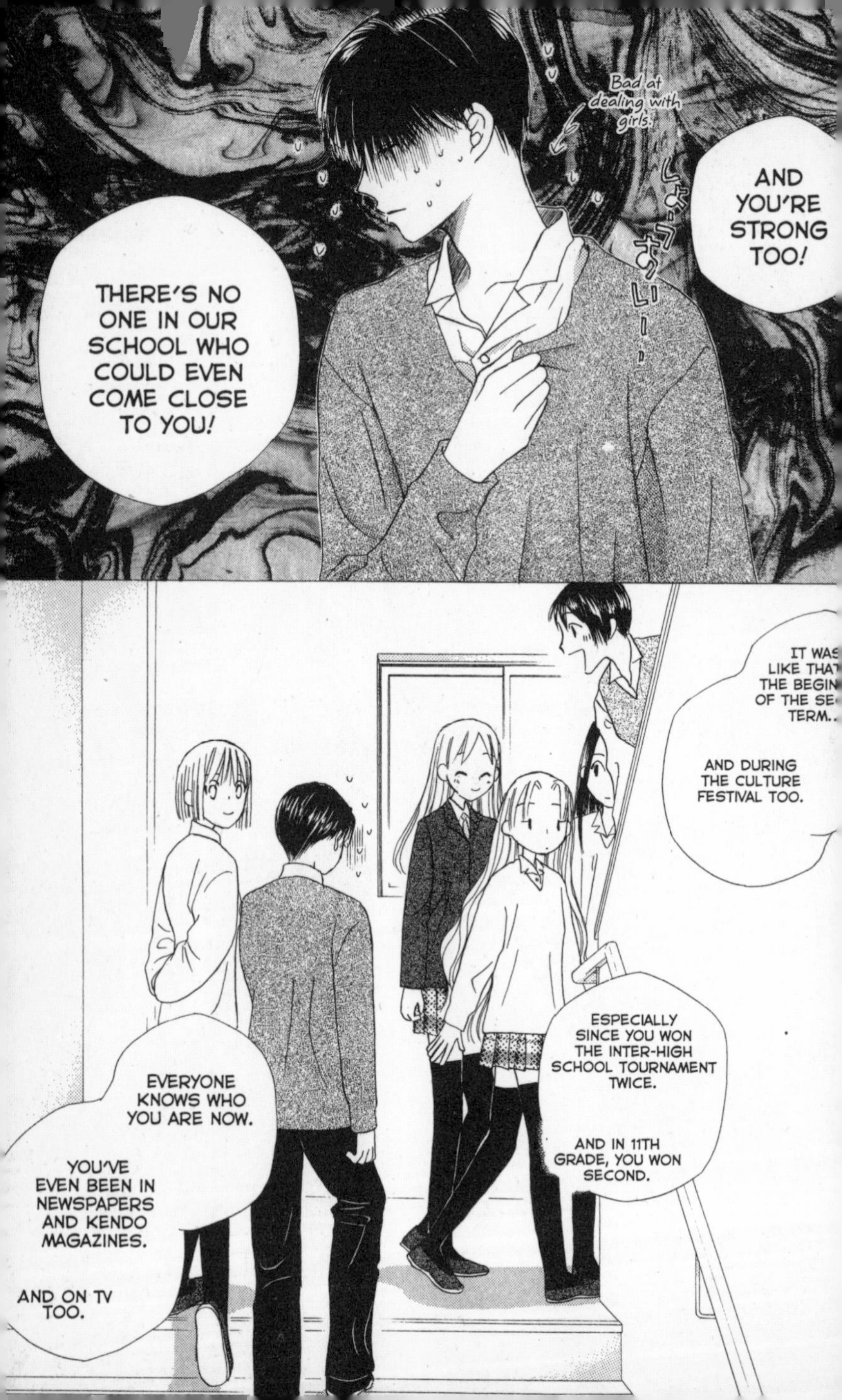
AND YOU'RE STRONG TOO!
Bad at dealing with girls.
THERE'S NO ONE IN OUR SCHOOL WHO COULD EVEN COME CLOSE TO YOU!
IT WAS LIKE THAT THE BEGIN OF THE SE TERM..
AND DURING THE CULTURE FESTIVAL TOO.
ESPECIALLY SINCE YOU WON THE INTER-HIGH SCHOOL TOURNAMENT TWICE.
AND IN 11TH GRADE, YOU WON SECOND.
EVERYONE KNOWS WHO YOU ARE NOW.
YOU'VE EVEN BEEN IN NEWSPAPERS AND KENDO MAGAZINES.
AND ON TV TOO.

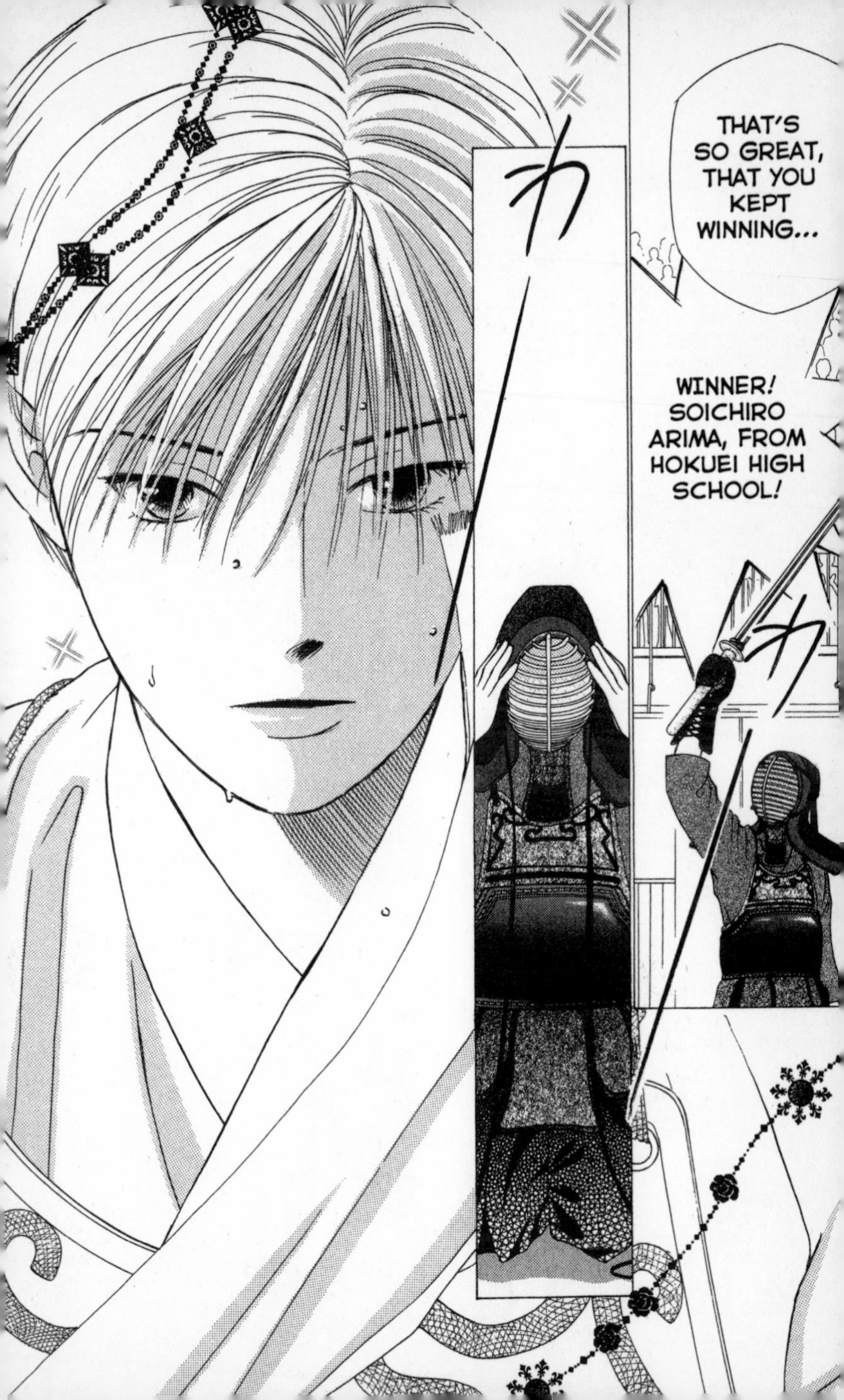
THAT'S SO GREAT, THAT YOU KEPT WINNING...
WINNER! SOICHIRO ARIMA, FROM HOKUEI HIGH SCHOOL!
わ
わ

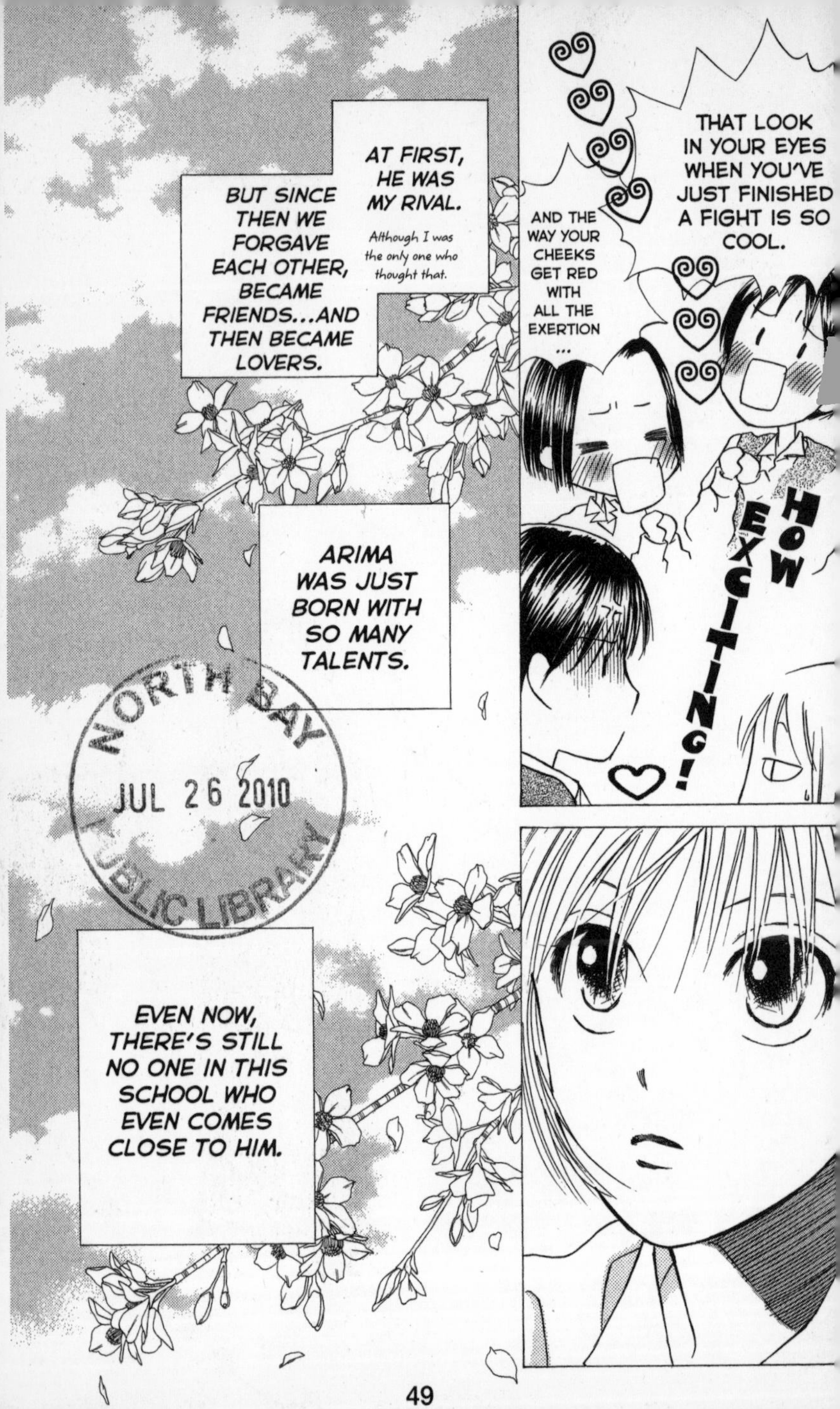
THAT LOOK IN YOUR EYES WHEN YOU'VE JUST FINISHED A FIGHT IS SO COOL.
AND THE WAY YOUR CHEEKS GET RED WITH ALL THE EXERTION...
HOW EXCITING!
AT FIRST, HE WAS MY RIVAL.
Although I was the only one who thought that.
BUT SINCE THEN WE FORGAVE EACH OTHER, BECAME FRIENDS...AND THEN BECAME LOVERS.
ARIMA WAS JUST BORN WITH SO MANY TALENTS.
EVEN NOW, THERE'S STILL NO ONE IN THIS SCHOOL WHO EVEN COMES CLOSE TO HIM.

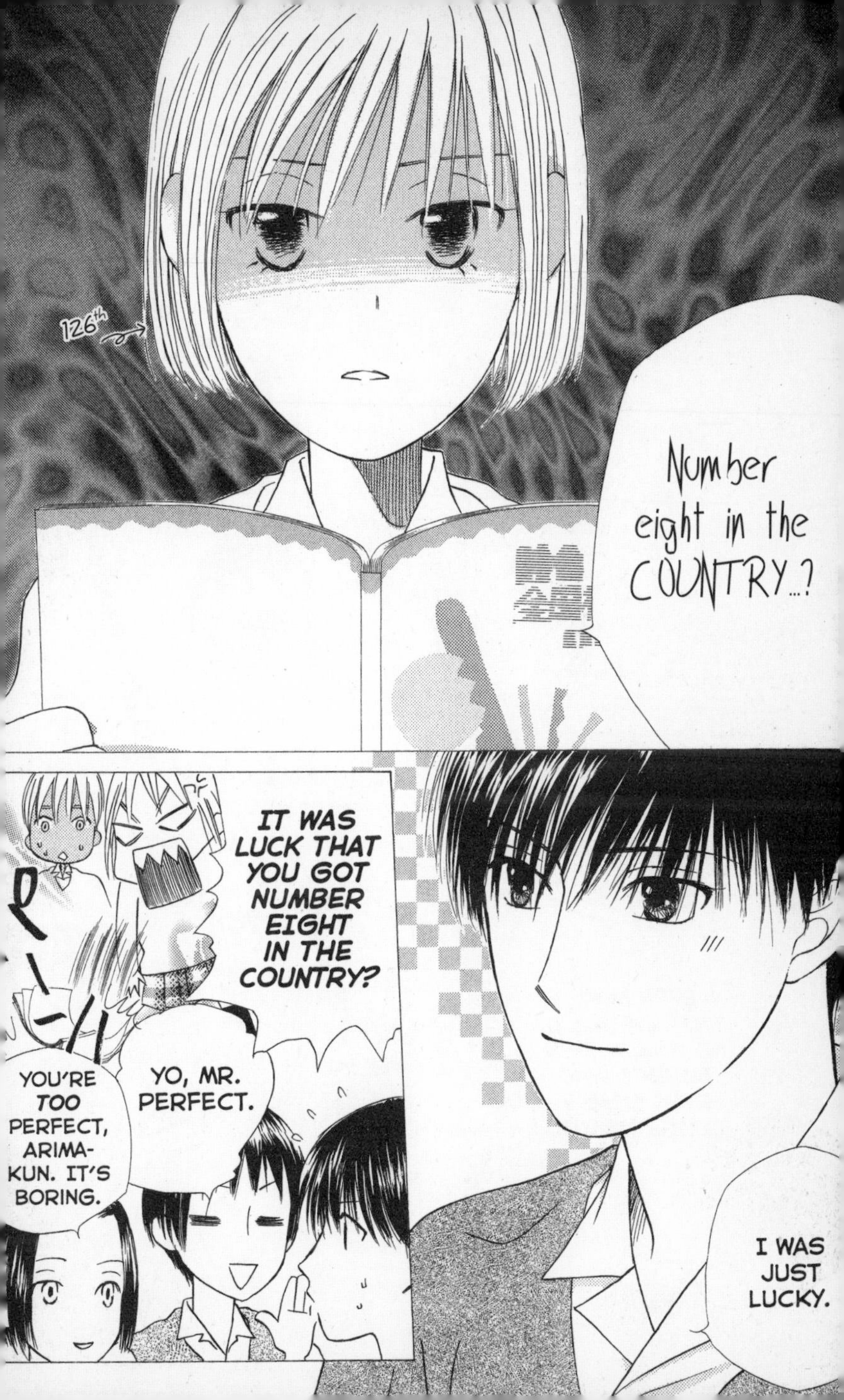
Number eight in the COUNTRY...?
126th
I WAS JUST LUCKY.
IT WAS LUCK THAT YOU GOT NUMBER EIGHT IN THE COUNTRY?
YO, MR. PERFECT.
YOU'RE *TOO* PERFECT, ARIMA-KUN. IT'S BORING.

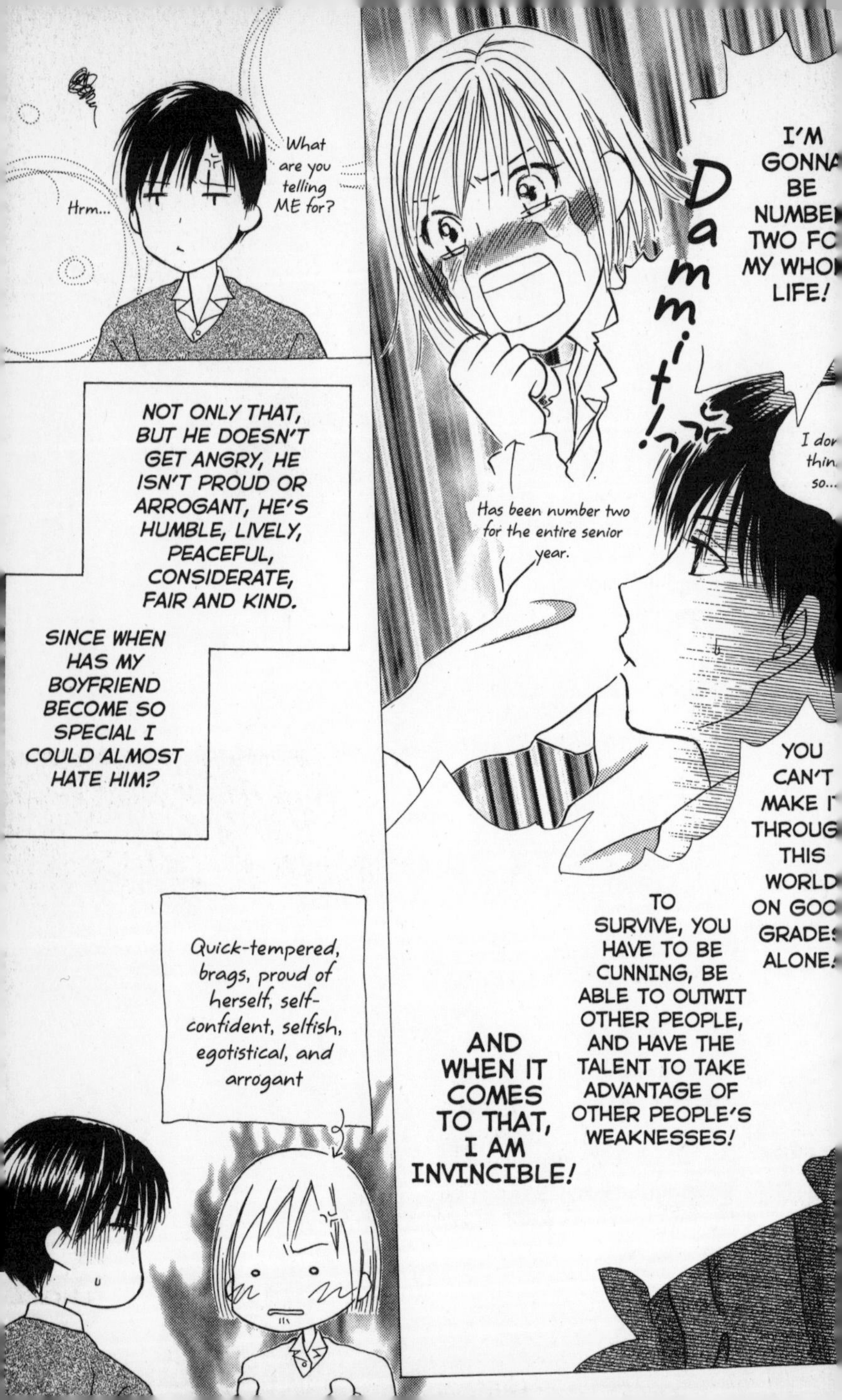
I'M GONNA BE NUMBE TWO FO MY WHOL LIFE!
Dammit!
Has been number two for the entire senior year.
I do thin so...
YOU CAN'T MAKE I THROUG THIS WORLD ON GOO GRADES ALONE!
TO SURVIVE, YOU HAVE TO BE CUNNING, BE ABLE TO OUTWIT OTHER PEOPLE, AND HAVE THE TALENT TO TAKE ADVANTAGE OF OTHER PEOPLE'S WEAKNESSES!
AND WHEN IT COMES TO THAT, I AM INVINCIBLE!
What are you telling ME for?
Hrm...
NOT ONLY THAT, BUT HE DOESN'T GET ANGRY, HE ISN'T PROUD OR ARROGANT, HE'S HUMBLE, LIVELY, PEACEFUL, CONSIDERATE, FAIR AND KIND.
SINCE WHEN HAS MY BOYFRIEND BECOME SO SPECIAL I COULD ALMOST HATE HIM?
Quick-tempered, brags, proud of herself, self-confident, selfish, egotistical, and arrogant

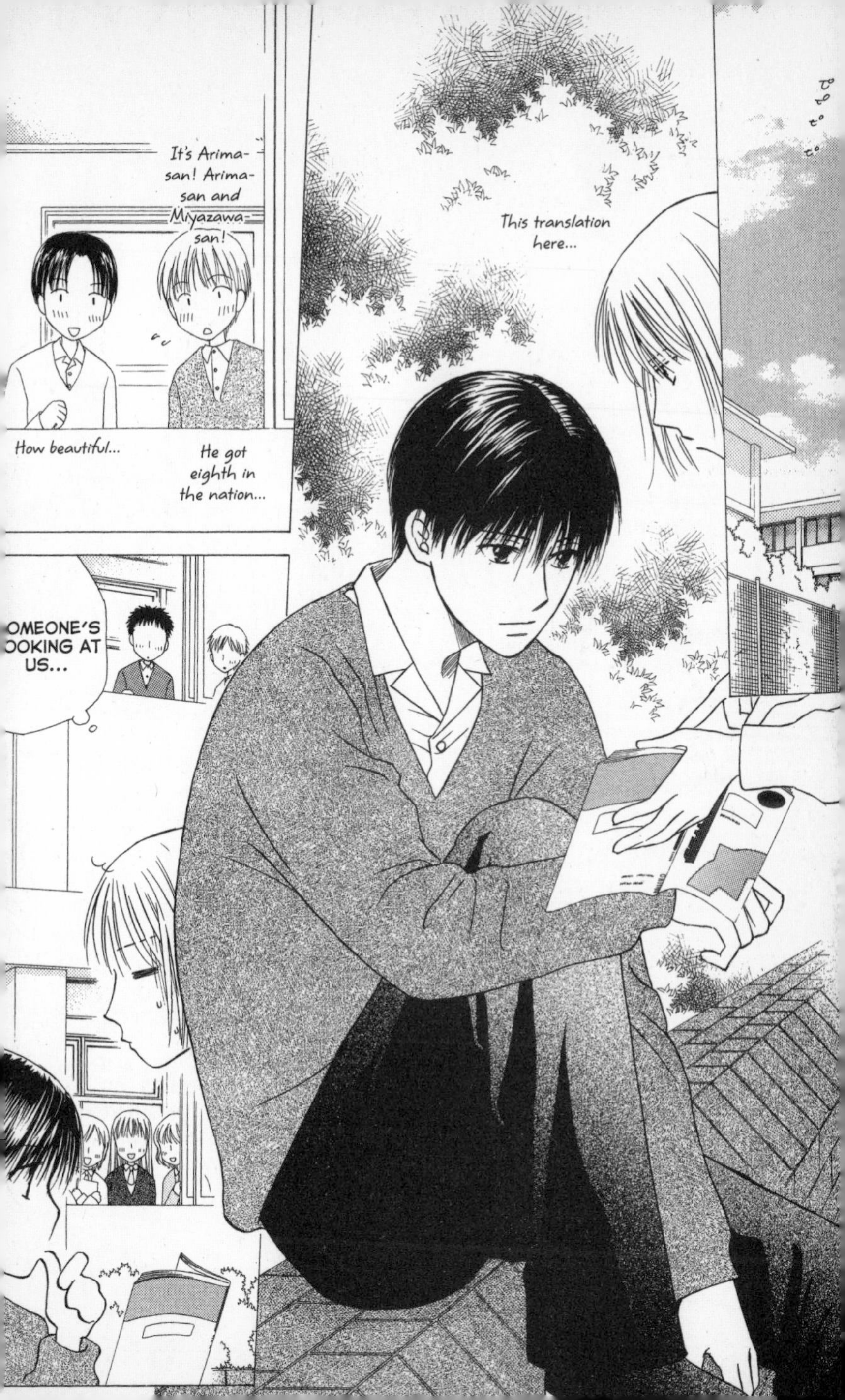
This translation here...
It's Arima-san! Arima-san and Miyazawa-san!
He got eighth in the nation...
How beautiful...
OMEONE'S OOKING AT US...

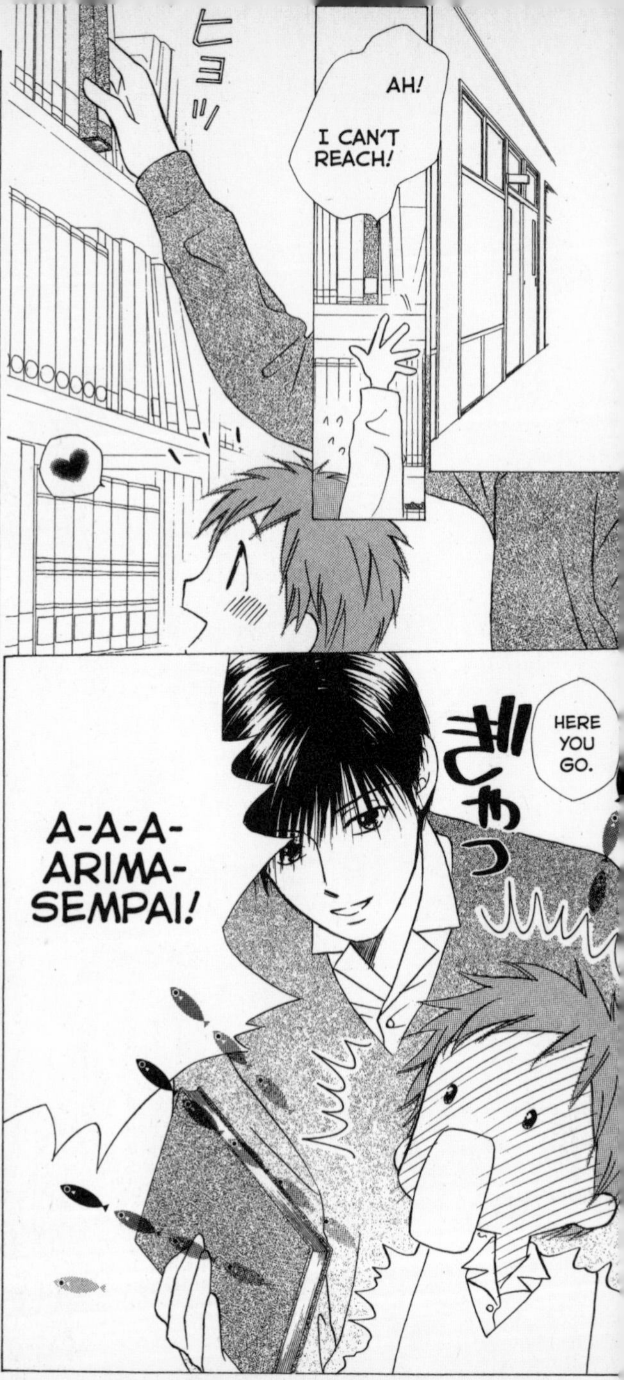
AH!
I CAN'T REACH!
ヒョッ
HERE YOU GO.
ぎゅっ
A-A-A-ARIMA-SEMPAI!

2

Ever since Volume 12, I've gotten lots of letters telling me where I can get great Raisin-wiches.

Thank you! They're SO good!

激うま。

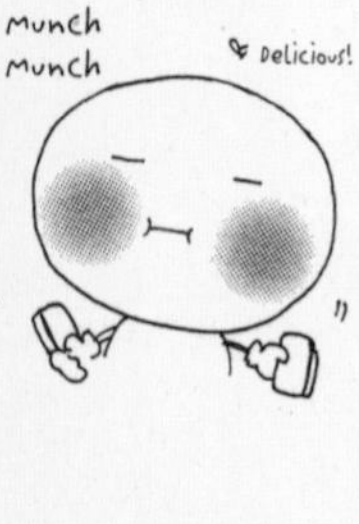
Munch Munch
Delicious!

As for chocolate, I've fallen in love with Lotte!

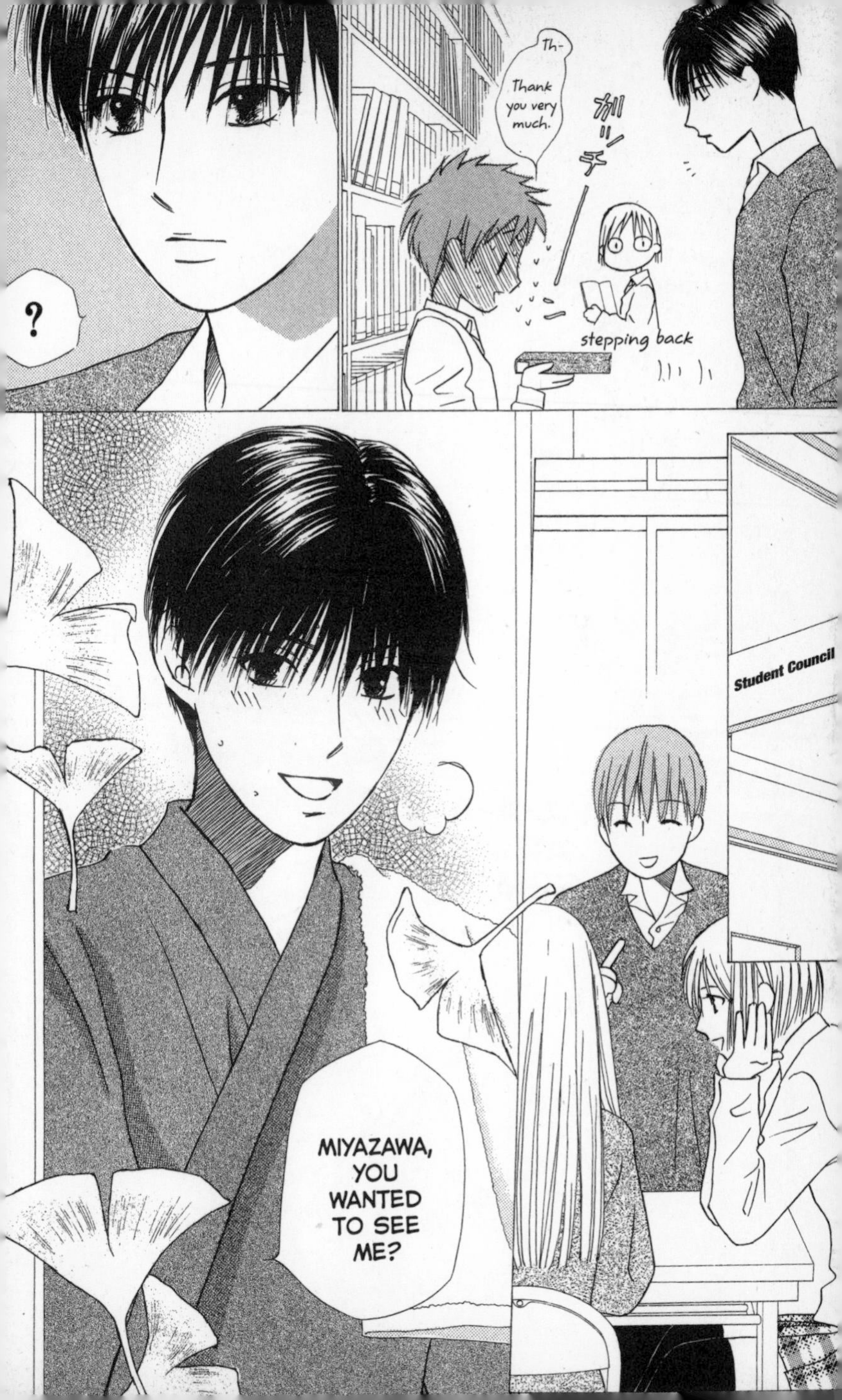
Th-
Thank you very much.
stepping back
?
Student Council
MIYAZAWA, YOU WANTED TO SEE ME?

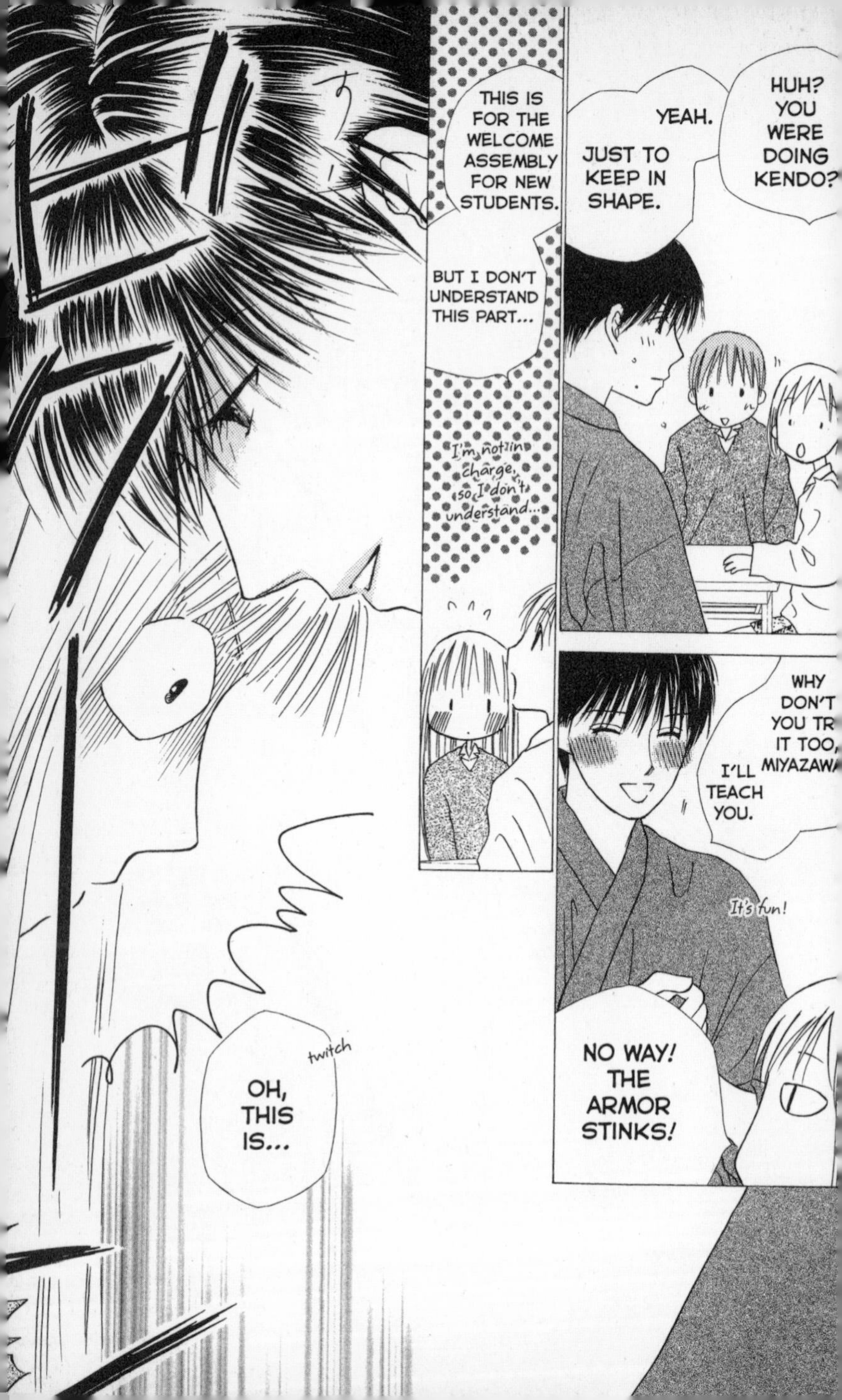
HUH? YOU WERE DOING KENDO?
YEAH.
JUST TO KEEP IN SHAPE.
WHY DON'T YOU TR IT TOO, MIYAZAW
I'LL TEACH YOU.
It's fun!
NO WAY! THE ARMOR STINKS!
THIS IS FOR THE WELCOME ASSEMBLY FOR NEW STUDENTS.
BUT I DON'T UNDERSTAND THIS PART...
I'm not in charge, so I don't understand...
twitch
OH, THIS IS...

SORRY.

DO I SMELL?

NO... I'M SORRY.

You don't stink at all.

IT'S ALL RIGHT. PLEASE, SHOW ME.

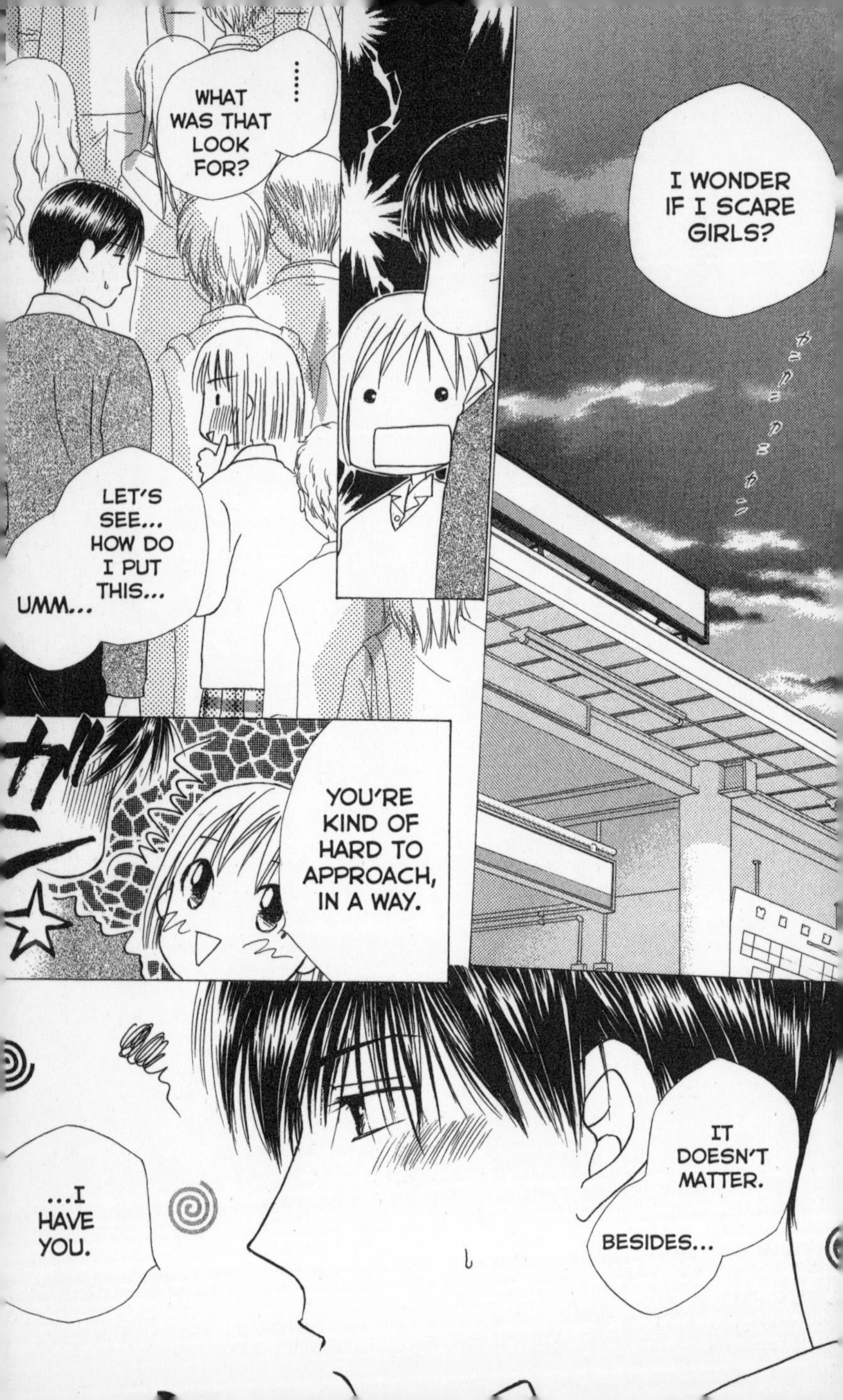
I WONDER IF I SCARE GIRLS?
......
WHAT WAS THAT LOOK FOR?
LET'S SEE... HOW DO I PUT THIS... UMM...
YOU'RE KIND OF HARD TO APPROACH, IN A WAY.
IT DOESN'T MATTER.
BESIDES...
...I HAVE YOU.

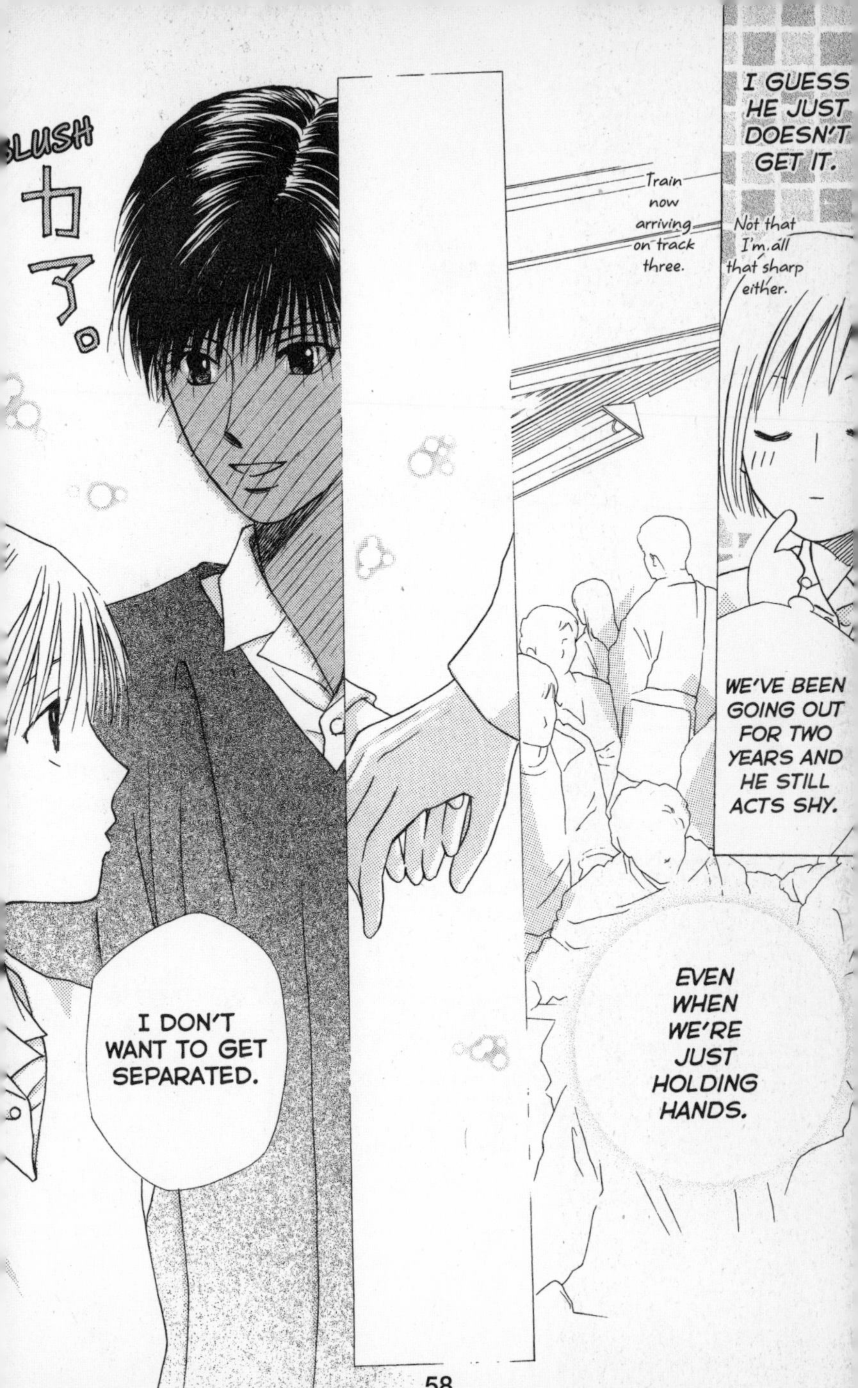
I GUESS HE JUST DOESN'T GET IT.
Not that I'm all that sharp either.
WE'VE BEEN GOING OUT FOR TWO YEARS AND HE STILL ACTS SHY.
Train now arriving on track three.
EVEN WHEN WE'RE JUST HOLDING HANDS.
BLUSH
カア。
I DON'T WANT TO GET SEPARATED.

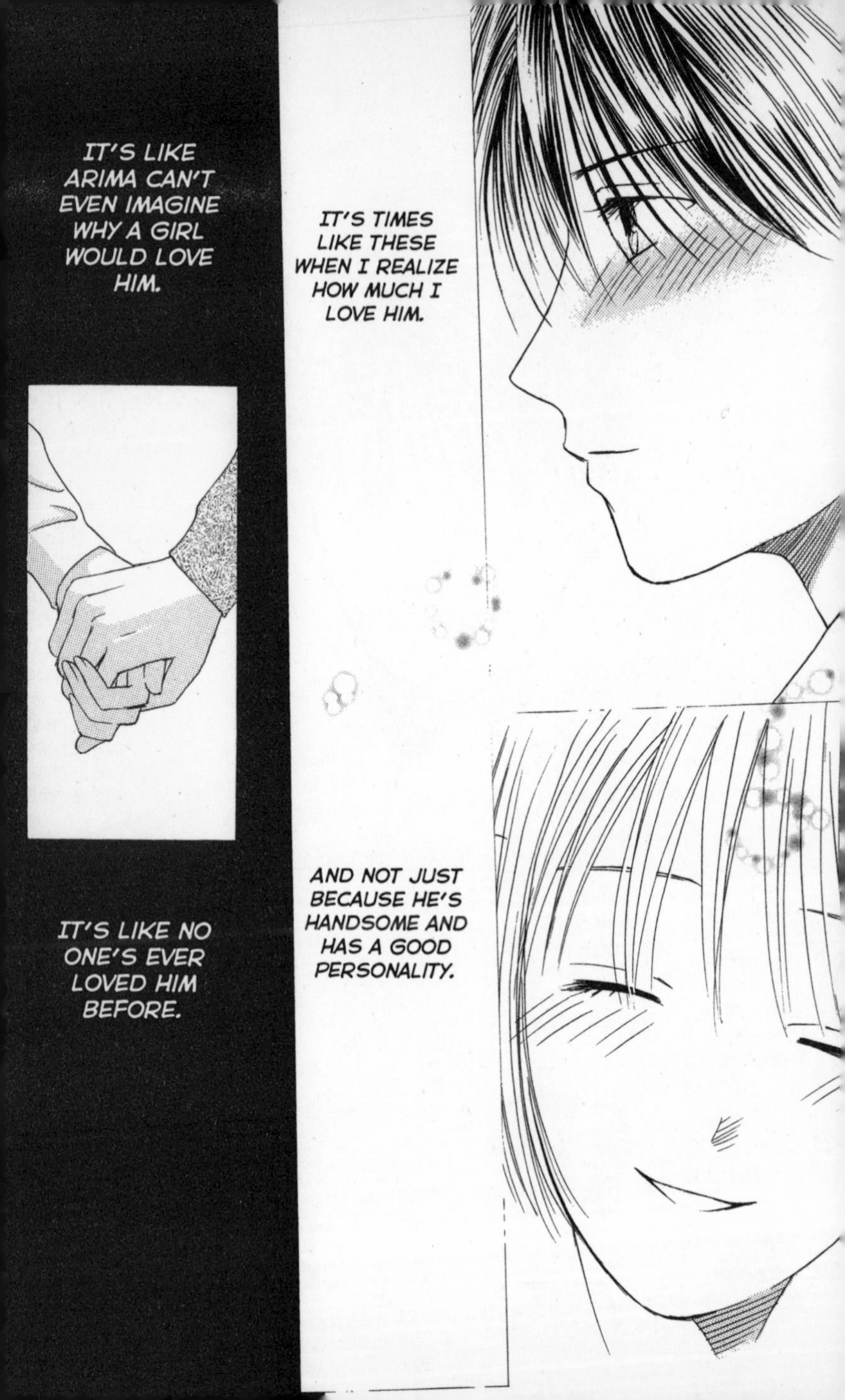
IT'S TIMES LIKE THESE WHEN I REALIZE HOW MUCH I LOVE HIM.
AND NOT JUST BECAUSE HE'S HANDSOME AND HAS A GOOD PERSONALITY.
IT'S LIKE ARIMA CAN'T EVEN IMAGINE WHY A GIRL WOULD LOVE HIM.
IT'S LIKE NO ONE'S EVER LOVED HIM BEFORE.

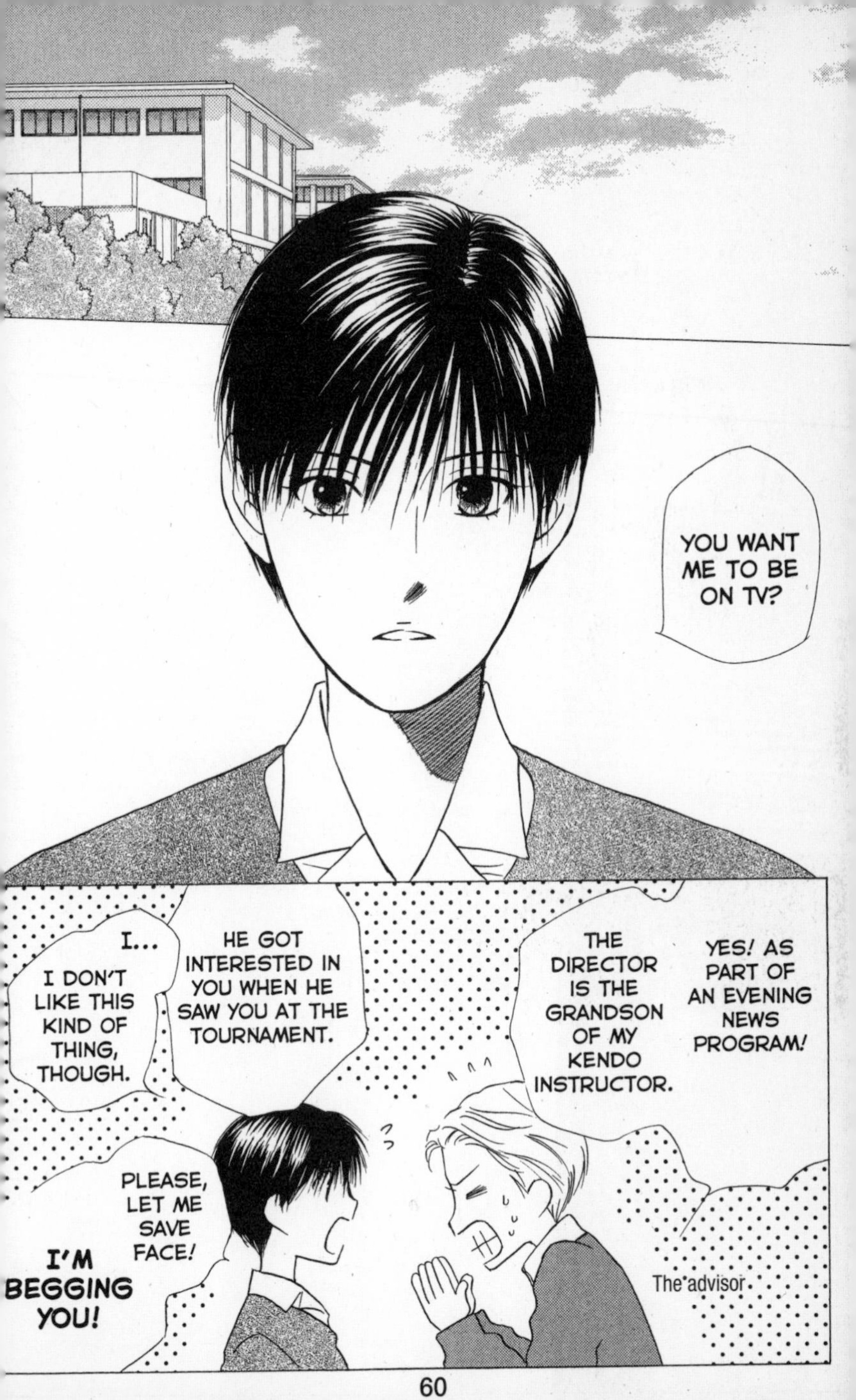
YOU WANT ME TO BE ON TV?
YES! AS PART OF AN EVENING NEWS PROGRAM!
THE DIRECTOR IS THE GRANDSON OF MY KENDO INSTRUCTOR.
HE GOT INTERESTED IN YOU WHEN HE SAW YOU AT THE TOURNAMENT.
I... I DON'T LIKE THIS KIND OF THING, THOUGH.
The advisor
PLEASE, LET ME SAVE FACE!
I'M BEGGING YOU!

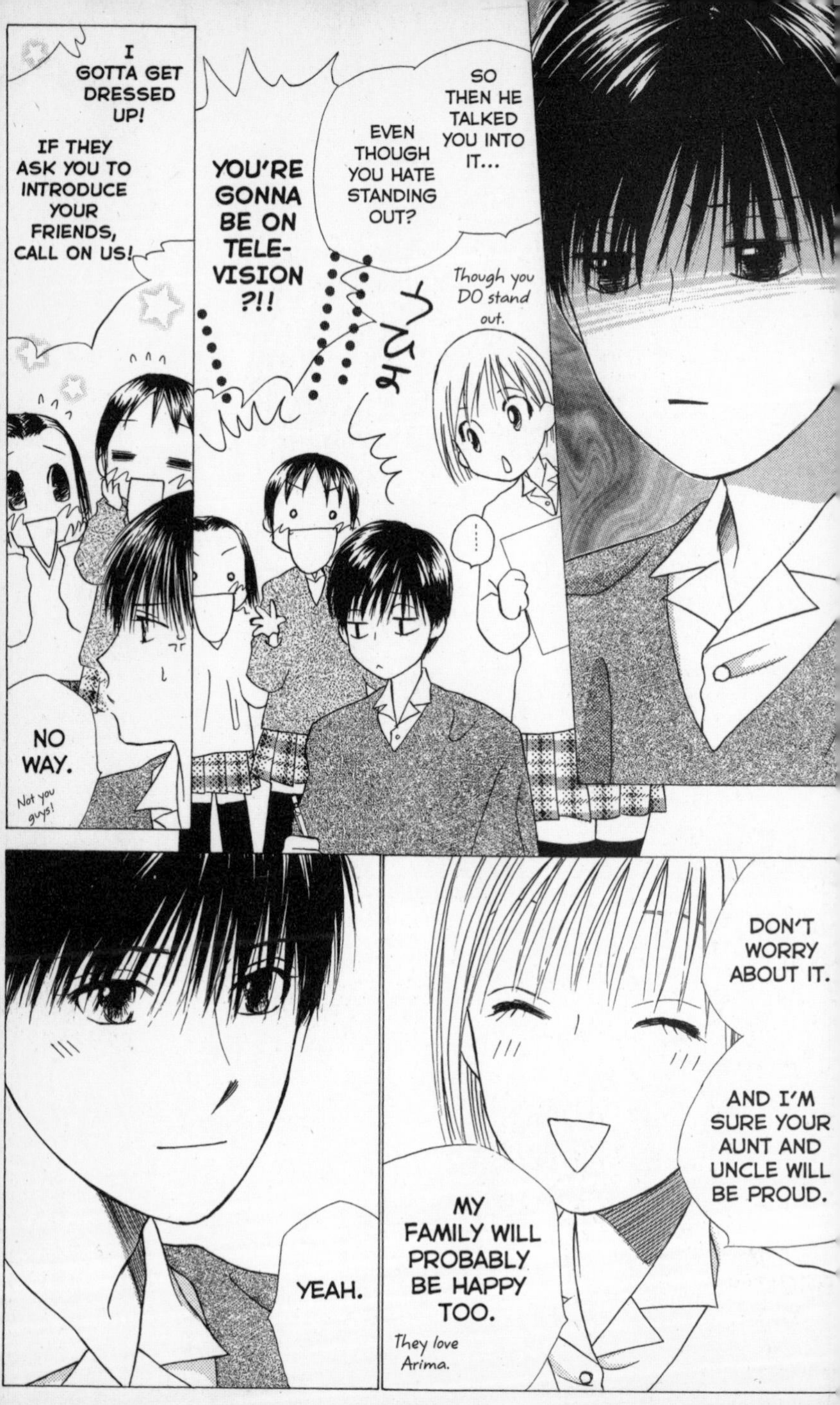
SO THEN HE TALKED YOU INTO IT...
EVEN THOUGH YOU HATE STANDING OUT?
Though you DO stand out.
YOU'RE GONNA BE ON TELE-VISION ?!!
...
I GOTTA GET DRESSED UP!
IF THEY ASK YOU TO INTRODUCE YOUR FRIENDS, CALL ON US!
NO WAY.
Not you guys!
DON'T WORRY ABOUT IT.
AND I'M SURE YOUR AUNT AND UNCLE WILL BE PROUD.
MY FAMILY WILL PROBABLY BE HAPPY TOO.
They love Arima.
YEAH.

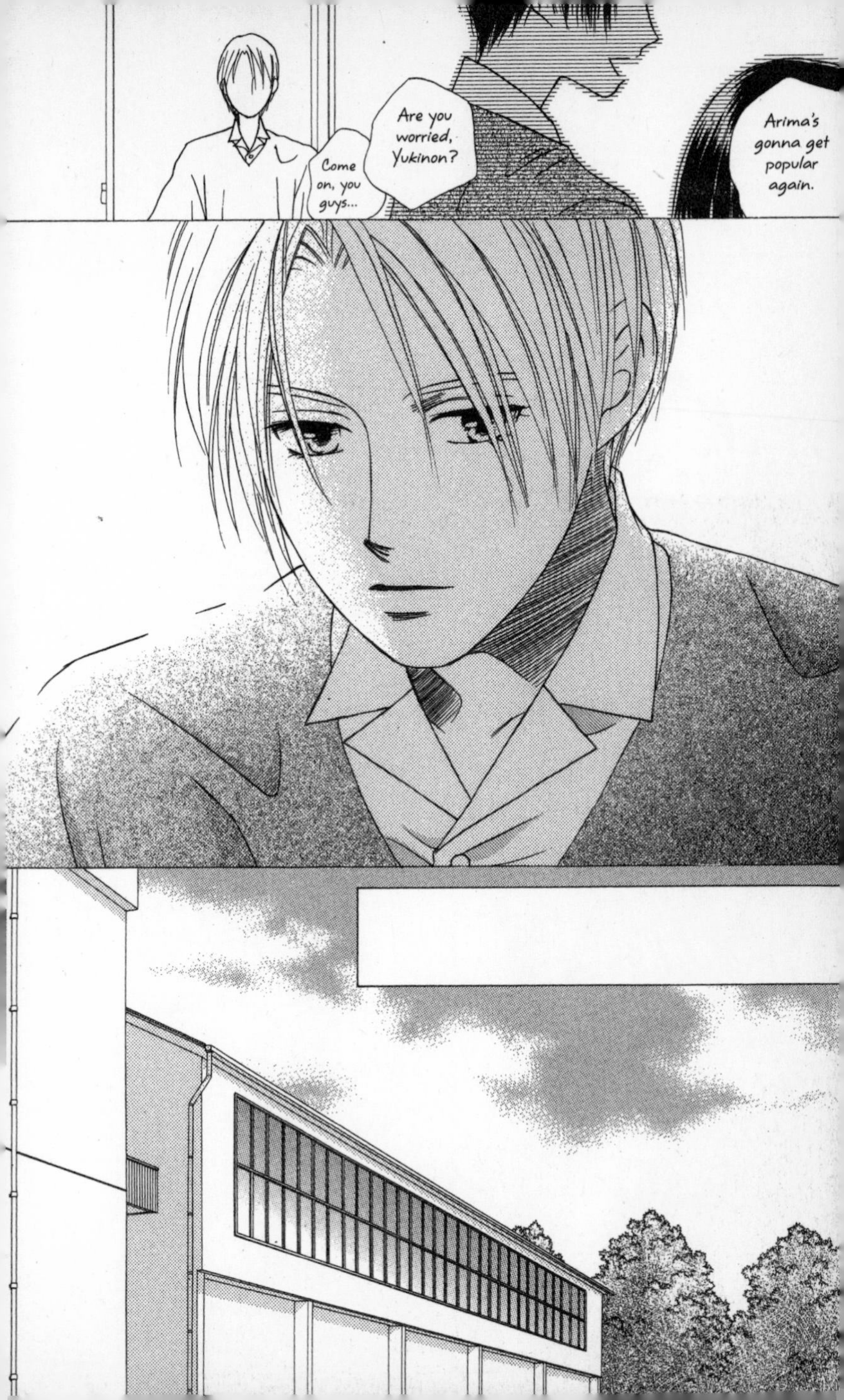
Arima's gonna get popular again.
Are you worried, Yukinon?
Come on, you guys...

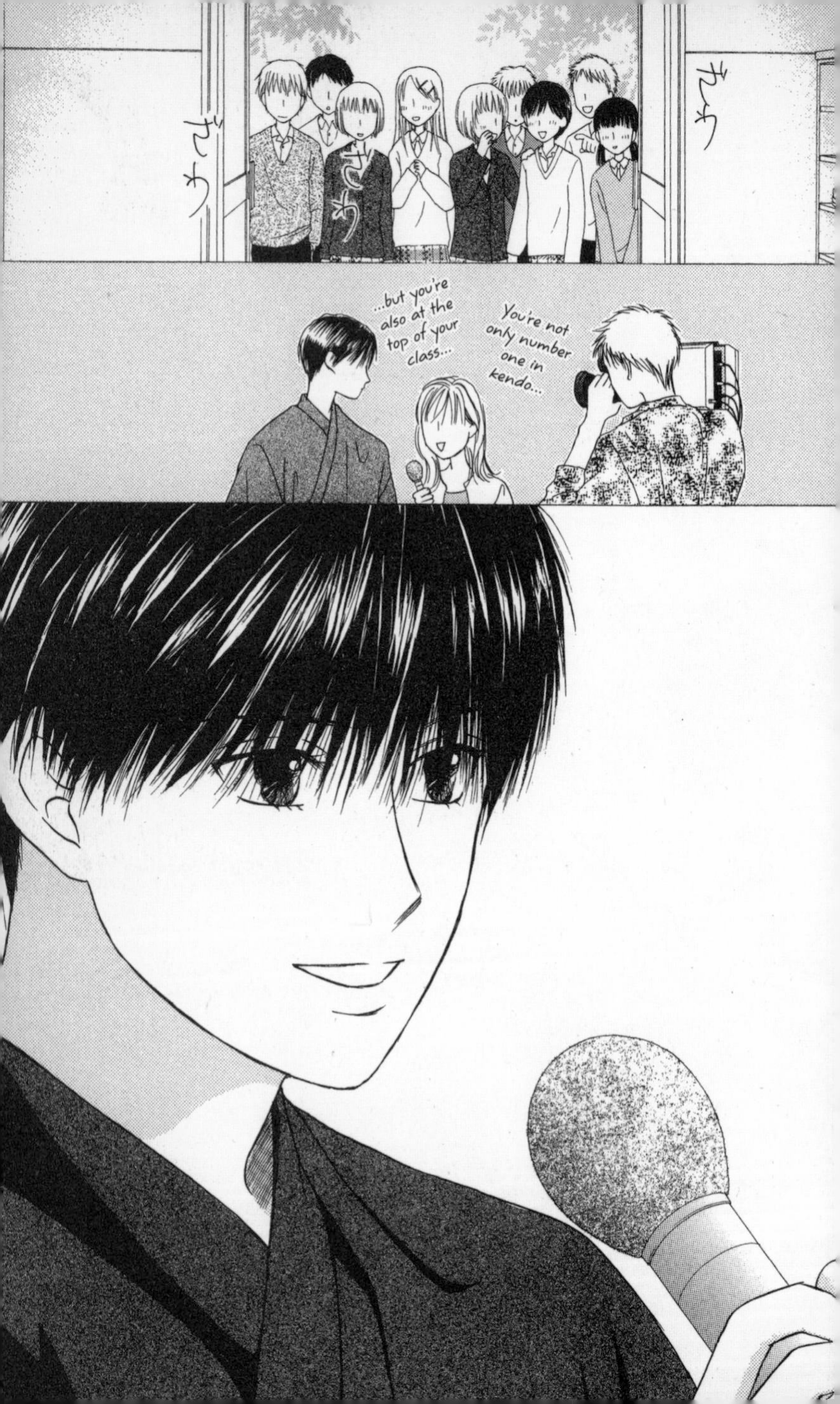
ざわ
ざわ
ざわ
You're not only number one in kendo...
...but you're also at the top of your class...

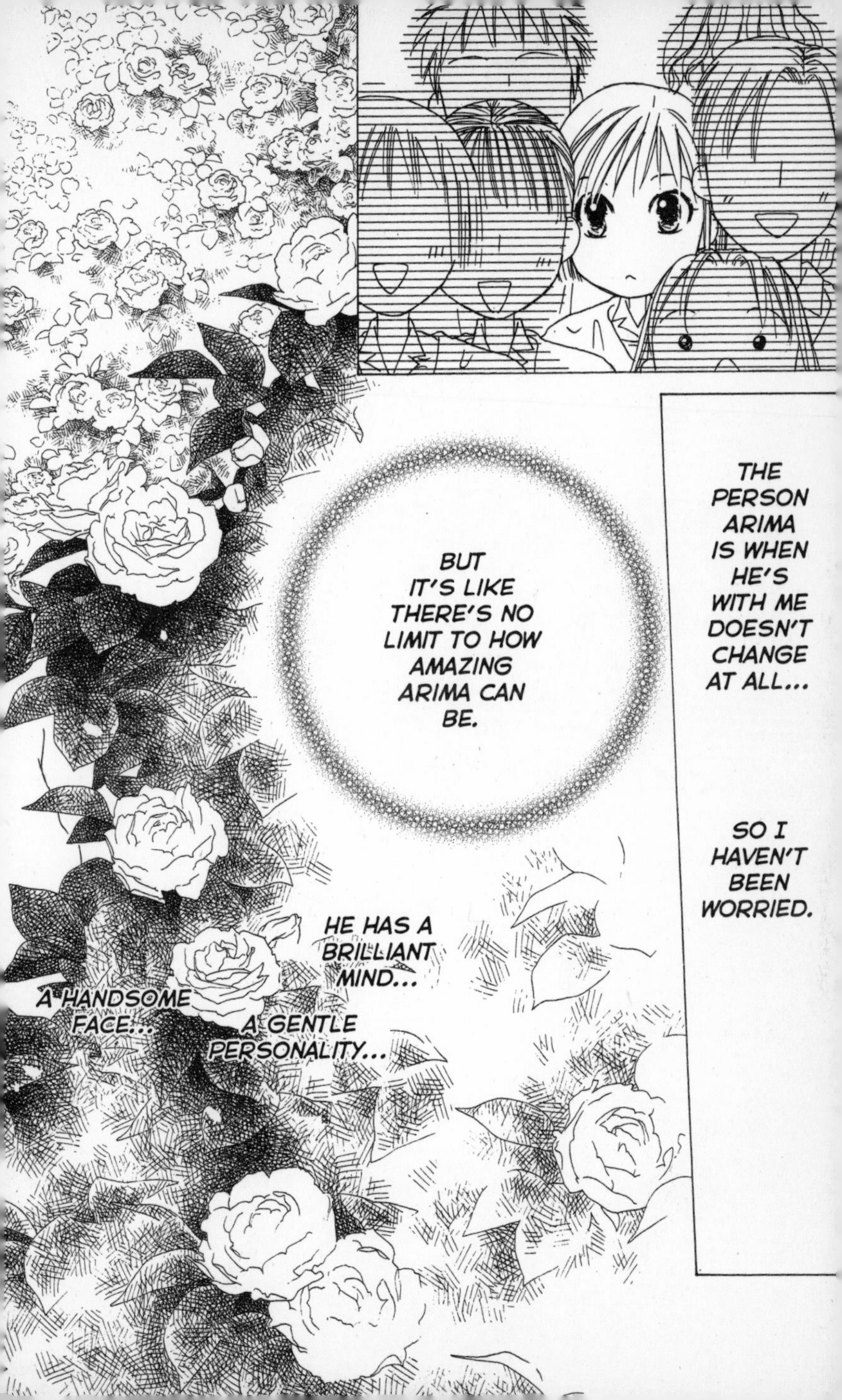
THE PERSON ARIMA IS WHEN HE'S WITH ME DOESN'T CHANGE AT ALL...
SO I HAVEN'T BEEN WORRIED.
BUT IT'S LIKE THERE'S NO LIMIT TO HOW AMAZING ARIMA CAN BE.
HE HAS A BRILLIANT MIND...
A HANDSOME FACE...
A GENTLE PERSONALITY...

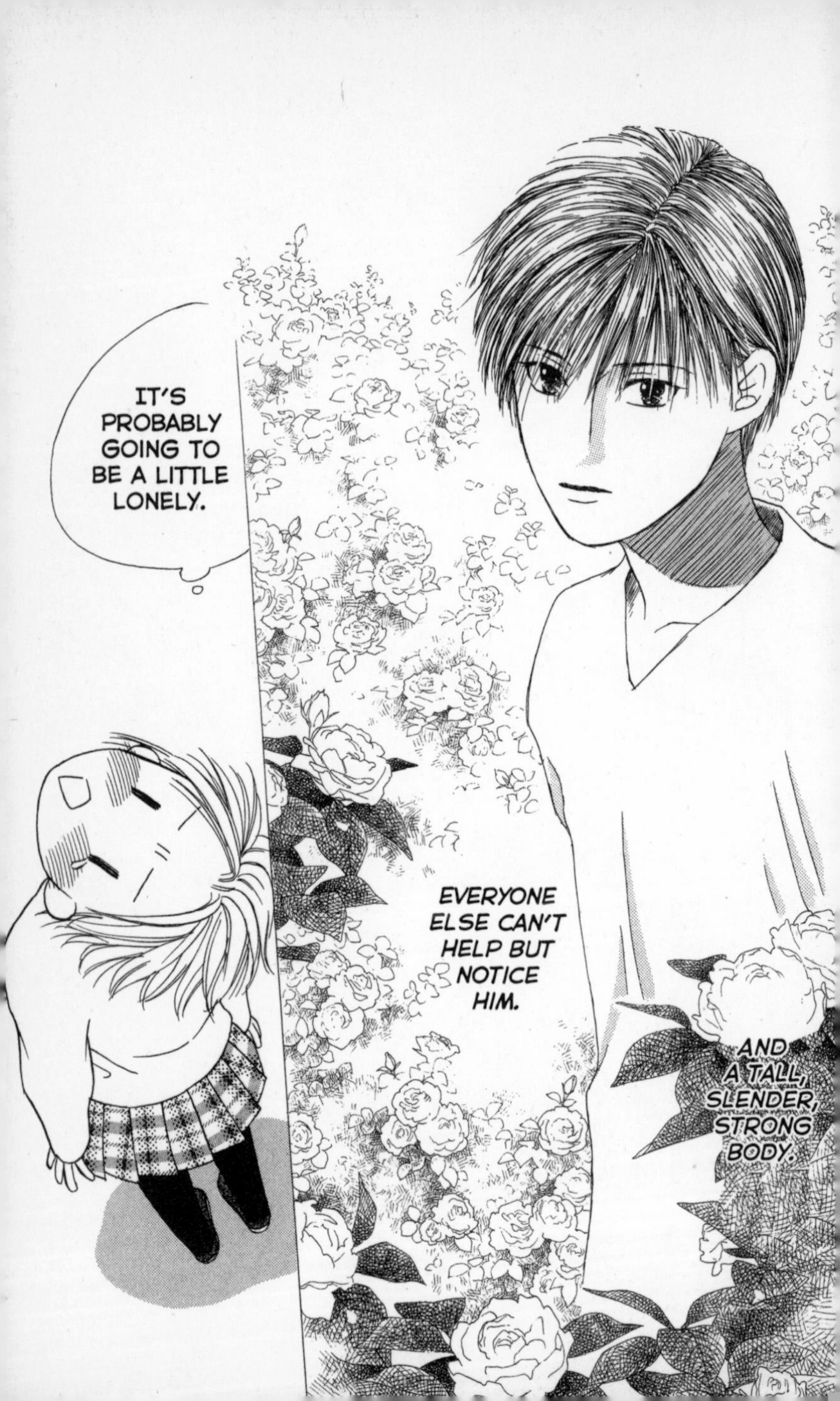
EVERYONE ELSE CAN'T HELP BUT NOTICE HIM.
AND A TALL, SLENDER, STRONG BODY.
IT'S PROBABLY GOING TO BE A LITTLE LONELY.

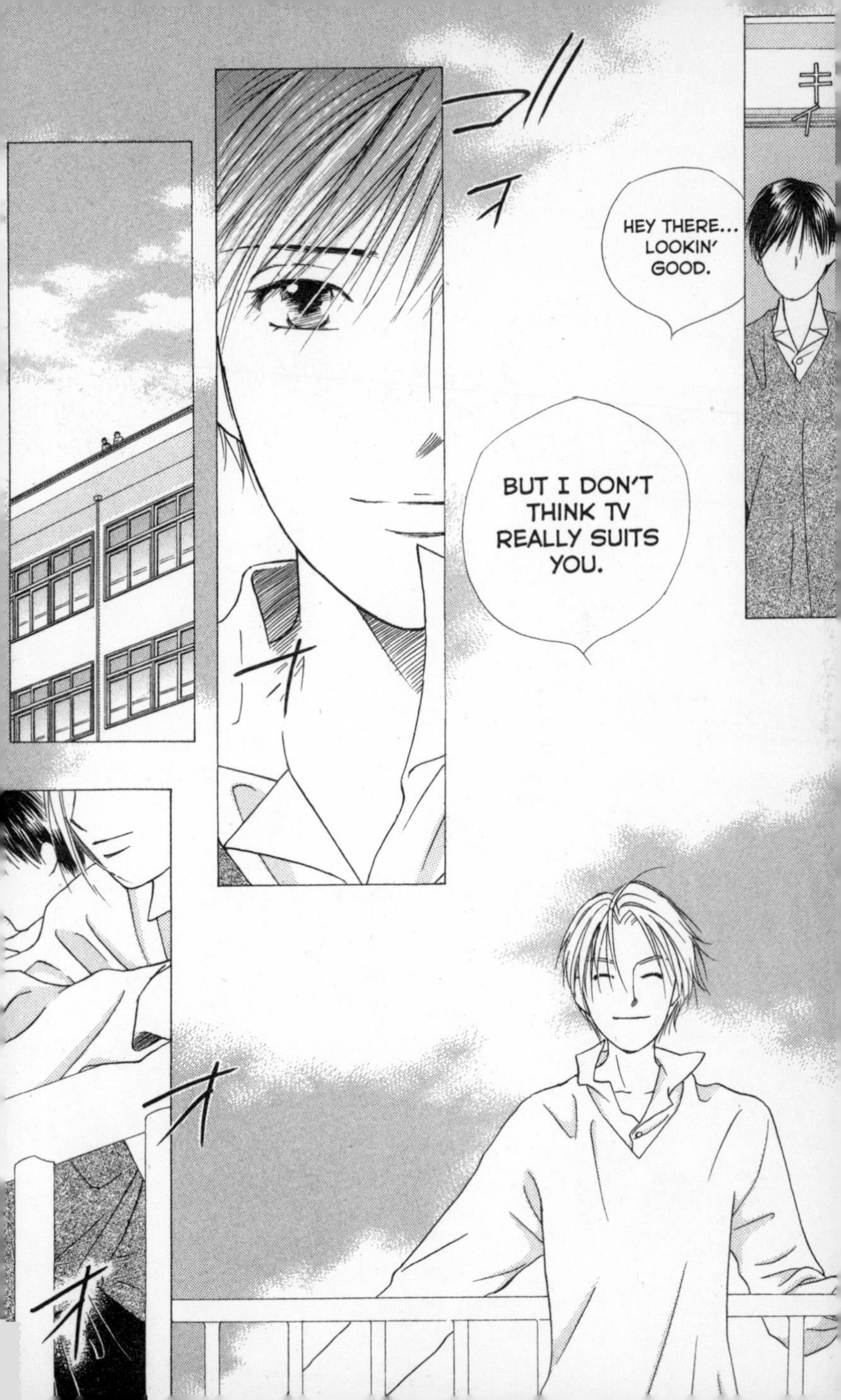
キィ
HEY THERE... LOOKIN' GOOD.
ゴソ
BUT I DON'T THINK TV REALLY SUITS YOU.

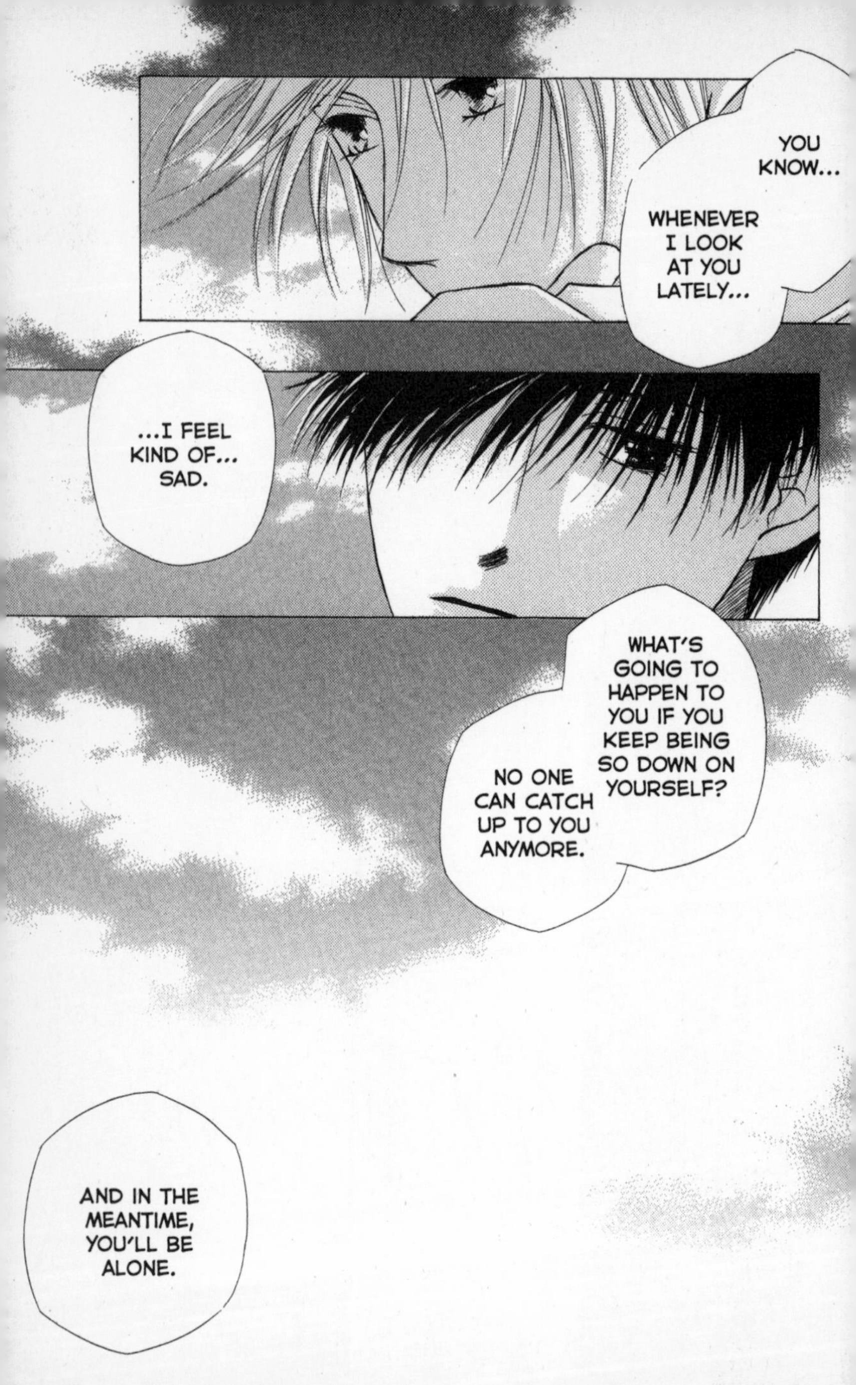
YOU KNOW...
WHENEVER I LOOK AT YOU LATELY...
...I FEEL KIND OF... SAD.
WHAT'S GOING TO HAPPEN TO YOU IF YOU KEEP BEING SO DOWN ON YOURSELF?
NO ONE CAN CATCH UP TO YOU ANYMORE.
AND IN THE MEANTIME, YOU'LL BE ALONE.

EVEN WITH MIYAZAWA.
MY HEART DIED ONCE.
CAN I BRING IT BACK TO LIFE?

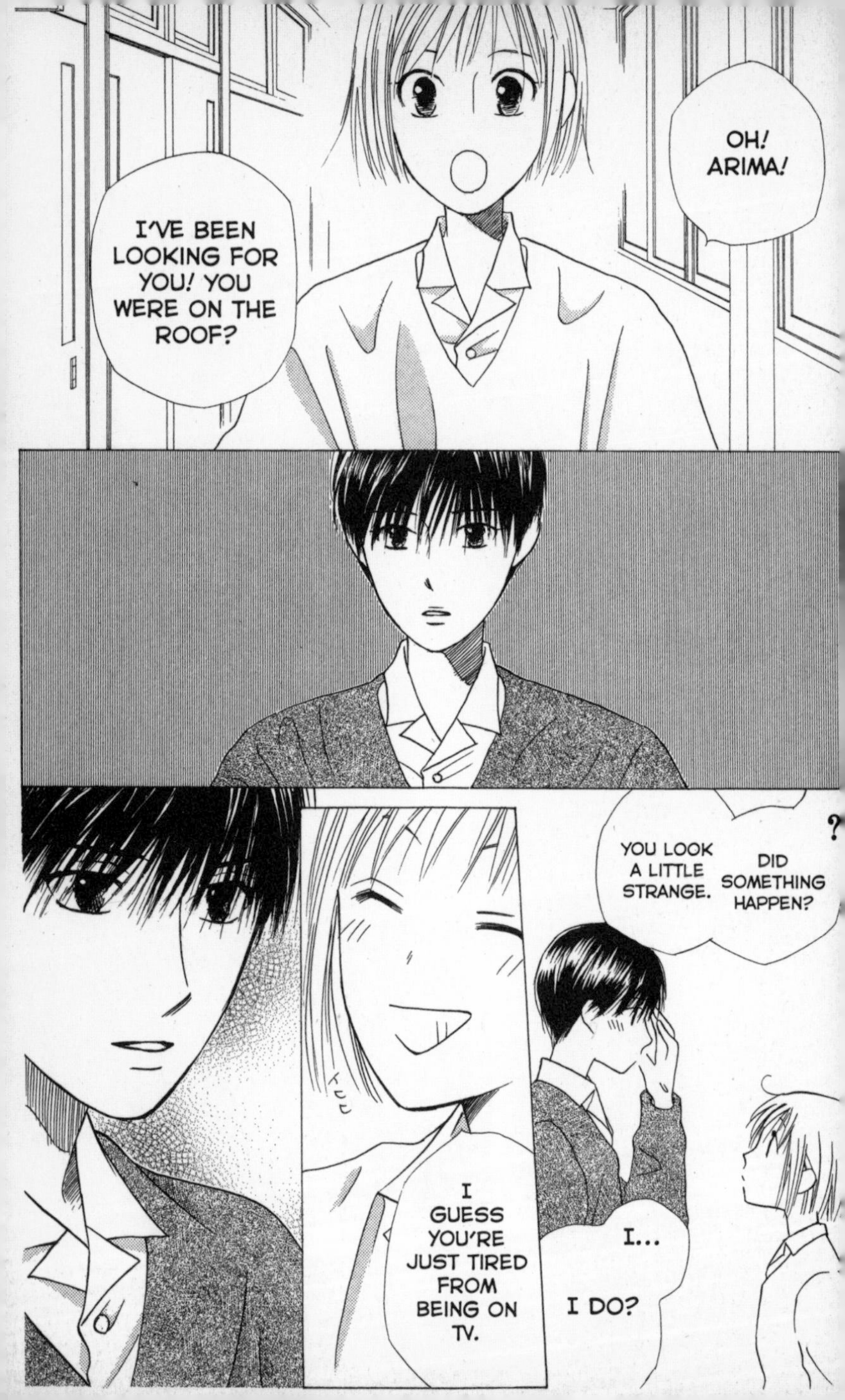
OH! ARIMA!
I'VE BEEN LOOKING FOR YOU! YOU WERE ON THE ROOF?
YOU LOOK A LITTLE STRANGE.
DID SOMETHING HAPPEN?
?
I...
I DO?
I GUESS YOU'RE JUST TIRED FROM BEING ON TV.

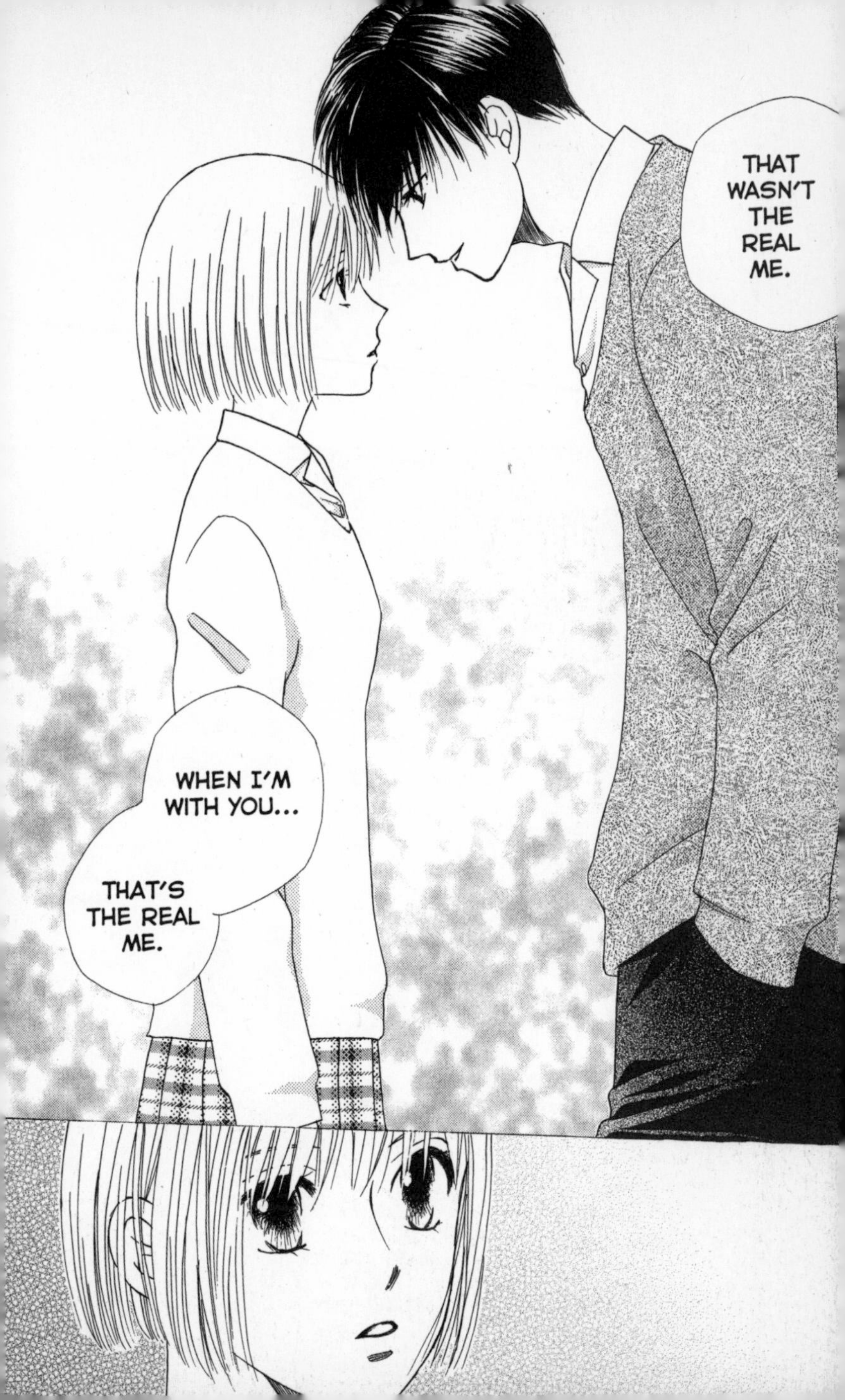
THAT WASN'T THE REAL ME.
WHEN I'M WITH YOU...
THAT'S THE REAL ME.

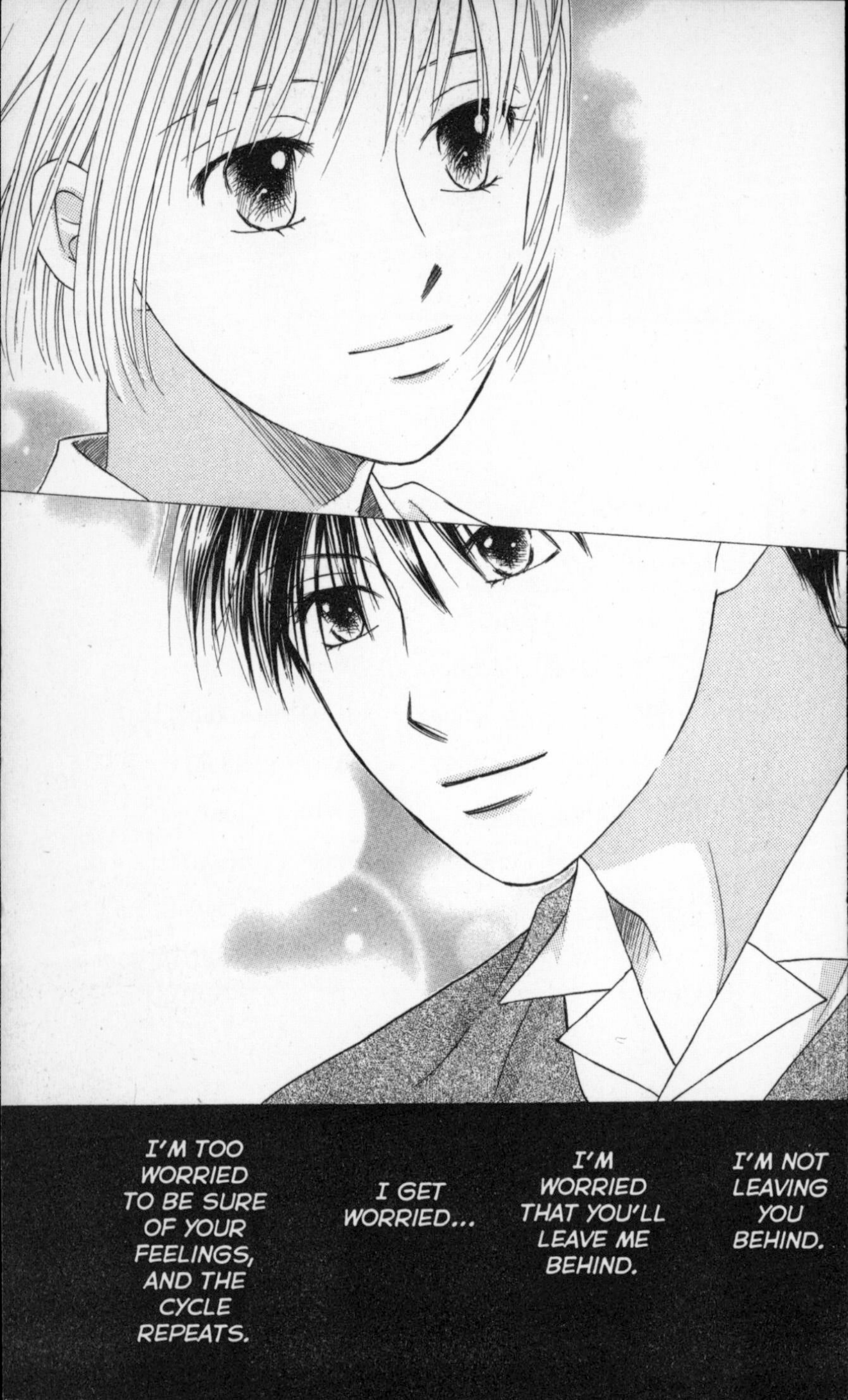
I'M NOT LEAVING YOU BEHIND.
I'M WORRIED THAT YOU'LL LEAVE ME BEHIND.
I GET WORRIED...
I'M TOO WORRIED TO BE SURE OF YOUR FEELINGS, AND THE CYCLE REPEATS.

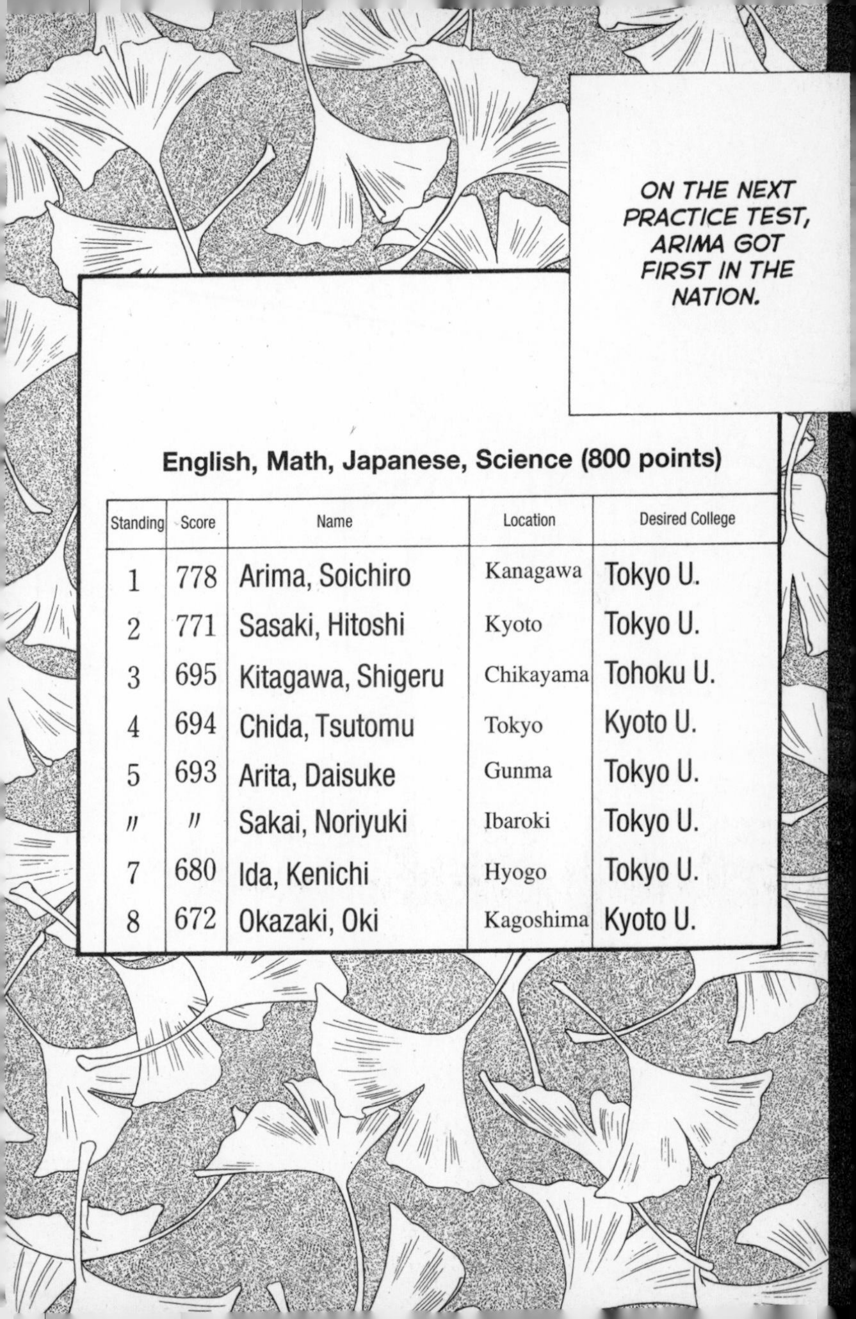
ON THE NEXT PRACTICE TEST, ARIMA GOT FIRST IN THE NATION.

English, Math, Japanese, Science (800 points)

Standing	Score	Name	Location	Desired College
1	778	Arima, Soichiro	Kanagawa	Tokyo U.
2	771	Sasaki, Hitoshi	Kyoto	Tokyo U.
3	695	Kitagawa, Shigeru	Chikayama	Tohoku U.
4	694	Chida, Tsutomu	Tokyo	Kyoto U.
5	693	Arita, Daisuke	Gunma	Tokyo U.
〃	〃	Sakai, Noriyuki	Ibaroki	Tokyo U.
7	680	Ida, Kenichi	Hyogo	Tokyo U.
8	672	Okazaki, Oki	Kagoshima	Kyoto U.

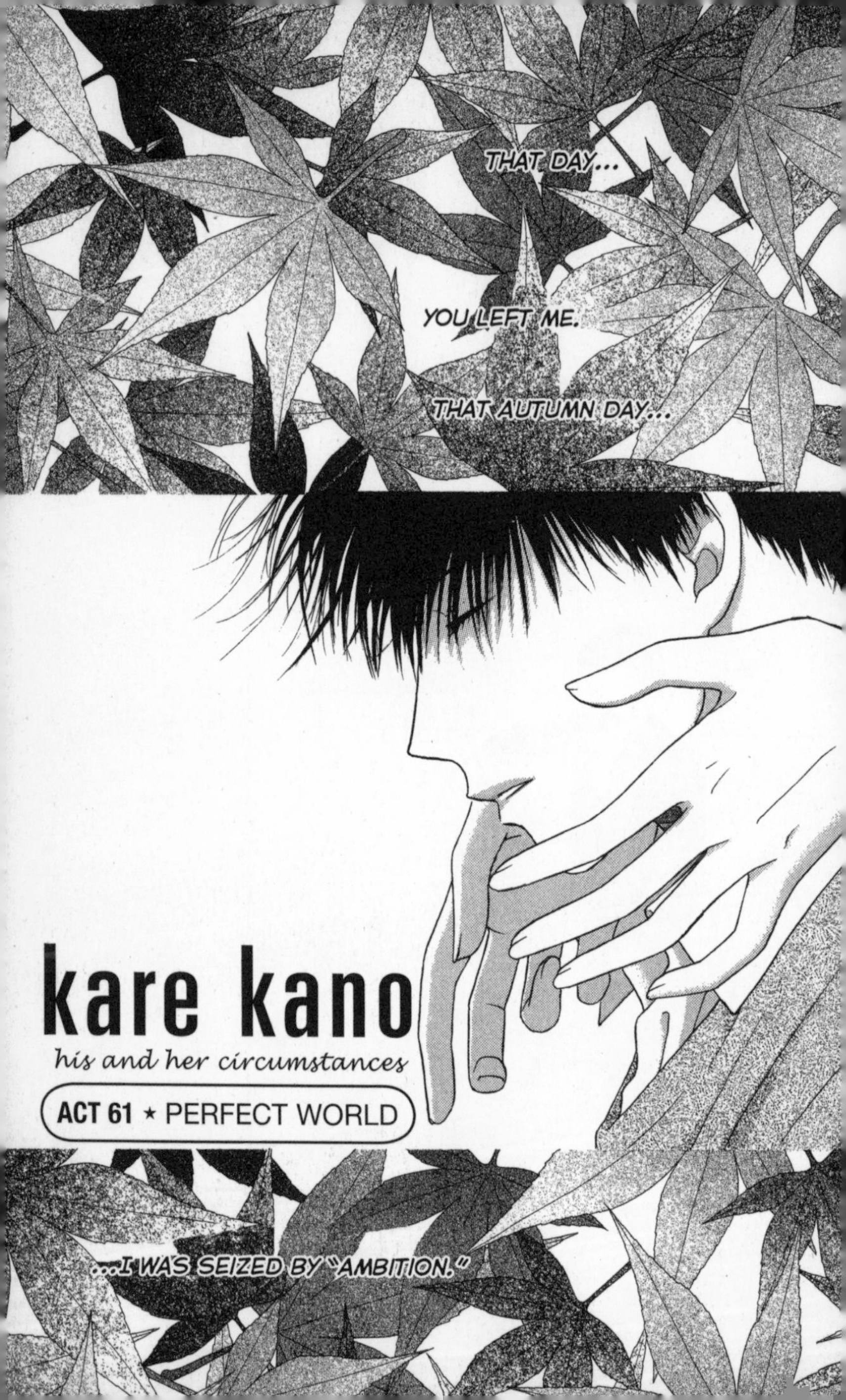
THAT DAY...
YOU LEFT ME.
THAT AUTUMN DAY...
kare kano
his and her circumstances
ACT 61 ★ PERFECT WORLD
...I WAS SEIZED BY "AMBITION."

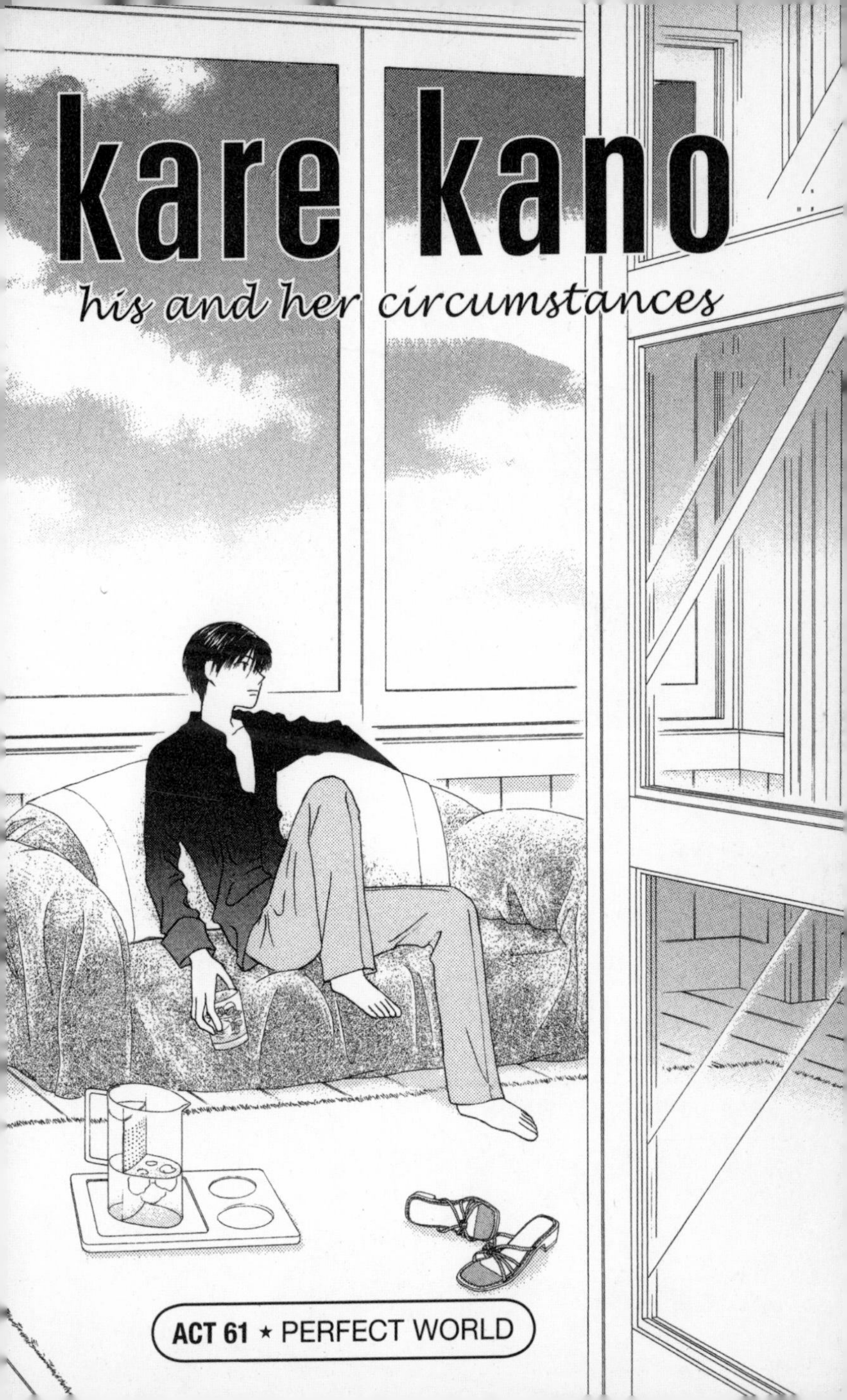
kare kano
his and her circumstances
ACT 61 ★ PERFECT WORLD

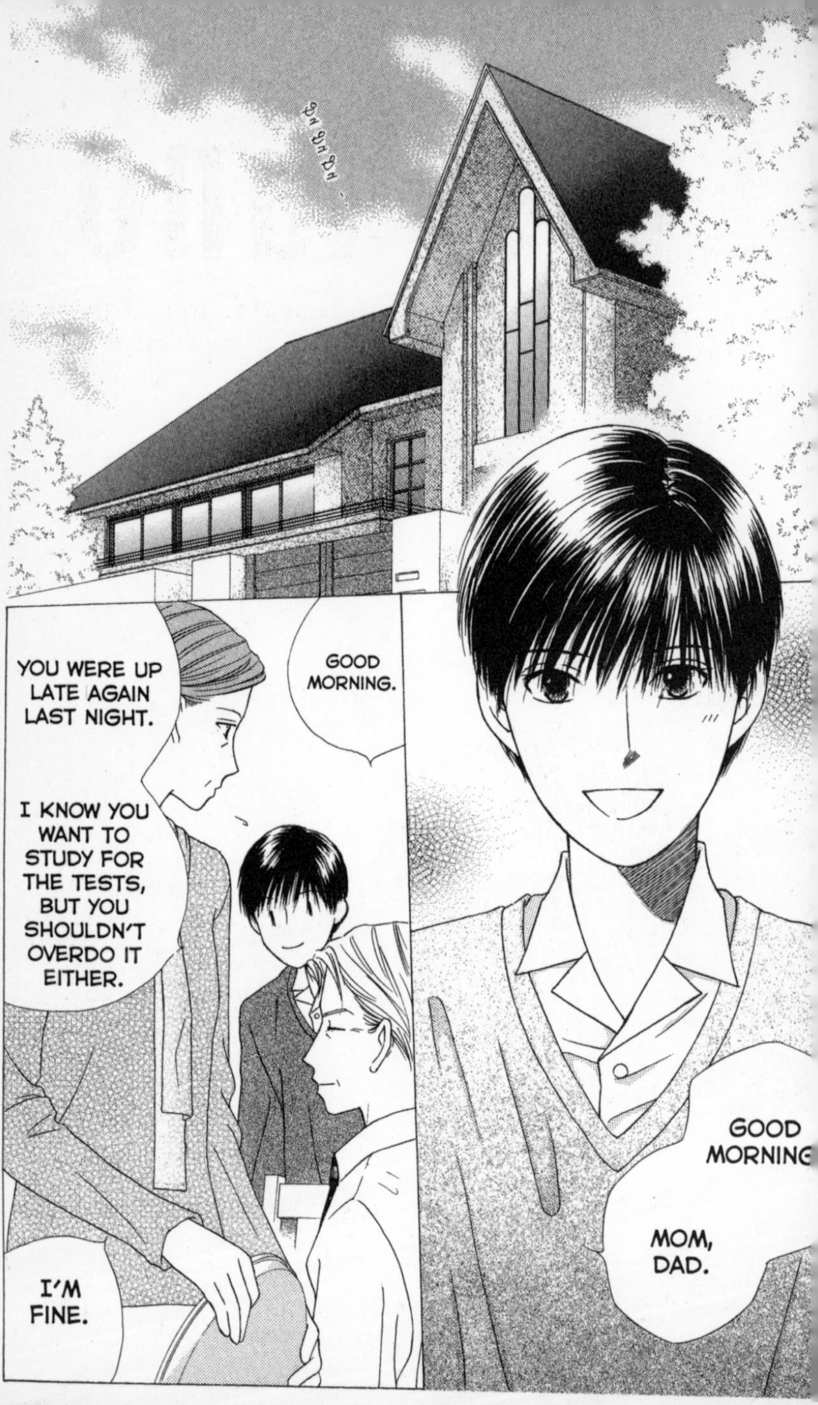
GOOD MORNING
MOM, DAD.
GOOD MORNING.
YOU WERE UP LATE AGAIN LAST NIGHT.
I KNOW YOU WANT TO STUDY FOR THE TESTS, BUT YOU SHOULDN'T OVERDO IT EITHER.
I'M FINE.

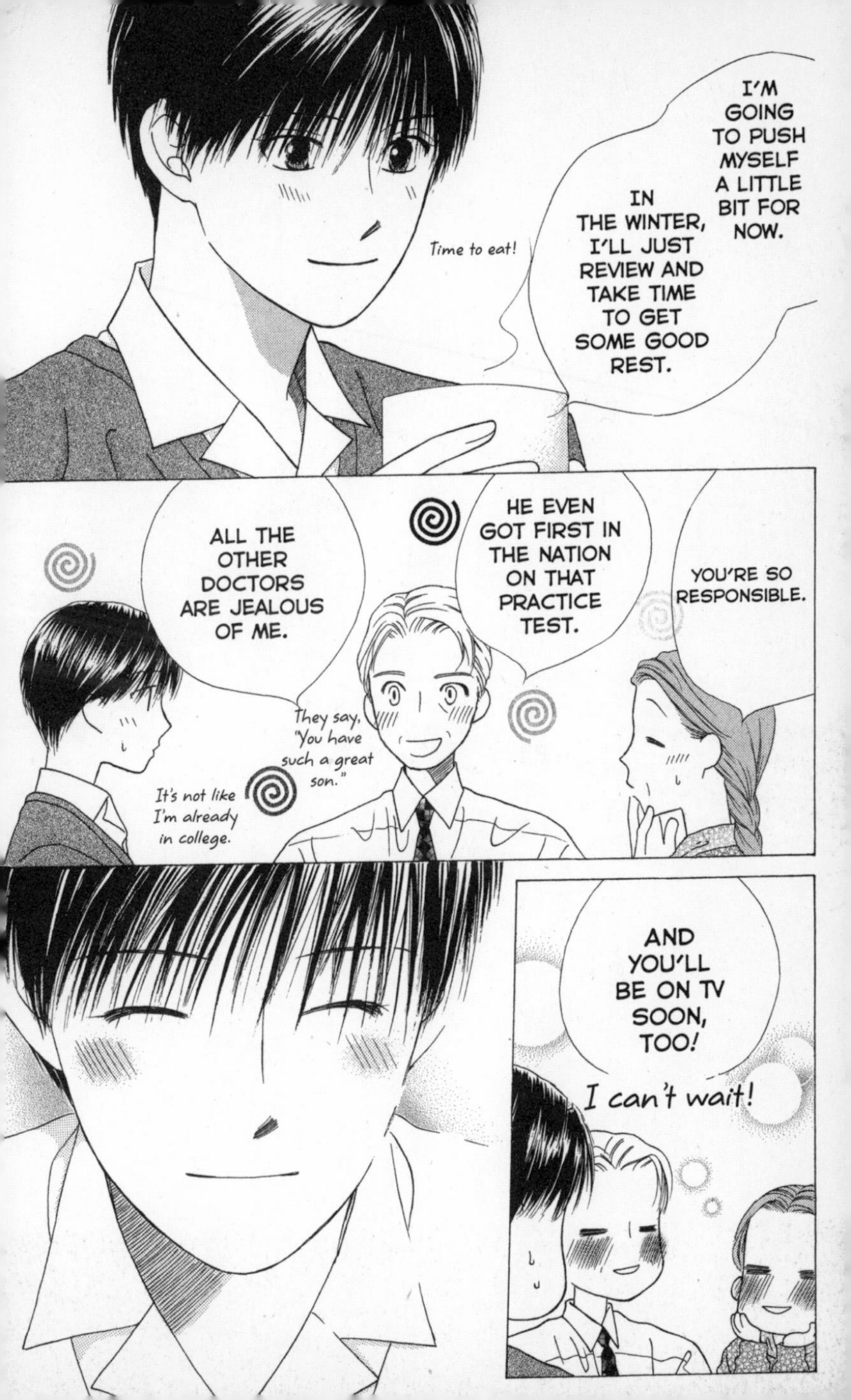
I'M GOING TO PUSH MYSELF A LITTLE BIT FOR NOW.
IN THE WINTER, I'LL JUST REVIEW AND TAKE TIME TO GET SOME GOOD REST.
Time to eat!
YOU'RE SO RESPONSIBLE.
HE EVEN GOT FIRST IN THE NATION ON THAT PRACTICE TEST.
ALL THE OTHER DOCTORS ARE JEALOUS OF ME.
They say, "You have such a great son."
It's not like I'm already in college.
AND YOU'LL BE ON TV SOON, TOO!
I can't wait!

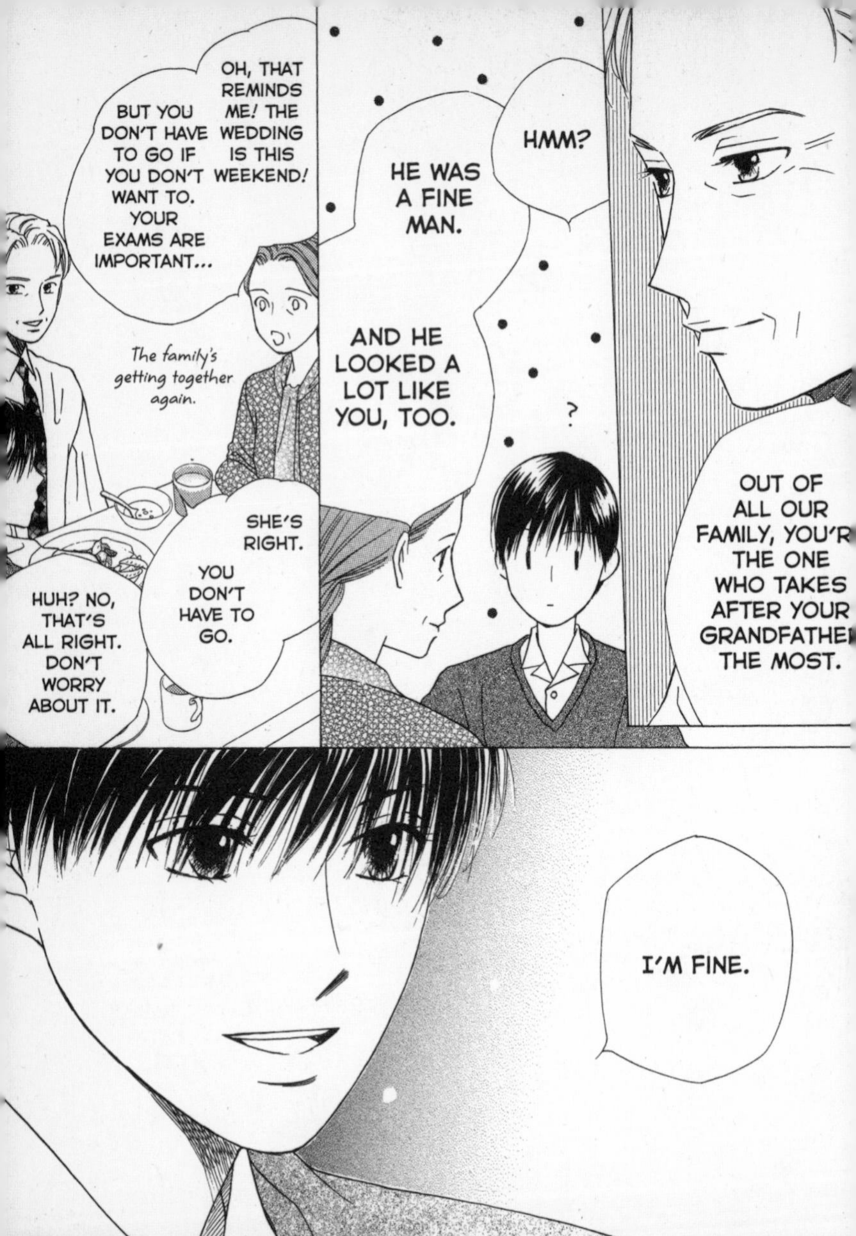
OUT OF ALL OUR FAMILY, YOU'R THE ONE WHO TAKES AFTER YOUR GRANDFATHE THE MOST.
HMM?
HE WAS A FINE MAN.
AND HE LOOKED A LOT LIKE YOU, TOO.
?
OH, THAT REMINDS ME! THE WEDDING IS THIS WEEKEND!
BUT YOU DON'T HAVE TO GO IF YOU DON'T WANT TO. YOUR EXAMS ARE IMPORTANT...
The family's getting together again.
SHE'S RIGHT.
YOU DON'T HAVE TO GO.
HUH? NO, THAT'S ALL RIGHT. DON'T WORRY ABOUT IT.
I'M FINE.

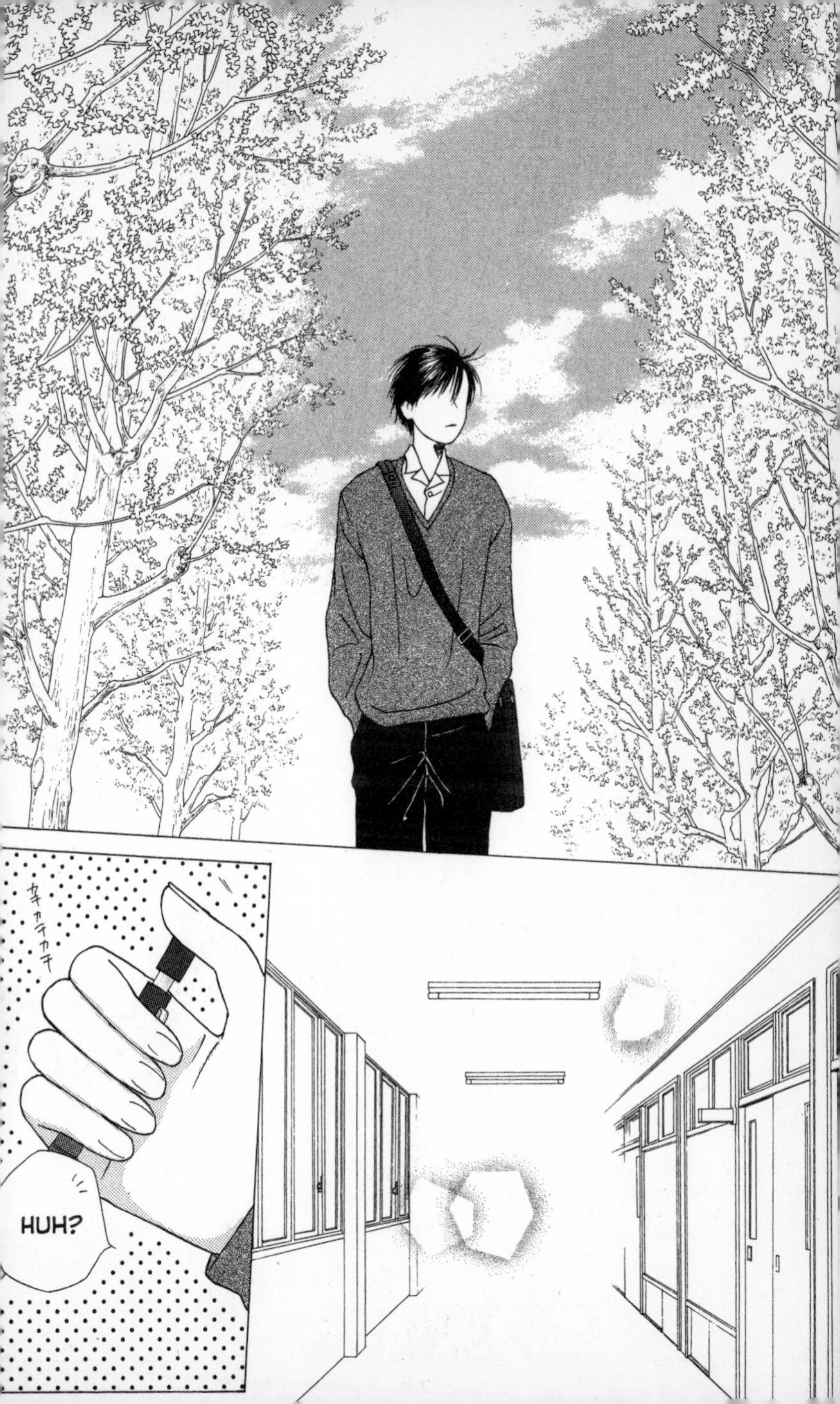
カチカチカチ
HUH?

3

As for music, at the moment I like Andre Gagnon. I love the song "Aprés la Pluie" (After the Rain). I really like songs like that, that are so quiet and beautiful, but with just a touch of madness. Like Michael Nyman's song "The Heart Asks Pleasure First."

↑
This has a lot of madness.

I had the pleasure of seeing that song performed in concert!
I want to see Andre Gagnon and Nikolai Tokarev in concert someday, too.

I'd love to hear Nikolai play "Danse Polovtsienne," one of my favorite songs.

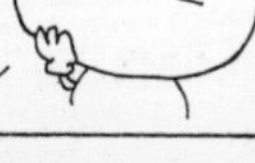

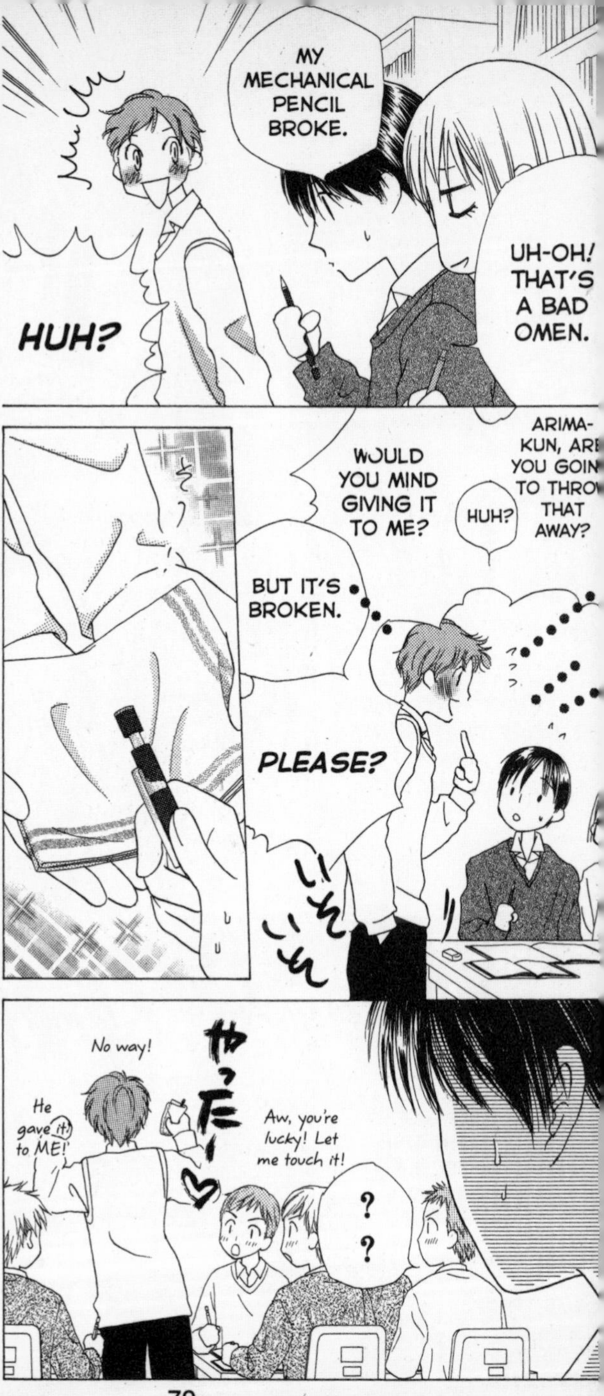
MY MECHANICAL PENCIL BROKE.
UH-OH! THAT'S A BAD OMEN.
HUH?
ARIMA-KUN, ARE YOU GOIN TO THRO THAT AWAY?
HUH?
WOULD YOU MIND GIVING IT TO ME?
BUT IT'S BROKEN.
PLEASE?
No way!
Aw, you're lucky! Let me touch it!
He gave it to ME!
?
?

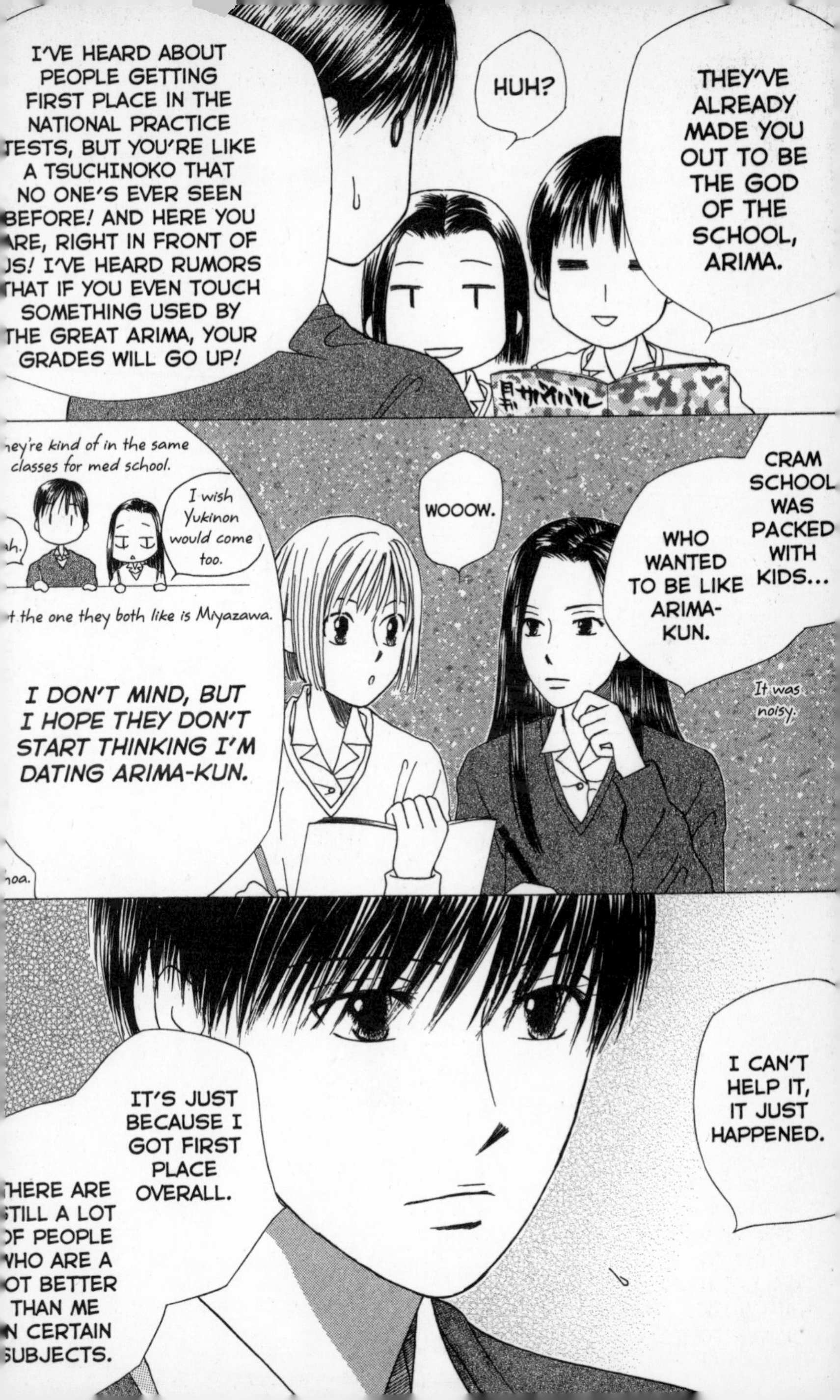

THEY'VE ALREADY MADE YOU OUT TO BE THE GOD OF THE SCHOOL, ARIMA.
HUH?
I'VE HEARD ABOUT PEOPLE GETTING FIRST PLACE IN THE NATIONAL PRACTICE TESTS, BUT YOU'RE LIKE A TSUCHINOKO THAT NO ONE'S EVER SEEN BEFORE! AND HERE YOU ARE, RIGHT IN FRONT OF US! I'VE HEARD RUMORS THAT IF YOU EVEN TOUCH SOMETHING USED BY THE GREAT ARIMA, YOUR GRADES WILL GO UP!
CRAM SCHOOL WAS PACKED WITH KIDS...
WHO WANTED TO BE LIKE ARIMA-KUN.
It was noisy.
WOOOW.
ey're kind of in the same classes for med school.
I wish Yukinon would come too.
t the one they both like is Miyazawa.
I DON'T MIND, BUT I HOPE THEY DON'T START THINKING I'M DATING ARIMA-KUN.
I CAN'T HELP IT, IT JUST HAPPENED.
IT'S JUST BECAUSE I GOT FIRST PLACE OVERALL.
THERE ARE STILL A LOT OF PEOPLE WHO ARE A LOT BETTER THAN ME IN CERTAIN SUBJECTS.

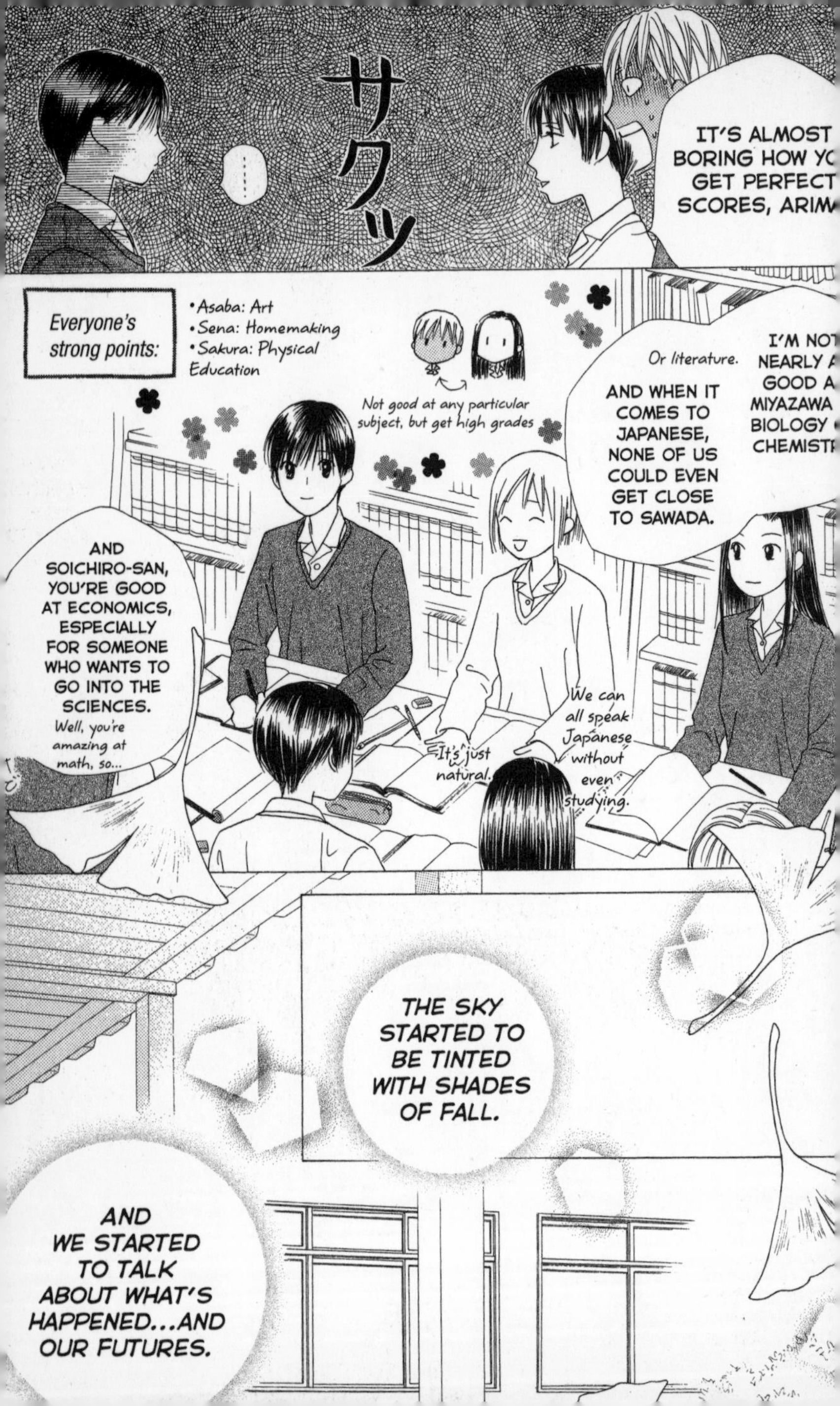

IT'S ALMOST BORING HOW YO GET PERFECT SCORES, ARIM
サクッ
......
I'M NOT NEARLY A GOOD A MIYAZAWA BIOLOGY CHEMISTR
Or literature.
AND WHEN IT COMES TO JAPANESE, NONE OF US COULD EVEN GET CLOSE TO SAWADA.
Not good at any particular subject, but get high grades
Everyone's strong points:
•Asaba: Art
•Sena: Homemaking
•Sakura: Physical Education
We can all speak Japanese without even studying.
It's just natural.
AND SOICHIRO-SAN, YOU'RE GOOD AT ECONOMICS, ESPECIALLY FOR SOMEONE WHO WANTS TO GO INTO THE SCIENCES.
Well, you're amazing at math, so...
THE SKY STARTED TO BE TINTED WITH SHADES OF FALL.
AND WE STARTED TO TALK ABOUT WHAT'S HAPPENED...AND OUR FUTURES.

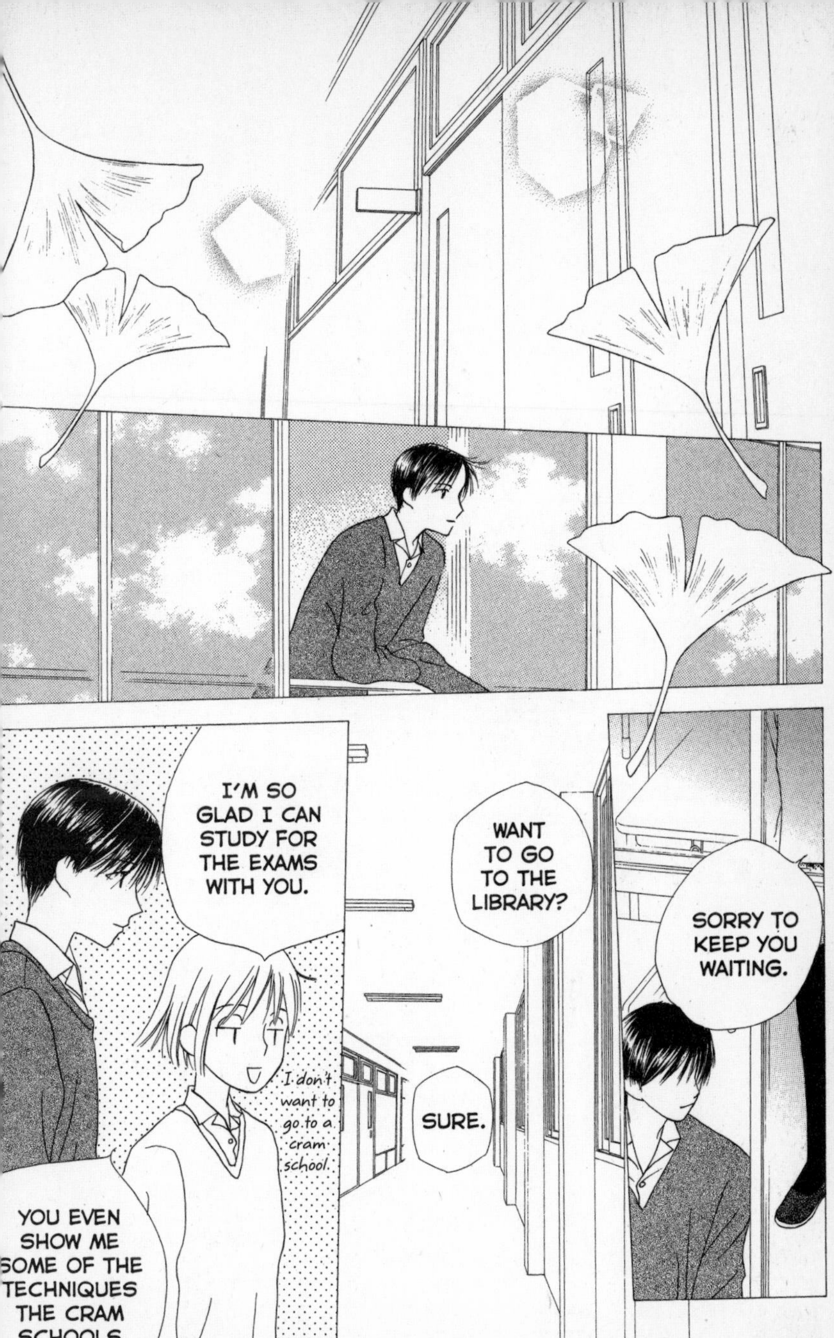
SORRY TO KEEP YOU WAITING.
WANT TO GO TO THE LIBRARY?
SURE.
I'M SO GLAD I CAN STUDY FOR THE EXAMS WITH YOU.
I don't want to go to a cram school.
YOU EVEN SHOW ME SOME OF THE TECHNIQUES THE CRAM SCHOOLS TEACH.

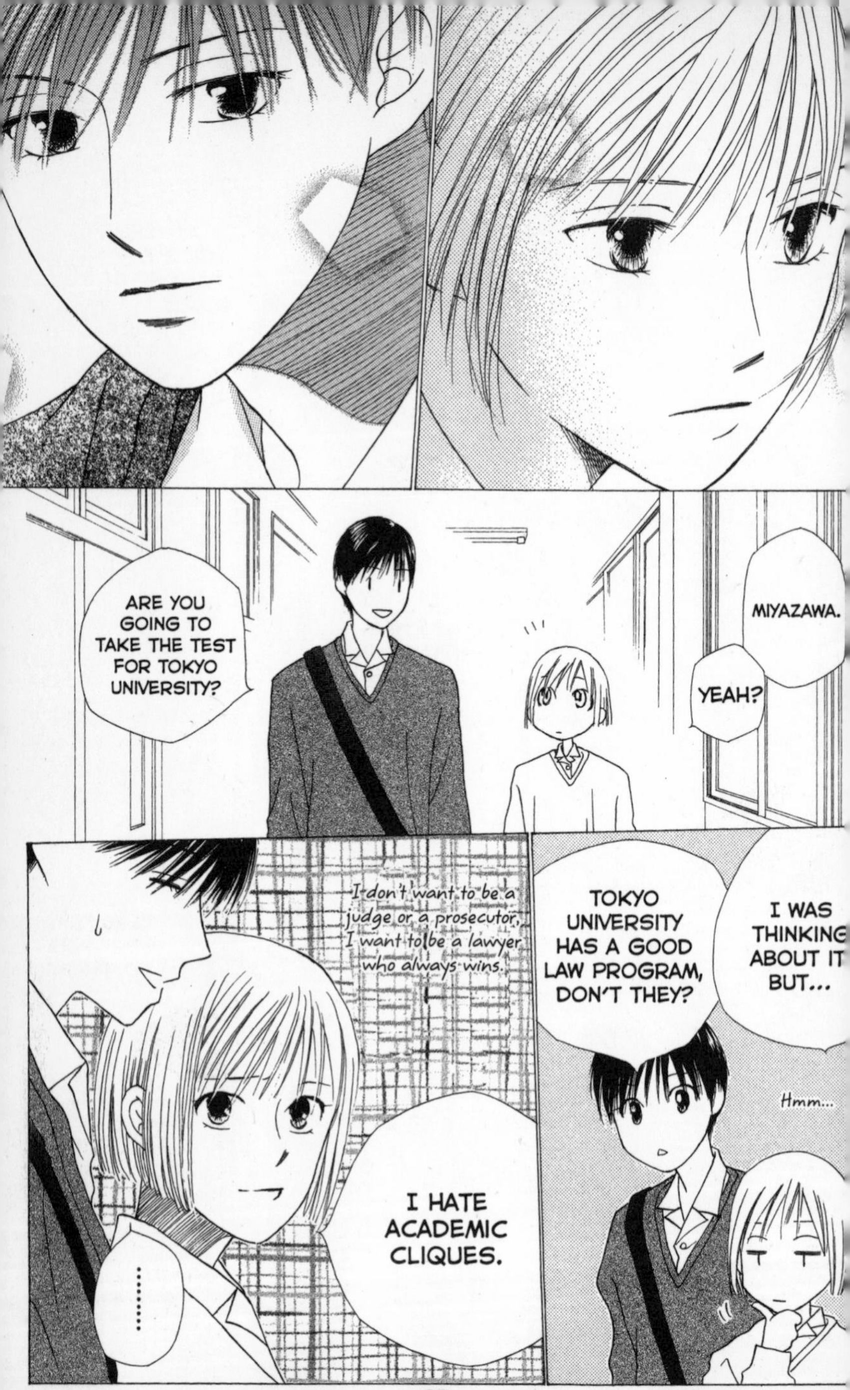
MIYAZAWA.
YEAH?
ARE YOU GOING TO TAKE THE TEST FOR TOKYO UNIVERSITY?
I WAS THINKING ABOUT IT BUT...
TOKYO UNIVERSITY HAS A GOOD LAW PROGRAM, DON'T THEY?
Hmm...
I don't want to be a judge or a prosecutor, I want to be a lawyer who always wins.
I HATE ACADEMIC CLIQUES.
......

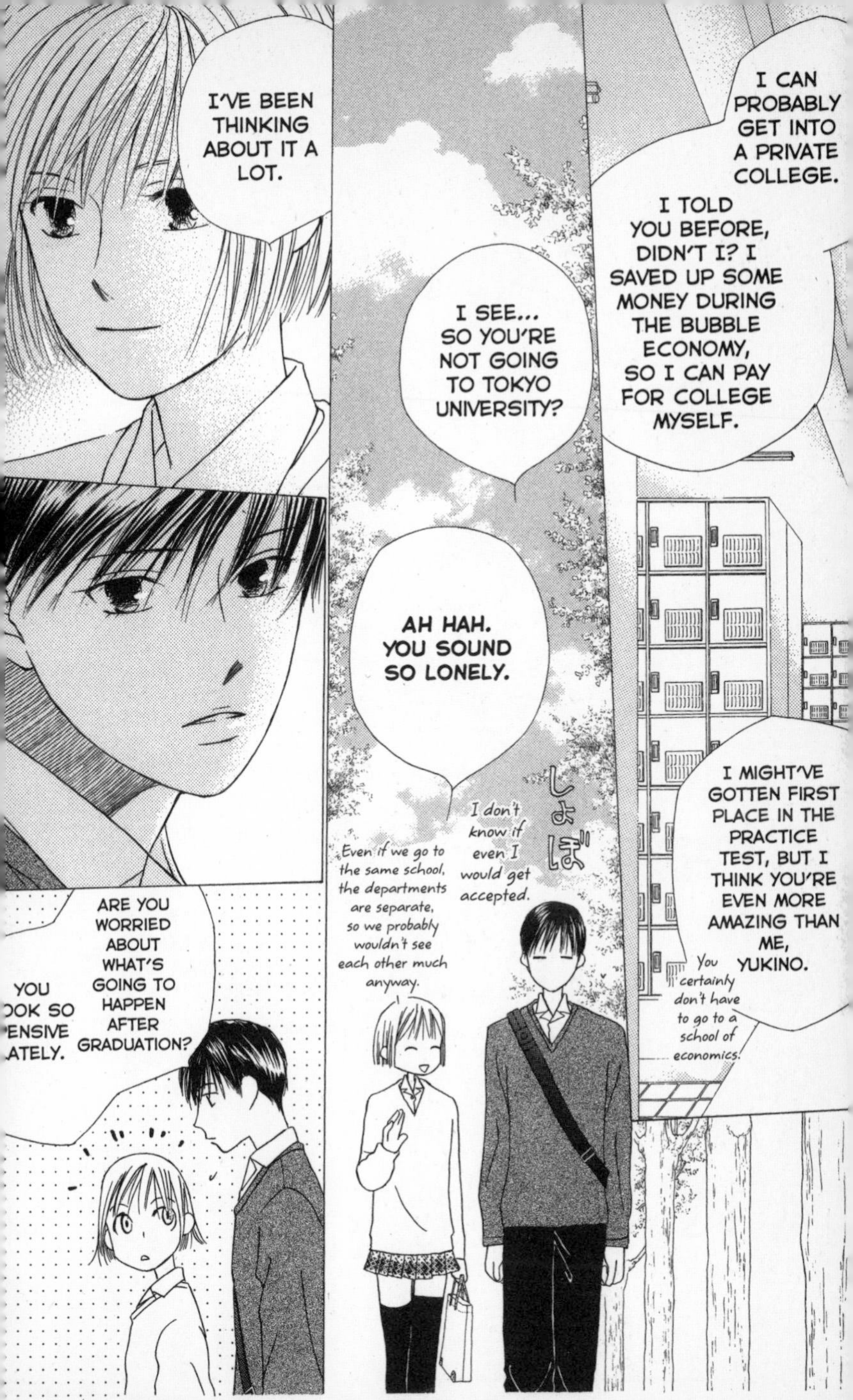
I CAN PROBABLY GET INTO A PRIVATE COLLEGE.
I TOLD YOU BEFORE, DIDN'T I? I SAVED UP SOME MONEY DURING THE BUBBLE ECONOMY, SO I CAN PAY FOR COLLEGE MYSELF.
I MIGHT'VE GOTTEN FIRST PLACE IN THE PRACTICE TEST, BUT I THINK YOU'RE EVEN MORE AMAZING THAN ME, YUKINO.
You certainly don't have to go to a school of economics.
I SEE... SO YOU'RE NOT GOING TO TOKYO UNIVERSITY?
AH HAH. YOU SOUND SO LONELY.
しょぼ
I don't know if even I would get accepted.
Even if we go to the same school, the departments are separate, so we probably wouldn't see each other much anyway.
I'VE BEEN THINKING ABOUT IT A LOT.
ARE YOU WORRIED ABOUT WHAT'S GOING TO HAPPEN AFTER GRADUATION?
YOU OOK SO ENSIVE ATELY.

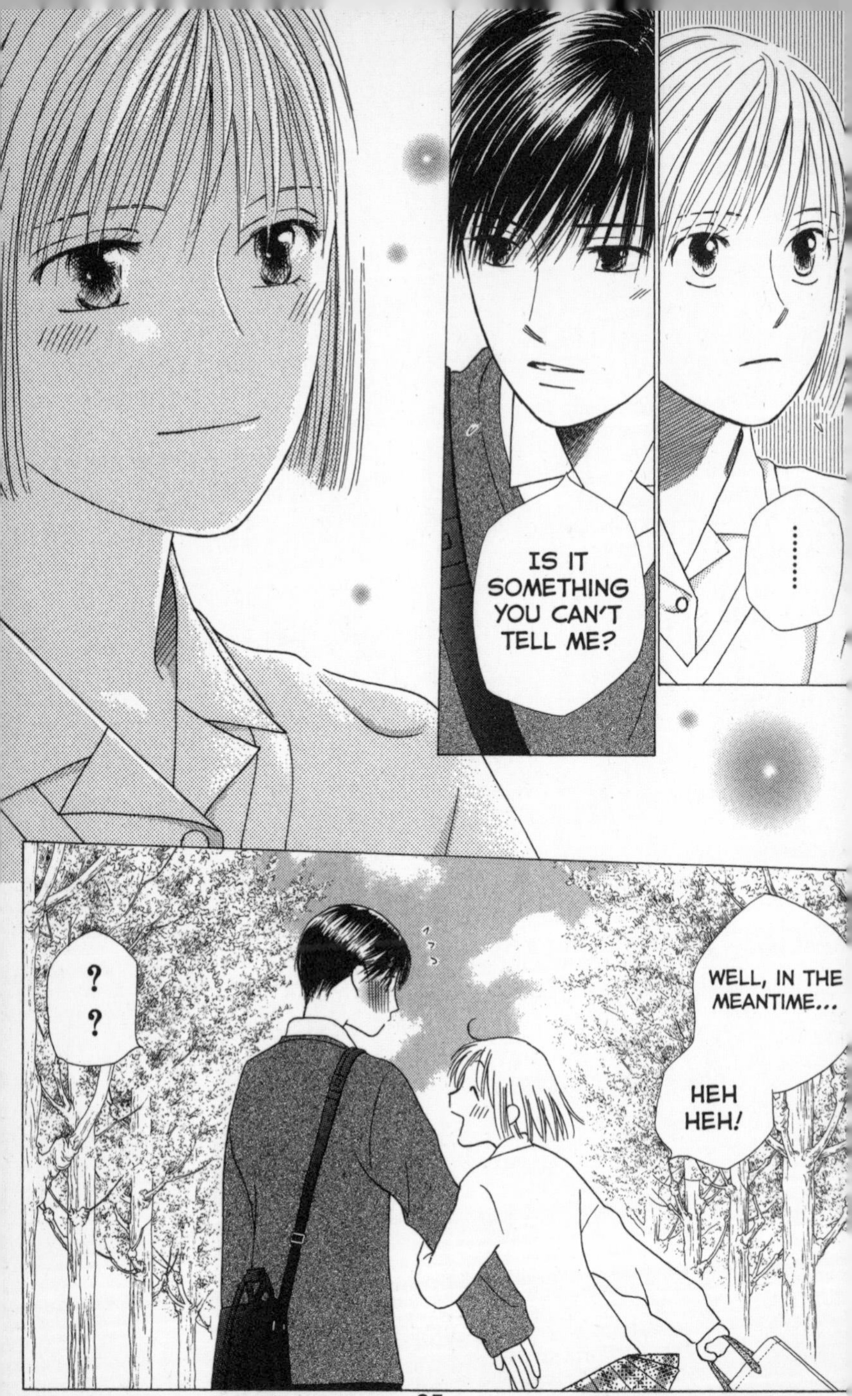

......
IS IT SOMETHING YOU CAN'T TELL ME?
WELL, IN THE MEANTIME...
HEH HEH!
? ?

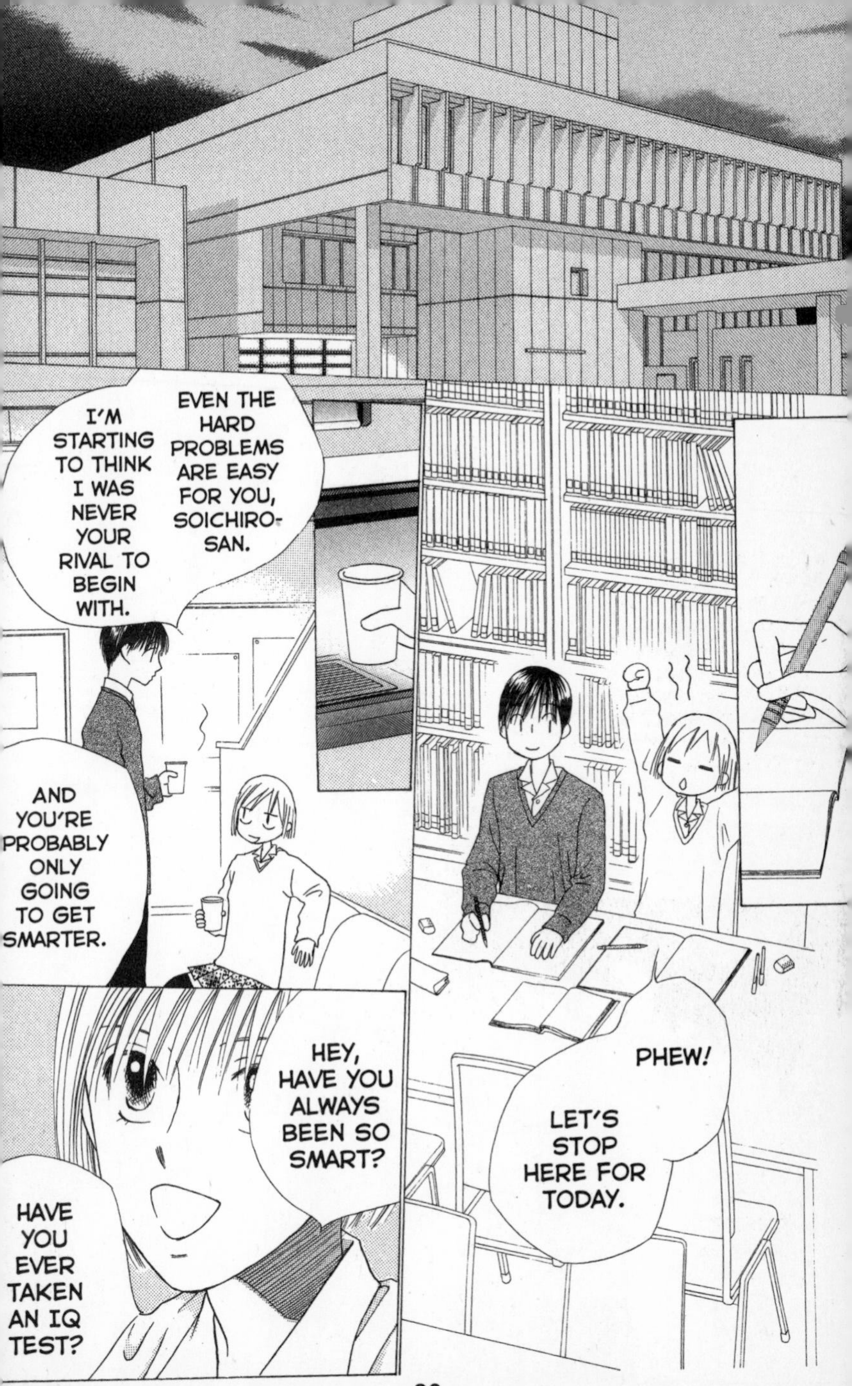
PHEW!
LET'S STOP HERE FOR TODAY.
EVEN THE HARD PROBLEMS ARE EASY FOR YOU, SOICHIRO-SAN.
I'M STARTING TO THINK I WAS NEVER YOUR RIVAL TO BEGIN WITH.
AND YOU'RE PROBABLY ONLY GOING TO GET SMARTER.
HEY, HAVE YOU ALWAYS BEEN SO SMART?
HAVE YOU EVER TAKEN AN IQ TEST?

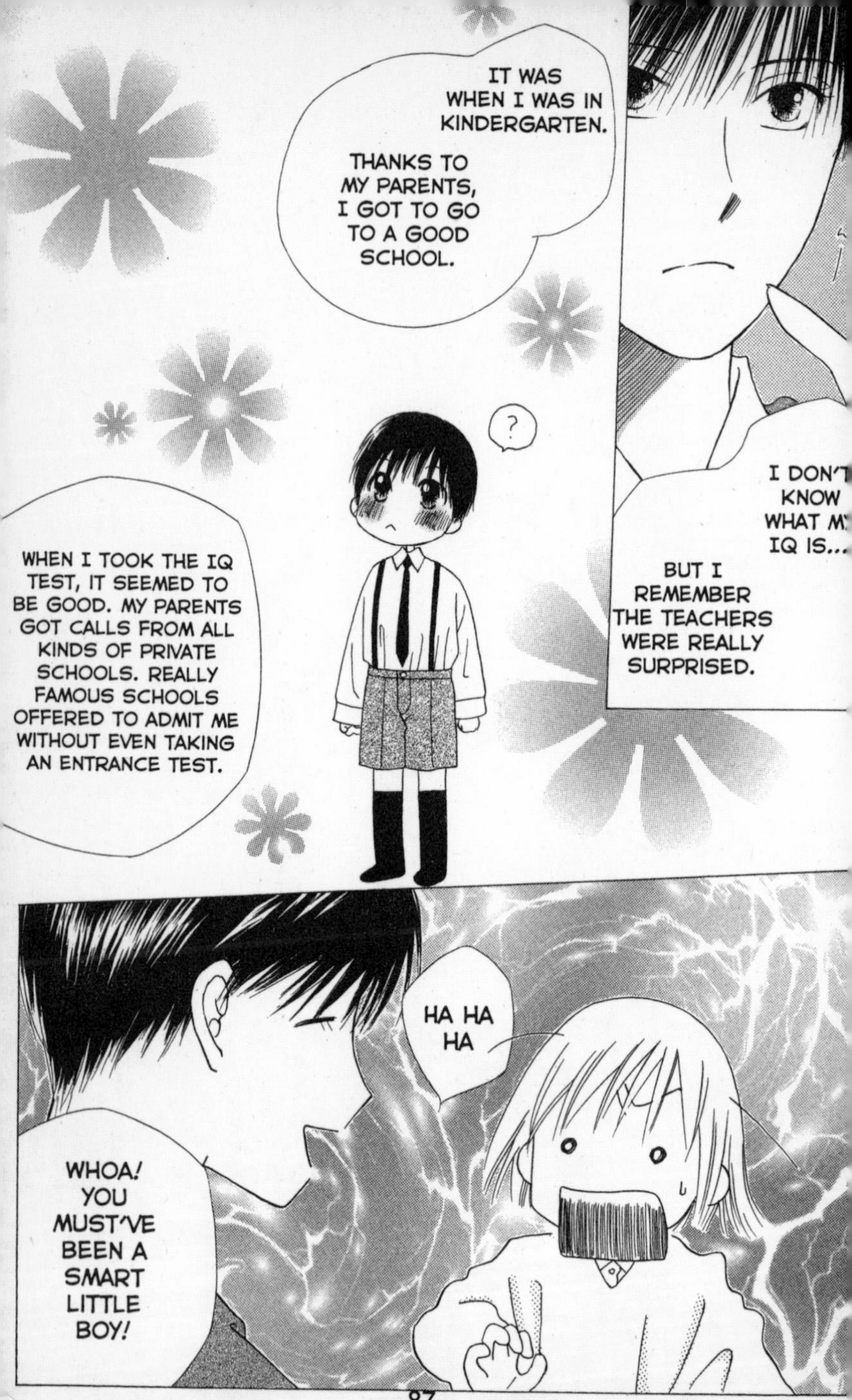
I DON'T KNOW WHAT MY IQ IS...
BUT I REMEMBER THE TEACHERS WERE REALLY SURPRISED.
IT WAS WHEN I WAS IN KINDERGARTEN.
THANKS TO MY PARENTS, I GOT TO GO TO A GOOD SCHOOL.
?
WHEN I TOOK THE IQ TEST, IT SEEMED TO BE GOOD. MY PARENTS GOT CALLS FROM ALL KINDS OF PRIVATE SCHOOLS. REALLY FAMOUS SCHOOLS OFFERED TO ADMIT ME WITHOUT EVEN TAKING AN ENTRANCE TEST.
HA HA HA
WHOA! YOU MUST'VE BEEN A SMART LITTLE BOY!

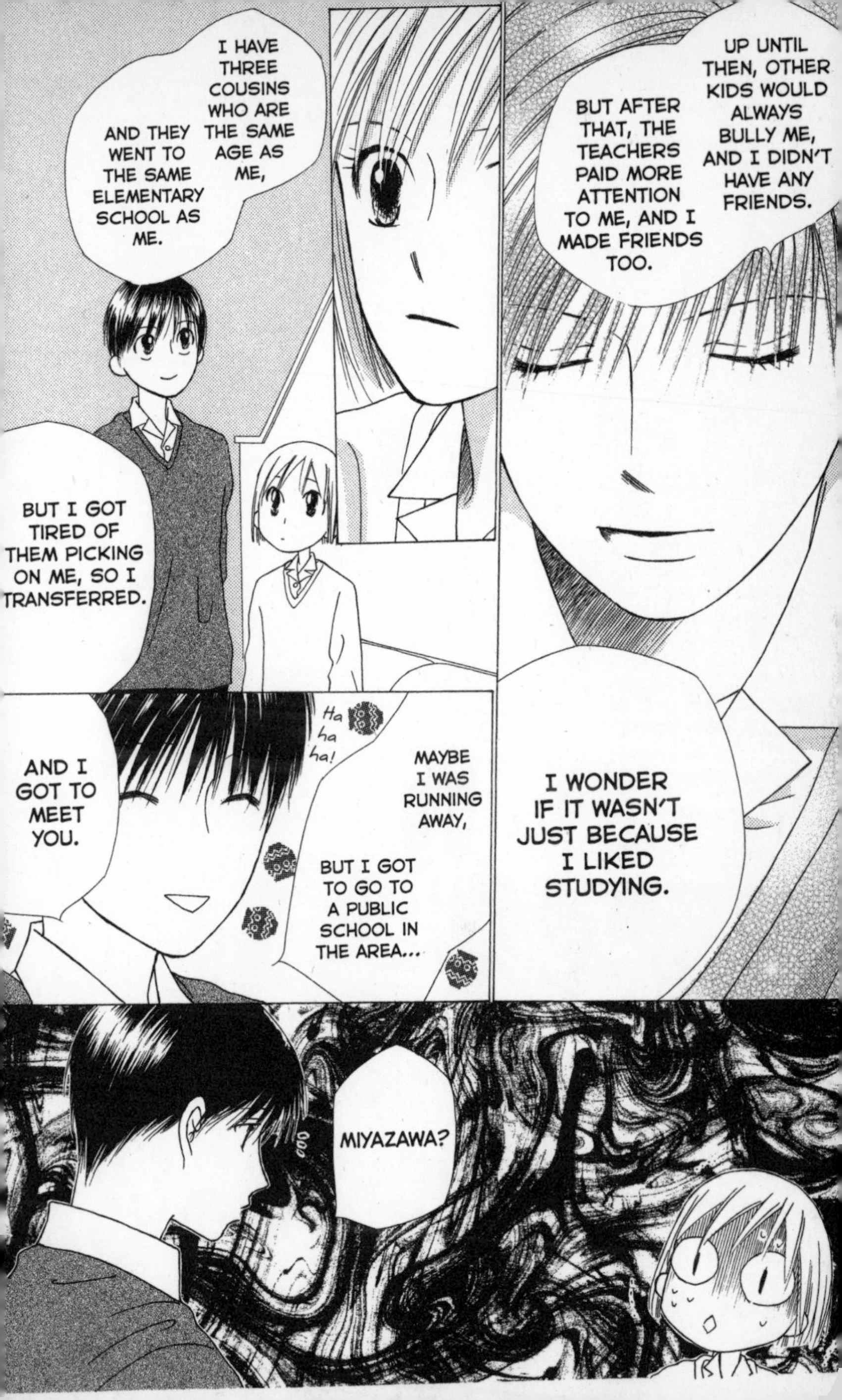
UP UNTIL THEN, OTHER KIDS WOULD ALWAYS BULLY ME, AND I DIDN'T HAVE ANY FRIENDS.
BUT AFTER THAT, THE TEACHERS PAID MORE ATTENTION TO ME, AND I MADE FRIENDS TOO.
I WONDER IF IT WASN'T JUST BECAUSE I LIKED STUDYING.
I HAVE THREE COUSINS WHO ARE THE SAME AGE AS ME,
AND THEY WENT TO THE SAME ELEMENTARY SCHOOL AS ME.
BUT I GOT TIRED OF THEM PICKING ON ME, SO I TRANSFERRED.
Ha ha ha!
MAYBE I WAS RUNNING AWAY,
BUT I GOT TO GO TO A PUBLIC SCHOOL IN THE AREA...
AND I GOT TO MEET YOU.
MIYAZAWA?

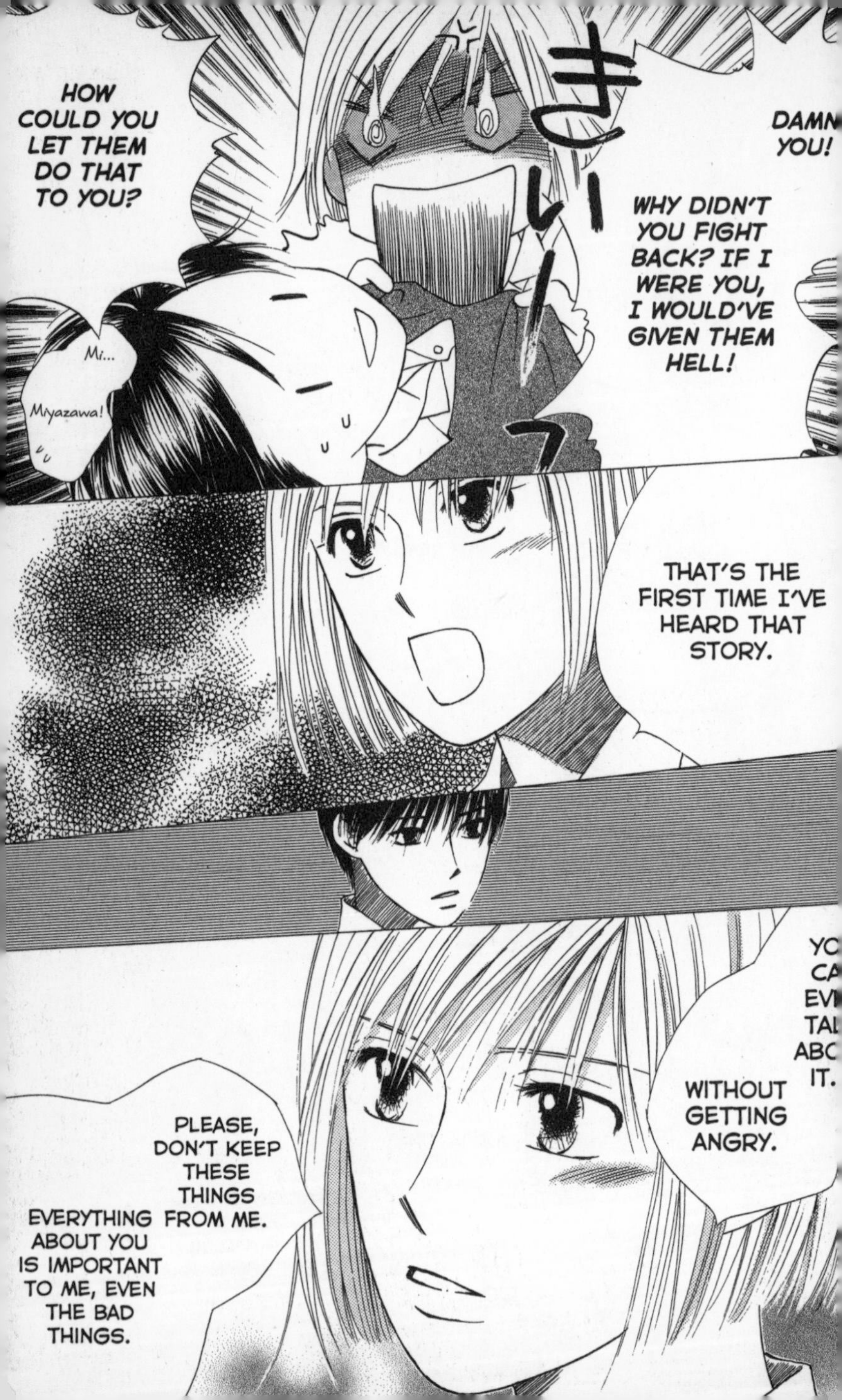
DAMN YOU!
きぃーっ
WHY DIDN'T YOU FIGHT BACK? IF I WERE YOU, I WOULD'VE GIVEN THEM HELL!
HOW COULD YOU LET THEM DO THAT TO YOU?
Mi...
Miyazawa!
THAT'S THE FIRST TIME I'VE HEARD THAT STORY.
YO CA EV TAL ABO IT.
WITHOUT GETTING ANGRY.
PLEASE, DON'T KEEP THESE THINGS FROM ME.
EVERYTHING ABOUT YOU IS IMPORTANT TO ME, EVEN THE BAD THINGS.

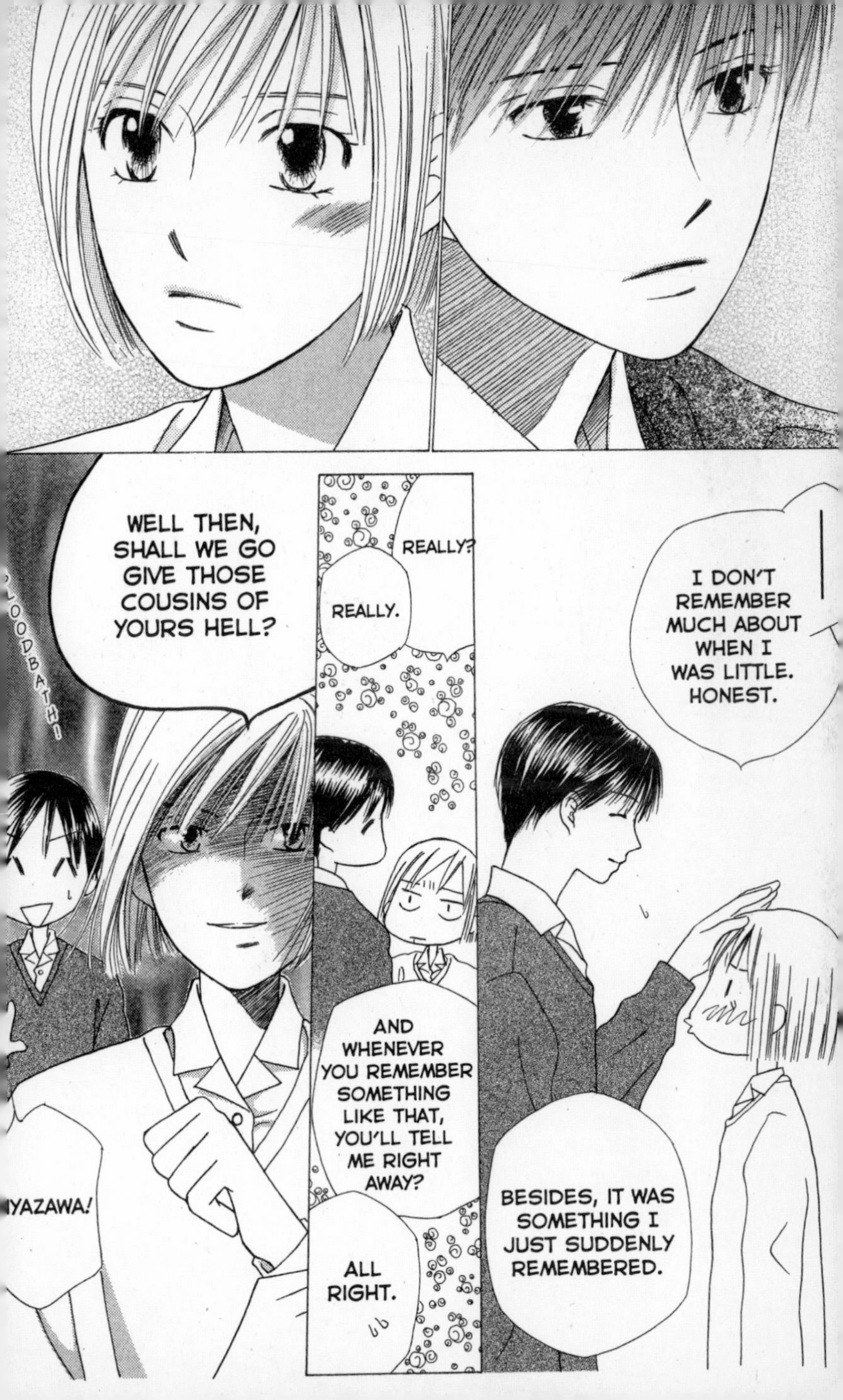
I DON'T REMEMBER MUCH ABOUT WHEN I WAS LITTLE. HONEST.
BESIDES, IT WAS SOMETHING I JUST SUDDENLY REMEMBERED.
REALLY?
REALLY.
AND WHENEVER YOU REMEMBER SOMETHING LIKE THAT, YOU'LL TELL ME RIGHT AWAY?
ALL RIGHT.
WELL THEN, SHALL WE GO GIVE THOSE COUSINS OF YOURS HELL?
LOODBATH!
YAZAWA!

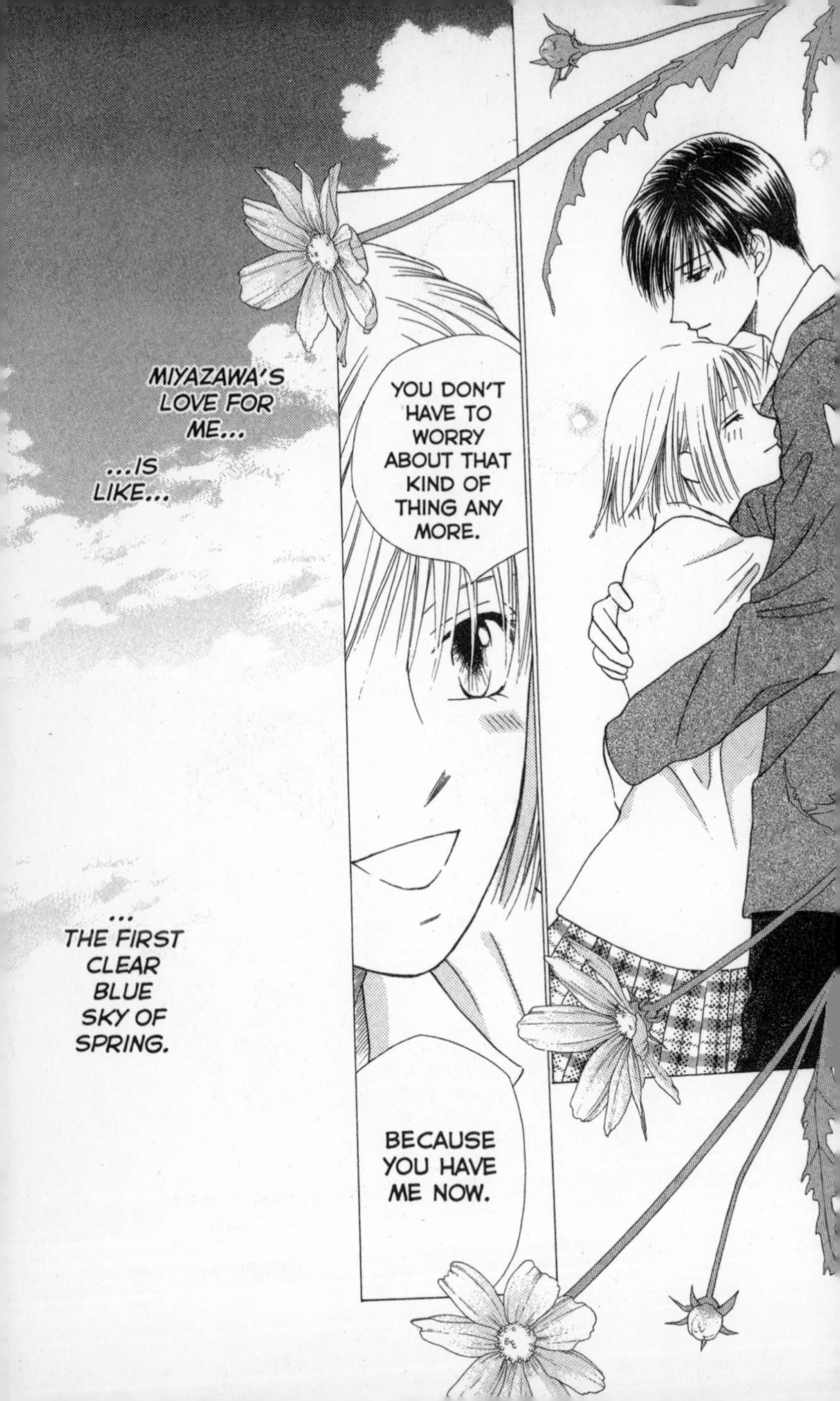
YOU DON'T HAVE TO WORRY ABOUT THAT KIND OF THING ANY MORE.
BECAUSE YOU HAVE ME NOW.
MIYAZAWA'S LOVE FOR ME...
...IS LIKE...
...THE FIRST CLEAR BLUE SKY OF SPRING.

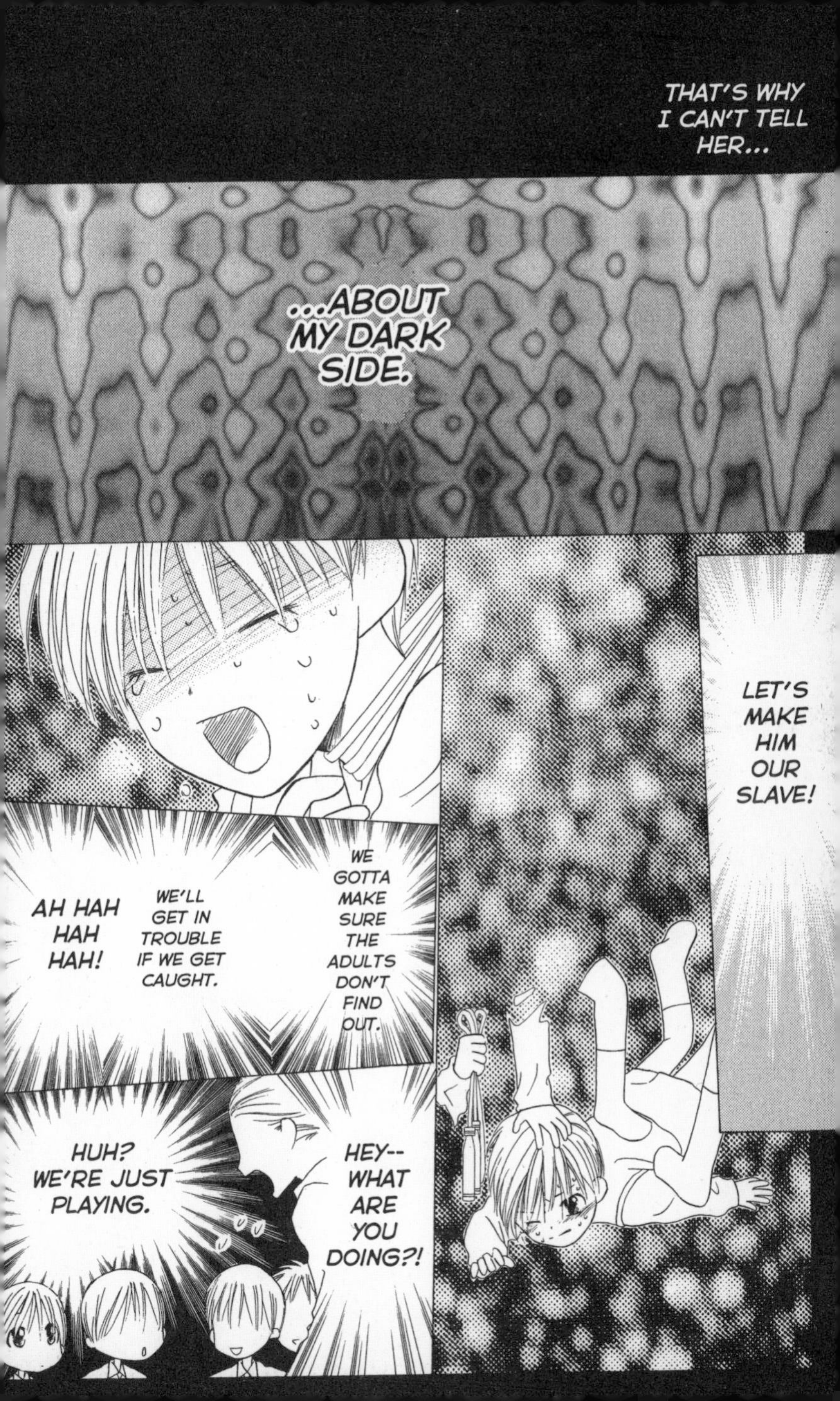
THAT'S WHY I CAN'T TELL HER...
...ABOUT MY DARK SIDE.
LET'S MAKE HIM OUR SLAVE!
WE GOTTA MAKE SURE THE ADULTS DON'T FIND OUT.
WE'LL GET IN TROUBLE IF WE GET CAUGHT.
AH HAH HAH HAH!
HEY-- WHAT ARE YOU DOING?!
HUH? WE'RE JUST PLAYING.

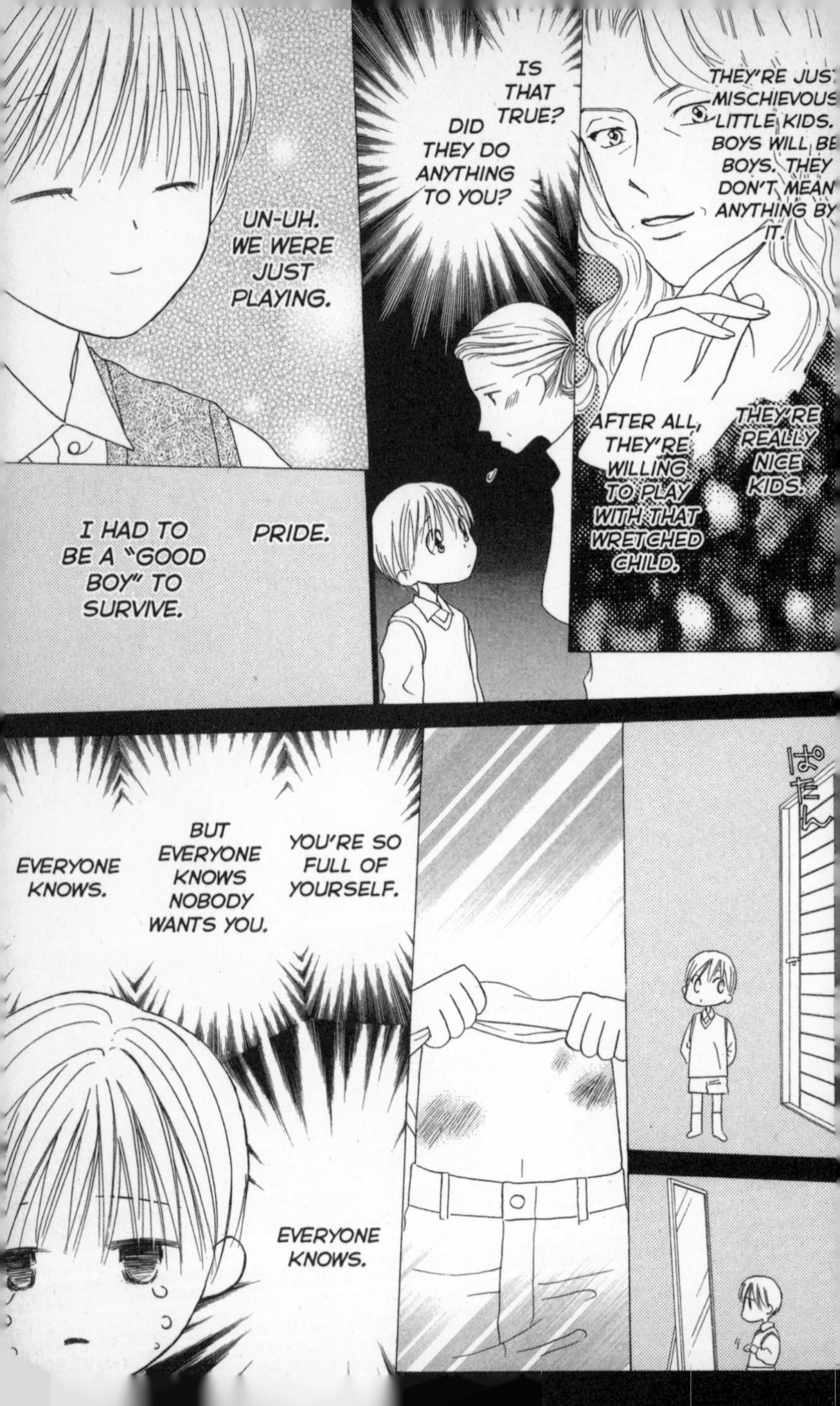
THEY'RE JUST MISCHIEVOUS LITTLE KIDS. BOYS WILL BE BOYS. THEY DON'T MEAN ANYTHING BY IT.
THEY'RE REALLY NICE KIDS.
AFTER ALL, THEY'RE WILLING TO PLAY WITH THAT WRETCHED CHILD.
IS THAT TRUE?
DID THEY DO ANYTHING TO YOU?
UN-UH. WE WERE JUST PLAYING.
PRIDE.
I HAD TO BE A "GOOD BOY" TO SURVIVE.
ぱたん
EVERYONE KNOWS.
YOU'RE SO FULL OF YOURSELF.
BUT EVERYONE KNOWS NOBODY WANTS YOU.
EVERYONE KNOWS.

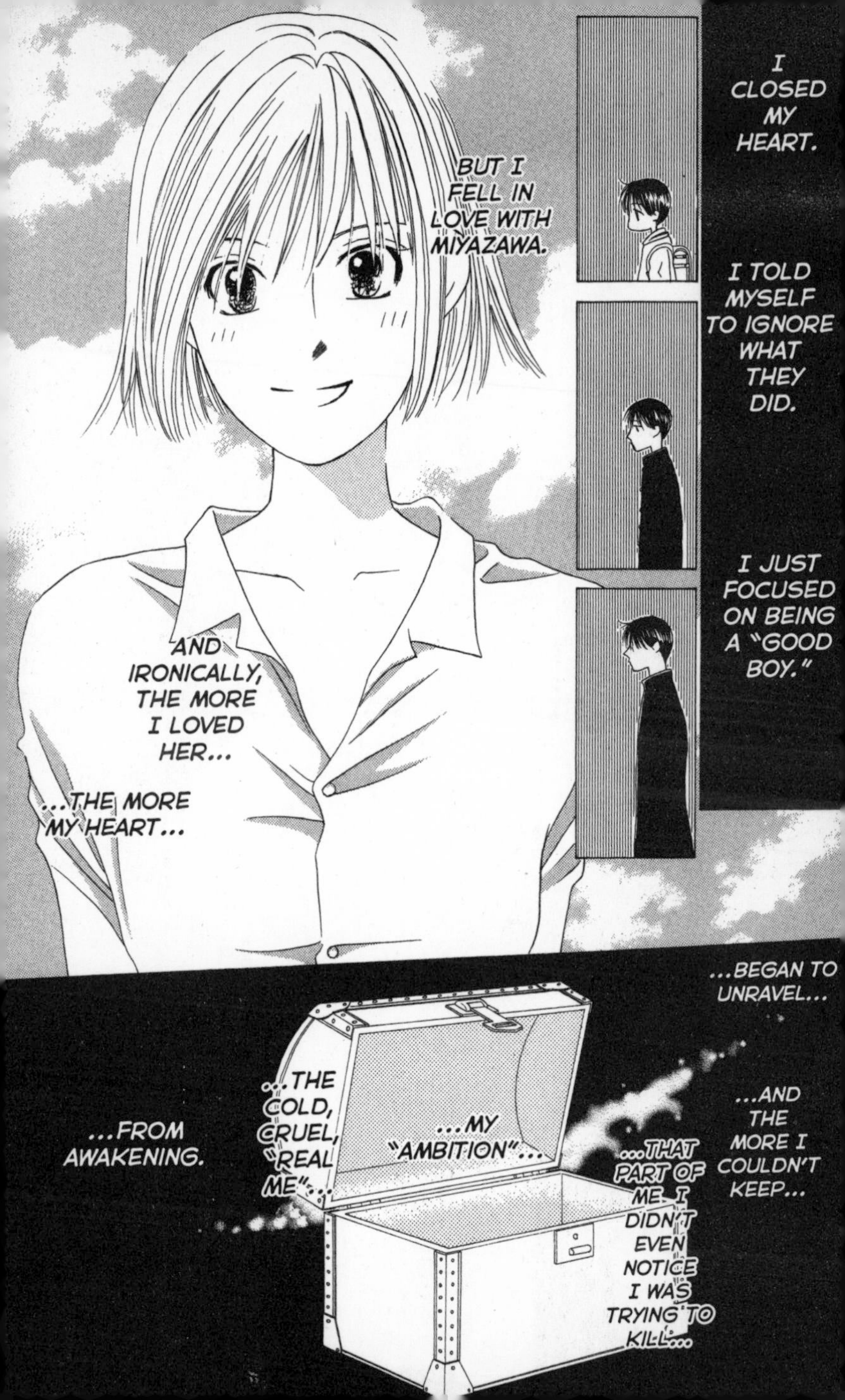
I CLOSED MY HEART.
I TOLD MYSELF TO IGNORE WHAT THEY DID.
I JUST FOCUSED ON BEING A "GOOD BOY."
BUT I FELL IN LOVE WITH MIYAZAWA.
AND IRONICALLY, THE MORE I LOVED HER...
...THE MORE MY HEART...
...BEGAN TO UNRAVEL...
...AND THE MORE I COULDN'T KEEP...
...THAT PART OF ME I DIDN'T EVEN NOTICE I WAS TRYING TO KILL...
...MY "AMBITION"...
...THE COLD, CRUEL, "REAL ME"...
...FROM AWAKENING.

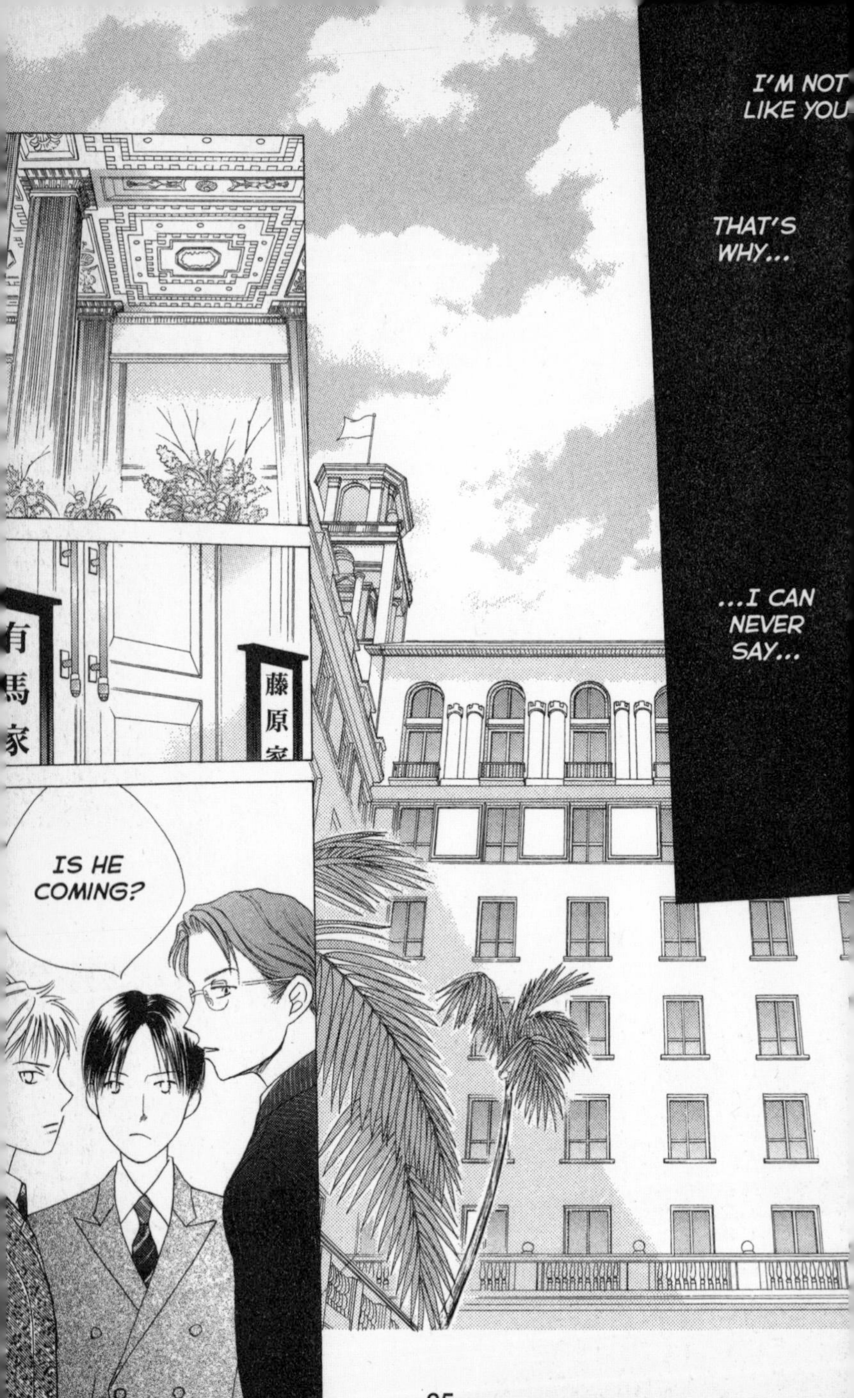
I'M NOT LIKE YOU
THAT'S WHY...
...I CAN NEVER SAY...
有馬家
藤原
IS HE COMING?

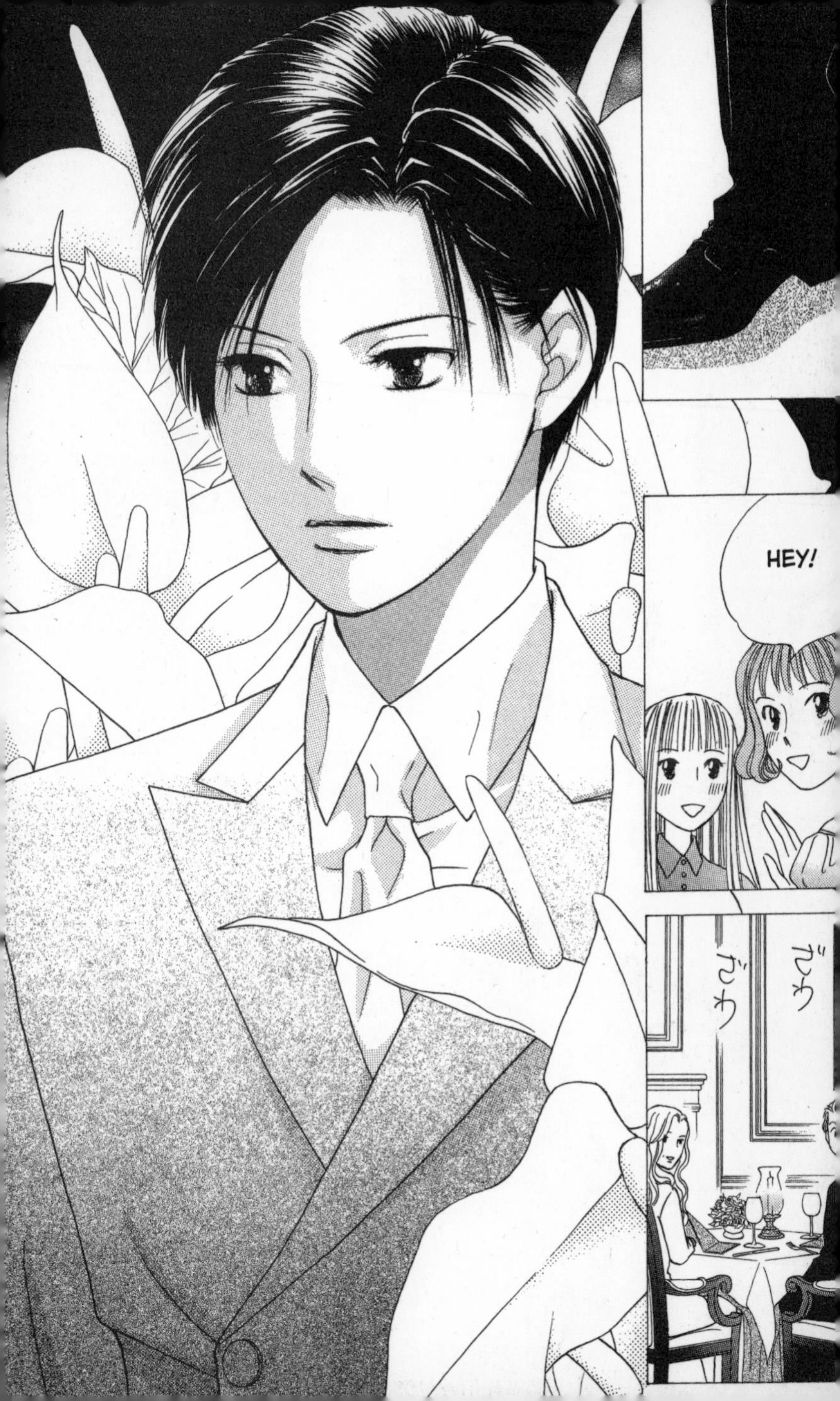
HEY!
ざわ
ざわ

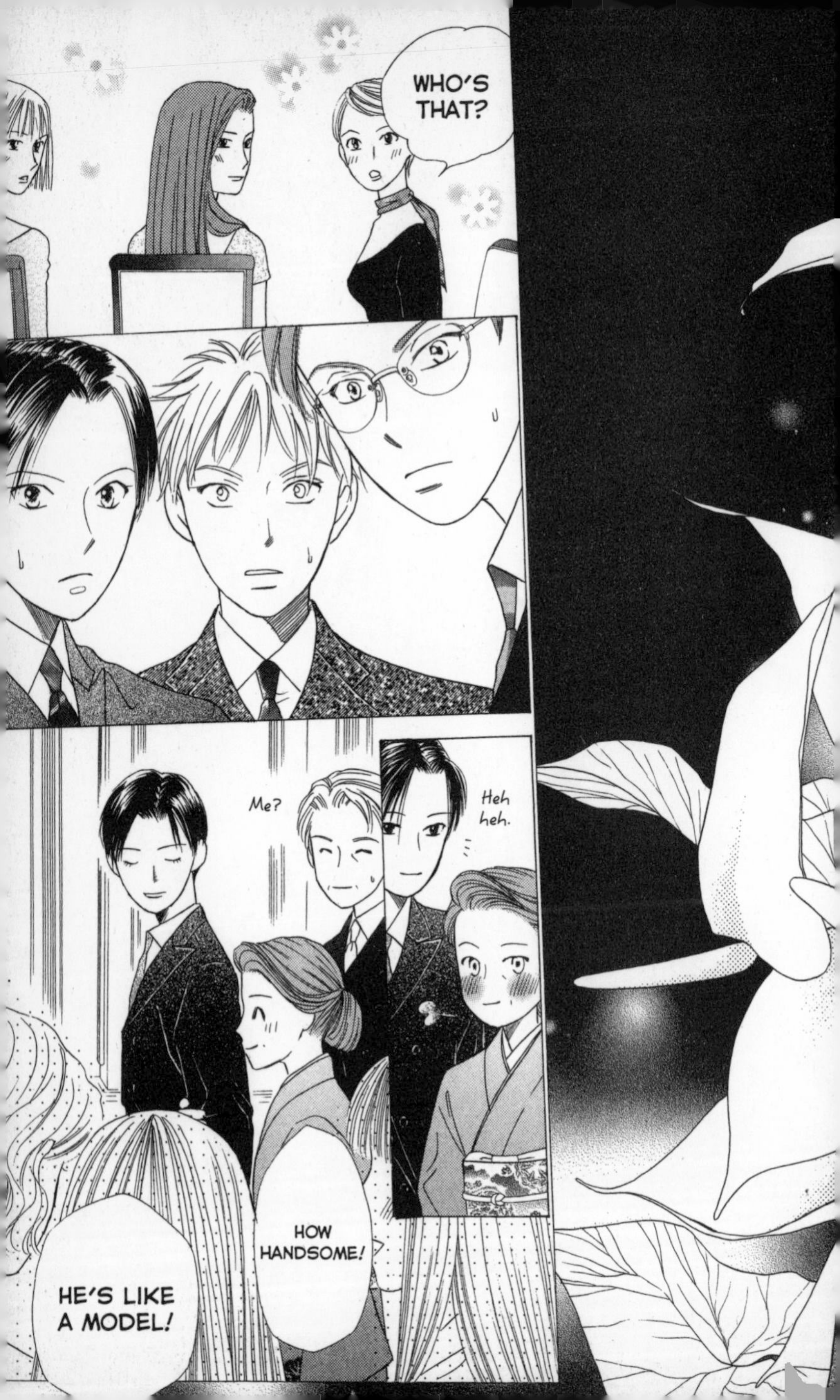
WHO'S THAT?
Heh heh.
Me?
HOW HANDSOME!
HE'S LIKE A MODEL!

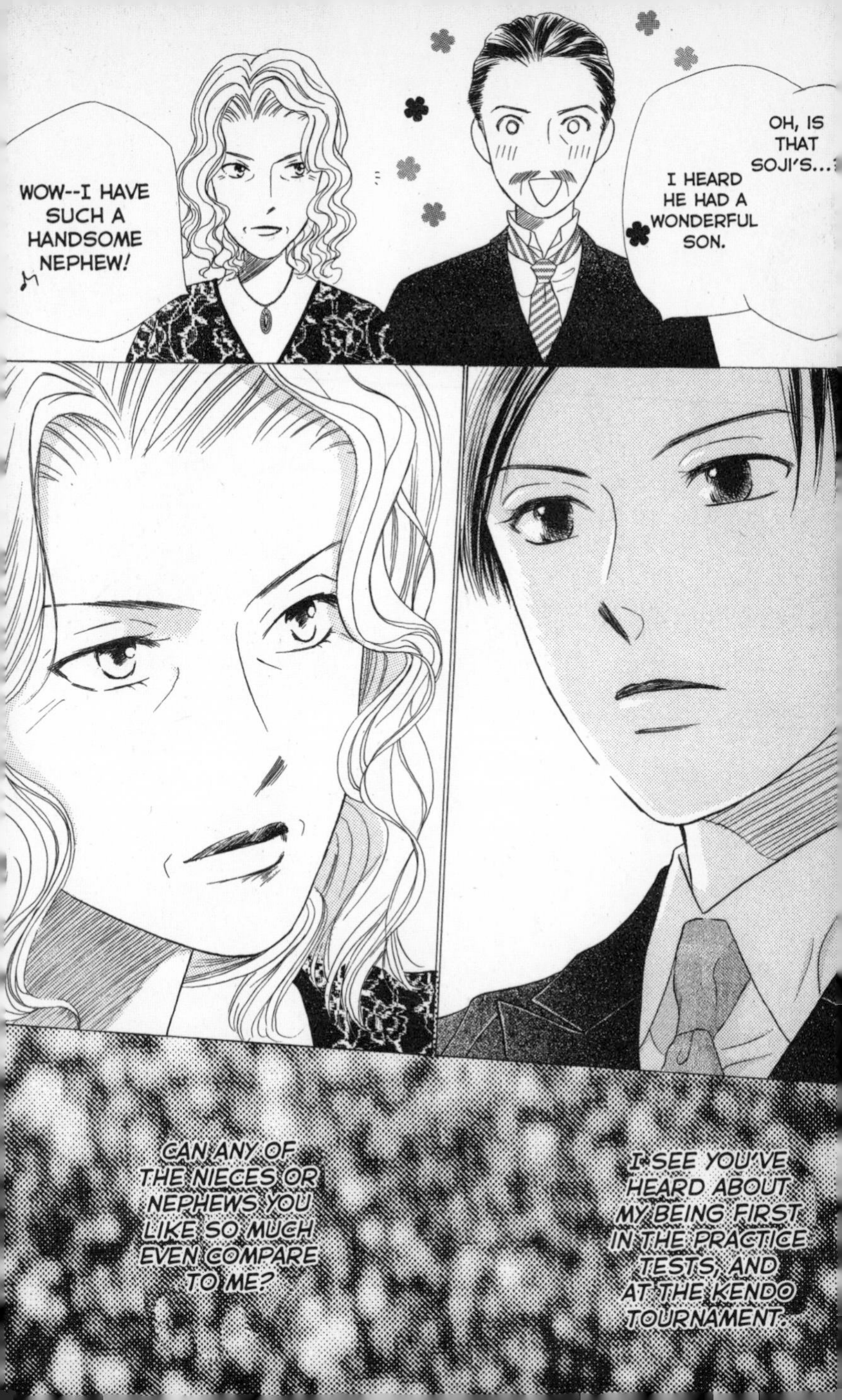
OH, IS THAT SOJI'S...
I HEARD HE HAD A WONDERFUL SON.
WOW--I HAVE SUCH A HANDSOME NEPHEW!
I SEE YOU'VE HEARD ABOUT MY BEING FIRST IN THE PRACTICE TESTS, AND AT THE KENDO TOURNAMENT.
CAN ANY OF THE NIECES OR NEPHEWS YOU LIKE SO MUCH EVEN COMPARE TO ME?

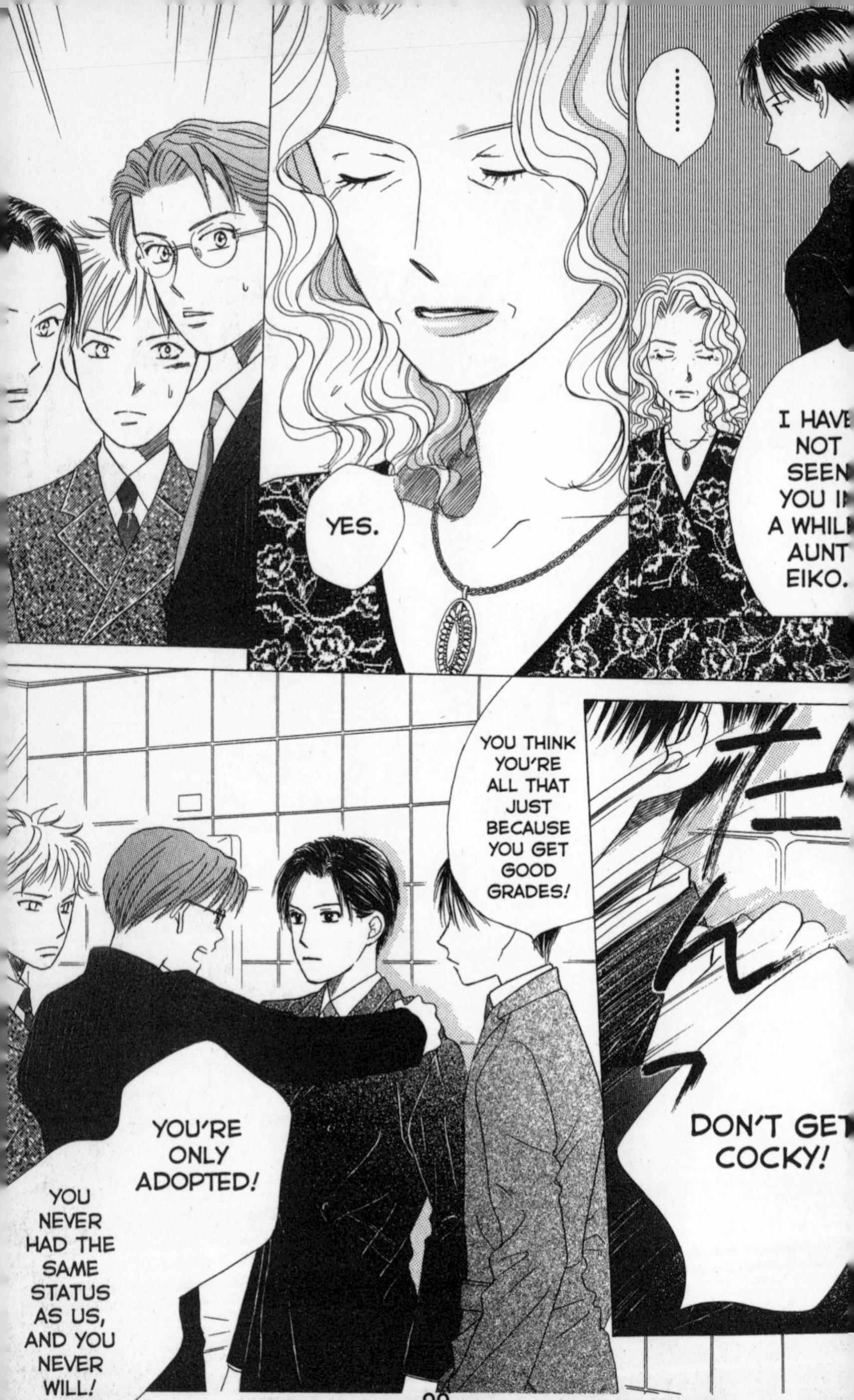

......
I HAVE NOT SEEN YOU I A WHIL AUNT EIKO.
YES.
DON'T GET COCKY!
YOU THINK YOU'RE ALL THAT JUST BECAUSE YOU GET GOOD GRADES!
YOU'RE ONLY ADOPTED!
YOU NEVER HAD THE SAME STATUS AS US, AND YOU NEVER WILL!

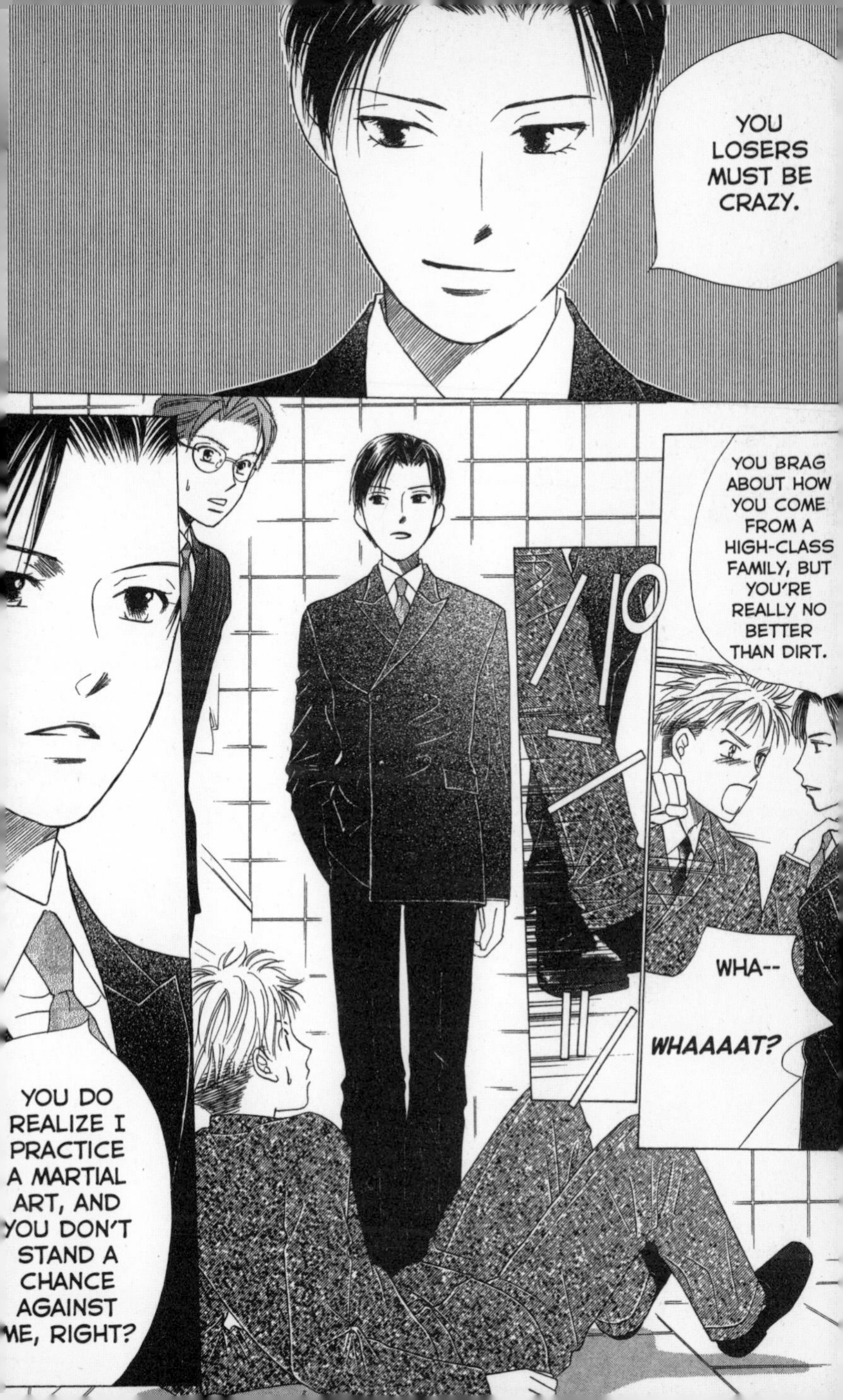
YOU LOSERS MUST BE CRAZY.
YOU BRAG ABOUT HOW YOU COME FROM A HIGH-CLASS FAMILY, BUT YOU'RE REALLY NO BETTER THAN DIRT.
WHA--
WHAAAAT?
YOU DO REALIZE I PRACTICE A MARTIAL ART, AND YOU DON'T STAND A CHANCE AGAINST ME, RIGHT?

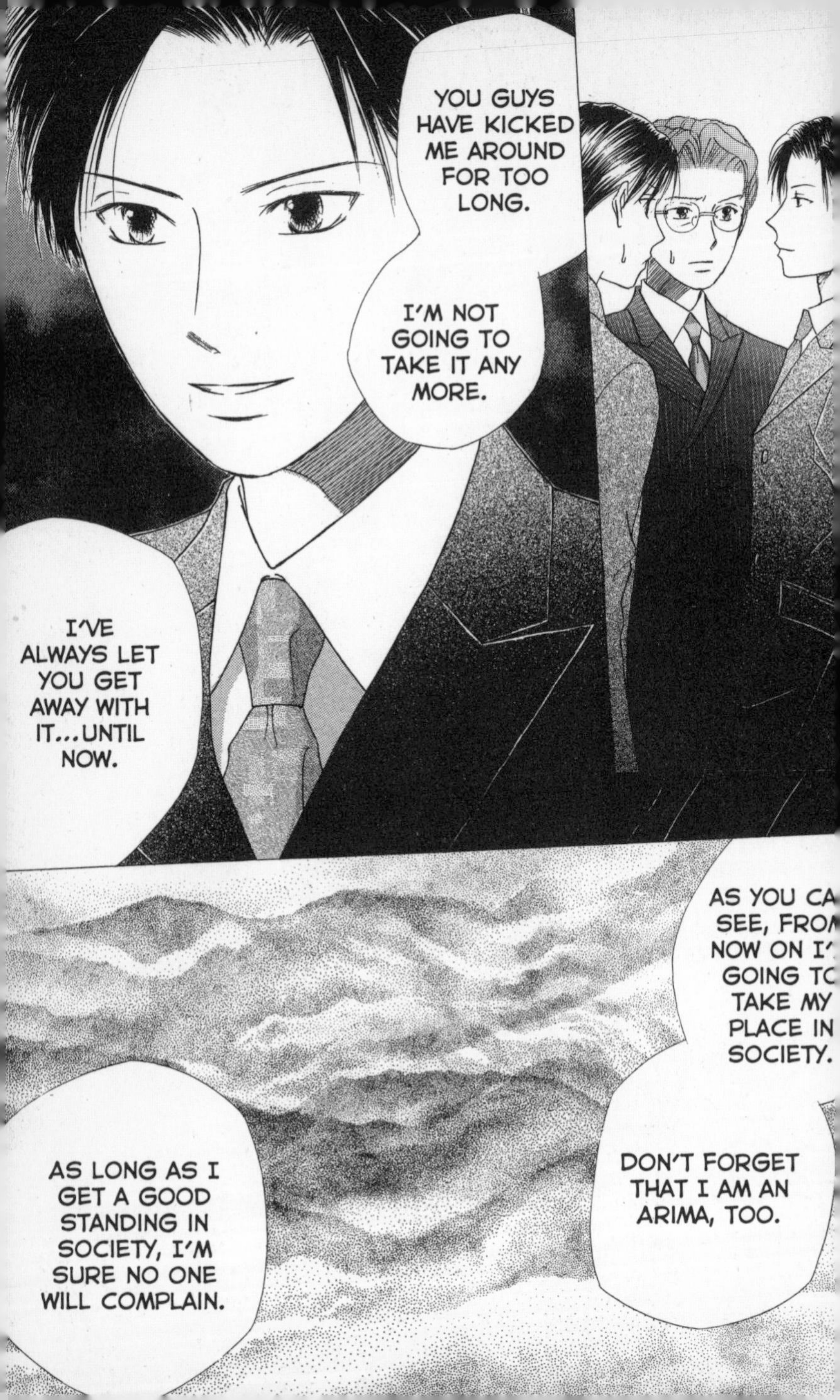
YOU GUYS HAVE KICKED ME AROUND FOR TOO LONG.
I'M NOT GOING TO TAKE IT ANY MORE.
I'VE ALWAYS LET YOU GET AWAY WITH IT...UNTIL NOW.
AS YOU CA SEE, FRO NOW ON I' GOING TO TAKE MY PLACE IN SOCIETY.
DON'T FORGET THAT I AM AN ARIMA, TOO.
AS LONG AS I GET A GOOD STANDING IN SOCIETY, I'M SURE NO ONE WILL COMPLAIN.

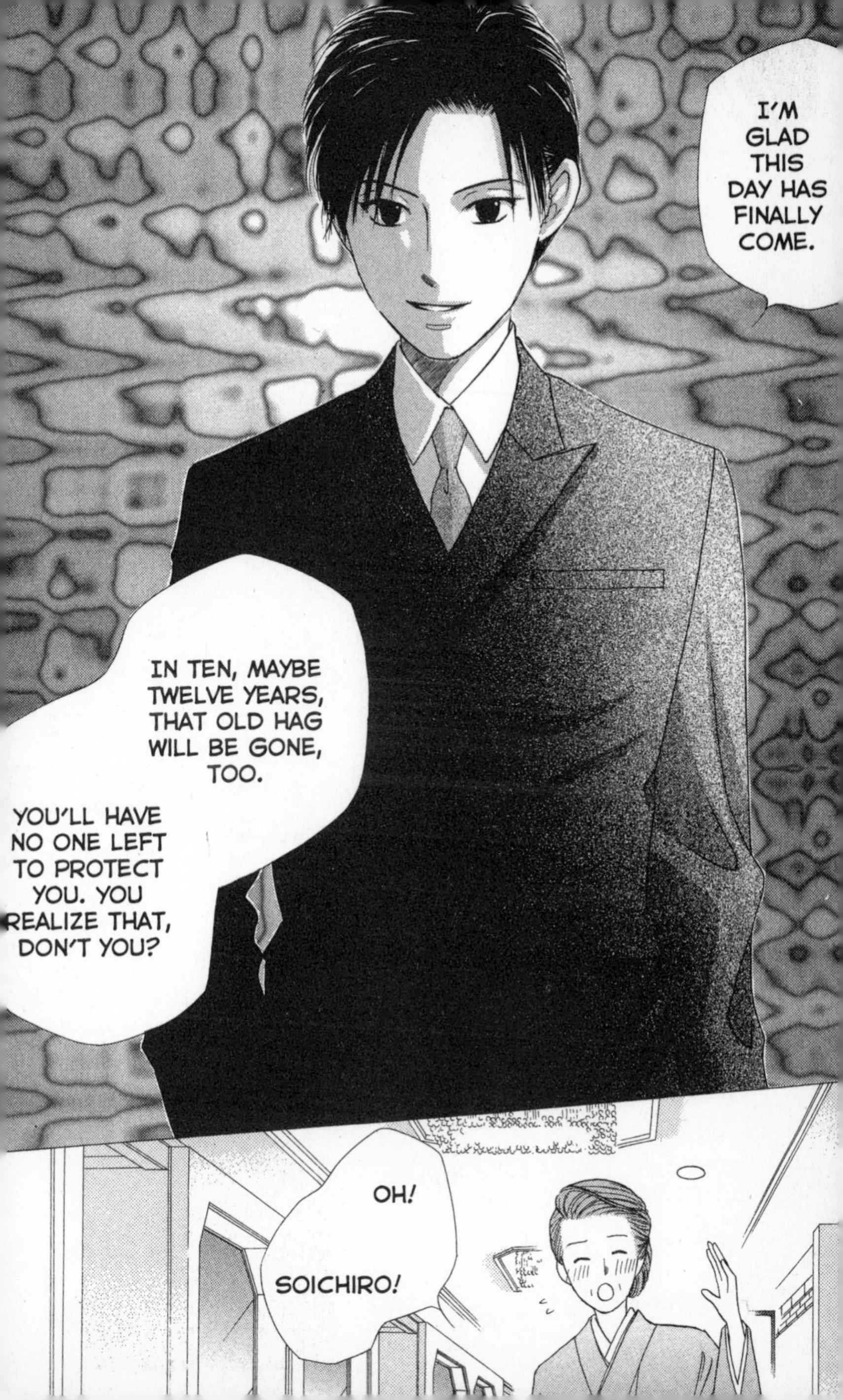
I'M GLAD THIS DAY HAS FINALLY COME.
IN TEN, MAYBE TWELVE YEARS, THAT OLD HAG WILL BE GONE, TOO.
YOU'LL HAVE NO ONE LEFT TO PROTECT YOU. YOU REALIZE THAT, DON'T YOU?
OH!
SOICHIRO!

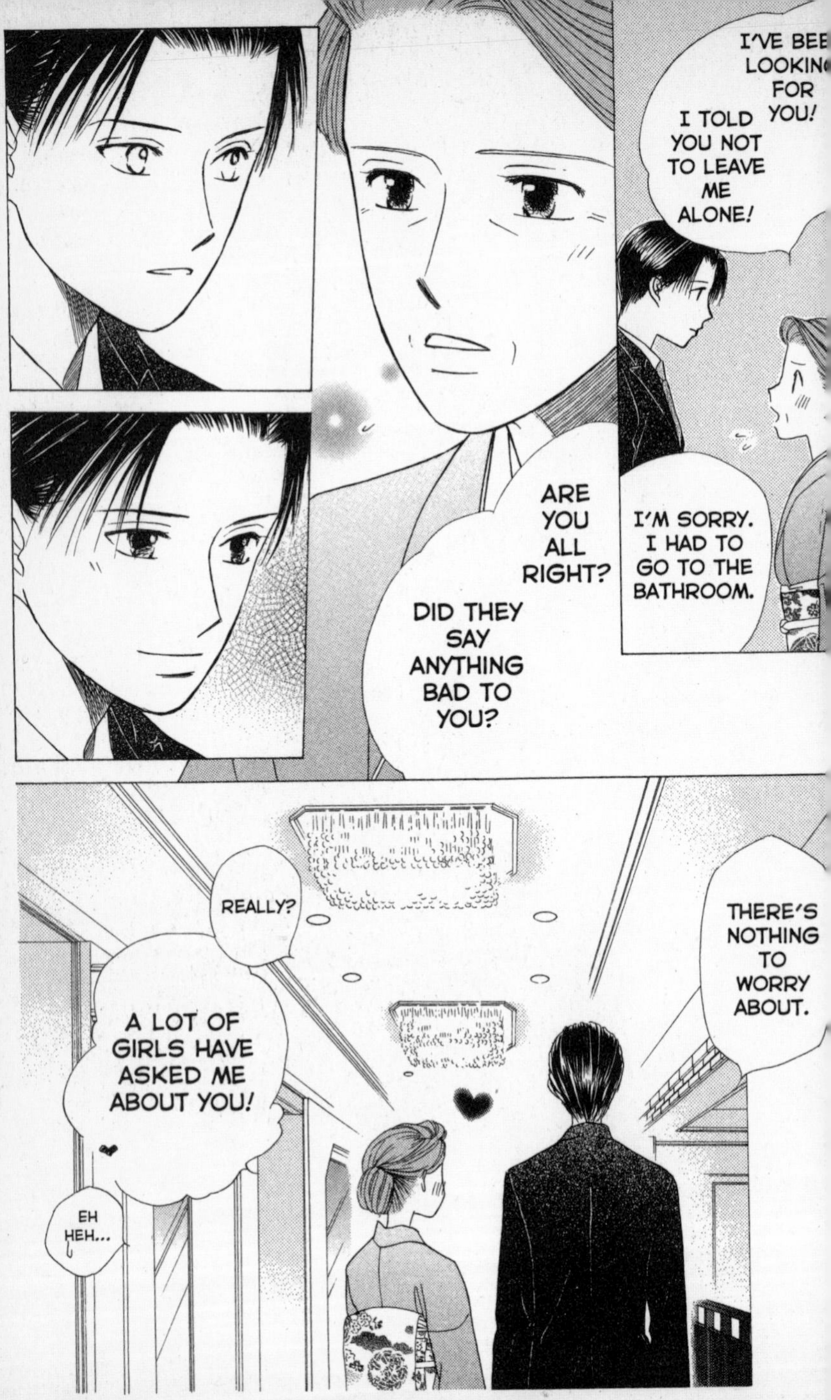
I'VE BEE LOOKIN FOR YOU!
I TOLD YOU NOT TO LEAVE ME ALONE!
I'M SORRY. I HAD TO GO TO THE BATHROOM.
ARE YOU ALL RIGHT?
DID THEY SAY ANYTHING BAD TO YOU?
THERE'S NOTHING TO WORRY ABOUT.
REALLY?
A LOT OF GIRLS HAVE ASKED ME ABOUT YOU!
EH HEH...

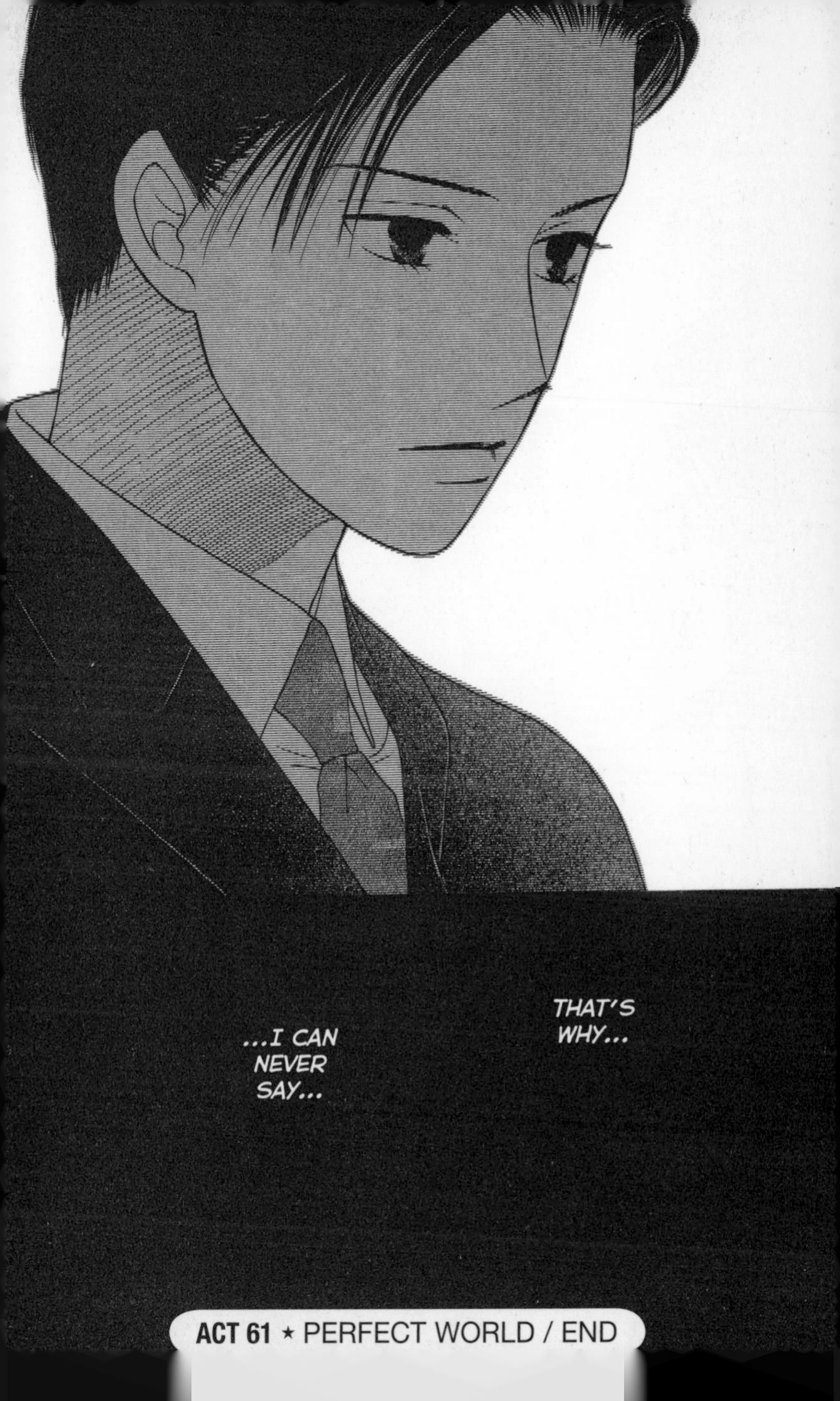
THAT'S WHY...
...I CAN NEVER SAY...
ACT 61 ★ PERFECT WORLD / END

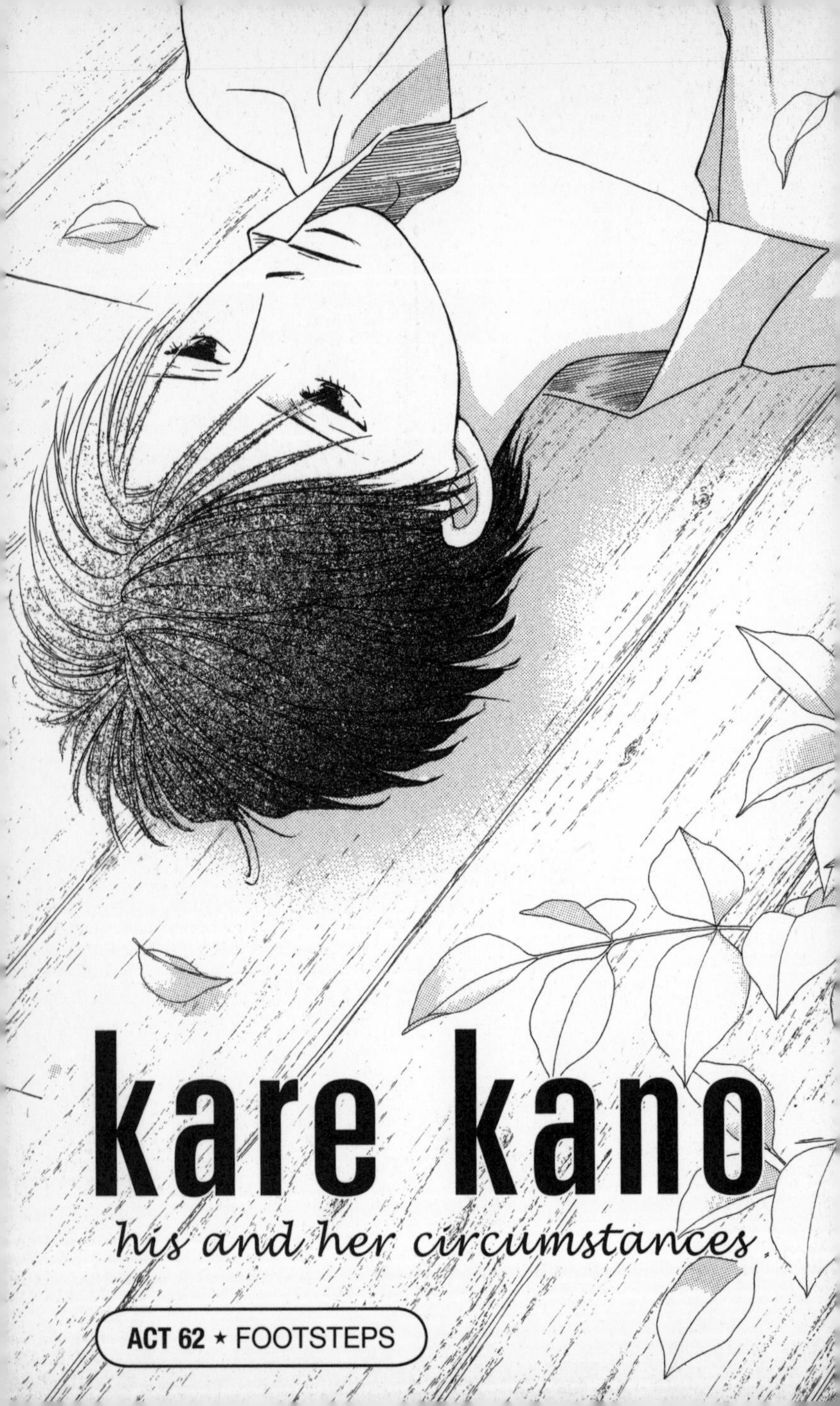
kare kano
his and her circumstances
ACT 62 ★ FOOTSTEPS

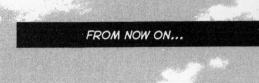

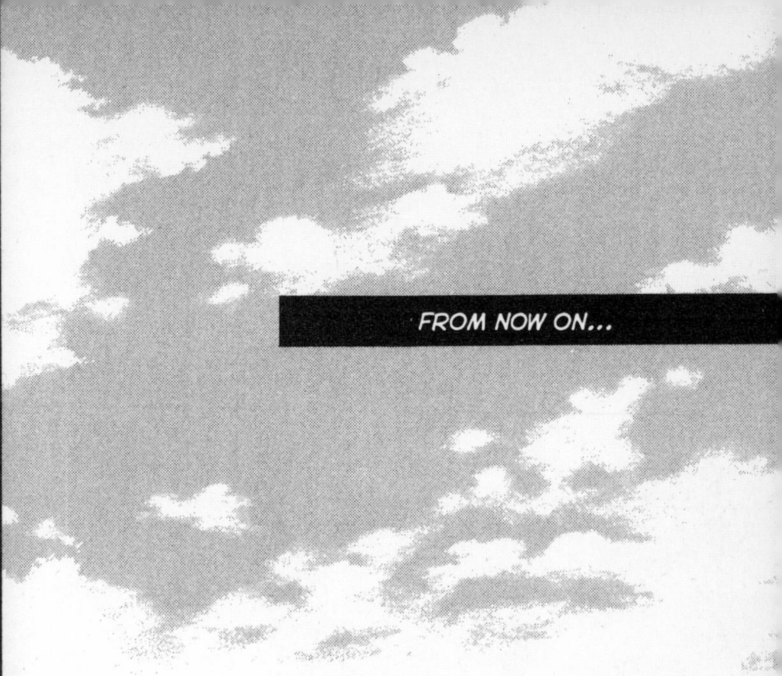

FROM NOW ON...

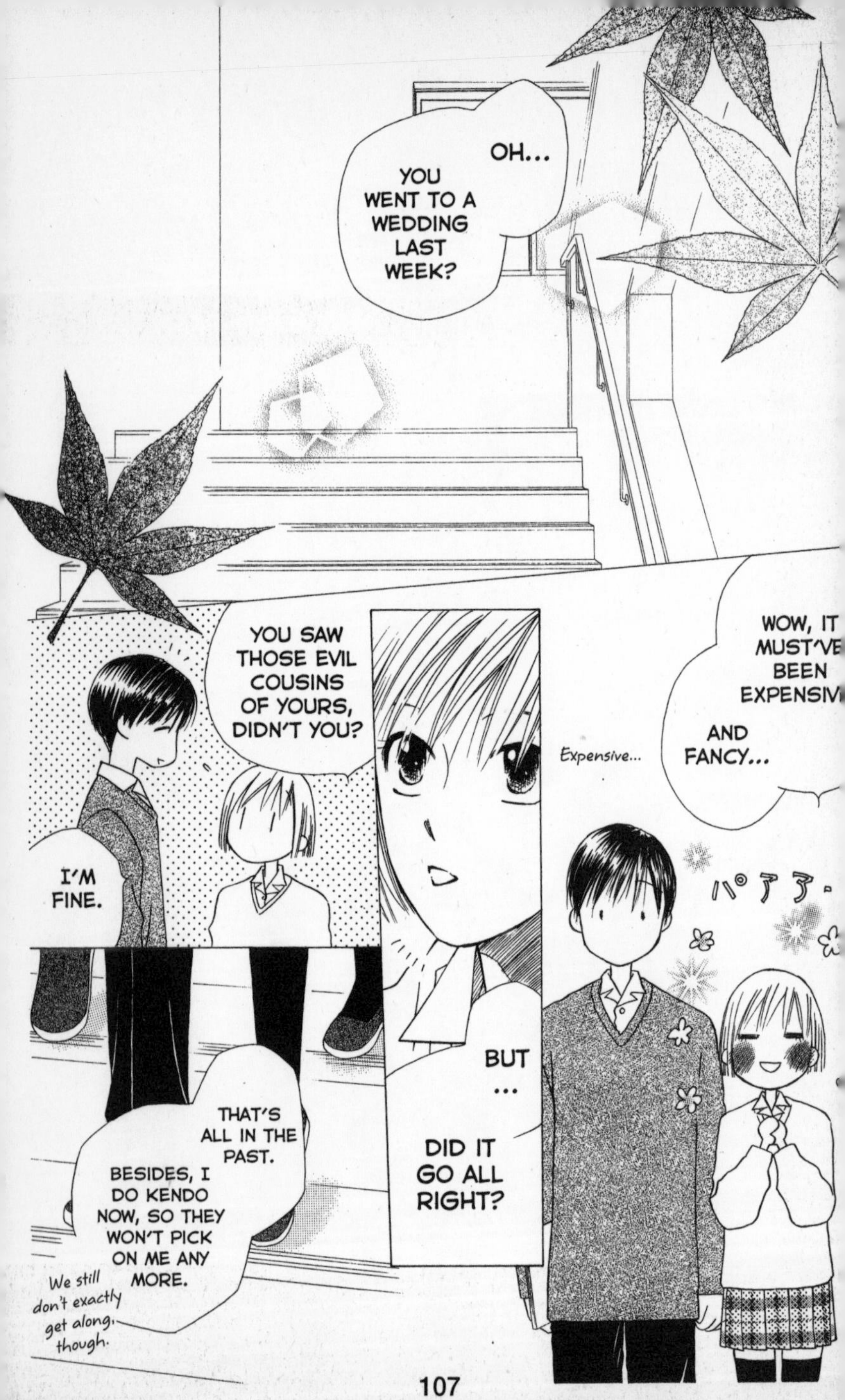
OH...
YOU WENT TO A WEDDING LAST WEEK?
WOW, IT MUST'VE BEEN EXPENSIV
AND FANCY...
Expensive...
パアア
BUT ...
DID IT GO ALL RIGHT?
YOU SAW THOSE EVIL COUSINS OF YOURS, DIDN'T YOU?
I'M FINE.
THAT'S ALL IN THE PAST.
BESIDES, I DO KENDO NOW, SO THEY WON'T PICK ON ME ANY MORE.
We still don't exactly get along, though.

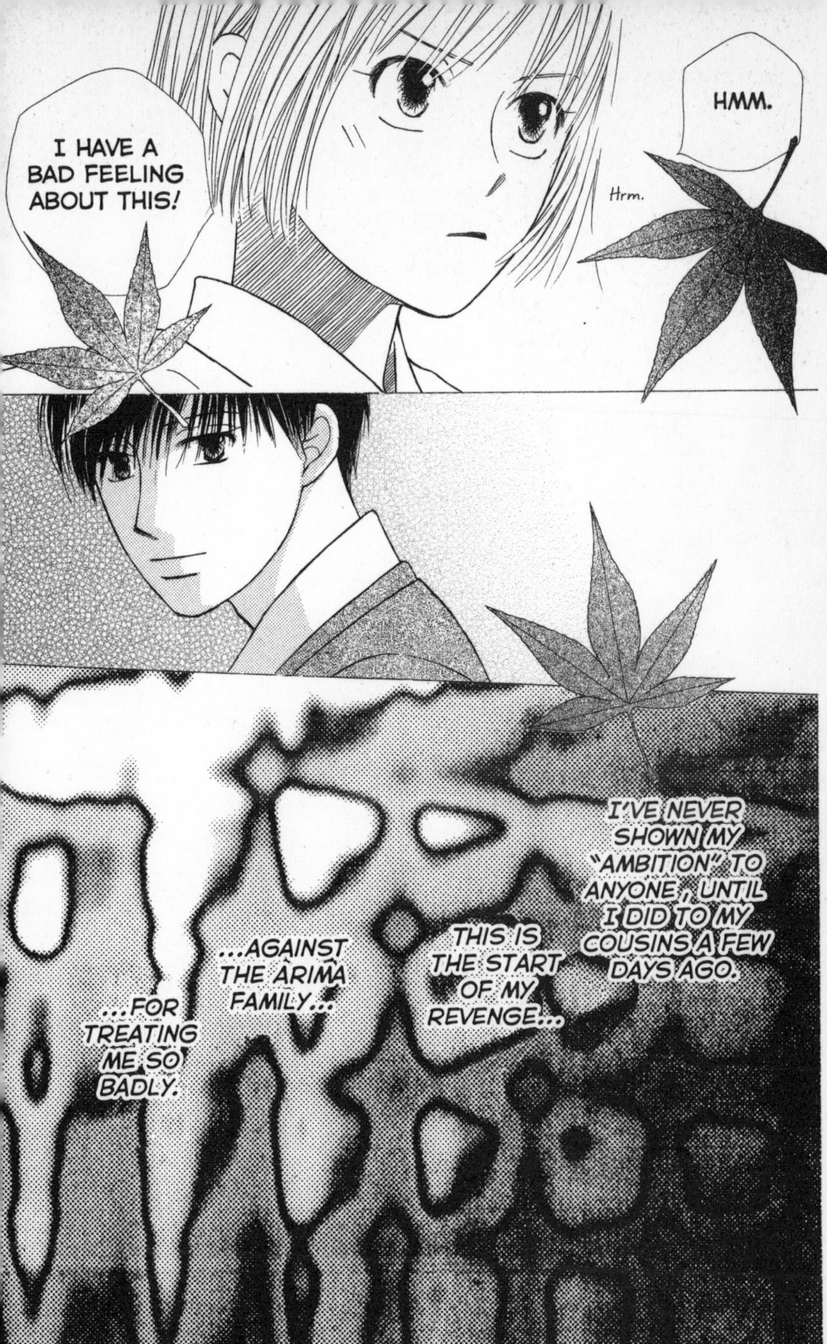
HMM.
Hrm.
I HAVE A BAD FEELING ABOUT THIS!
I'VE NEVER SHOWN MY "AMBITION" TO ANYONE, UNTIL I DID TO MY COUSINS A FEW DAYS AGO.
THIS IS THE START OF MY REVENGE...
...AGAINST THE ARIMA FAMILY...
...FOR TREATING ME SO BADLY.

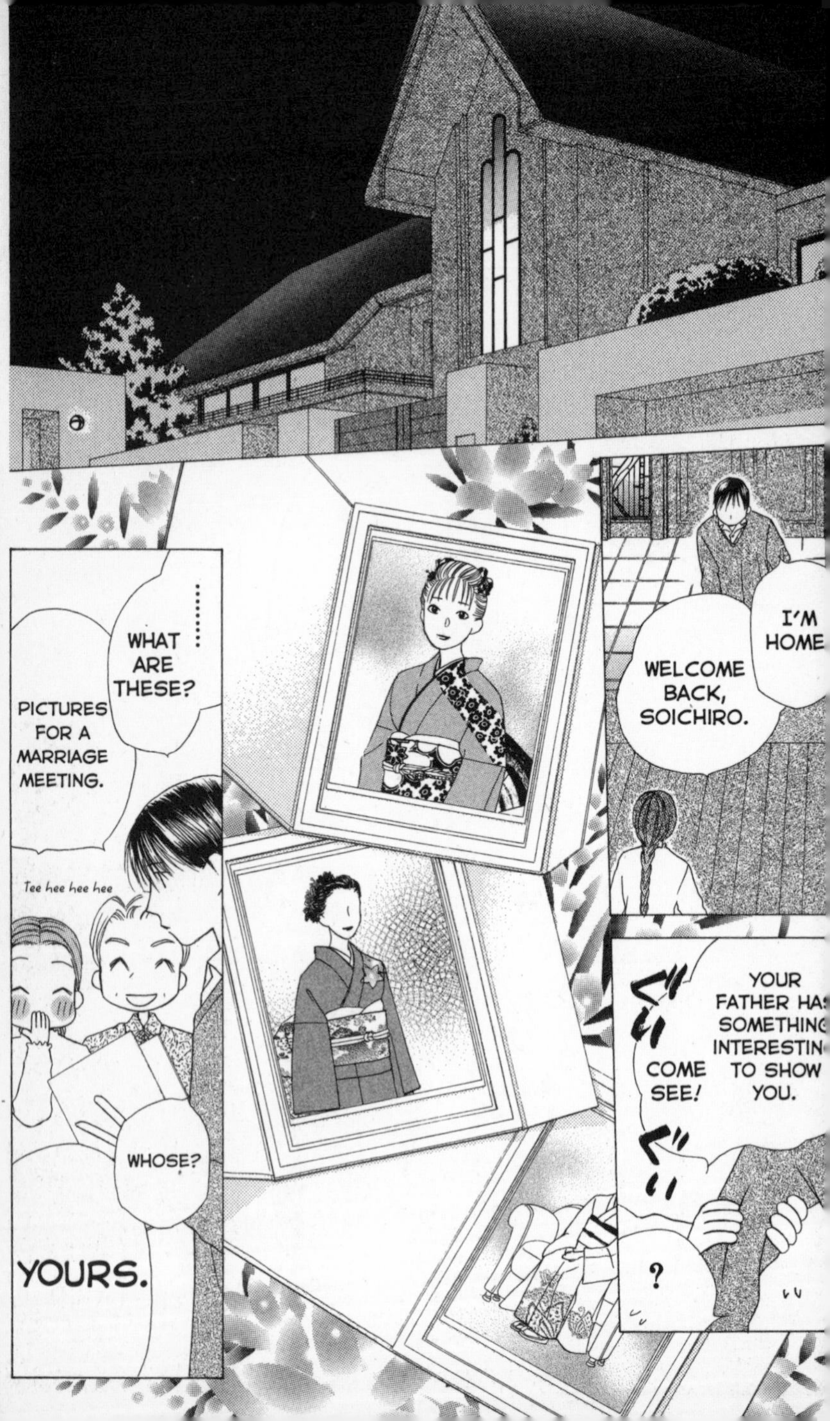
I'M HOME
WELCOME BACK, SOICHIRO.
YOUR FATHER HA SOMETHING INTERESTIN TO SHOW YOU.
ぐい
COME SEE!
ぐい
?
......
WHAT ARE THESE?
PICTURES FOR A MARRIAGE MEETING.
Tee hee hee hee
WHOSE?
YOURS.

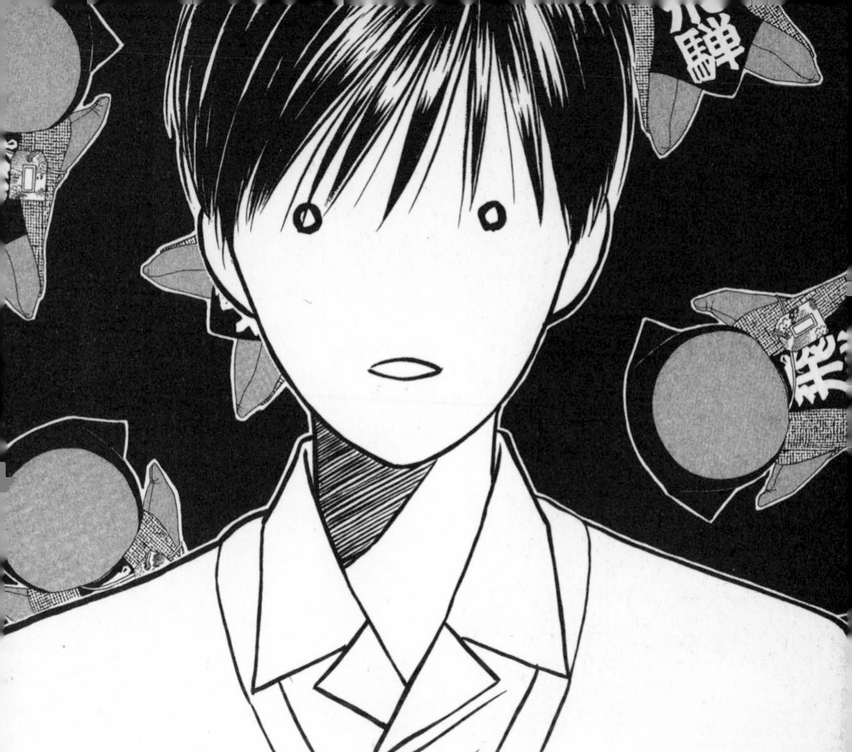
(Sarubobo dolls he got as a gift)
YOUR RELATIVES SURE HAVE SHARP EYES, DON'T THEY?
What?
はっはっはっ
WHEN THEY SAW YOU WHEN WE ADOPTED YOU, THEY KNEW RIGHT AWAY YOU'D GROW UP TO BE A GREAT MAN, SO THEY DIDN'T WASTE ANY TIME GETTING THESE ALL TOGETHER.
はっはっはっはっ
OF COURSE, YOU HAVE MIYAZAWA-SAN, SO I REFUSED AT FIRST.
BUT THEN I WAS SO SURPRISED I BROUGHT THEM BACK.
You should see your face!
ほほほ
OH, DEAR.

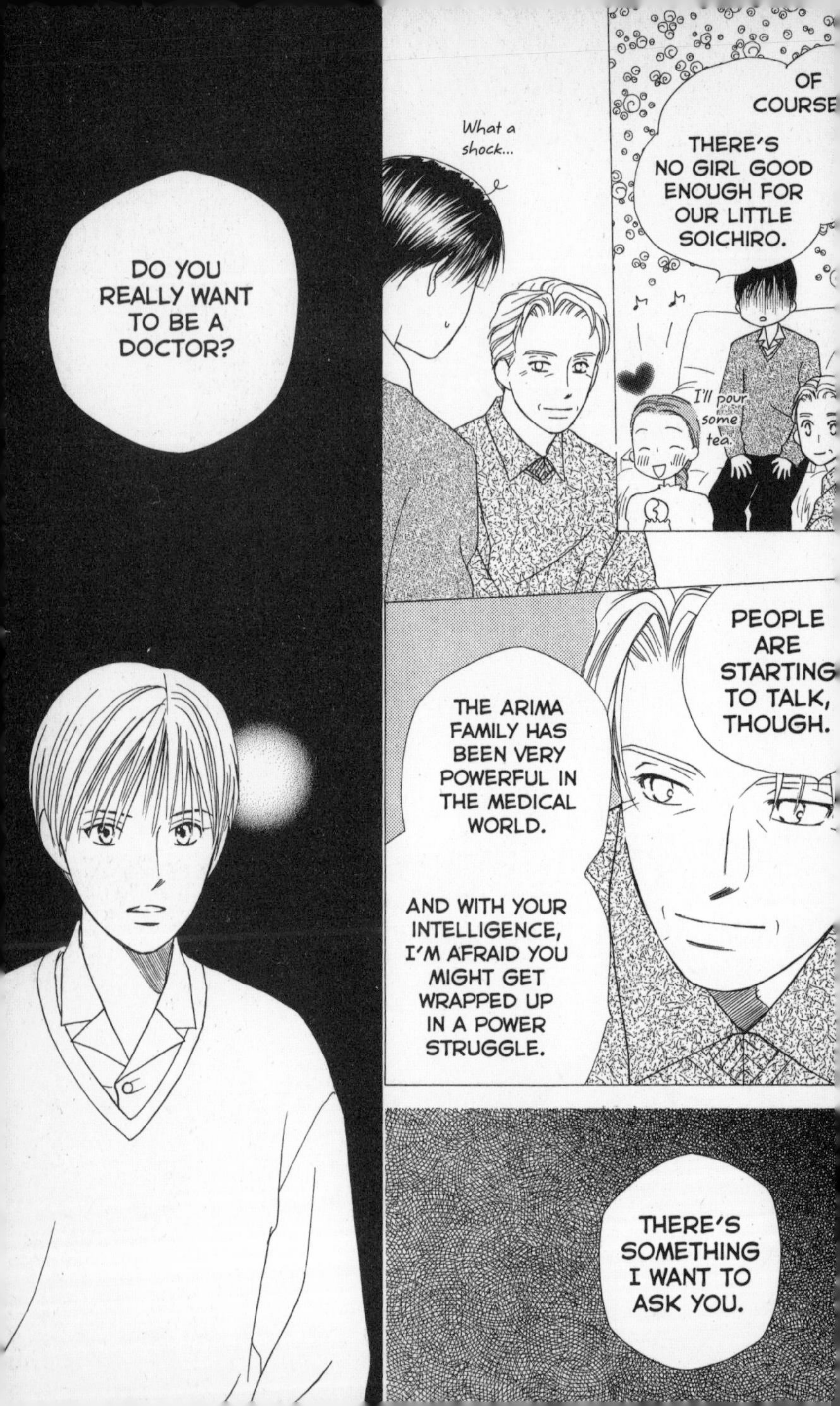
OF COURSE THERE'S NO GIRL GOOD ENOUGH FOR OUR LITTLE SOICHIRO.
I'll pour some tea.
What a shock...
PEOPLE ARE STARTING TO TALK, THOUGH.
THE ARIMA FAMILY HAS BEEN VERY POWERFUL IN THE MEDICAL WORLD.
AND WITH YOUR INTELLIGENCE, I'M AFRAID YOU MIGHT GET WRAPPED UP IN A POWER STRUGGLE.
THERE'S SOMETHING I WANT TO ASK YOU.
DO YOU REALLY WANT TO BE A DOCTOR?

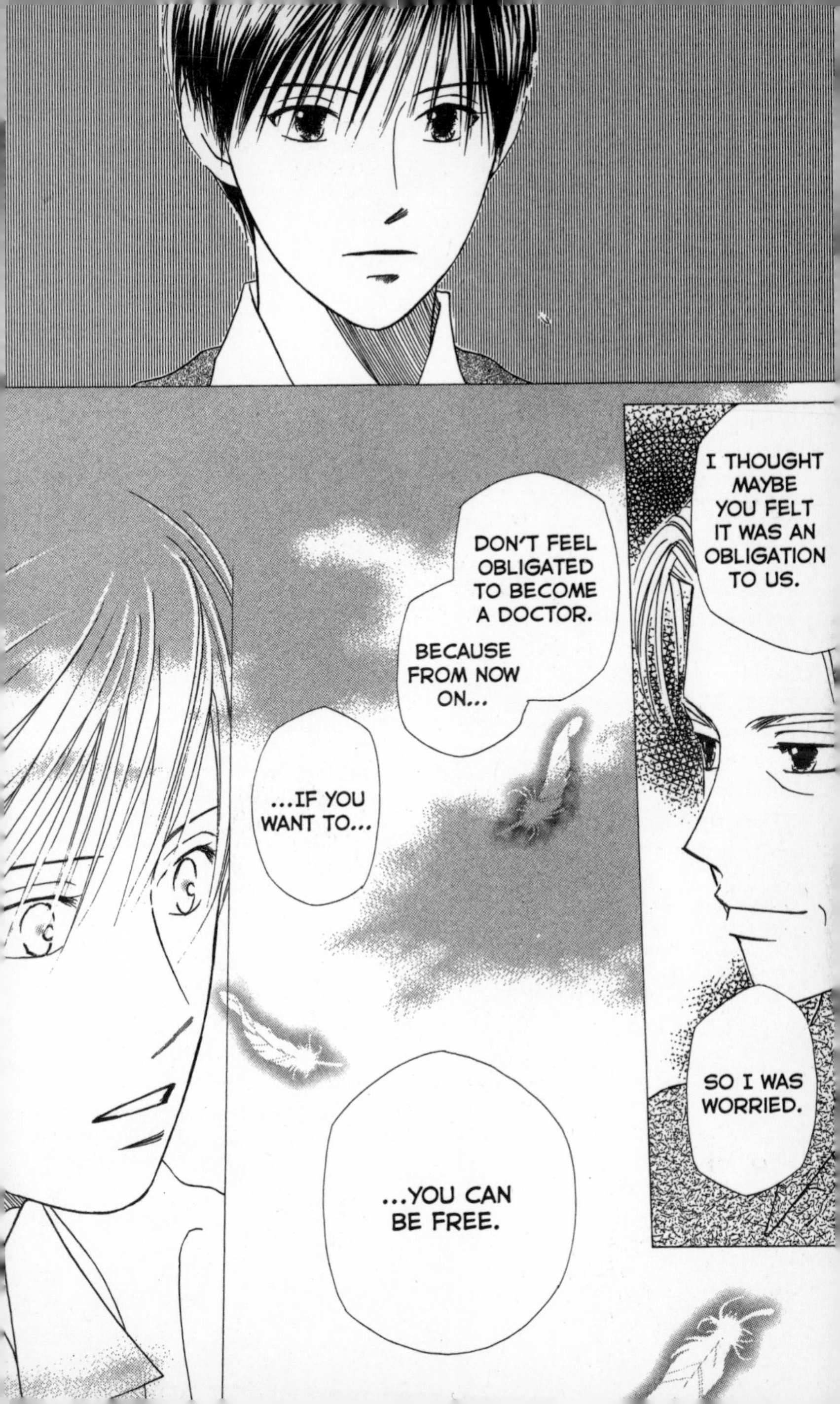
I THOUGHT MAYBE YOU FELT IT WAS AN OBLIGATION TO US.
SO I WAS WORRIED.
DON'T FEEL OBLIGATED TO BECOME A DOCTOR.
BECAUSE FROM NOW ON...
...IF YOU WANT TO...
...YOU CAN BE FREE.

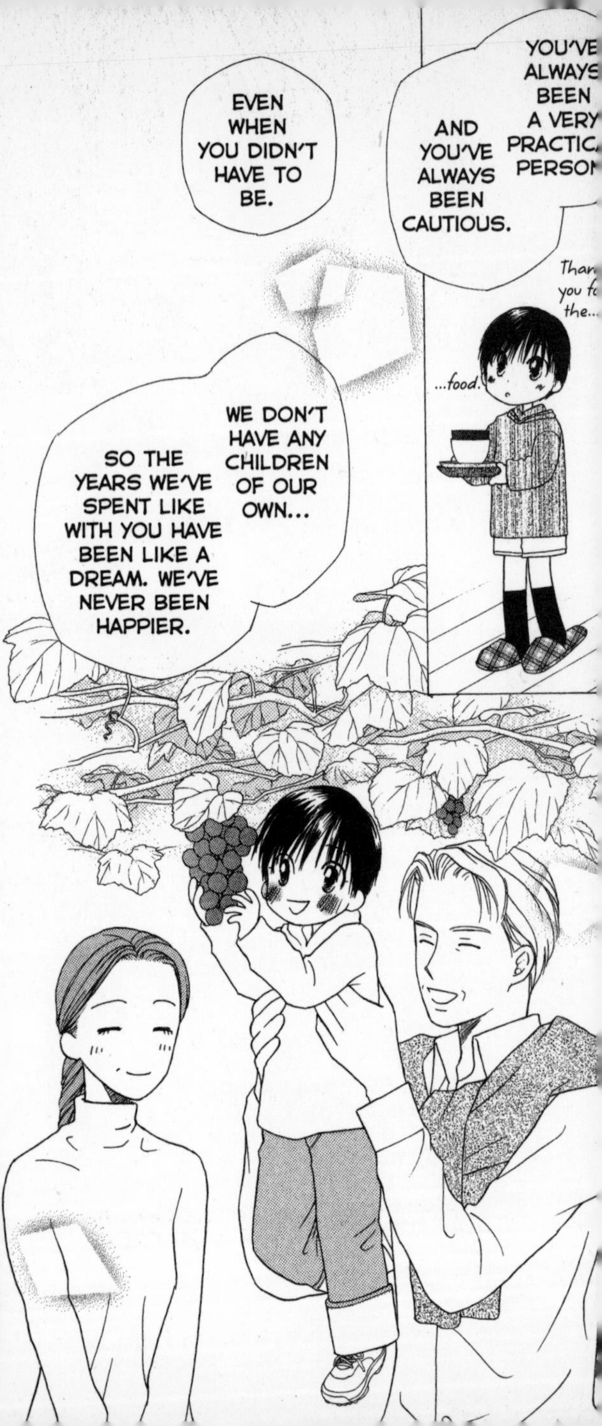
YOU'VE ALWAYS BEEN A VERY PRACTIC PERSO
AND YOU'VE ALWAYS BEEN CAUTIOUS.
EVEN WHEN YOU DIDN'T HAVE TO BE.
Than you fo the...
...food.
WE DON'T HAVE ANY CHILDREN OF OUR OWN...
SO THE YEARS WE'VE SPENT LIKE WITH YOU HAVE BEEN LIKE A DREAM. WE'VE NEVER BEEN HAPPIER.

4

Lately, my interests have been turning toward Japanese things. So I thought, "Maybe I'm really getting into those kinds of things now," and sure enough, I was.

KABUKICHO! ♥

I feel so great now.

I usually work from the first to the 21st or 22nd of the month. The final day of the sumo tournament at Kabukicho is on the 26th, so I'm going to

REALLY CONCENTRATE

to get my work done and go to Kabukicho. In July, I'm going to go to Tokyo and see Tamasaburo. I'm gonna try my best!

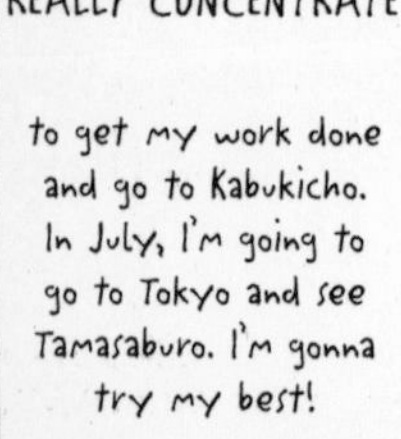

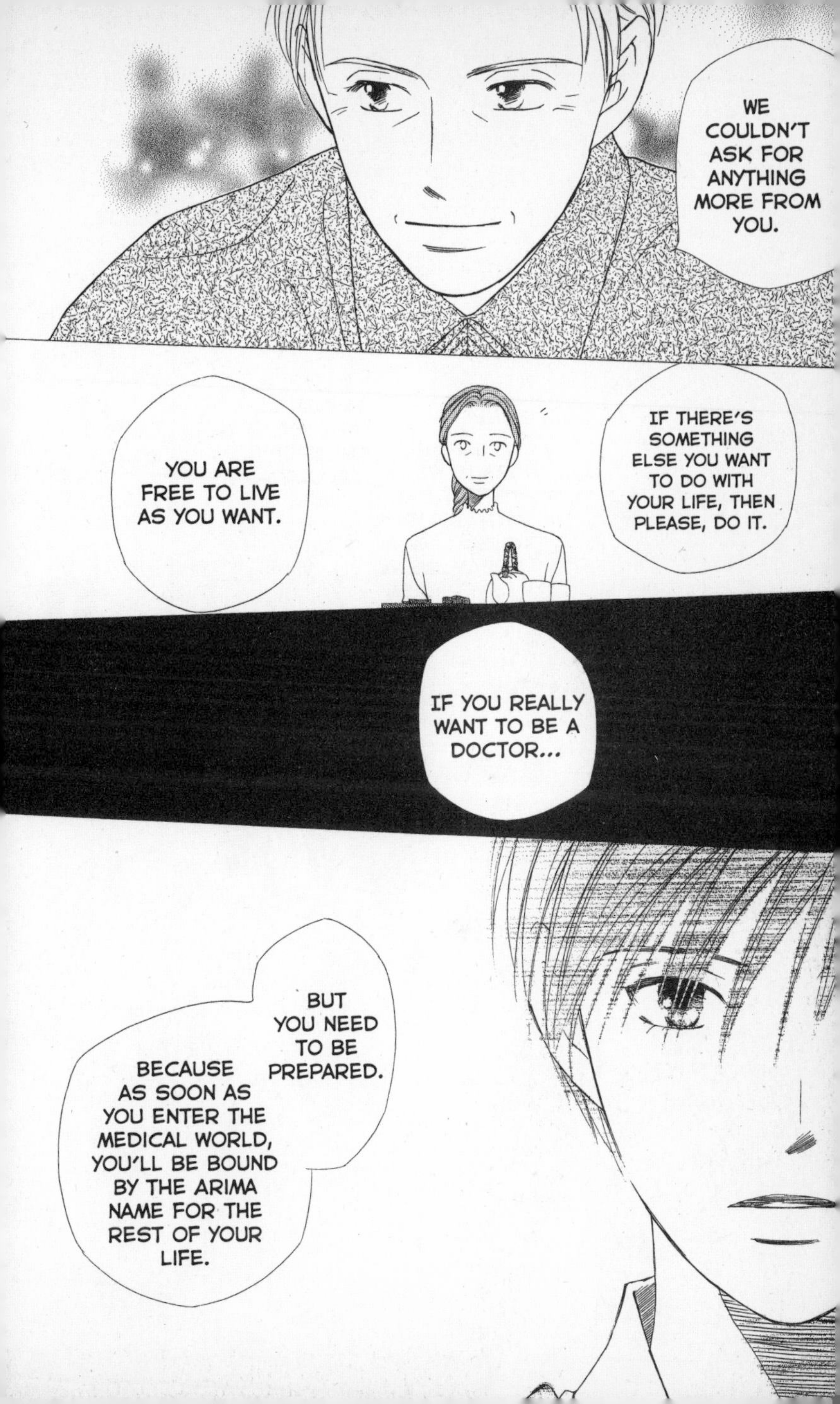
WE COULDN'T ASK FOR ANYTHING MORE FROM YOU.
IF THERE'S SOMETHING ELSE YOU WANT TO DO WITH YOUR LIFE, THEN PLEASE, DO IT.
YOU ARE FREE TO LIVE AS YOU WANT.
IF YOU REALLY WANT TO BE A DOCTOR...
BUT YOU NEED TO BE PREPARED.
BECAUSE AS SOON AS YOU ENTER THE MEDICAL WORLD, YOU'LL BE BOUND BY THE ARIMA NAME FOR THE REST OF YOUR LIFE.

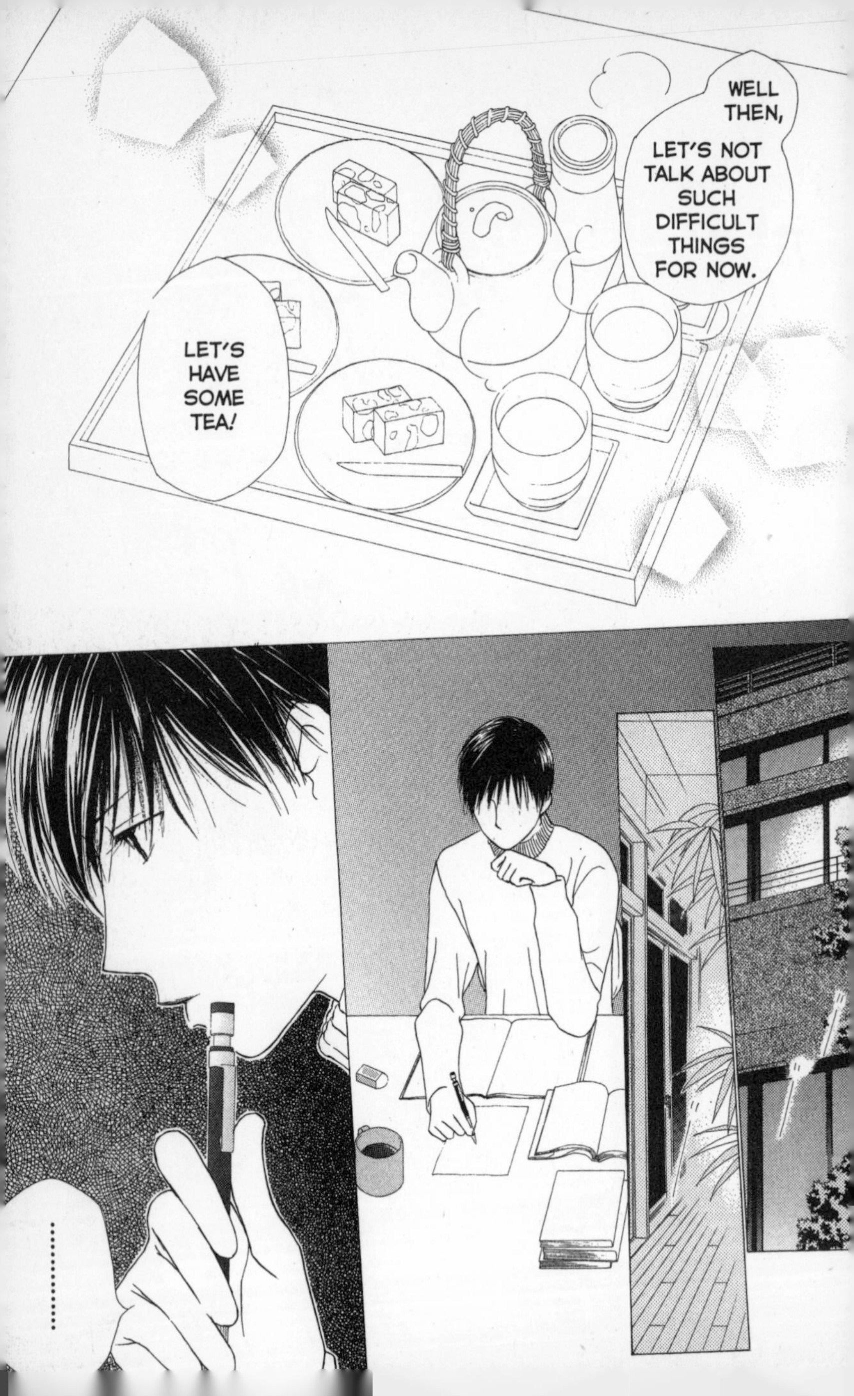
WELL THEN,
LET'S NOT TALK ABOUT SUCH DIFFICULT THINGS FOR NOW.
LET'S HAVE SOME TEA!

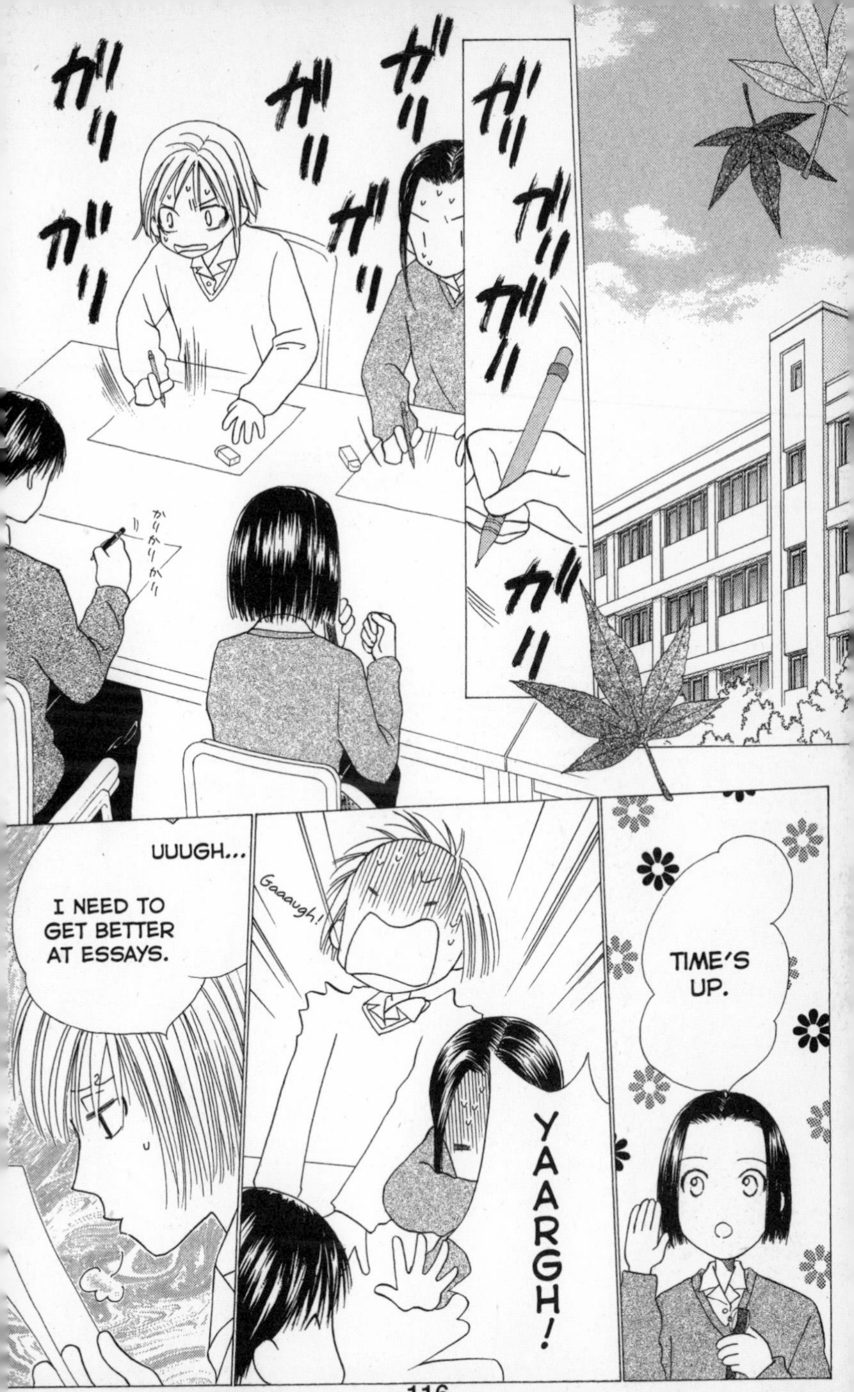
ガリガリガリ
ガリ
ガリガリ
ガリガリ
ガリガリ
かりかりかり
TIME'S UP.
Gaaaugh!
YAARGH!
UUUGH...
I NEED TO GET BETTER AT ESSAYS.

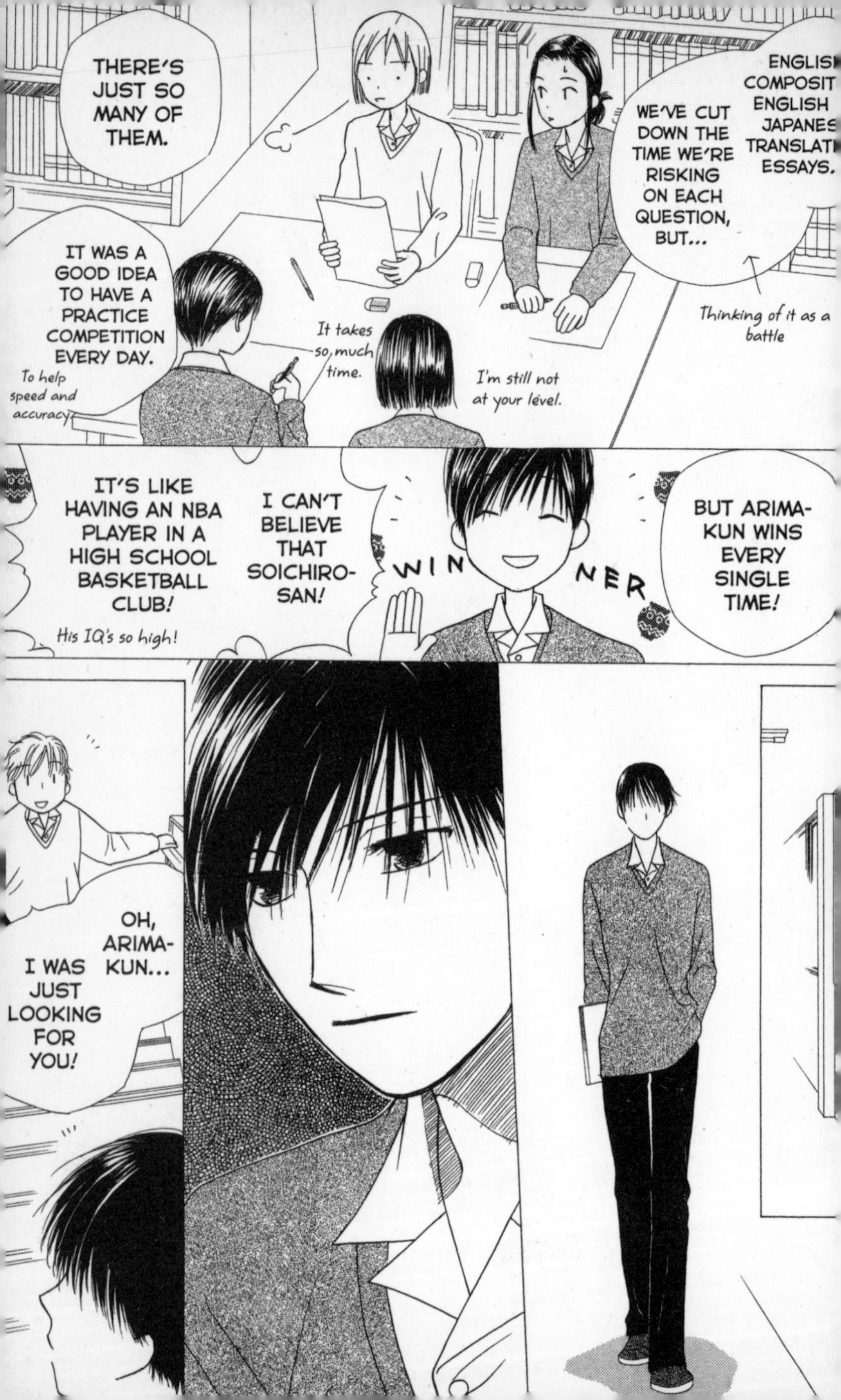
ENGLISH COMPOSIT ENGLISH JAPANES TRANSLAT ESSAYS.
WE'VE CUT DOWN THE TIME WE'RE RISKING ON EACH QUESTION, BUT...
Thinking of it as a battle
I'm still not at your level.
It takes so much time.
THERE'S JUST SO MANY OF THEM.
IT WAS A GOOD IDEA TO HAVE A PRACTICE COMPETITION EVERY DAY.
To help speed and accuracy.
BUT ARIMA-KUN WINS EVERY SINGLE TIME!
WIN NER
I CAN'T BELIEVE THAT SOICHIRO-SAN!
IT'S LIKE HAVING AN NBA PLAYER IN A HIGH SCHOOL BASKETBALL CLUB!
His IQ's so high!
OH, ARIMA-KUN...
I WAS JUST LOOKING FOR YOU!

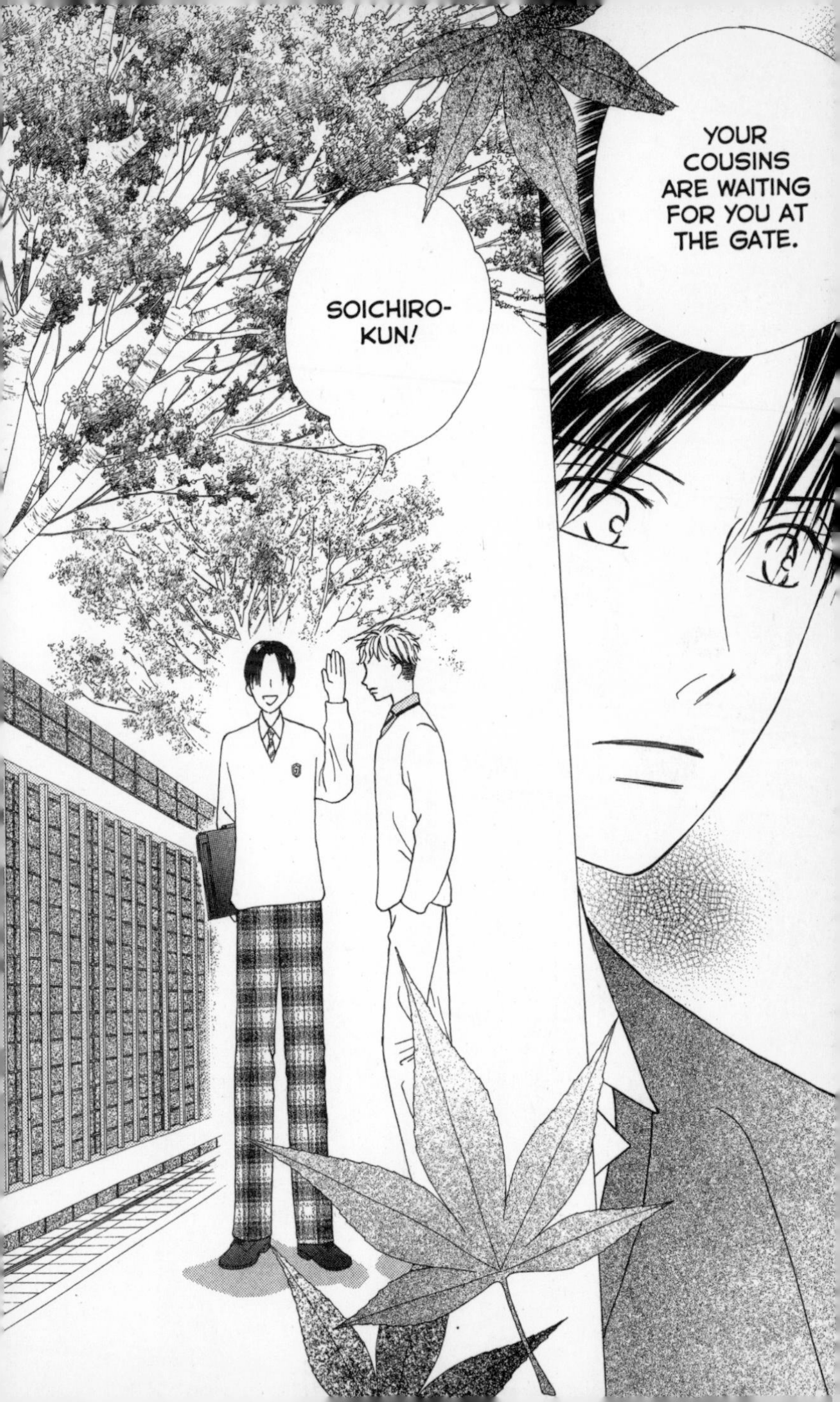
YOUR COUSINS ARE WAITING FOR YOU AT THE GATE.
SOICHIRO-KUN!

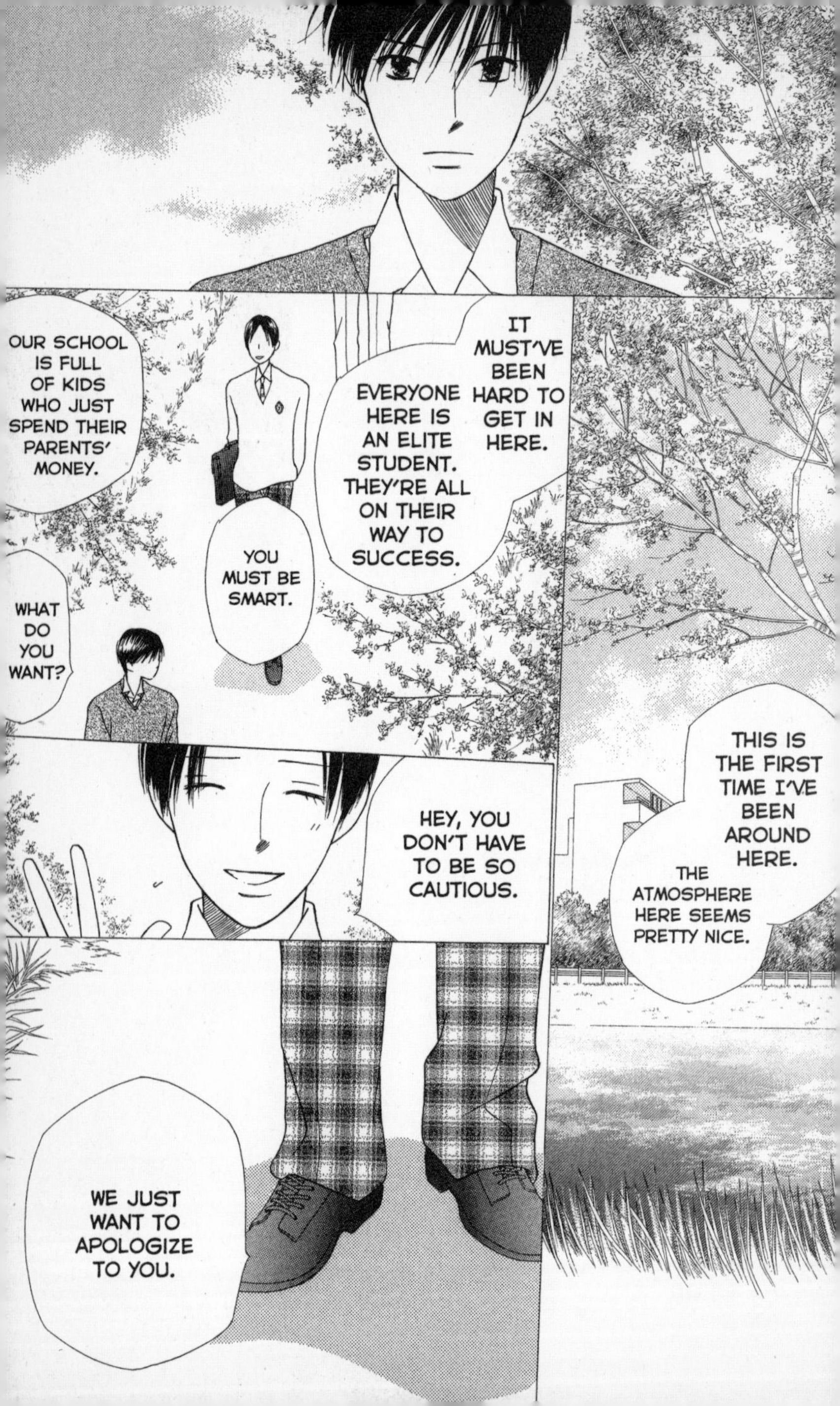
THIS IS THE FIRST TIME I'VE BEEN AROUND HERE.
THE ATMOSPHERE HERE SEEMS PRETTY NICE.
IT MUST'VE BEEN HARD TO GET IN HERE.
EVERYONE HERE IS AN ELITE STUDENT. THEY'RE ALL ON THEIR WAY TO SUCCESS.
OUR SCHOOL IS FULL OF KIDS WHO JUST SPEND THEIR PARENTS' MONEY.
YOU MUST BE SMART.
WHAT DO YOU WANT?
HEY, YOU DON'T HAVE TO BE SO CAUTIOUS.
WE JUST WANT TO APOLOGIZE TO YOU.

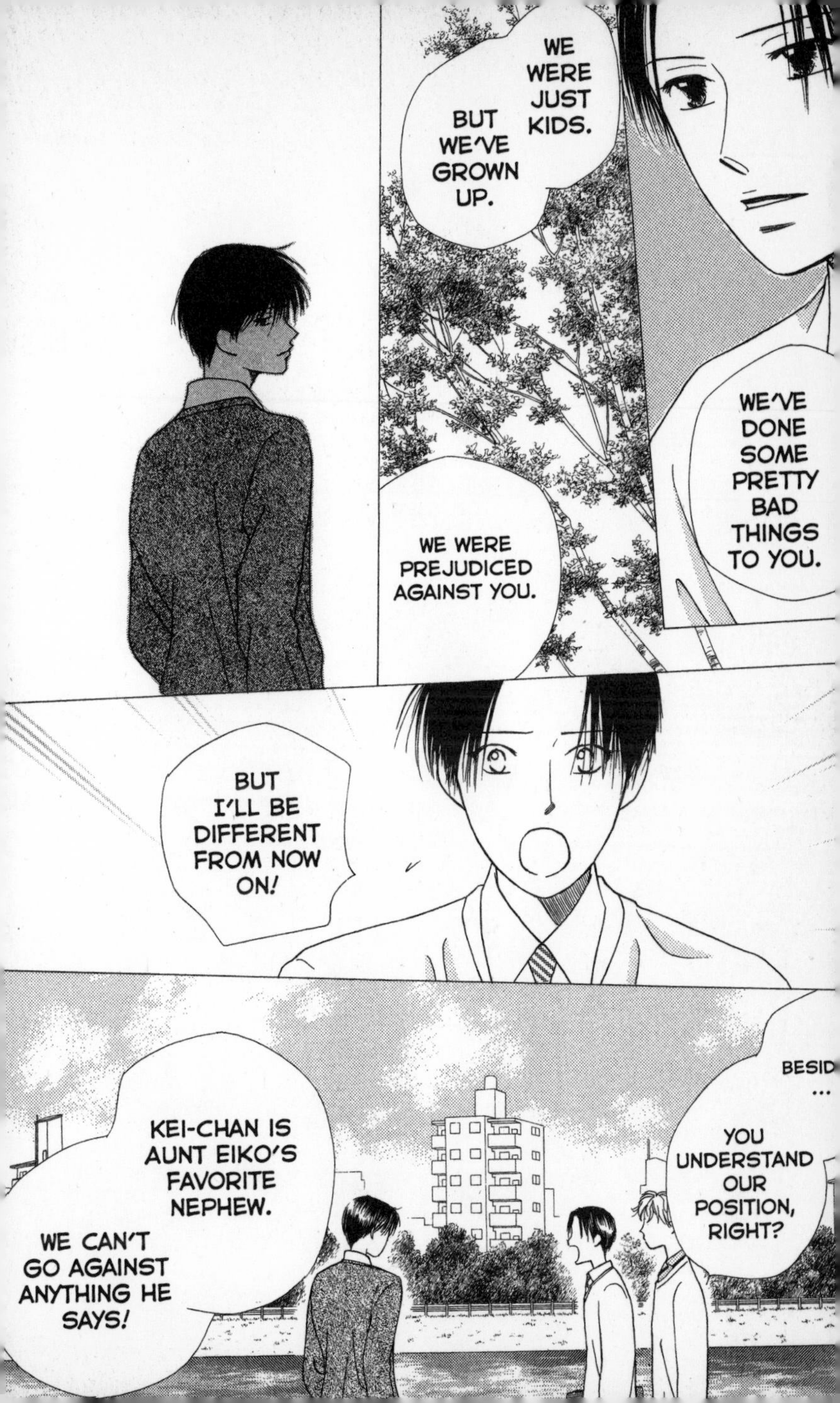
WE WERE JUST KIDS.
BUT WE'VE GROWN UP.
WE'VE DONE SOME PRETTY BAD THINGS TO YOU.
WE WERE PREJUDICED AGAINST YOU.
BUT I'LL BE DIFFERENT FROM NOW ON!
BESID ...
YOU UNDERSTAND OUR POSITION, RIGHT?
KEI-CHAN IS AUNT EIKO'S FAVORITE NEPHEW.
WE CAN'T GO AGAINST ANYTHING HE SAYS!

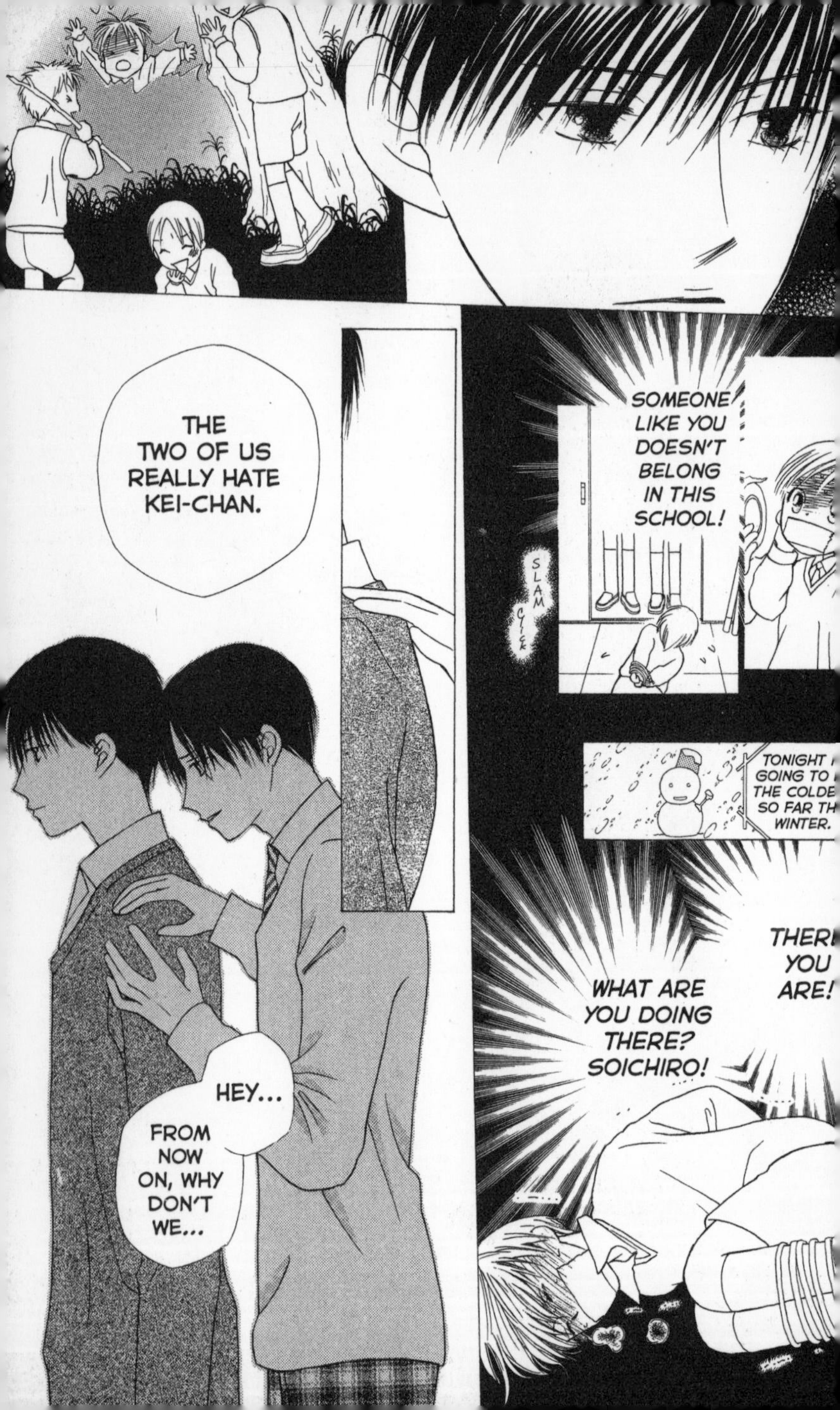
SOMEONE LIKE YOU DOESN'T BELONG IN THIS SCHOOL!
SLAM
CLICK
TONIGHT
GOING TO
THE COLDE
SO FAR TH
WINTER.
THER
YOU ARE!
WHAT ARE YOU DOING THERE? SOICHIRO!
THE TWO OF US REALLY HATE KEI-CHAN.
HEY...
FROM NOW ON, WHY DON'T WE...

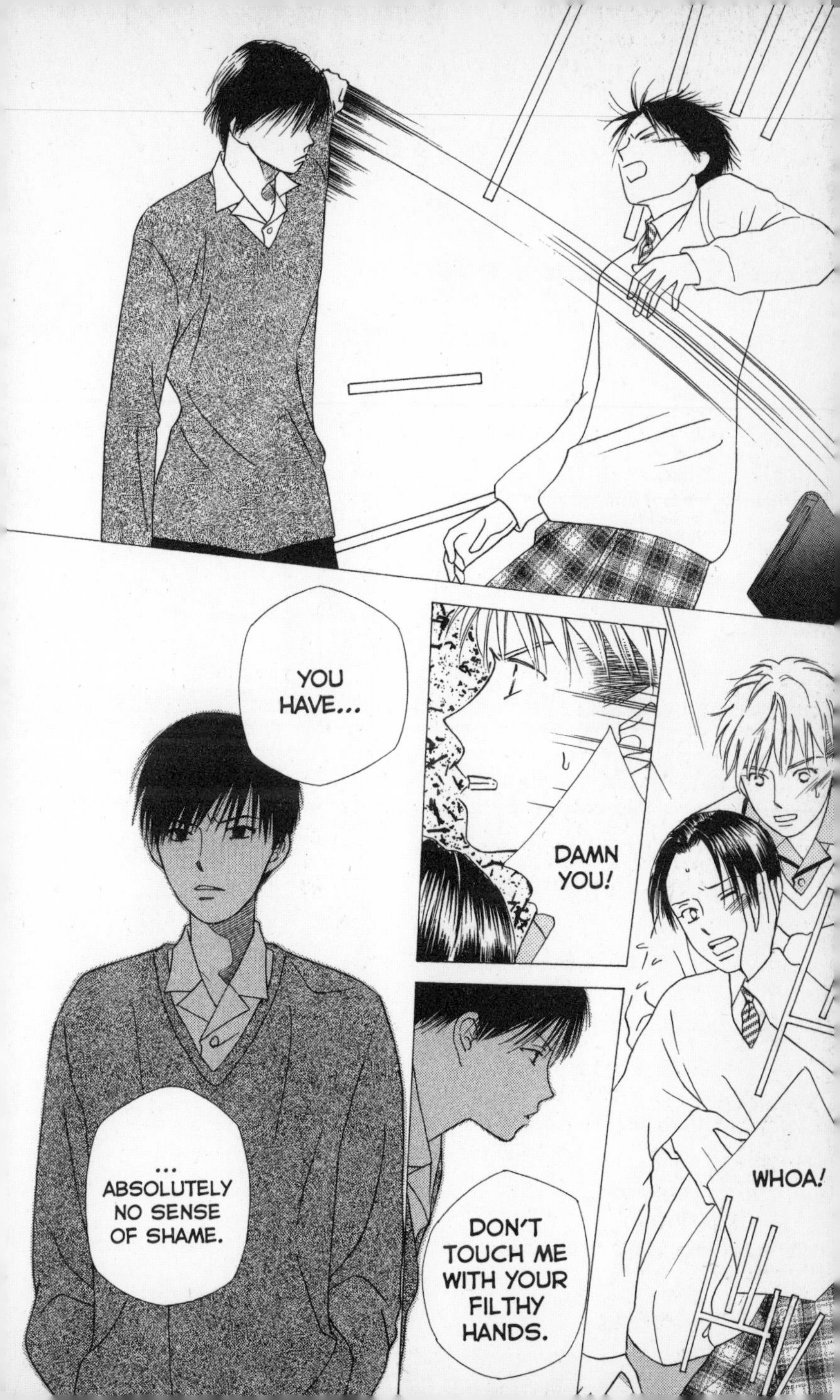
WHOA!
DAMN YOU!
DON'T TOUCH ME WITH YOUR FILTHY HANDS.
YOU HAVE...
...ABSOLUTELY NO SENSE OF SHAME.

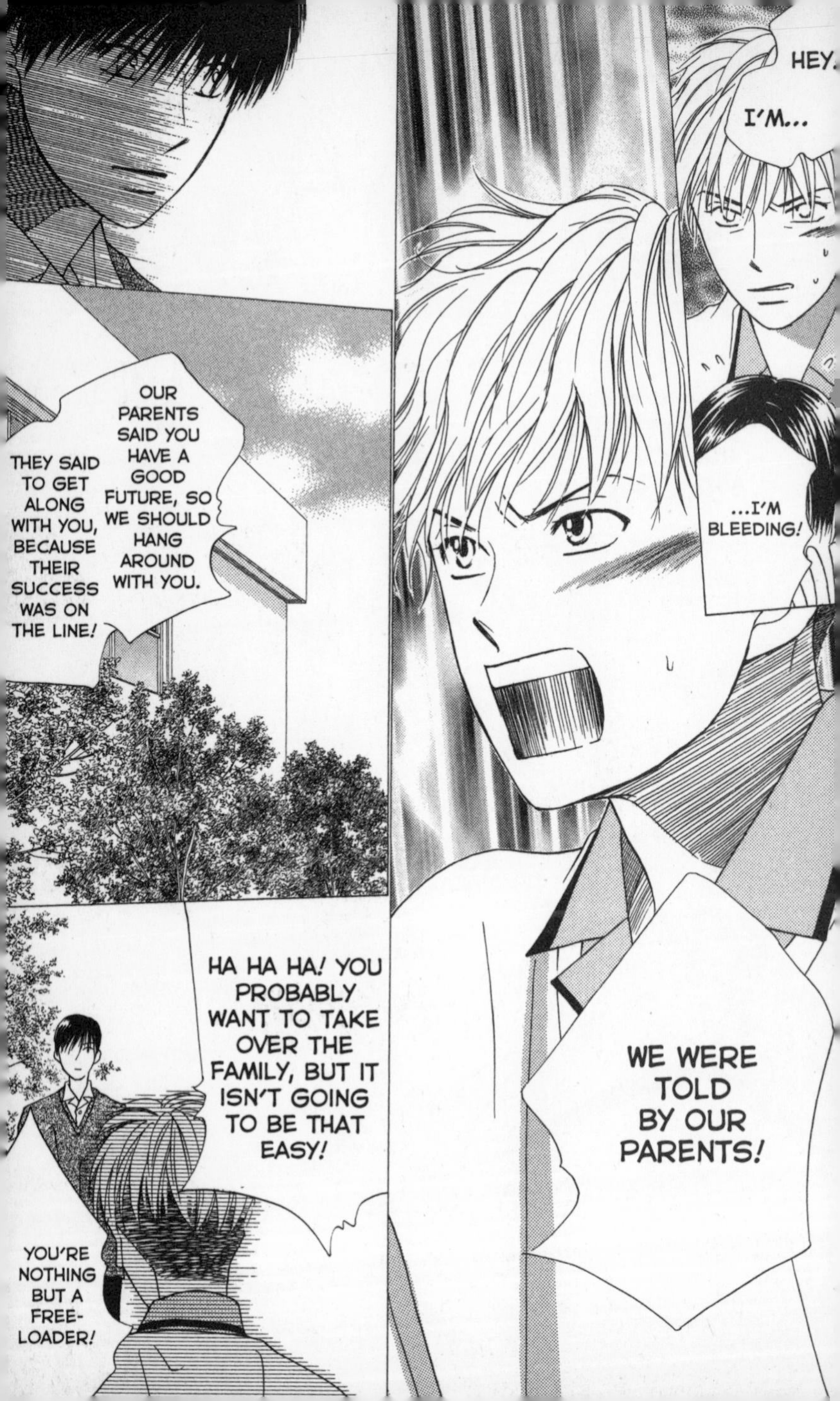
HEY.
I'M...
...I'M BLEEDING!
WE WERE TOLD BY OUR PARENTS!
OUR PARENTS SAID YOU HAVE A GOOD FUTURE, SO WE SHOULD HANG AROUND WITH YOU.
THEY SAID TO GET ALONG WITH YOU, BECAUSE THEIR SUCCESS WAS ON THE LINE!
HA HA HA! YOU PROBABLY WANT TO TAKE OVER THE FAMILY, BUT IT ISN'T GOING TO BE THAT EASY!
YOU'RE NOTHING BUT A FREE-LOADER!

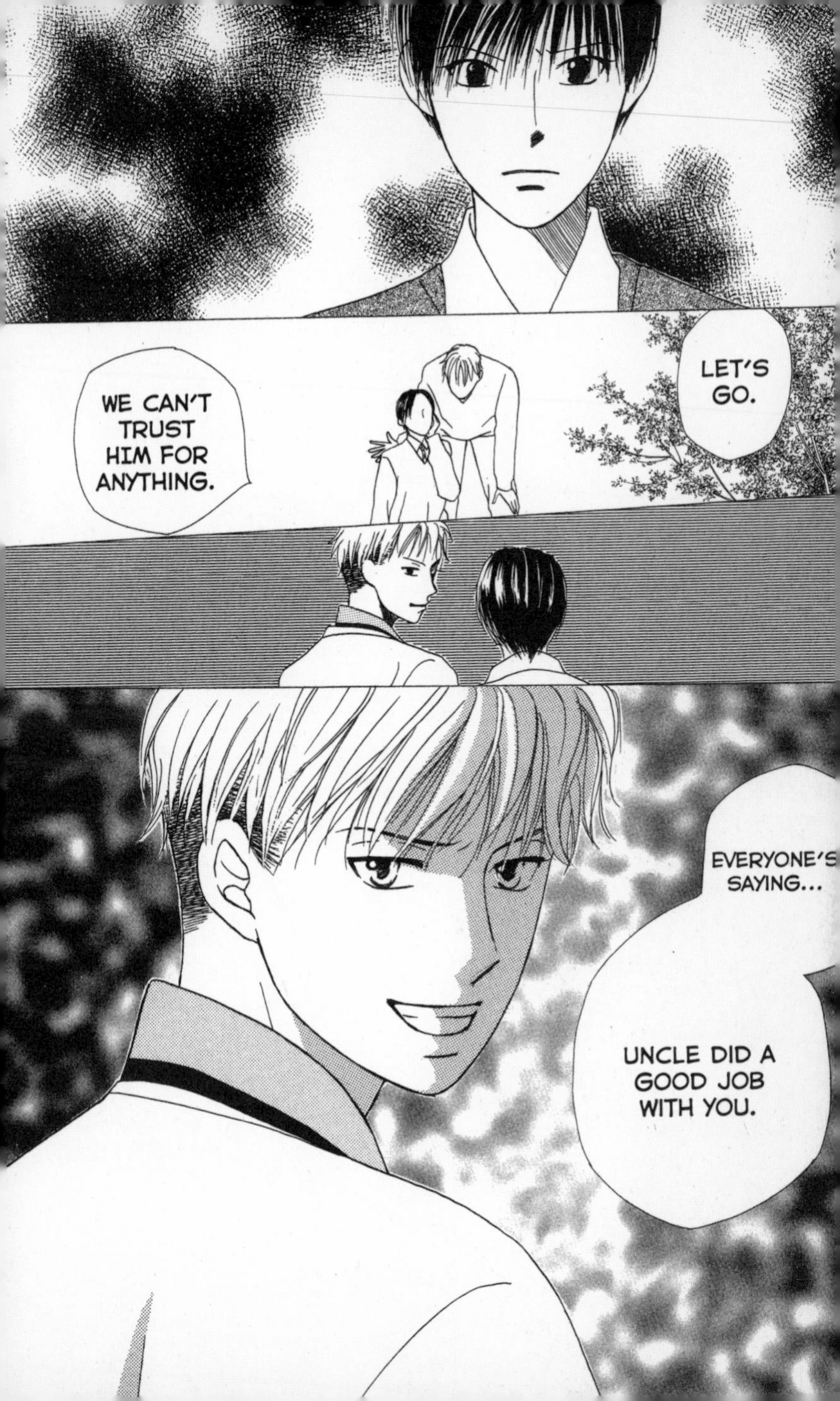
LET'S GO.
WE CAN'T TRUST HIM FOR ANYTHING.
EVERYONE'S SAYING...
UNCLE DID A GOOD JOB WITH YOU.

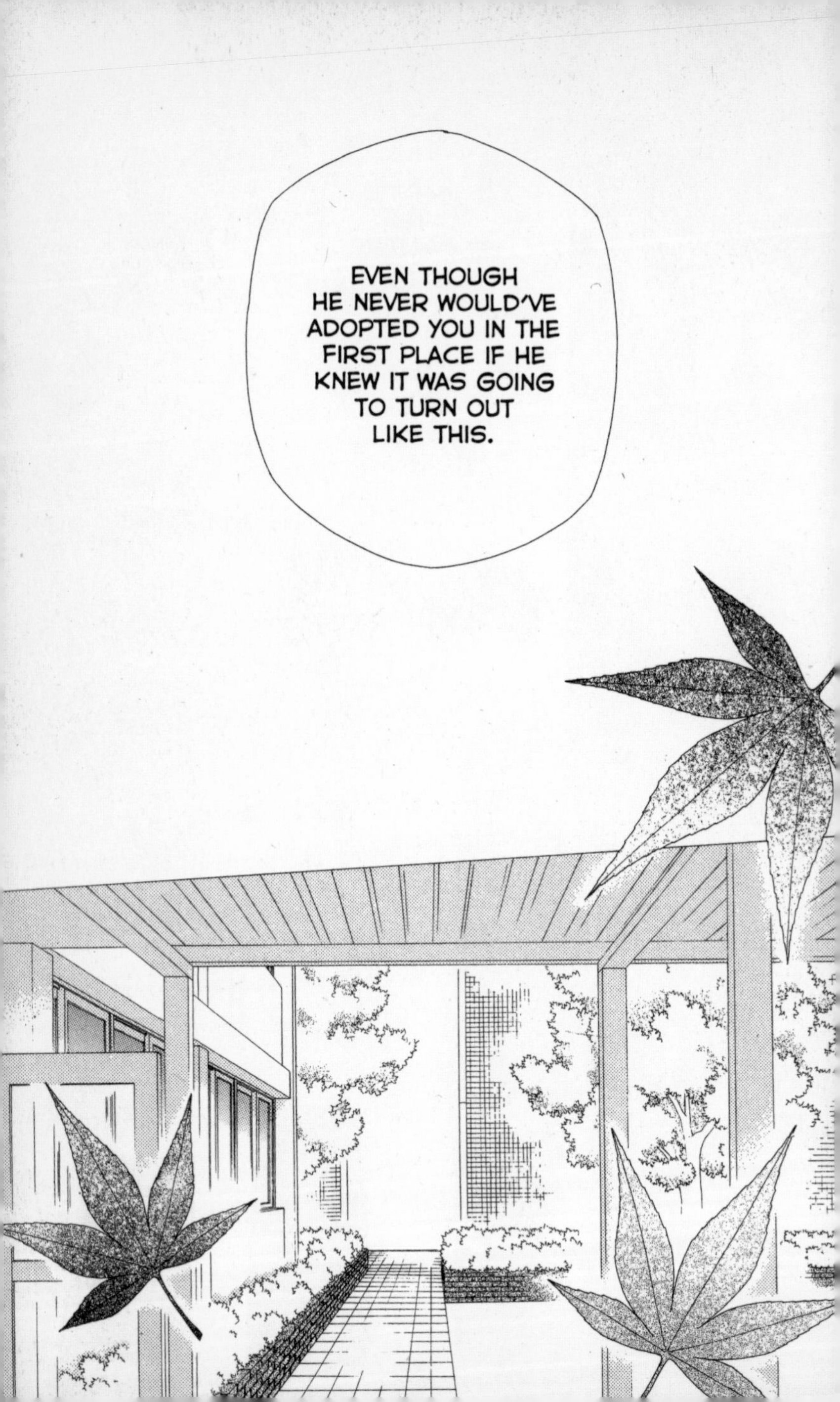
EVEN THOUGH HE NEVER WOULD'VE ADOPTED YOU IN THE FIRST PLACE IF HE KNEW IT WAS GOING TO TURN OUT LIKE THIS.

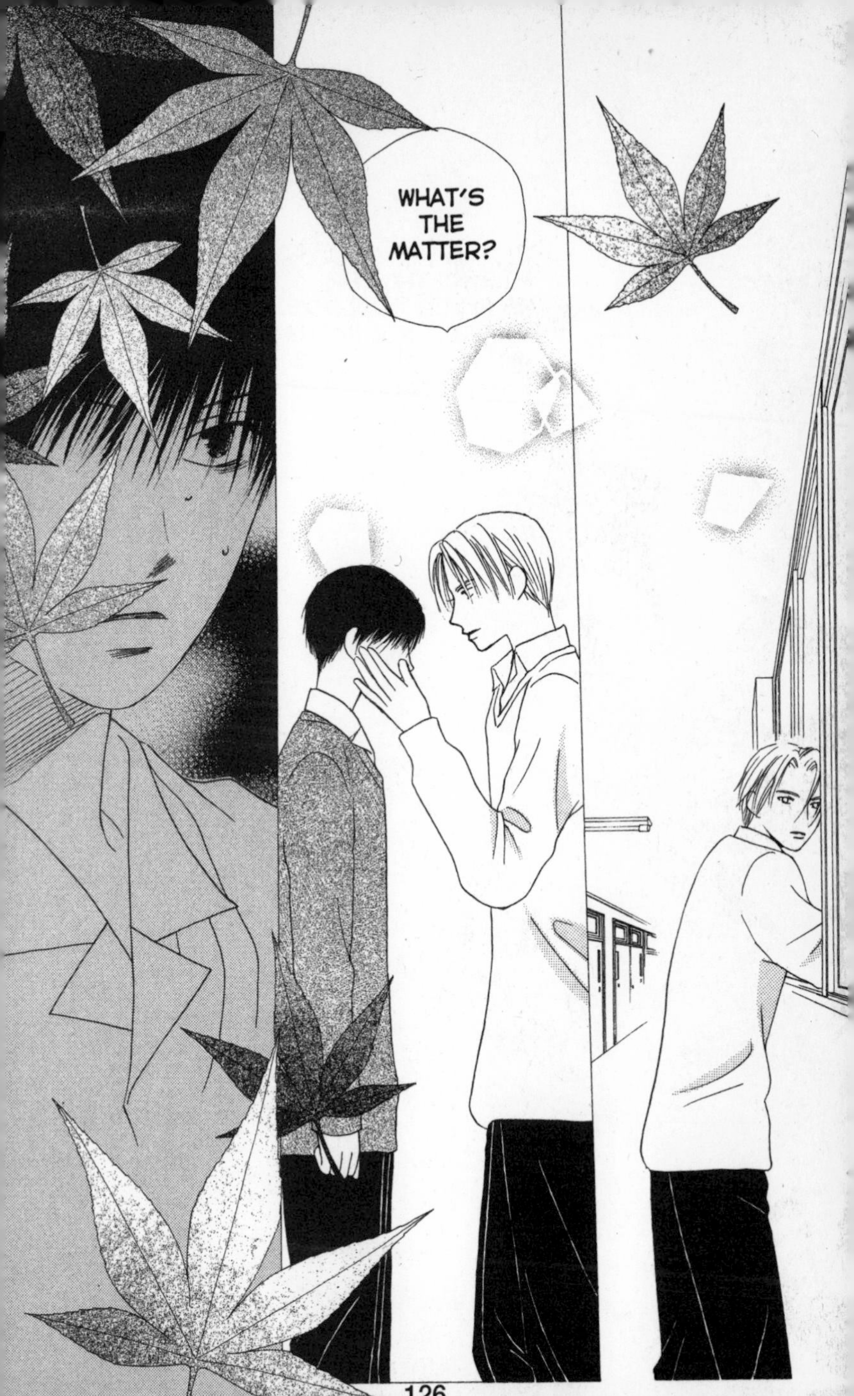
WHAT'S THE MATTER?

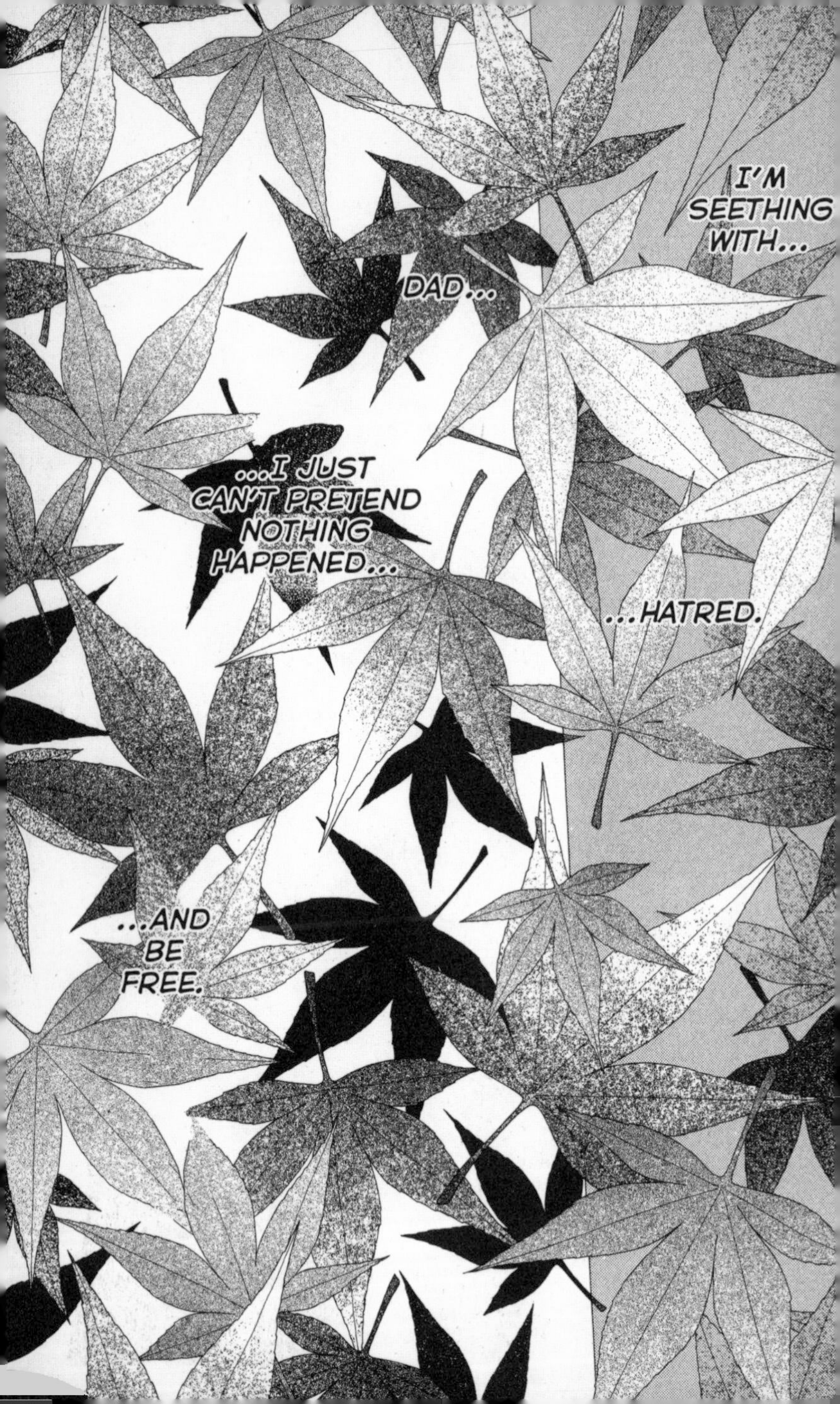

I'M SEETHING WITH...
DAD...
...I JUST CAN'T PRETEND NOTHING HAPPENED...
...HATRED.
...AND BE FREE.

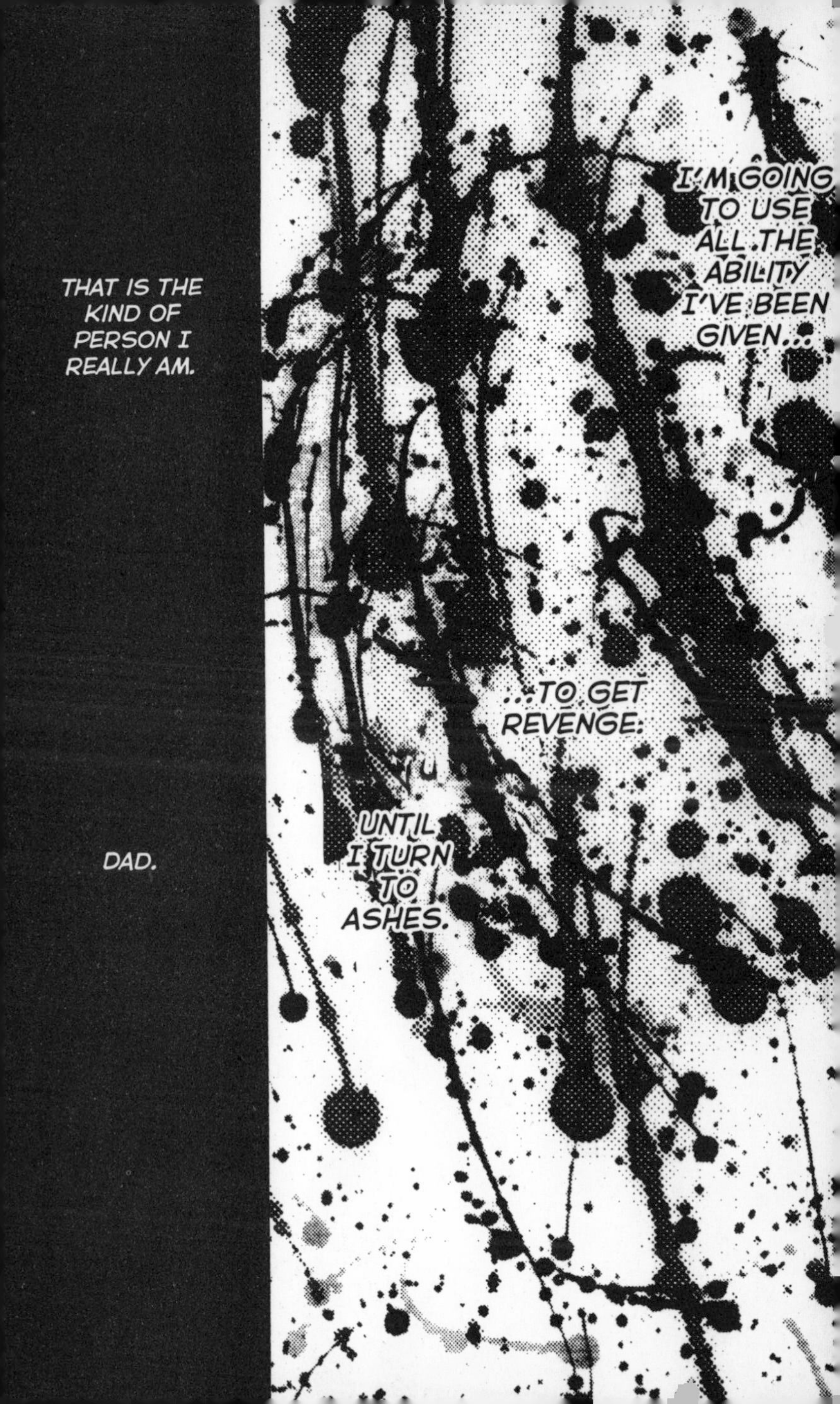
I'M GOING TO USE ALL THE ABILITY I'VE BEEN GIVEN...
...TO GET REVENGE.
UNTIL I TURN TO ASHES.
THAT IS THE KIND OF PERSON I REALLY AM.
DAD.

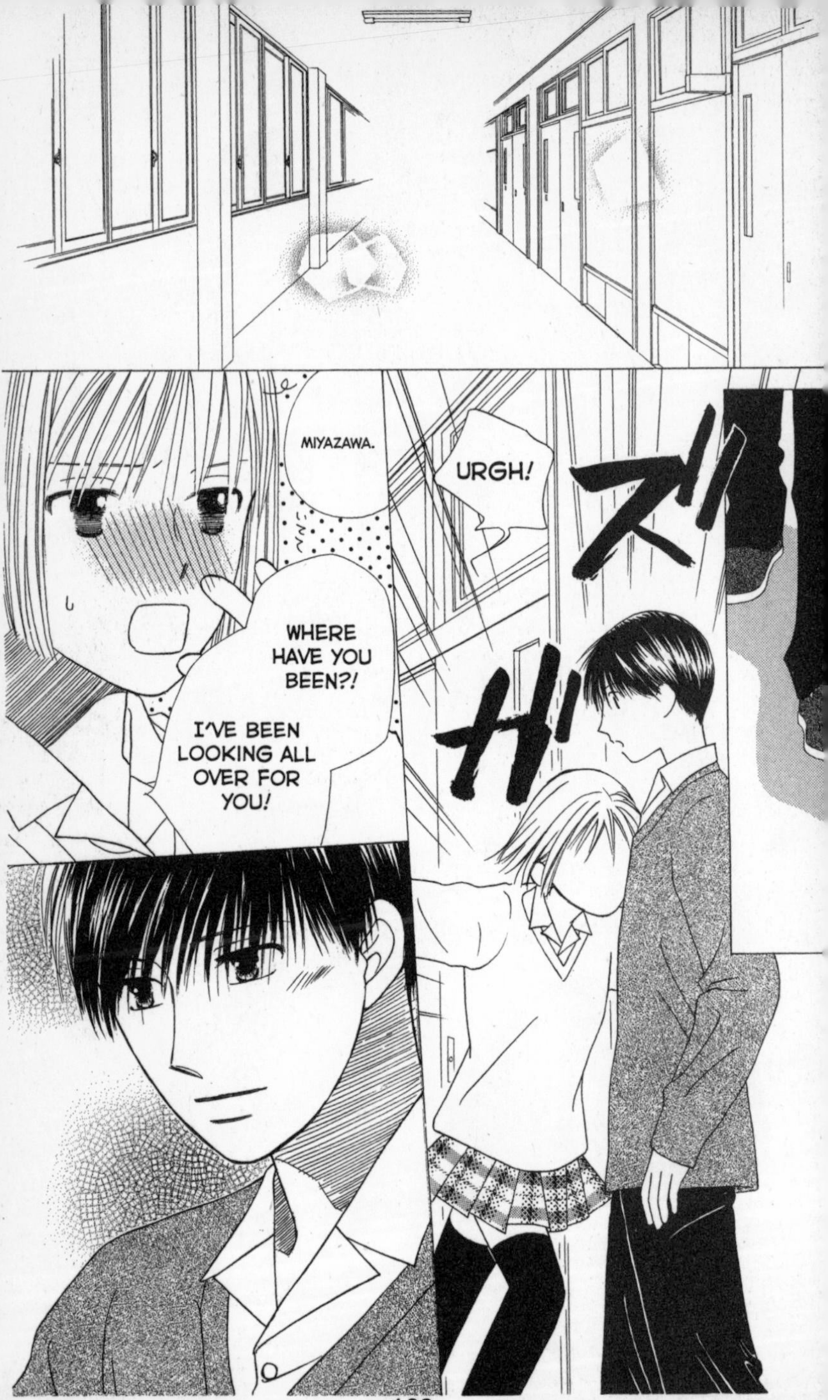
URGH!
MIYAZAWA.
WHERE HAVE YOU BEEN?!
I'VE BEEN LOOKING ALL OVER FOR YOU!

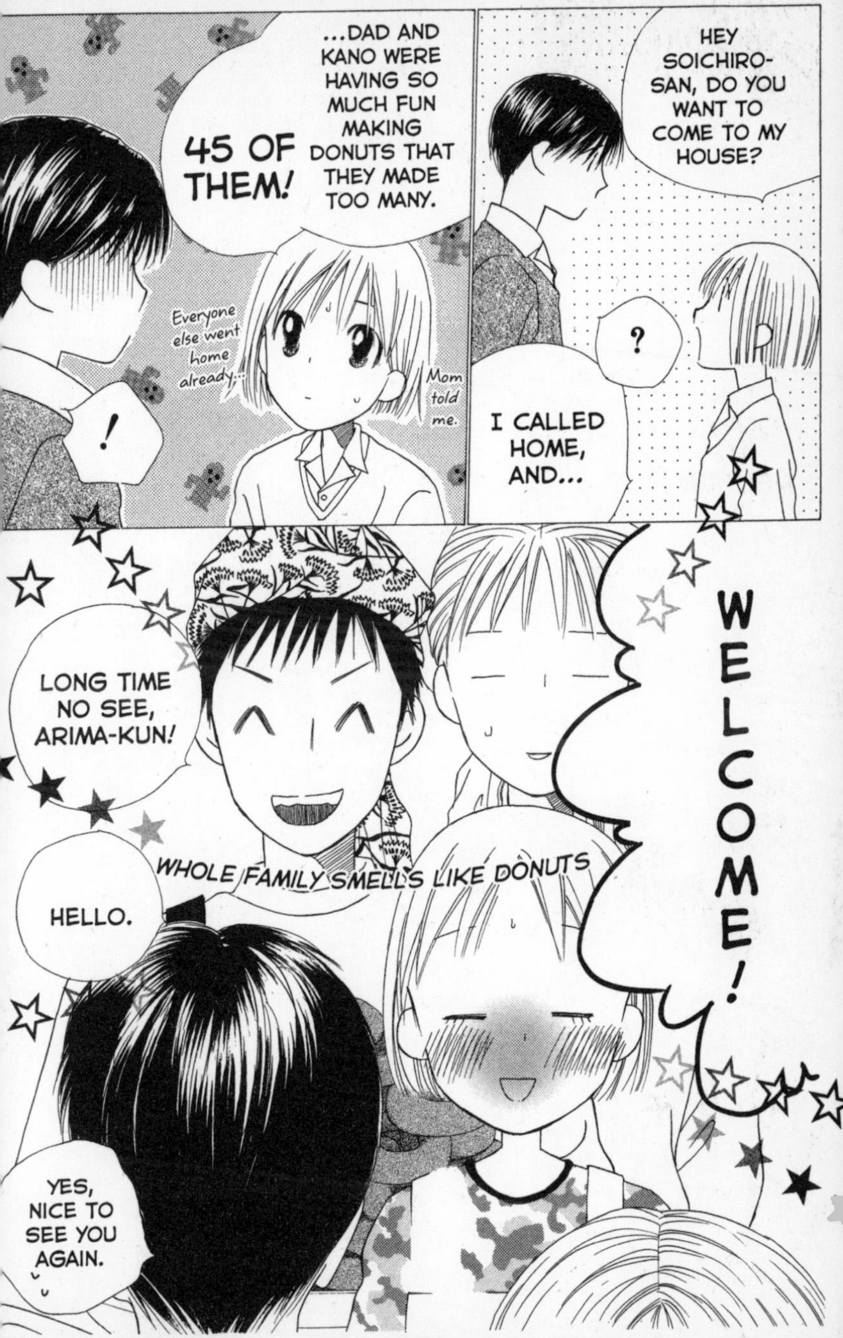
HEY SOICHIRO-SAN, DO YOU WANT TO COME TO MY HOUSE?
?
I CALLED HOME, AND...
...DAD AND KANO WERE HAVING SO MUCH FUN MAKING DONUTS THAT THEY MADE TOO MANY.
45 OF THEM!
Mom told me.
Everyone else went home already...
!
WELCOME!
LONG TIME NO SEE, ARIMA-KUN!
WHOLE FAMILY SMELLS LIKE DONUTS
HELLO.
YES, NICE TO SEE YOU AGAIN.

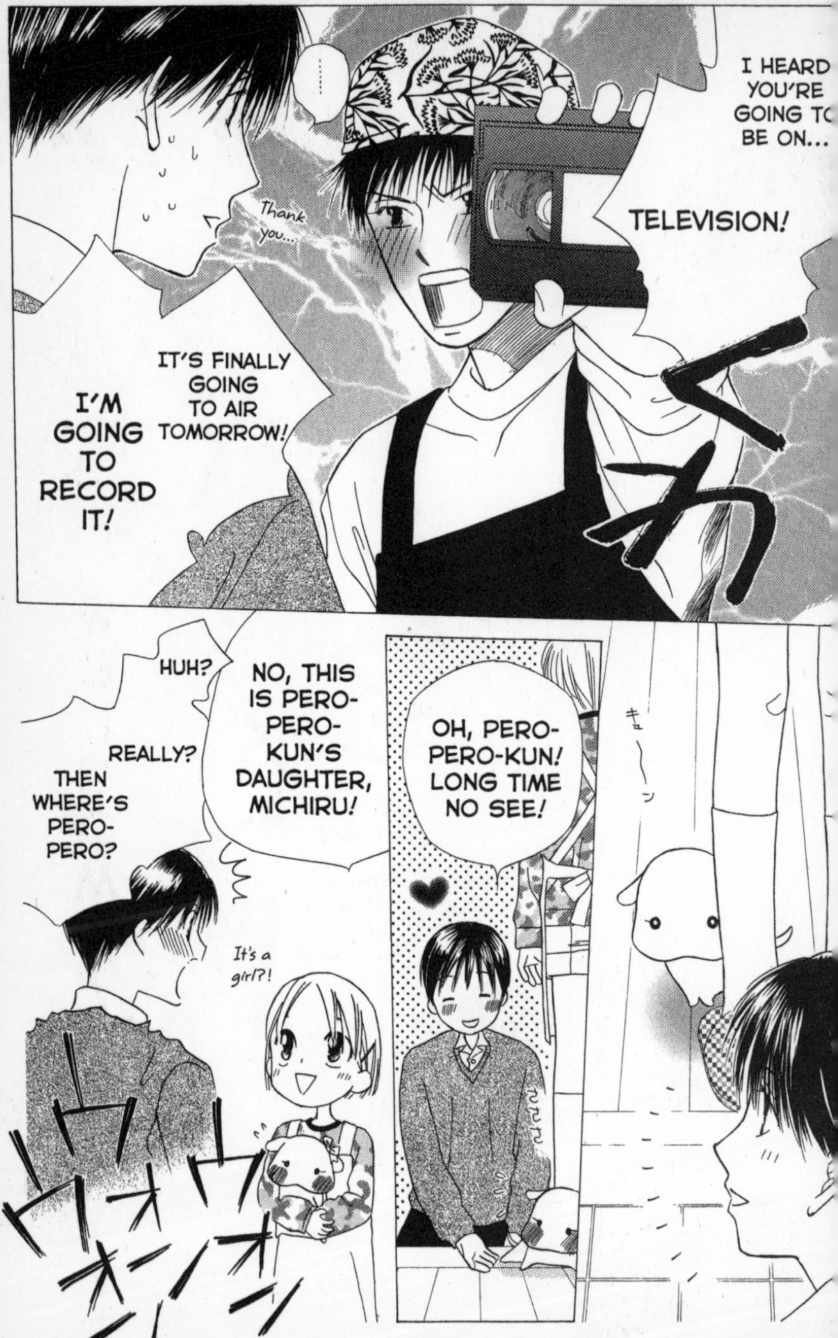
I HEARD YOU'RE GOING TO BE ON...
TELEVISION!
Thank you...
IT'S FINALLY GOING TO AIR TOMORROW!
I'M GOING TO RECORD IT!
OH, PERO-PERO-KUN! LONG TIME NO SEE!
NO, THIS IS PERO-PERO-KUN'S DAUGHTER, MICHIRU!
HUH?
REALLY? THEN WHERE'S PERO-PERO?
It's a girl?!

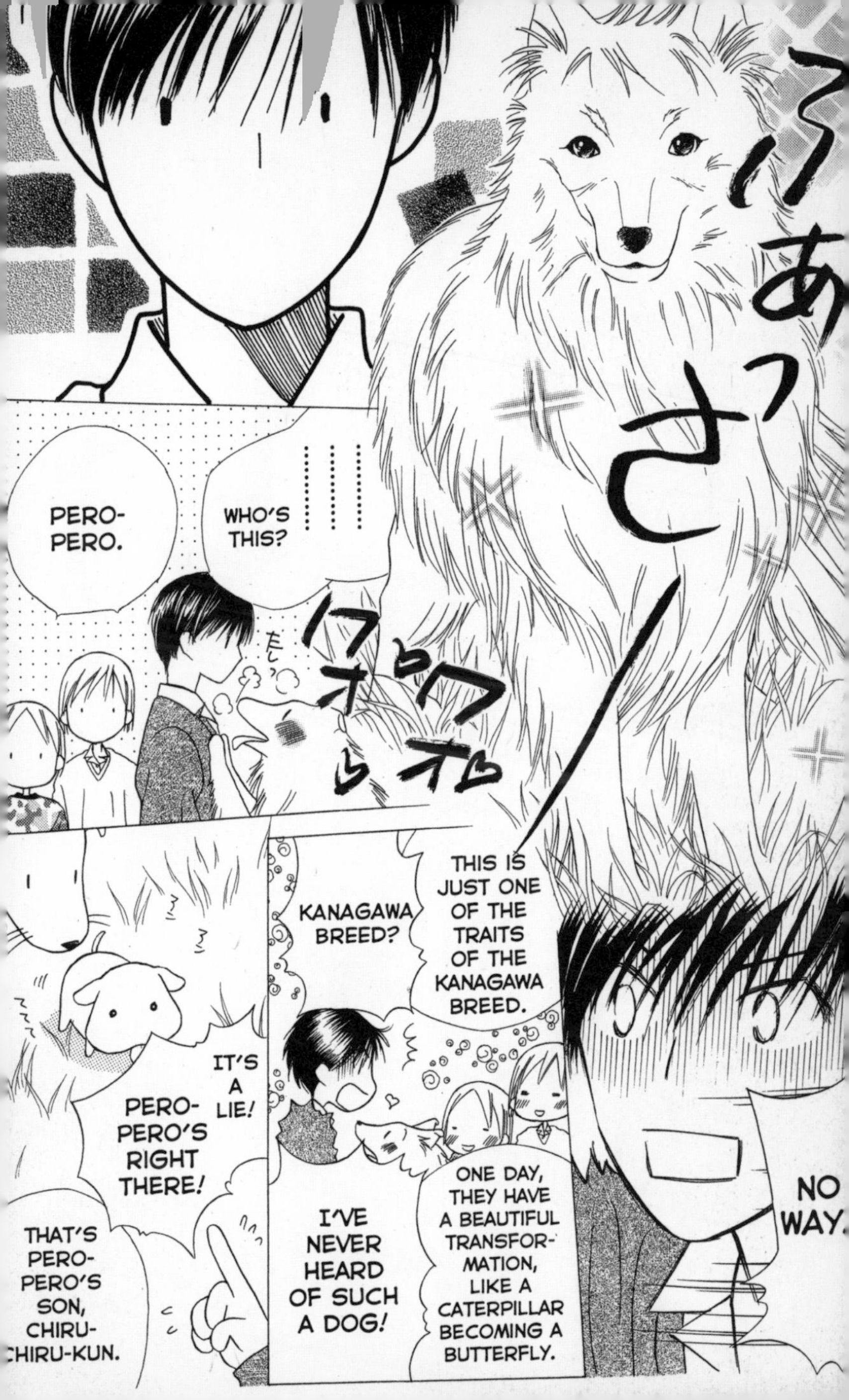
ふあっさー
WHO'S THIS?
......
PERO-PERO.
ワオ♡ワオ♡
NO WAY.
THIS IS JUST ONE OF THE TRAITS OF THE KANAGAWA BREED.
KANAGAWA BREED?
ONE DAY, THEY HAVE A BEAUTIFUL TRANSFORMATION, LIKE A CATERPILLAR BECOMING A BUTTERFLY.
I'VE NEVER HEARD OF SUCH A DOG!
IT'S A LIE!
PERO-PERO'S RIGHT THERE!
THAT'S PERO-PERO'S SON, CHIRU-CHIRU-KUN.

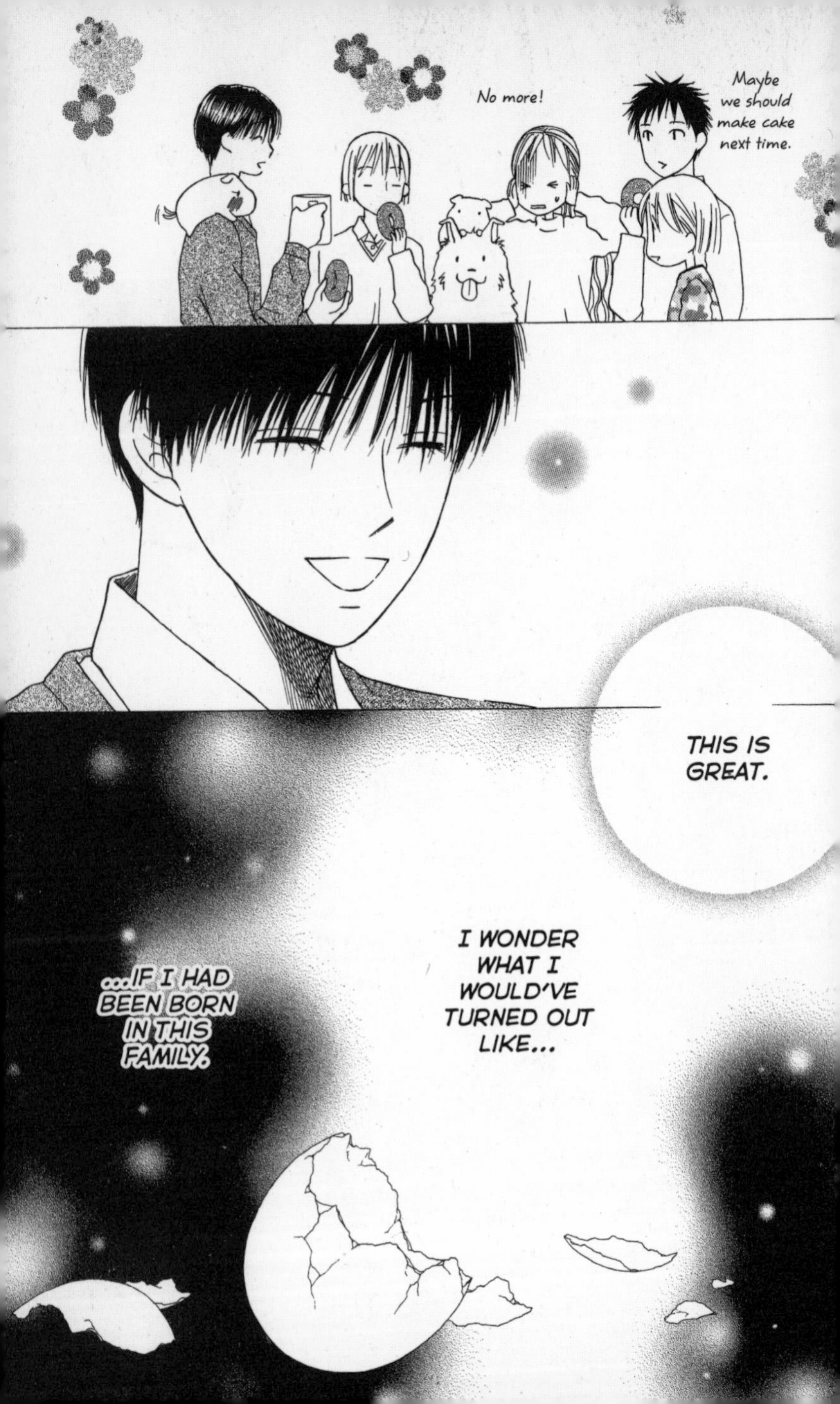
Maybe we should make cake next time.
No more!
THIS IS GREAT.
I WONDER WHAT I WOULD'VE TURNED OUT LIKE...
...IF I HAD BEEN BORN IN THIS FAMILY.

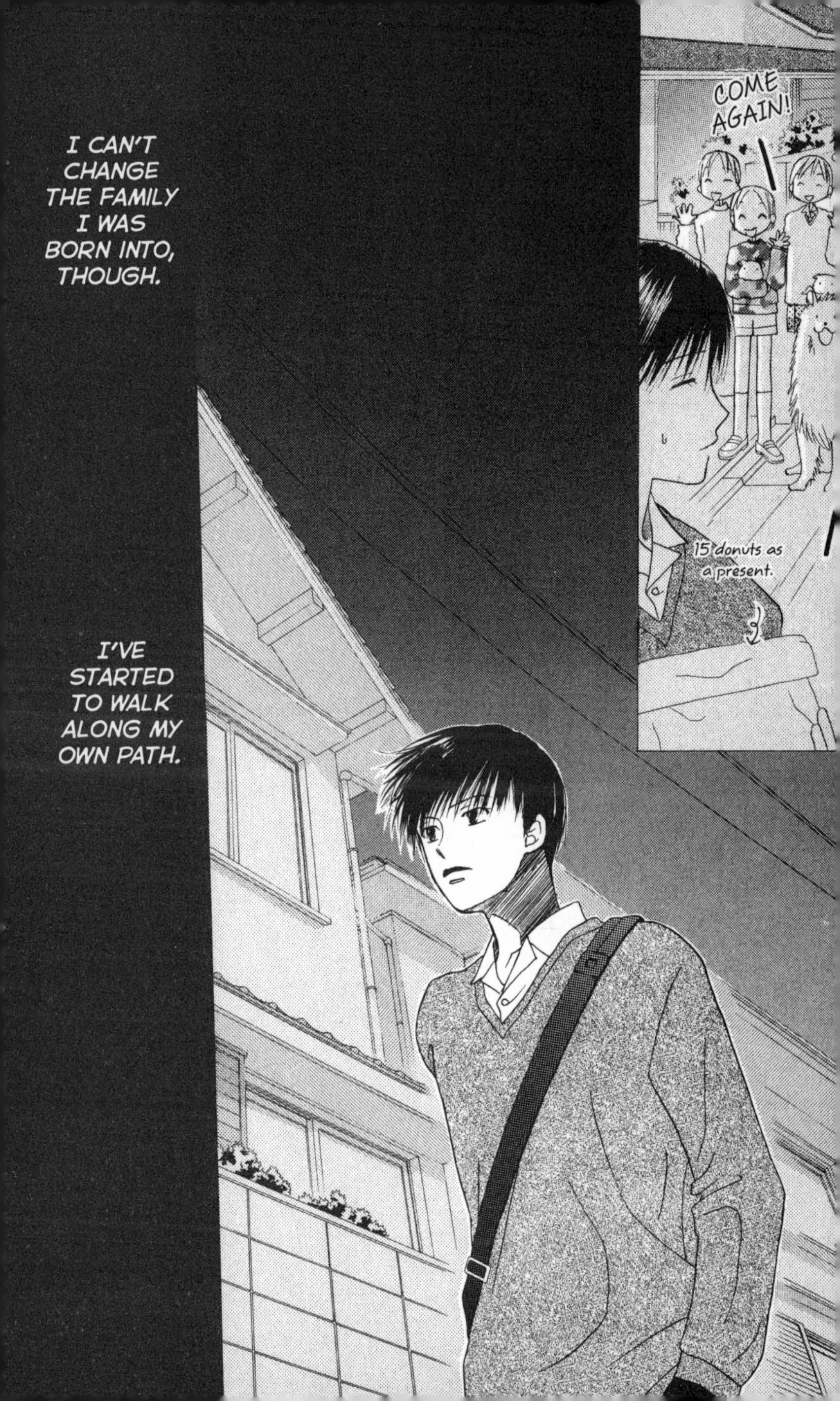

COME AGAIN!
15 donuts as a present.
I CAN'T CHANGE THE FAMILY I WAS BORN INTO, THOUGH.
I'VE STARTED TO WALK ALONG MY OWN PATH.

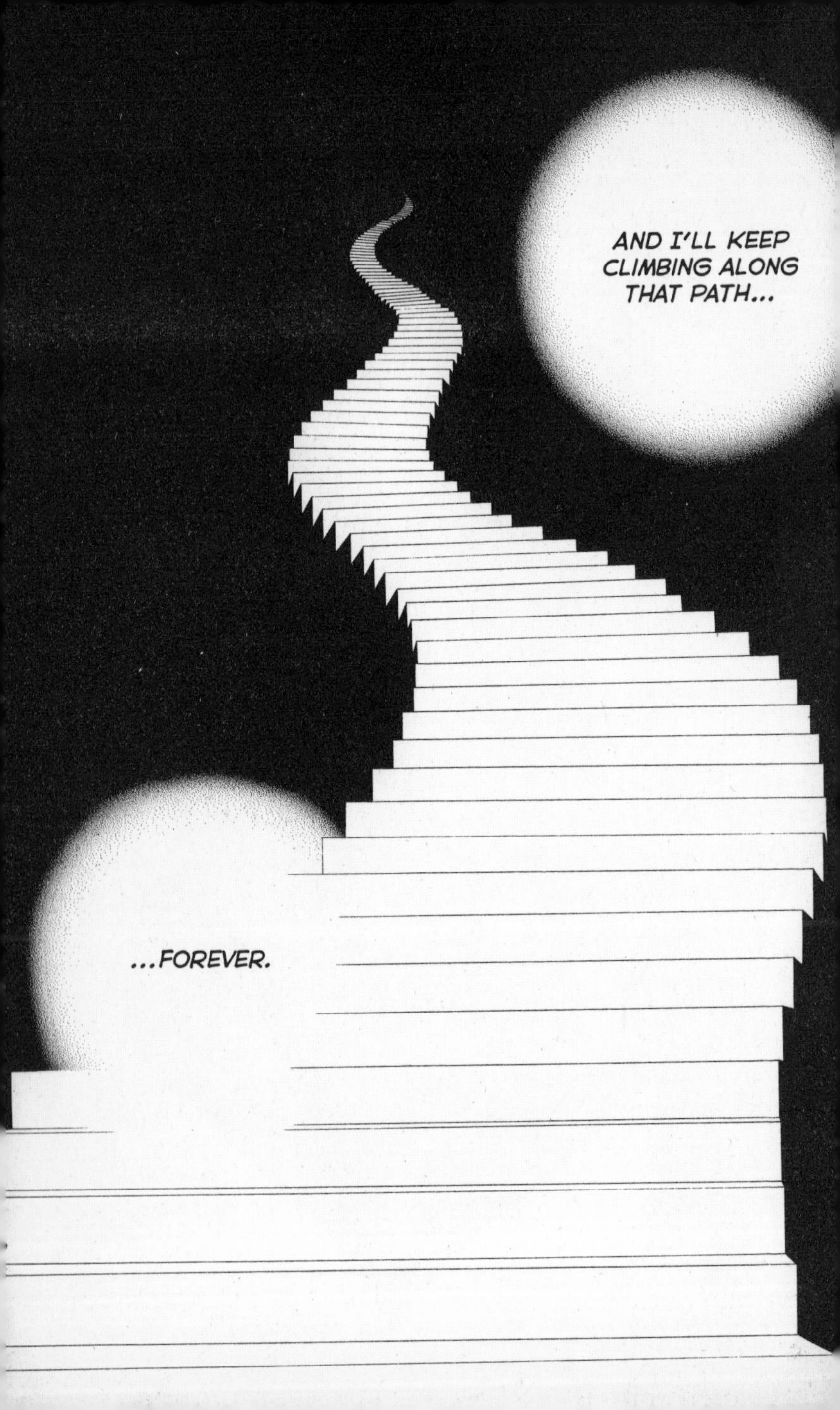
AND I'LL KEEP CLIMBING ALONG THAT PATH...
...FOREVER.

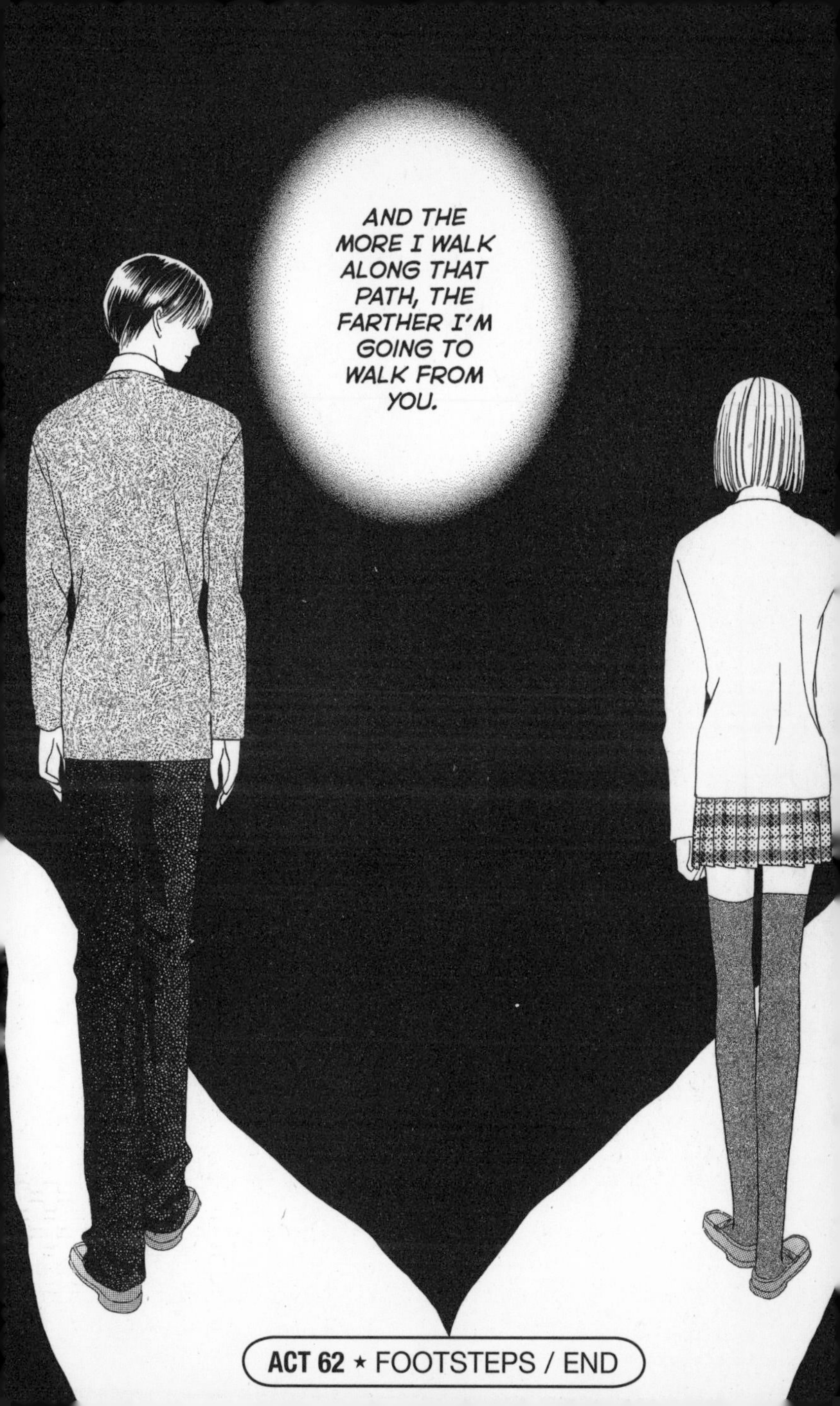
AND THE MORE I WALK ALONG THAT PATH, THE FARTHER I'M GOING TO WALK FROM YOU.

ACT 62 ★ FOOTSTEPS / END

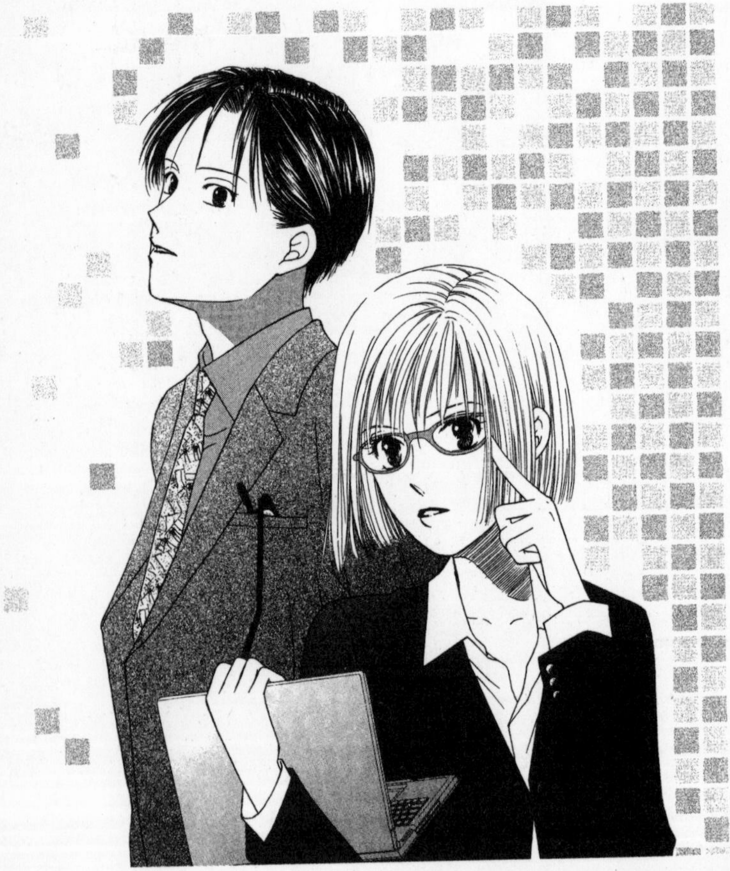

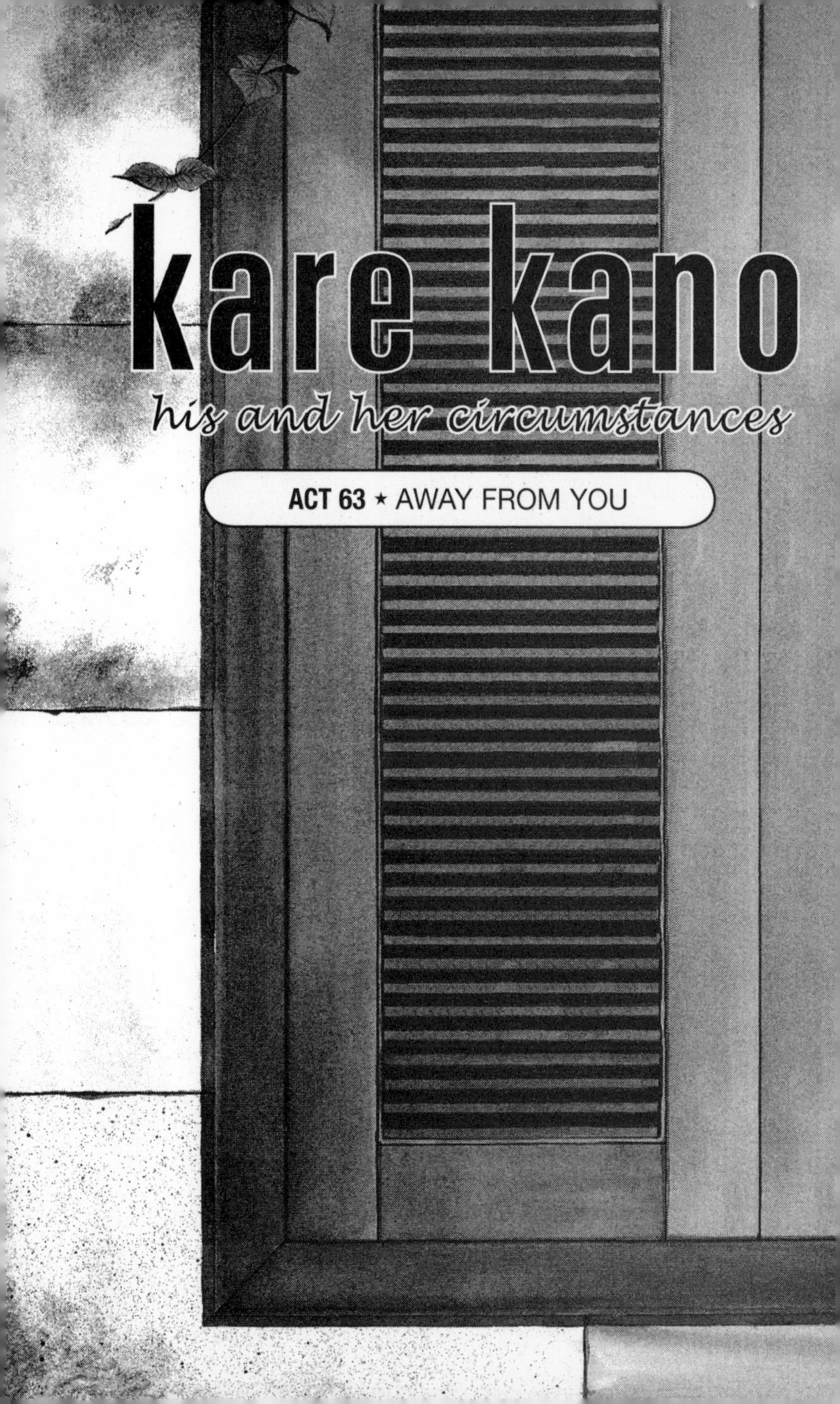
kare kano
his and her circumstances
ACT 63 ★ AWAY FROM YOU

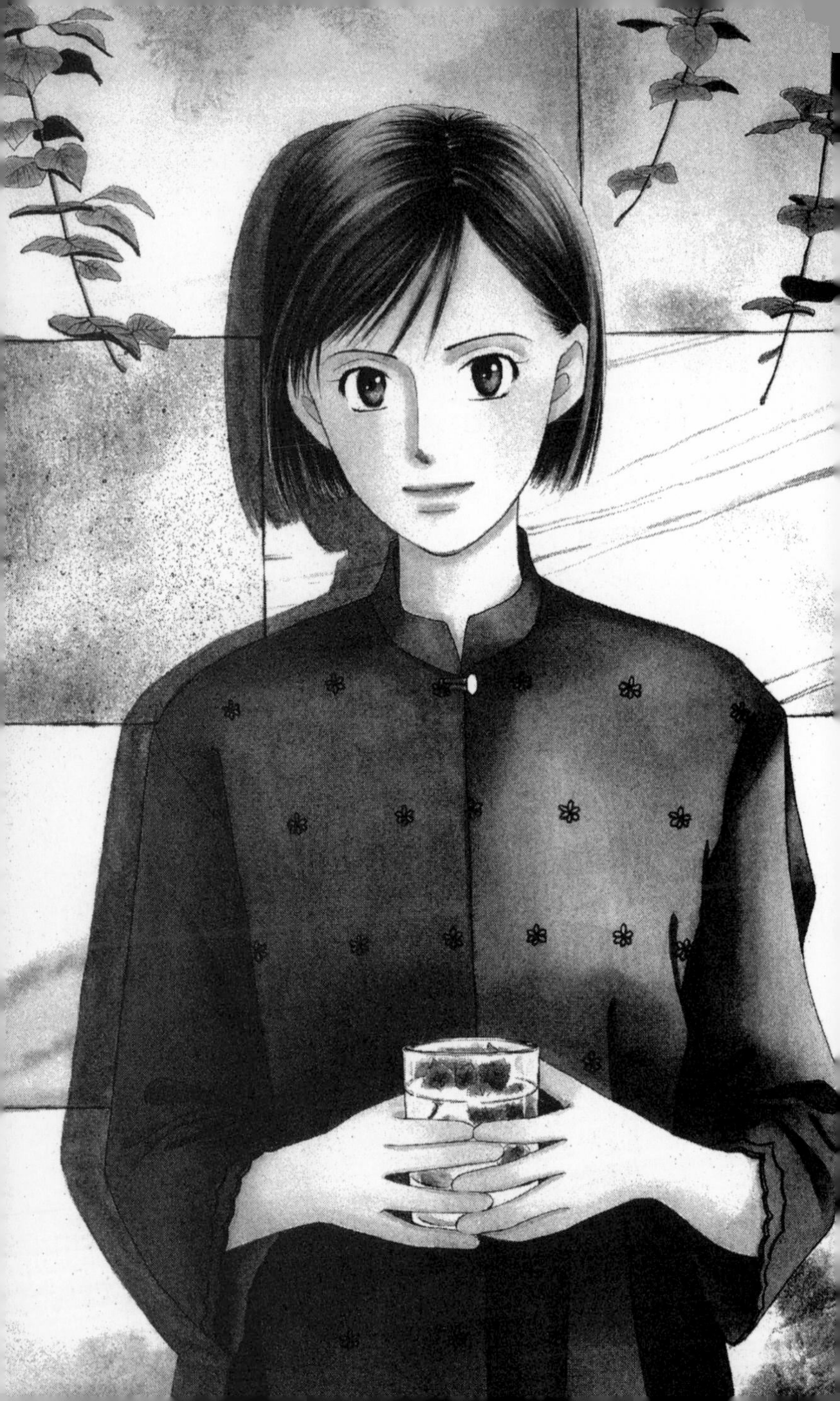

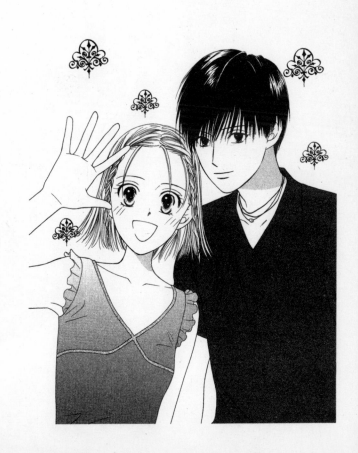

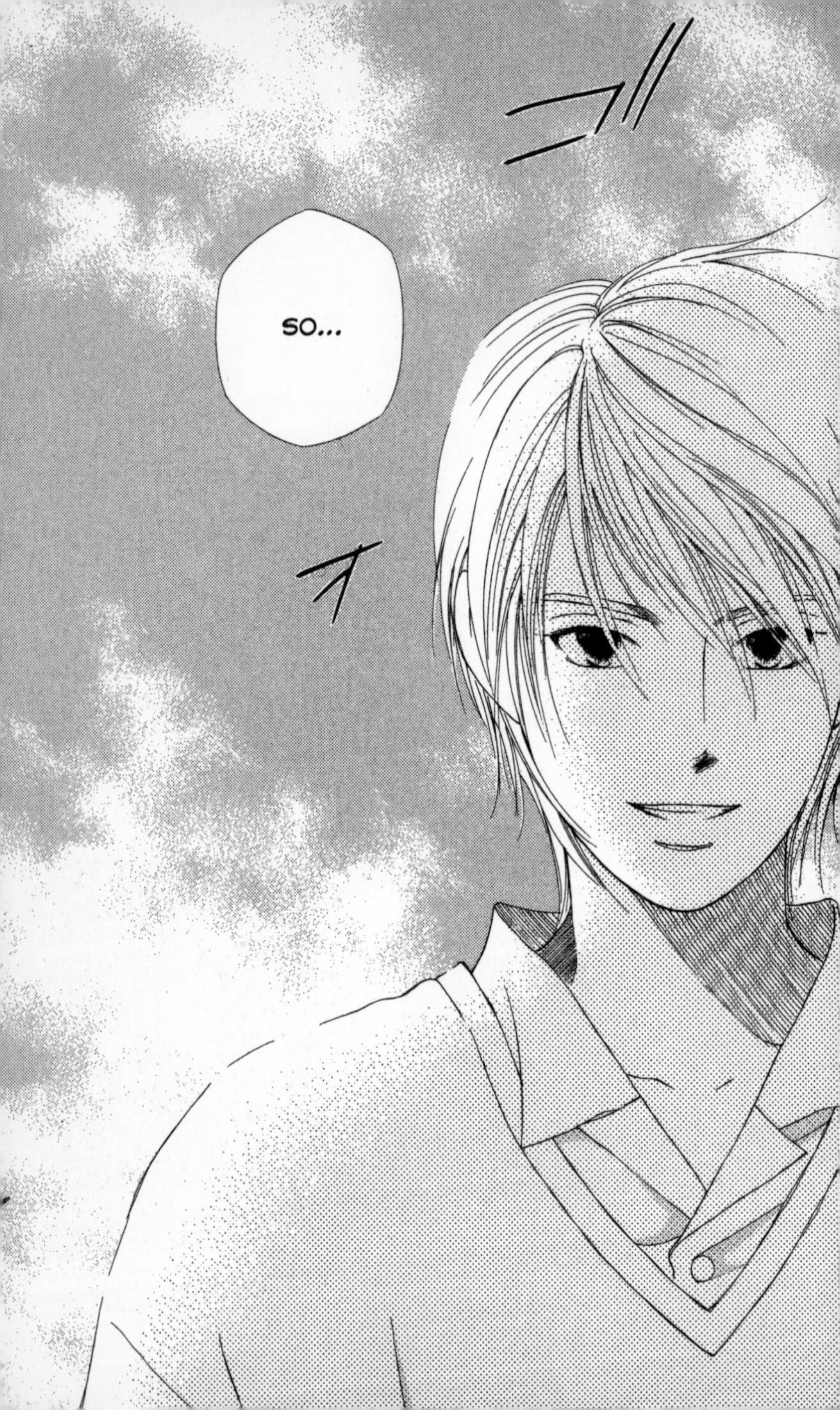
SO...

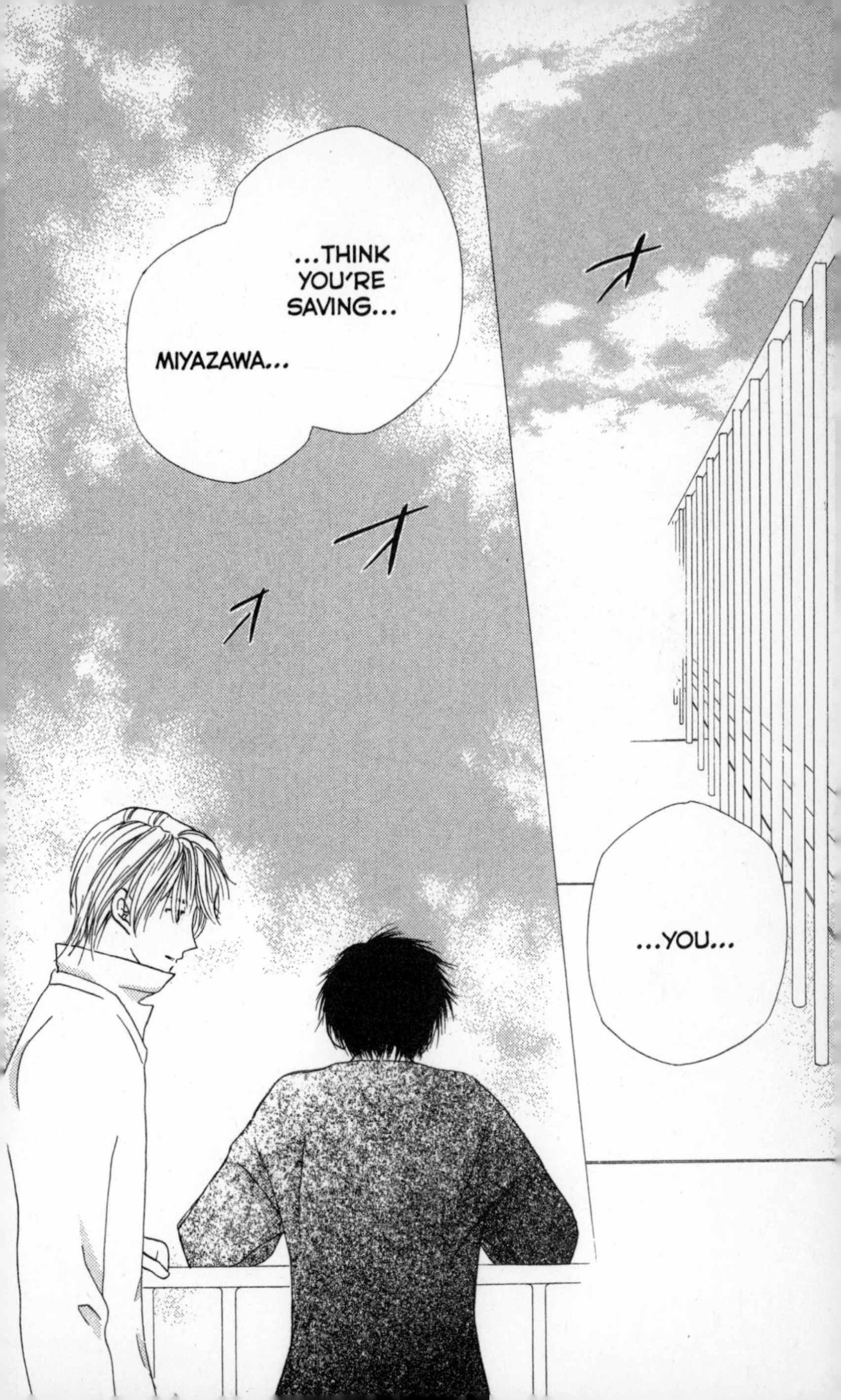
...YOU...
...THINK YOU'RE SAVING...
MIYAZAWA...

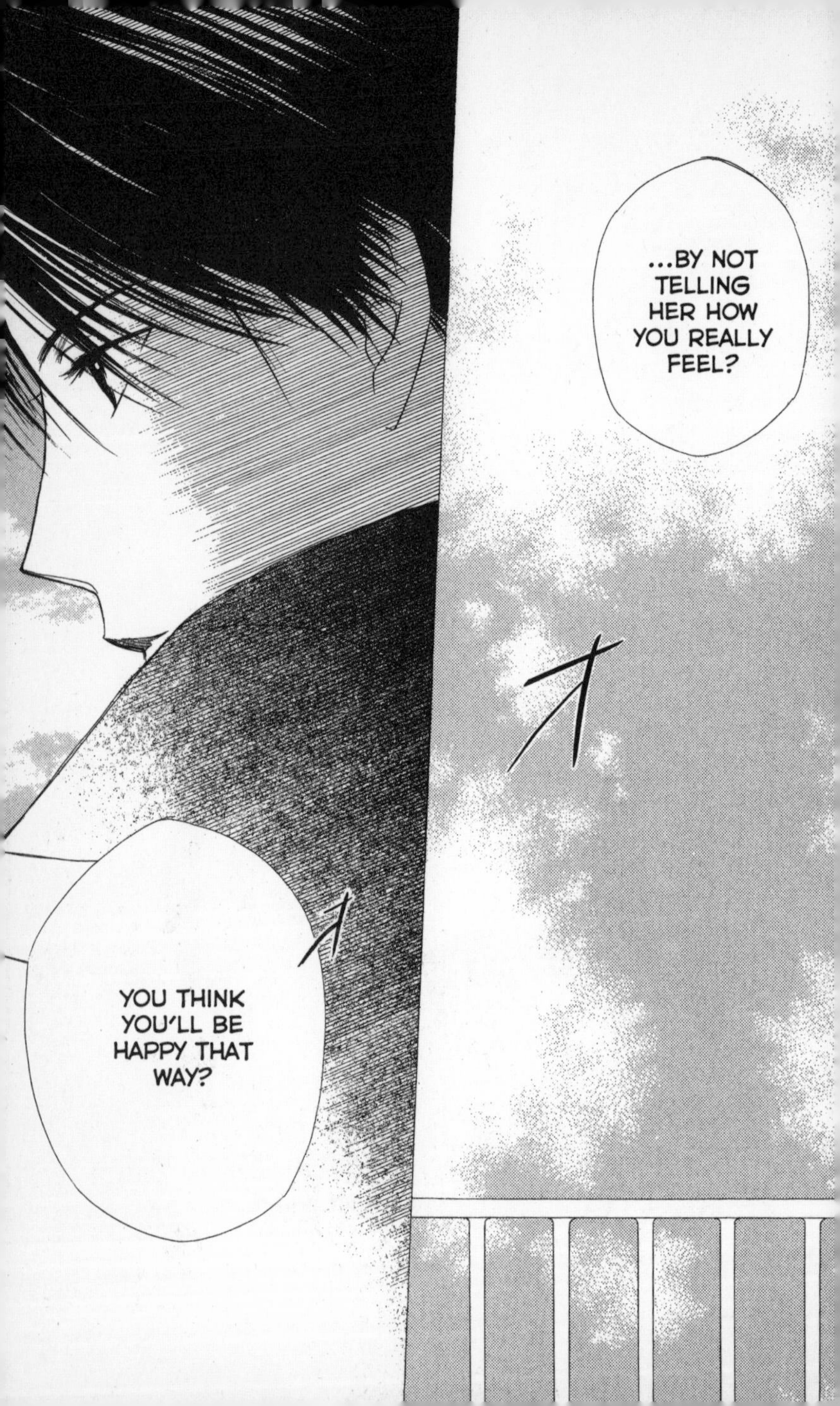
...BY NOT TELLING HER HOW YOU REALLY FEEL?
YOU THINK YOU'LL BE HAPPY THAT WAY?

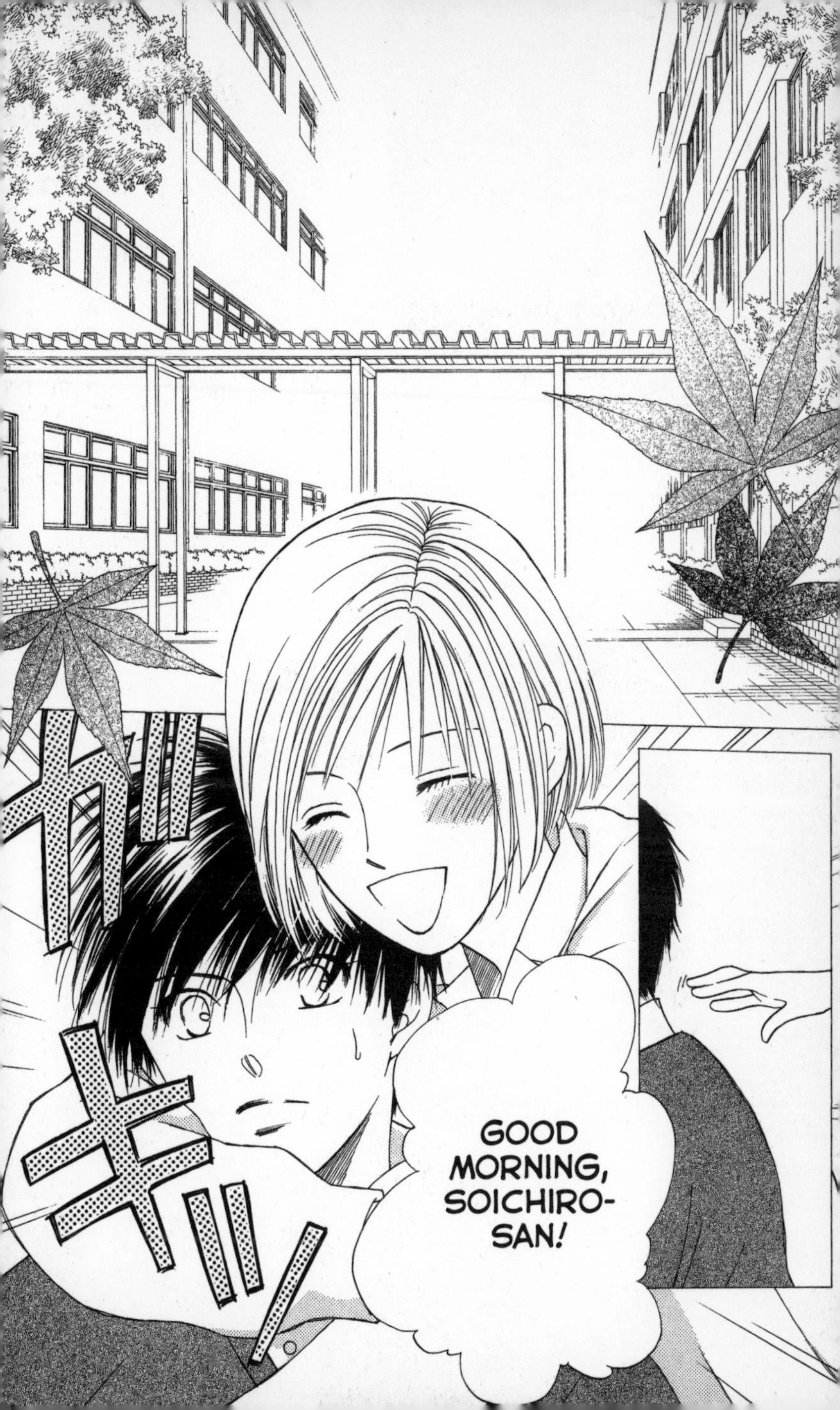
GOOD MORNING, SOICHIRO-SAN!

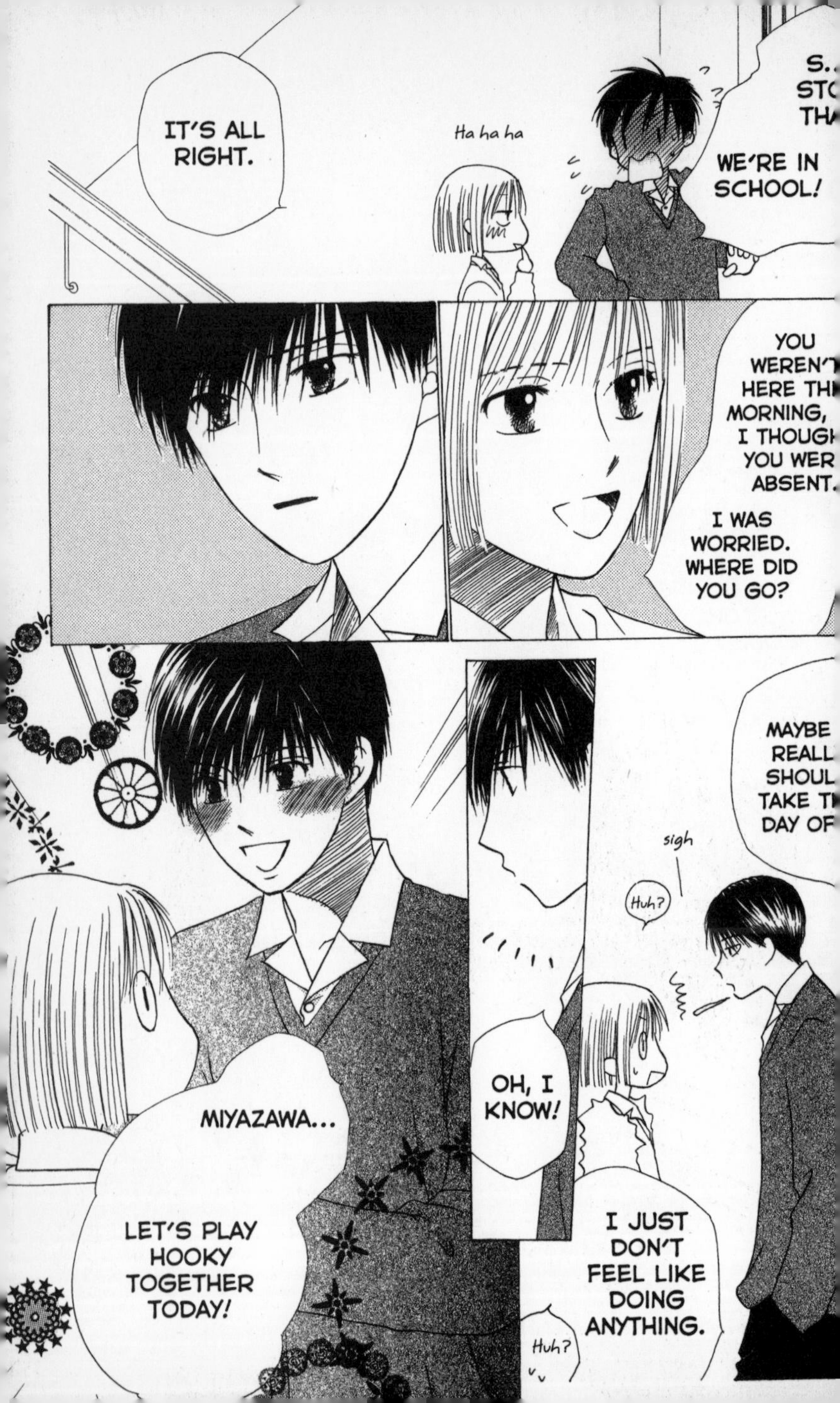

S.. STO TH
WE'RE IN SCHOOL!
Ha ha ha
IT'S ALL RIGHT.
YOU WEREN'T HERE TH MORNING, I THOUG YOU WER ABSENT.
I WAS WORRIED. WHERE DID YOU GO?
MAYBE REALL SHOUL TAKE T DAY OF
sigh
Huh?
I JUST DON'T FEEL LIKE DOING ANYTHING.
Huh?
OH, I KNOW!
MIYAZAWA...
LET'S PLAY HOOKY TOGETHER TODAY!

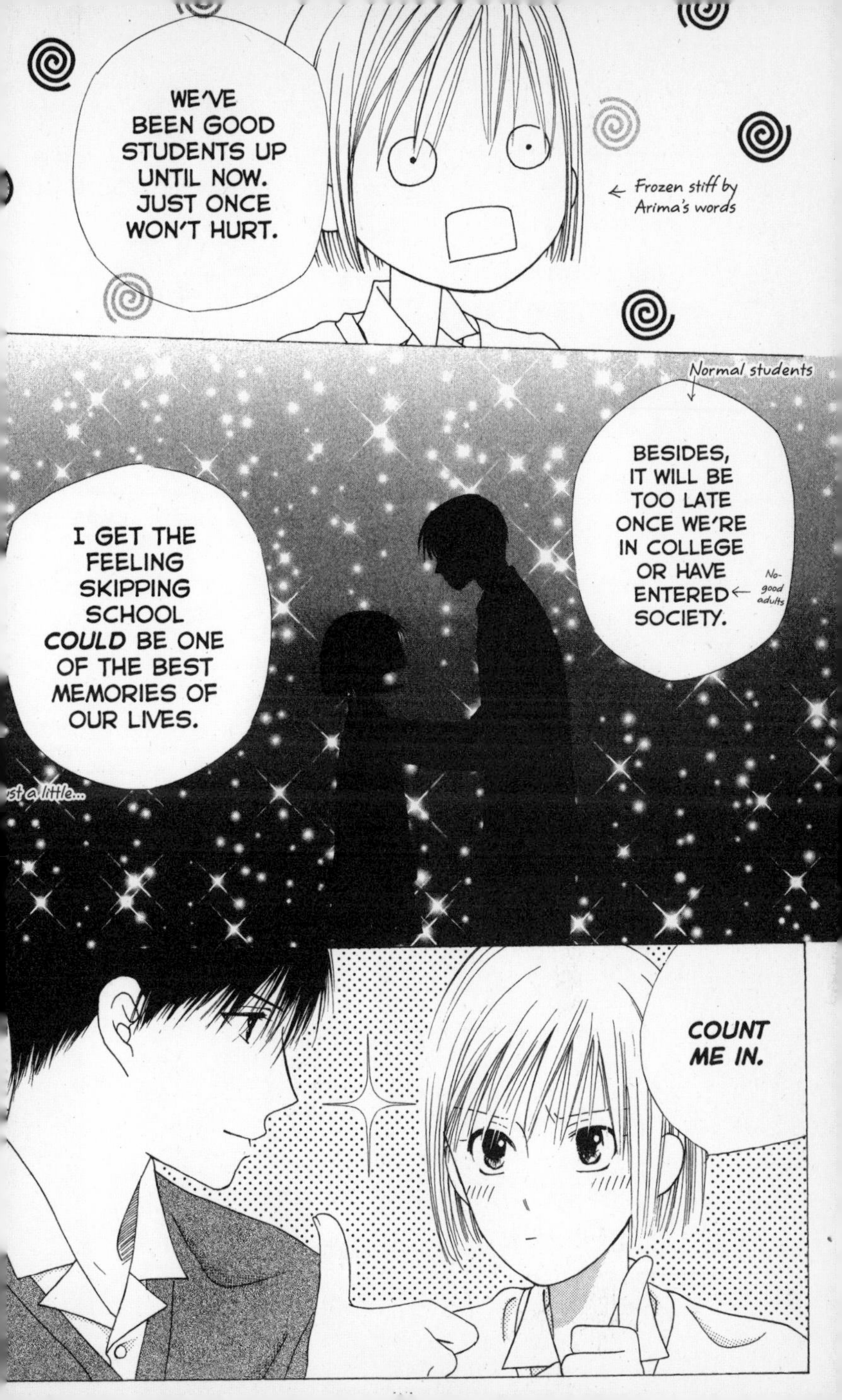
← Frozen stiff by Arima's words
WE'VE BEEN GOOD STUDENTS UP UNTIL NOW. JUST ONCE WON'T HURT.
Normal students
BESIDES, IT WILL BE TOO LATE ONCE WE'RE IN COLLEGE OR HAVE ENTERED SOCIETY.
No-good adults
I GET THE FEELING SKIPPING SCHOOL *COULD* BE ONE OF THE BEST MEMORIES OF OUR LIVES.
COUNT ME IN.

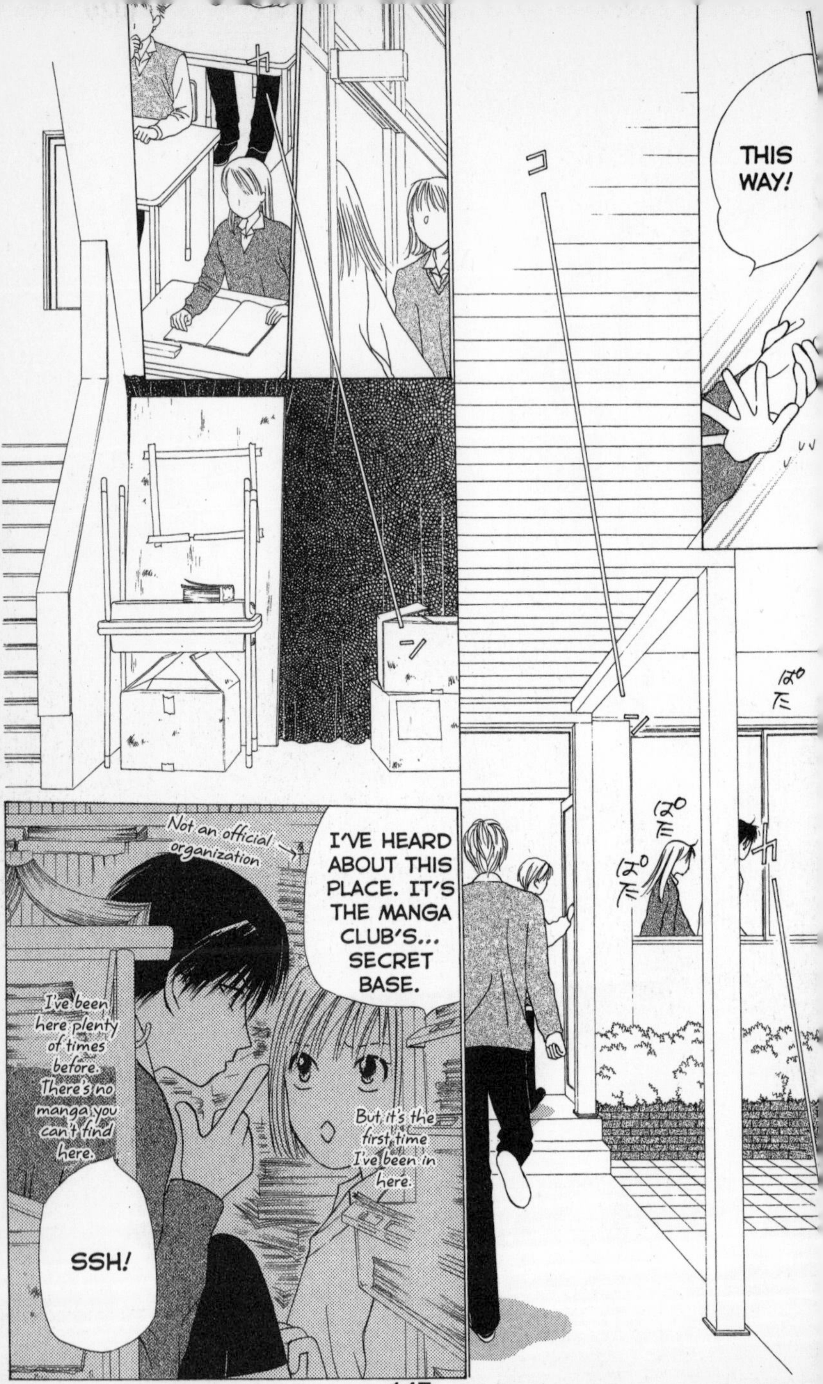
THIS WAY!
ぱた
ぱた
ぱた
I'VE HEARD ABOUT THIS PLACE. IT'S THE MANGA CLUB'S... SECRET BASE.
Not an official organization
I've been here plenty of times before. There's no manga you can't find here.
But it's the first time I've been in here.
SSH!

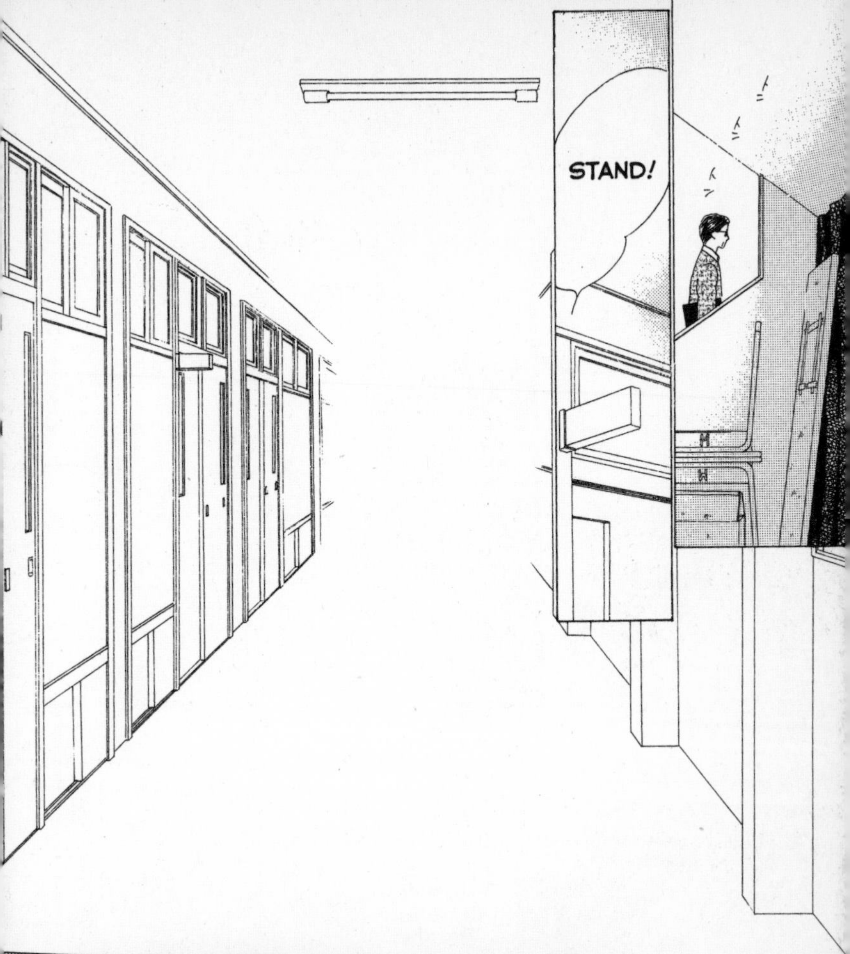
STAND!
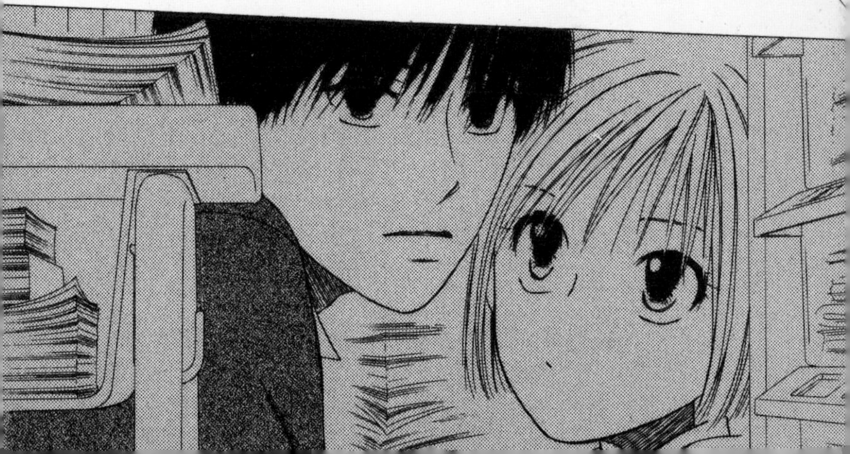

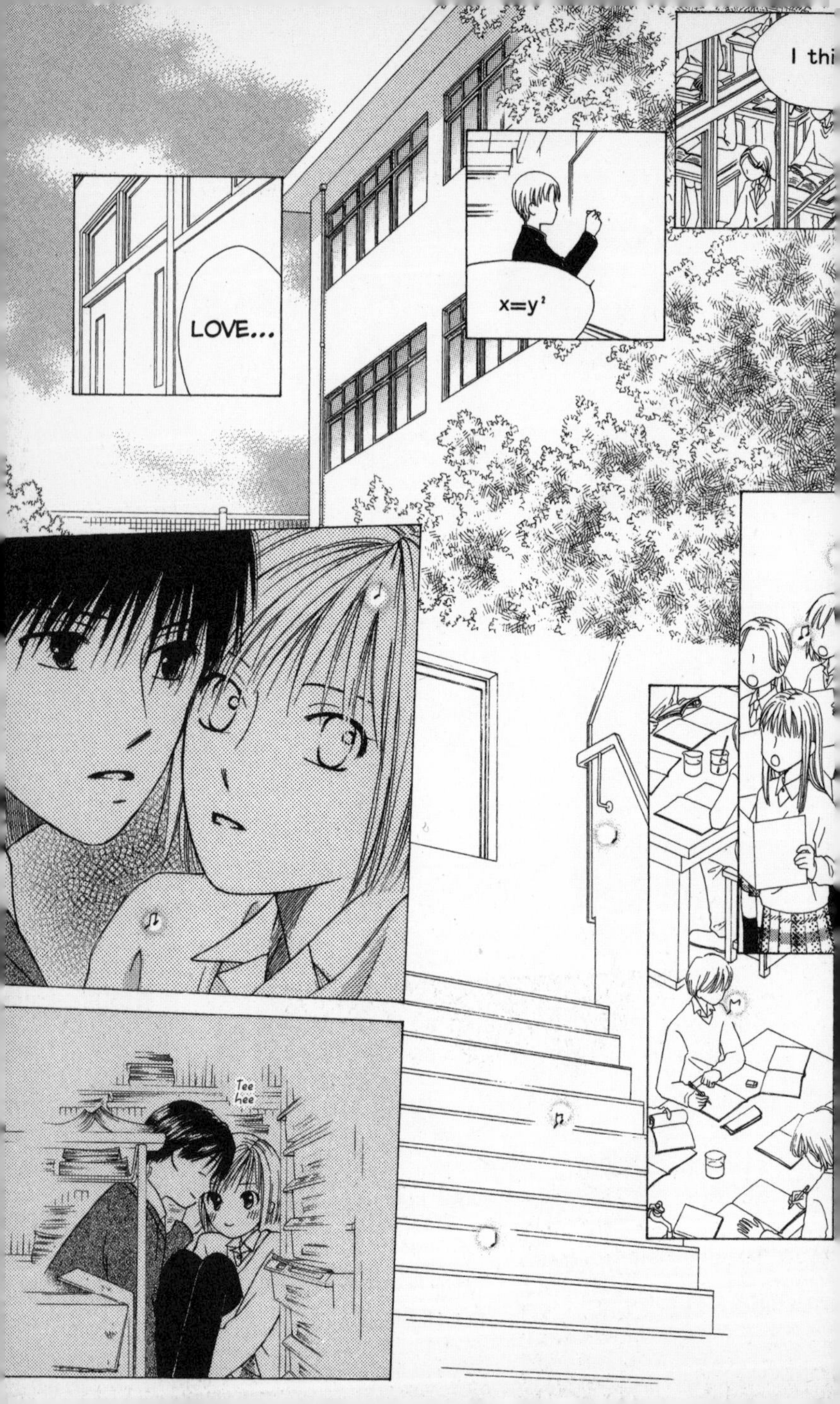
I thi
x=y²
LOVE...
Tee hee

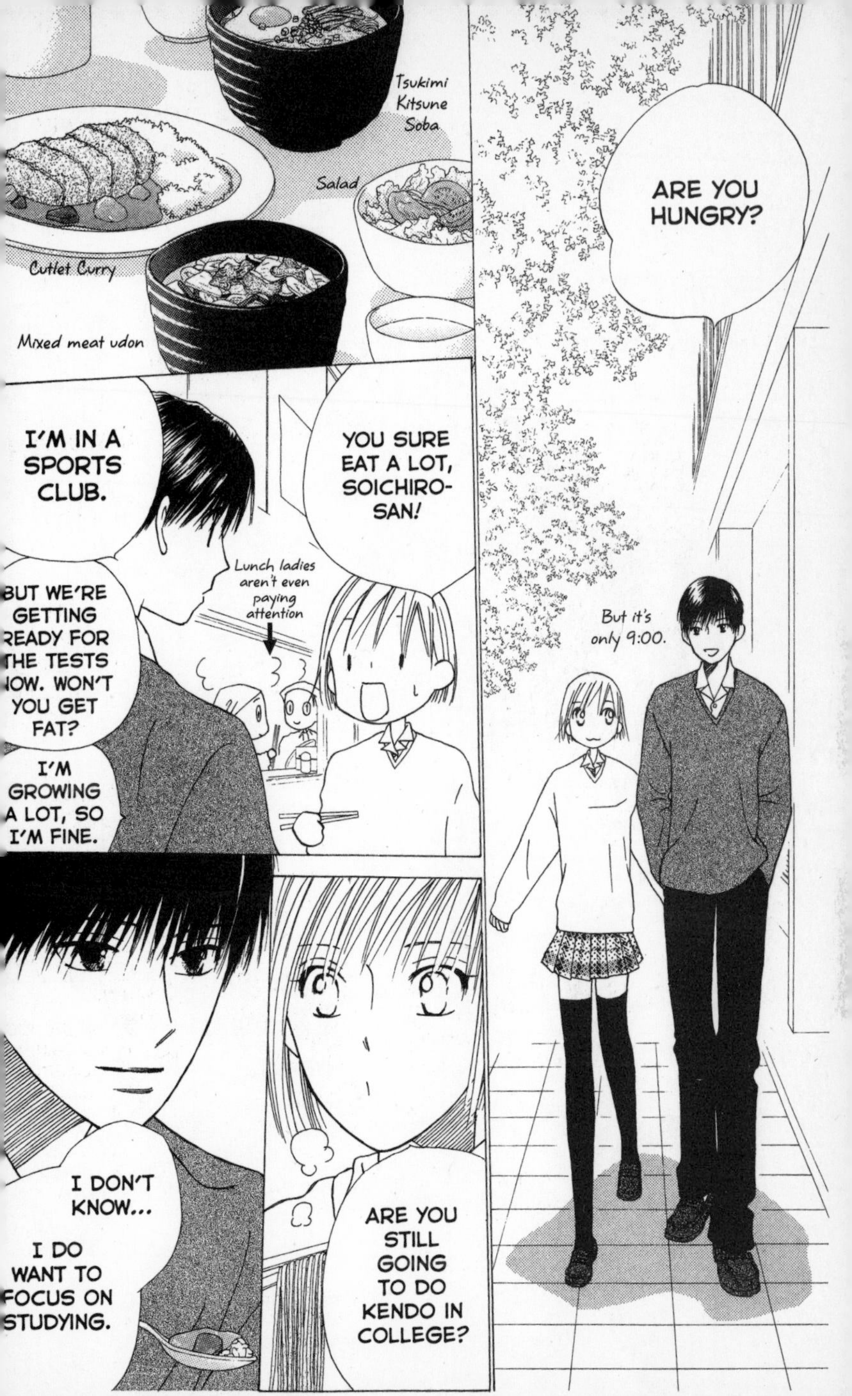
ARE YOU HUNGRY?
But it's only 9:00.
Tsukimi Kitsune Soba
Salad
Cutlet Curry
Mixed meat udon
YOU SURE EAT A LOT, SOICHIRO-SAN!
Lunch ladies aren't even paying attention
I'M IN A SPORTS CLUB.
BUT WE'RE GETTING READY FOR THE TESTS NOW. WON'T YOU GET FAT?
I'M GROWING A LOT, SO I'M FINE.
ARE YOU STILL GOING TO DO KENDO IN COLLEGE?
I DON'T KNOW...
I DO WANT TO FOCUS ON STUDYING.

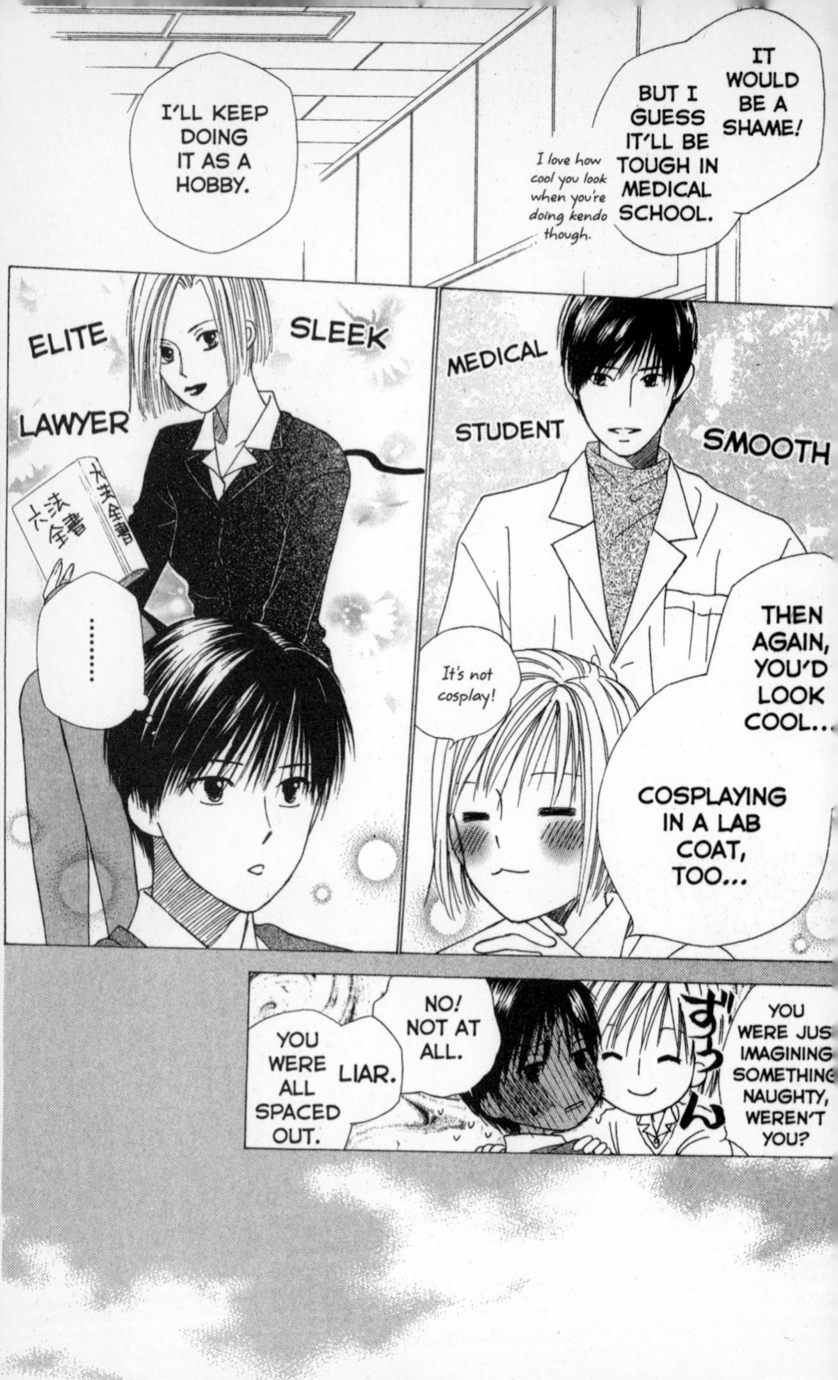
IT WOULD BE A SHAME!
BUT I GUESS IT'LL BE TOUGH IN MEDICAL SCHOOL.
I love how cool you look when you're doing kendo though.
I'LL KEEP DOING IT AS A HOBBY.
MEDICAL STUDENT
SMOOTH
THEN AGAIN, YOU'D LOOK COOL...
COSPLAYING IN A LAB COAT, TOO...
It's not cosplay!
SLEEK
ELITE LAWYER
六法全書
....
YOU WERE JUS IMAGINING SOMETHING NAUGHTY, WEREN'T YOU?
NO! NOT AT ALL.
LIAR.
YOU WERE ALL SPACED OUT.

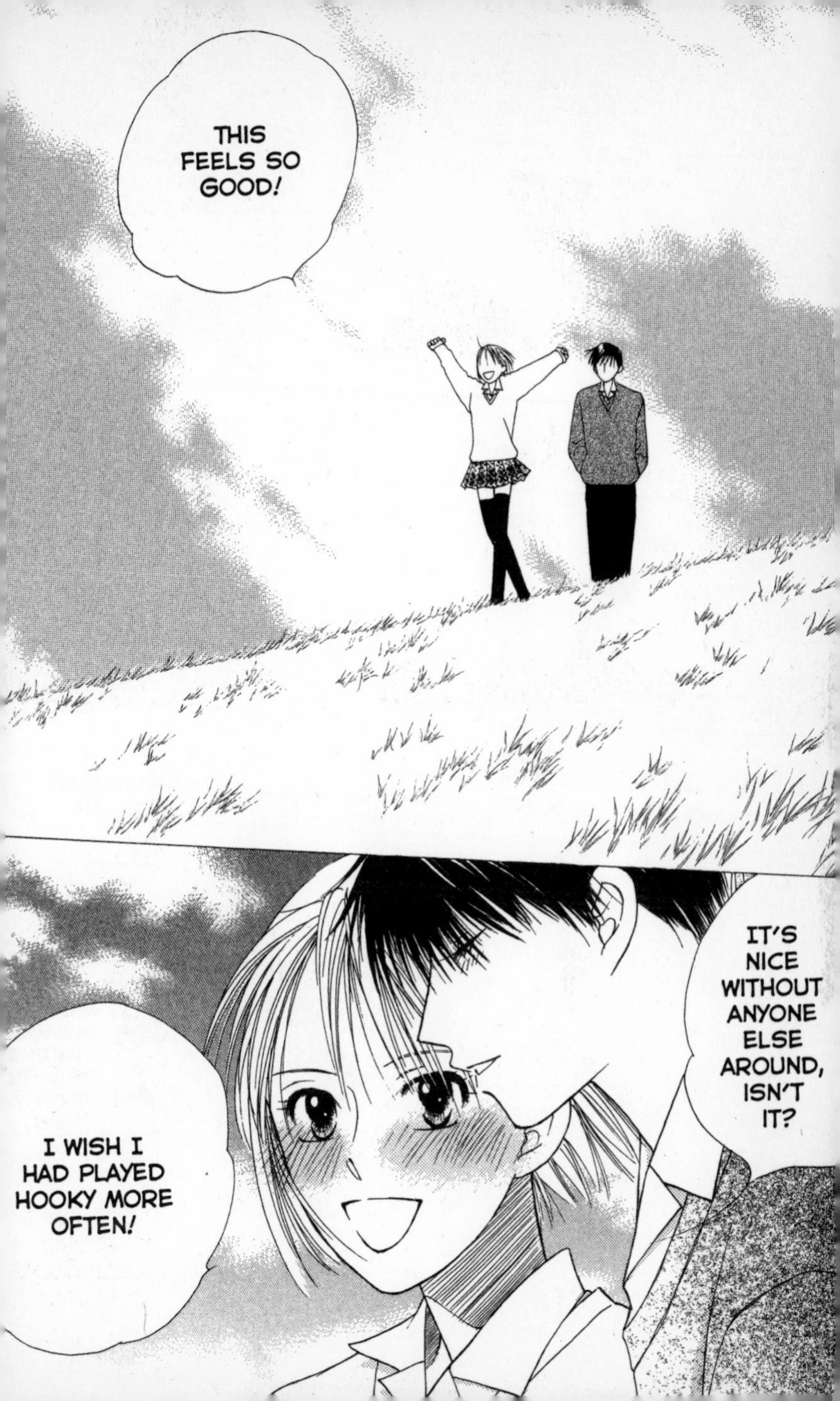
THIS FEELS SO GOOD!
IT'S NICE WITHOUT ANYONE ELSE AROUND, ISN'T IT?
I WISH I HAD PLAYED HOOKY MORE OFTEN!

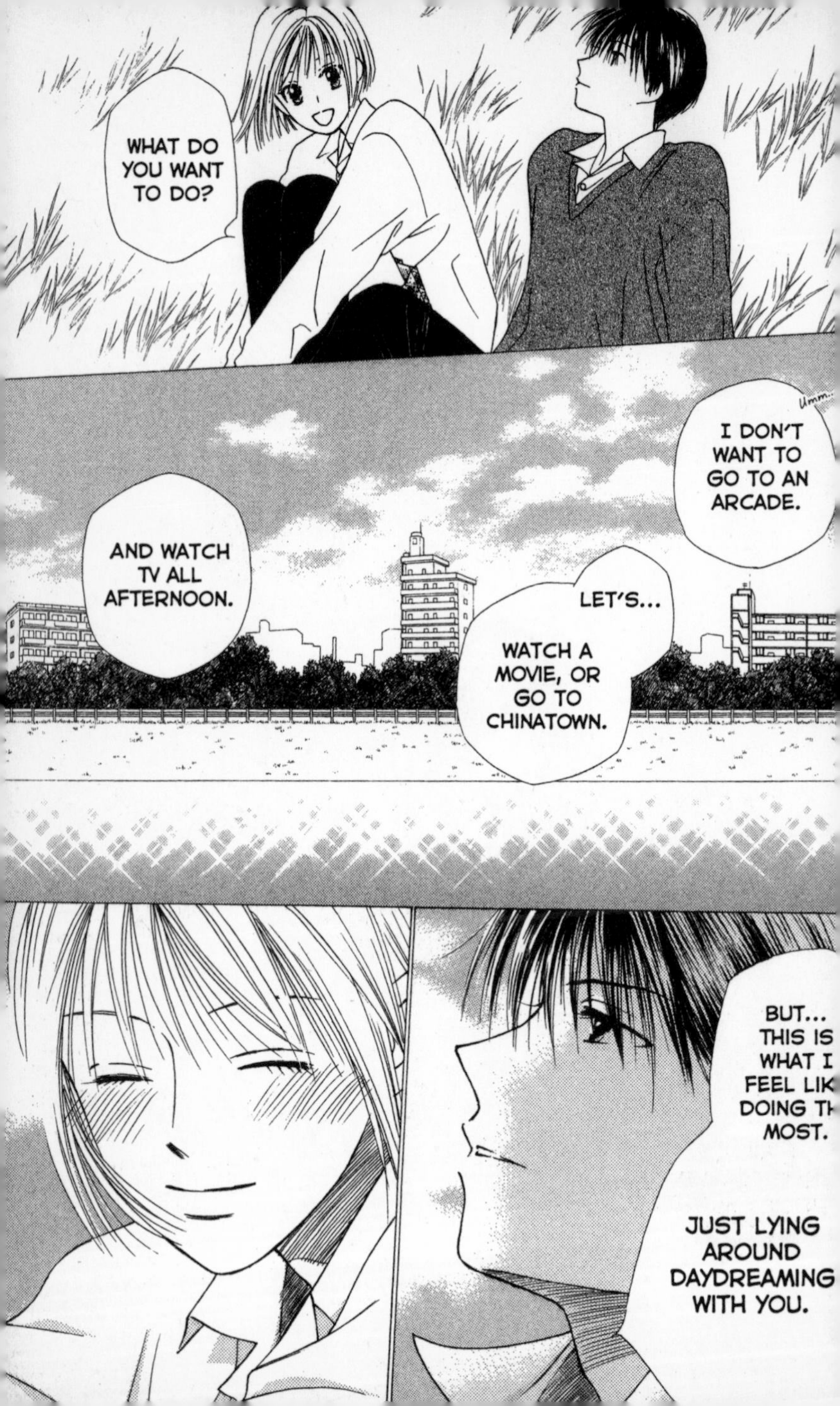
WHAT DO YOU WANT TO DO?
Umm...
I DON'T WANT TO GO TO AN ARCADE.
LET'S...
WATCH A MOVIE, OR GO TO CHINATOWN.
AND WATCH TV ALL AFTERNOON.
BUT... THIS IS WHAT I FEEL LIK DOING TH MOST.
JUST LYING AROUND DAYDREAMING WITH YOU.

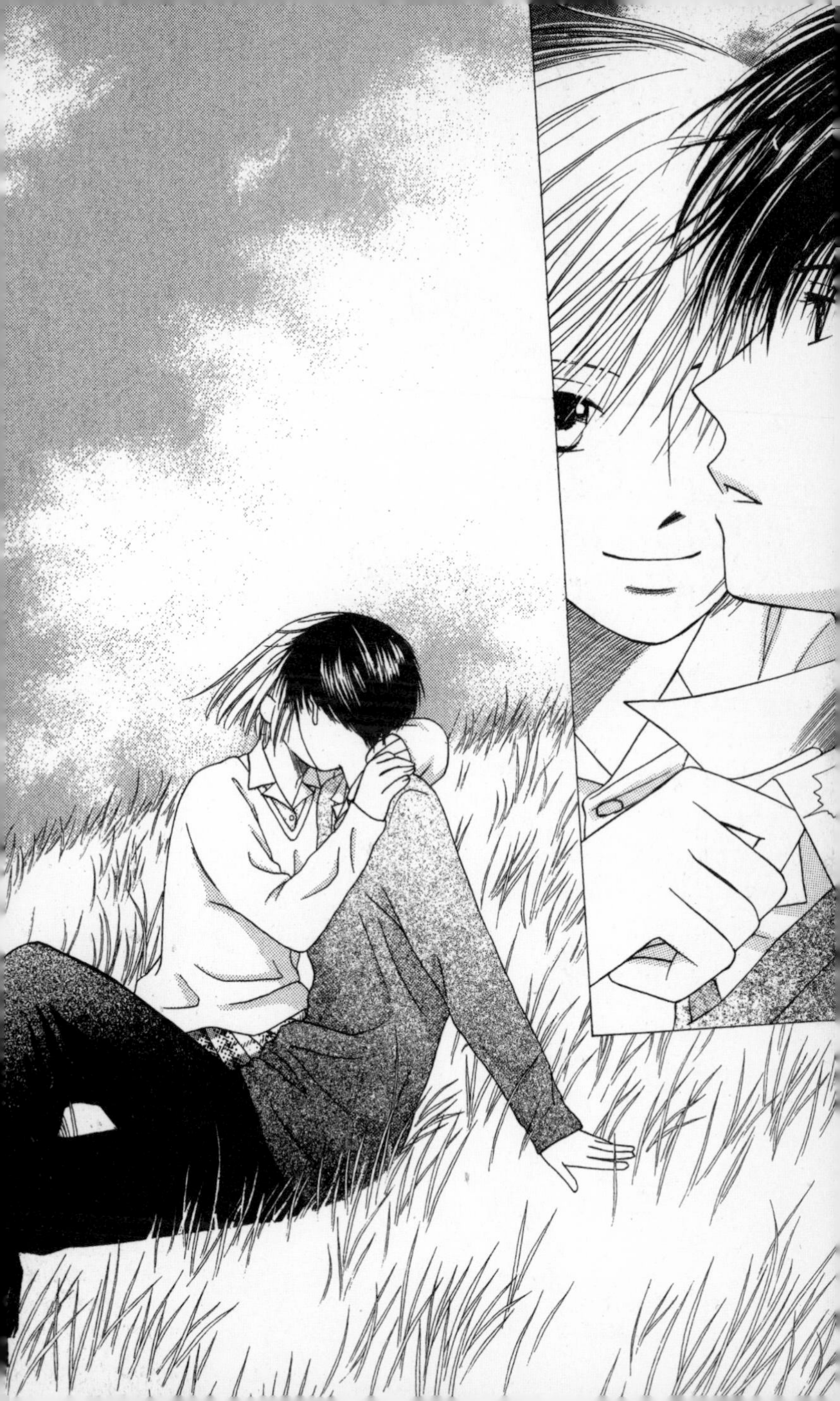

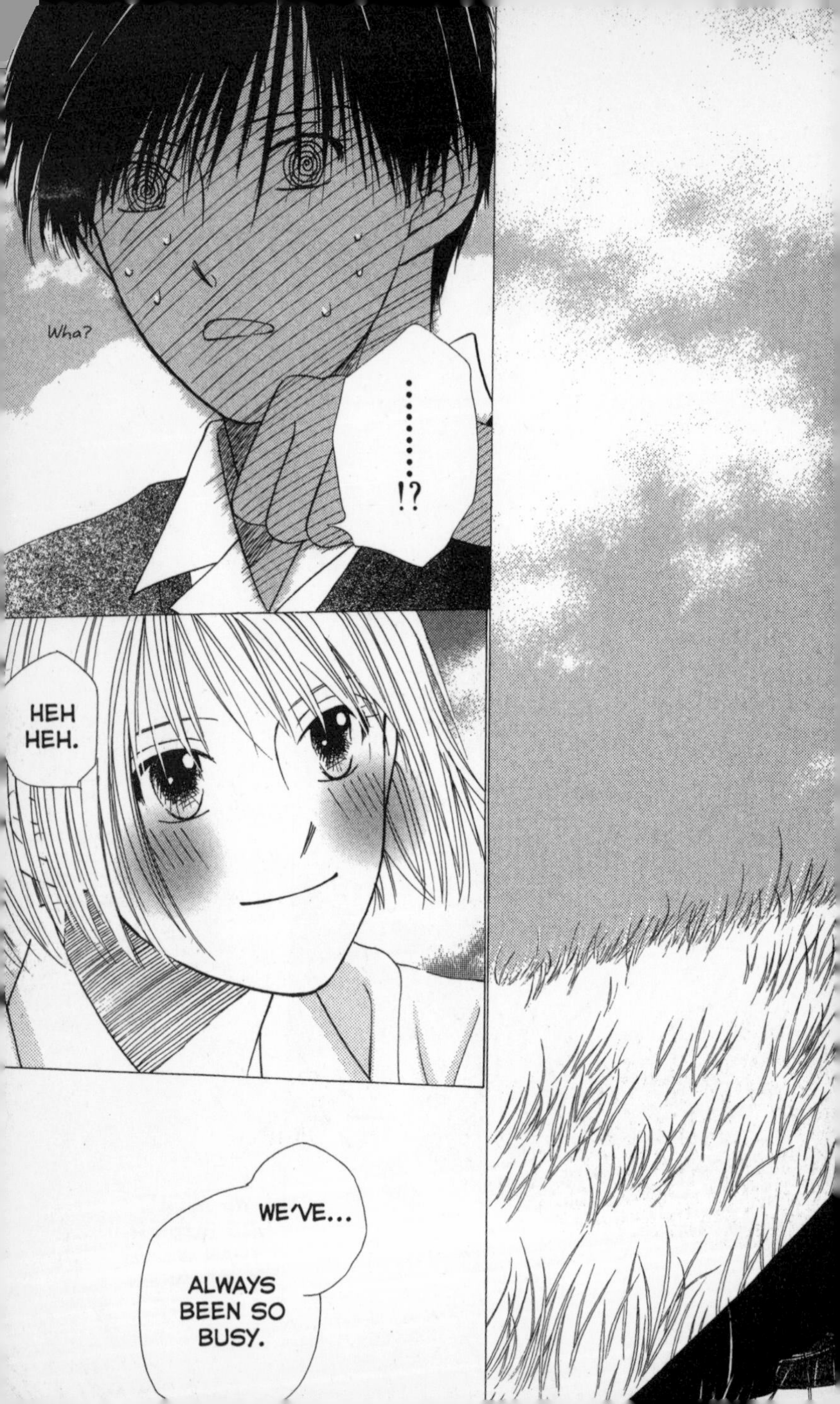
……!?
Wha?
HEH HEH.
WE'VE...
ALWAYS BEEN SO BUSY.

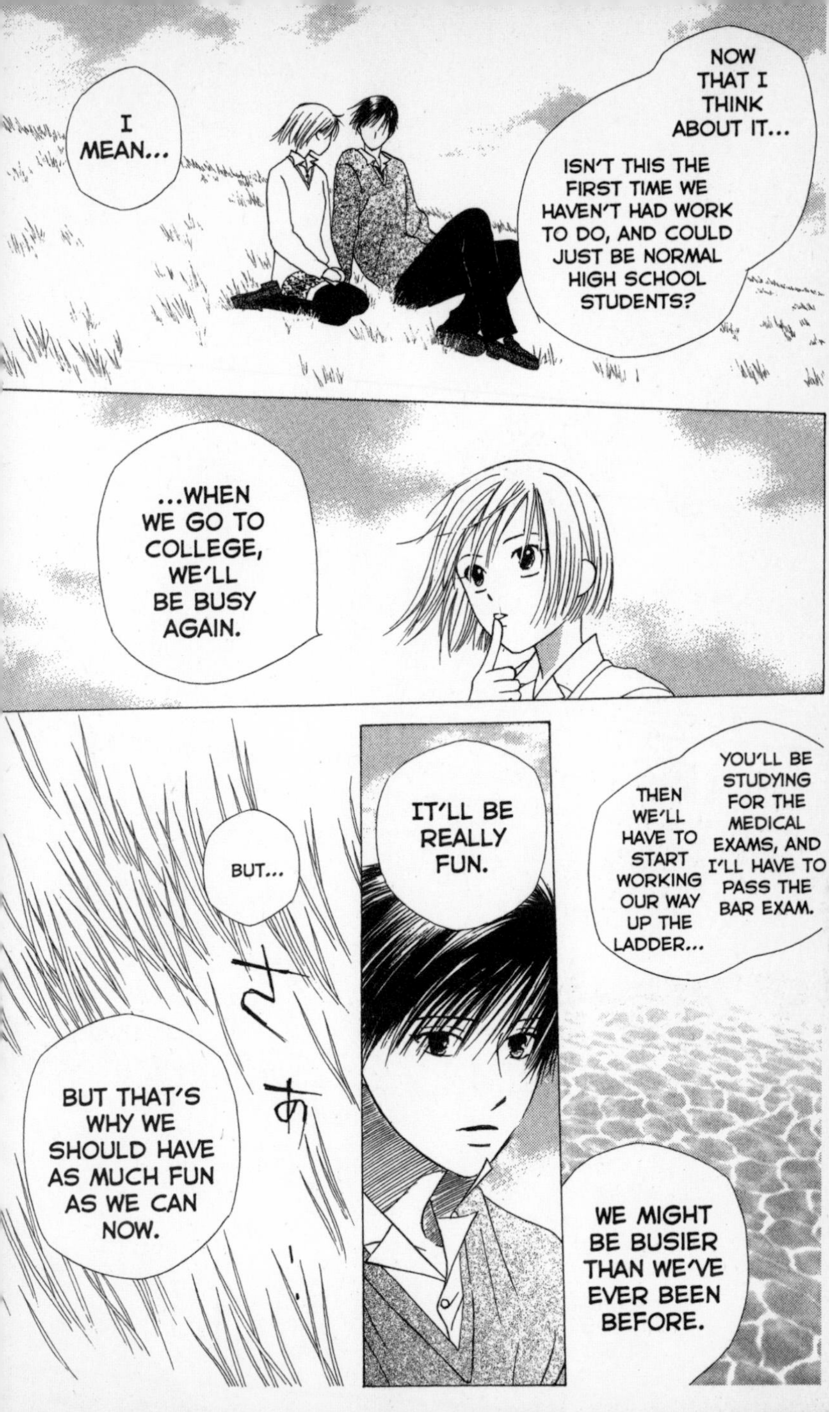
NOW THAT I THINK ABOUT IT...
ISN'T THIS THE FIRST TIME WE HAVEN'T HAD WORK TO DO, AND COULD JUST BE NORMAL HIGH SCHOOL STUDENTS?
I MEAN...
...WHEN WE GO TO COLLEGE, WE'LL BE BUSY AGAIN.
YOU'LL BE STUDYING FOR THE MEDICAL EXAMS, AND I'LL HAVE TO PASS THE BAR EXAM.
THEN WE'LL HAVE TO START WORKING OUR WAY UP THE LADDER...
WE MIGHT BE BUSIER THAN WE'VE EVER BEEN BEFORE.
IT'LL BE REALLY FUN.
BUT...
BUT THAT'S WHY WE SHOULD HAVE AS MUCH FUN AS WE CAN NOW.

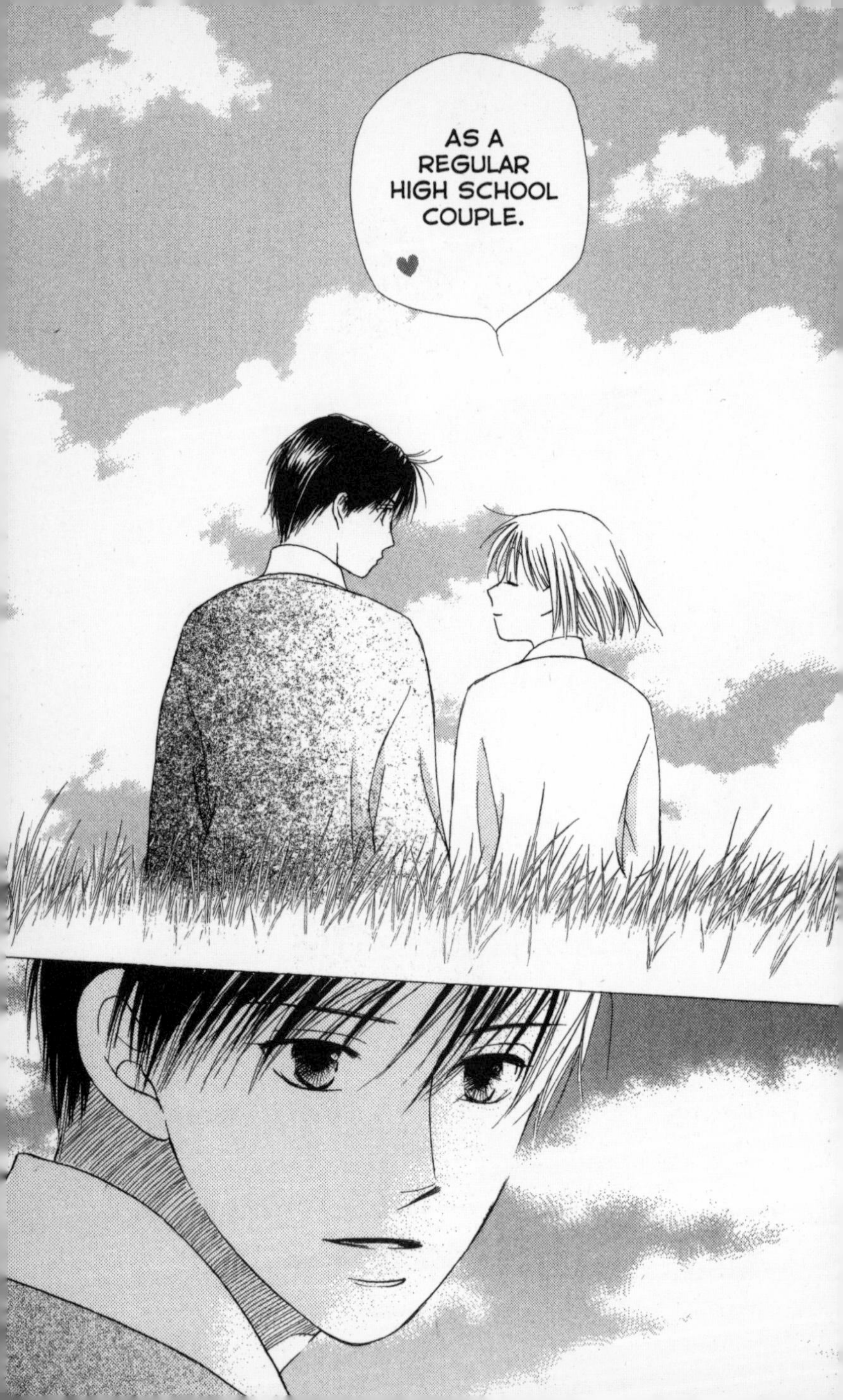
AS A REGULAR HIGH SCHOOL COUPLE.

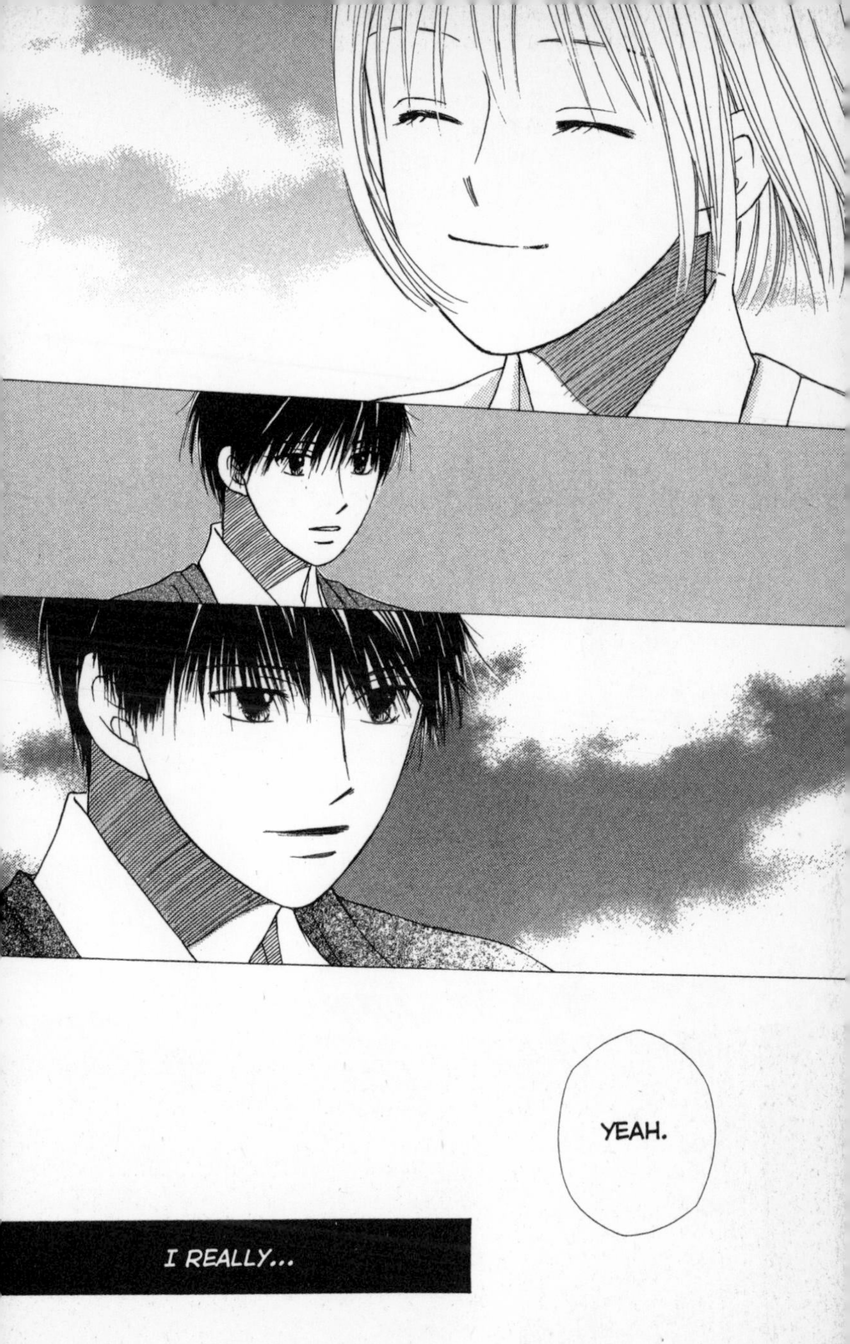
YEAH.
I REALLY...

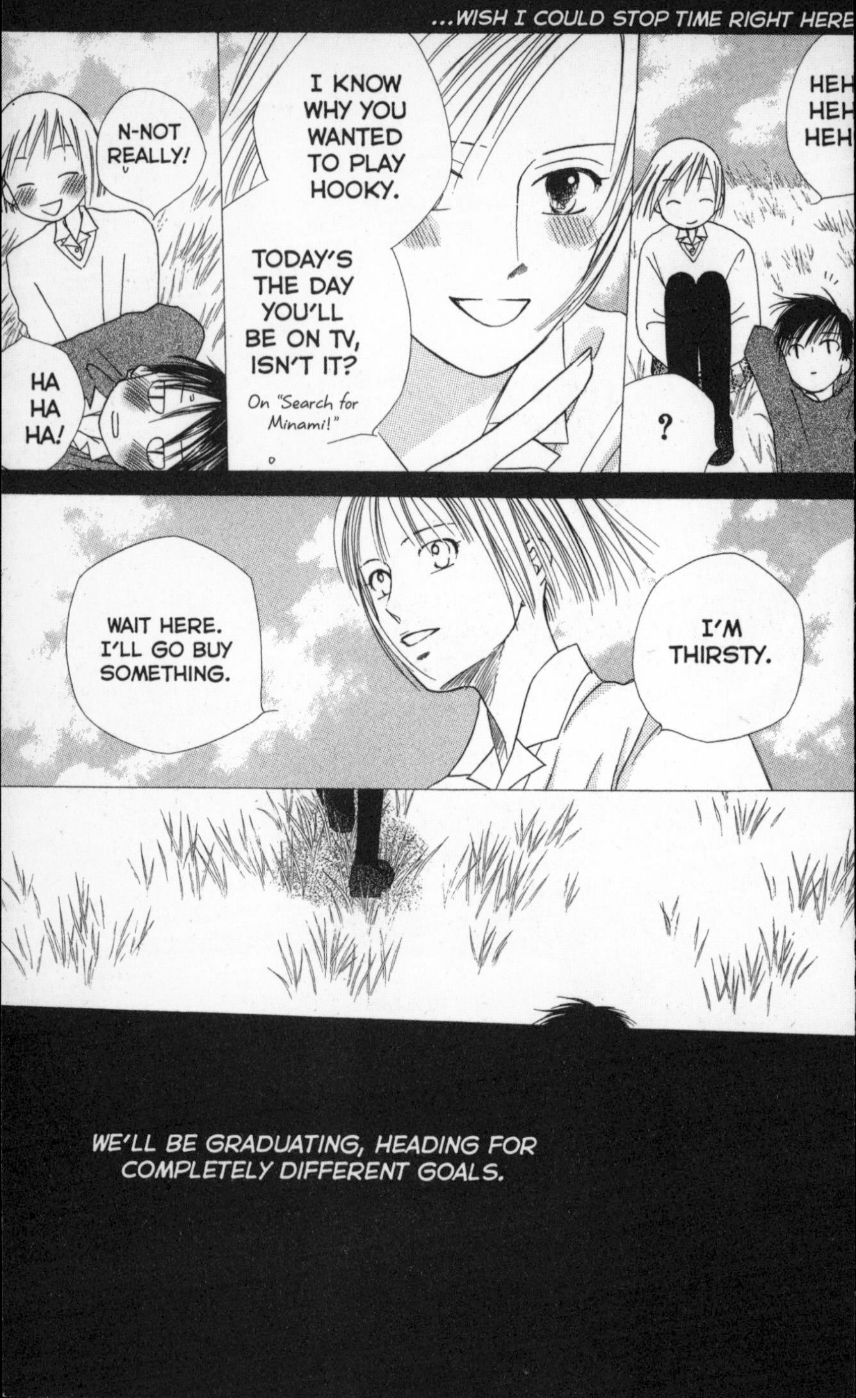
...WISH I COULD STOP TIME RIGHT HERE
HEH HEH HEH
?
I KNOW WHY YOU WANTED TO PLAY HOOKY.
TODAY'S THE DAY YOU'LL BE ON TV, ISN'T IT?
On "Search for Minami!"
N-NOT REALLY!
HA HA HA!
I'M THIRSTY.
WAIT HERE. I'LL GO BUY SOMETHING.
WE'LL BE GRADUATING, HEADING FOR COMPLETELY DIFFERENT GOALS.

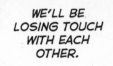

WE'LL BE LOSING TOUCH WITH EACH OTHER.

MIYAZAWA.

I THOUGHT I COULD CHANGE IF I WERE WITH YOU, BUT...

...I WAS WRONG.

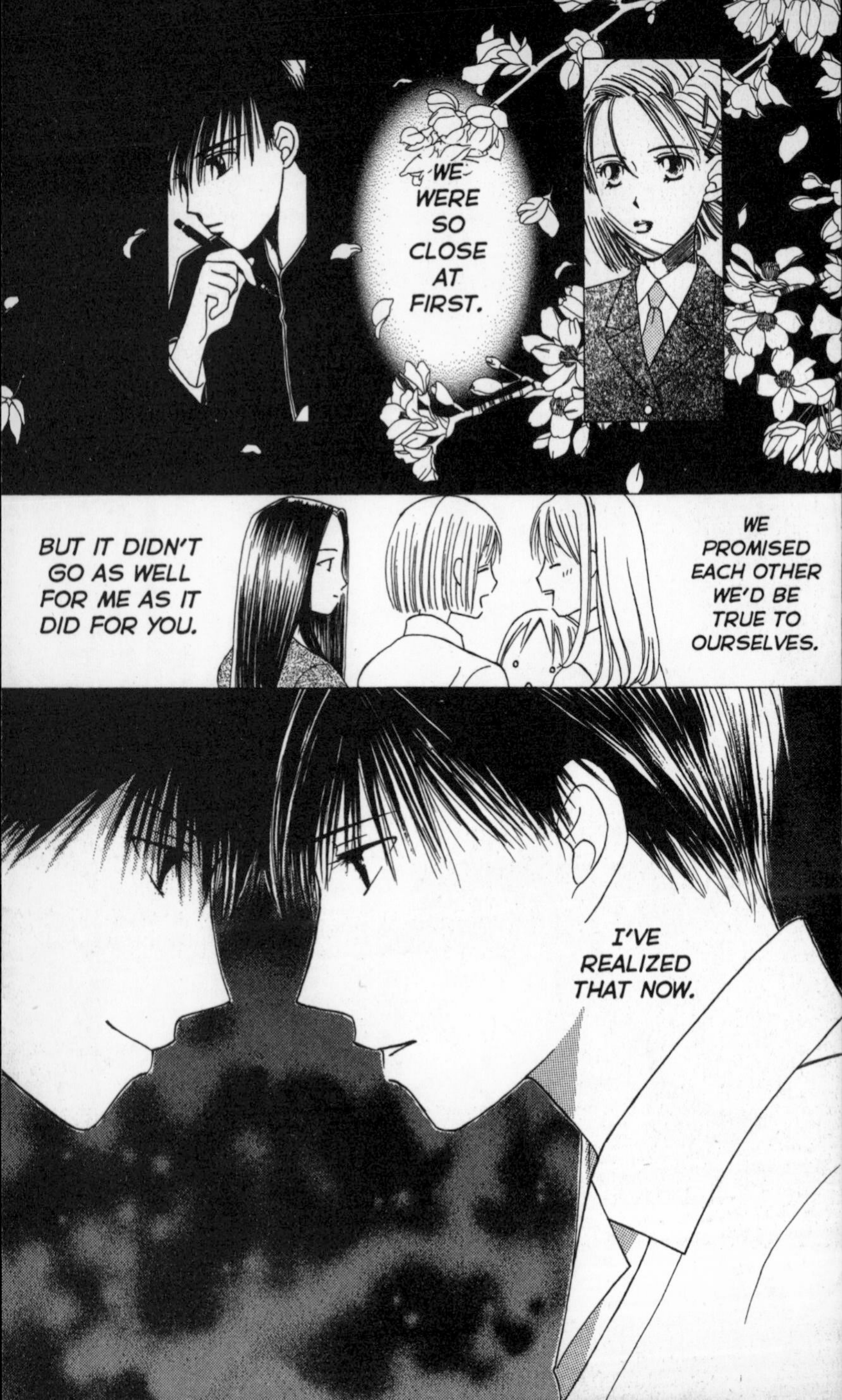
WE WERE SO CLOSE AT FIRST.
WE PROMISED EACH OTHER WE'D BE TRUE TO OURSELVES.
BUT IT DIDN'T GO AS WELL FOR ME AS IT DID FOR YOU.
I'VE REALIZED THAT NOW.

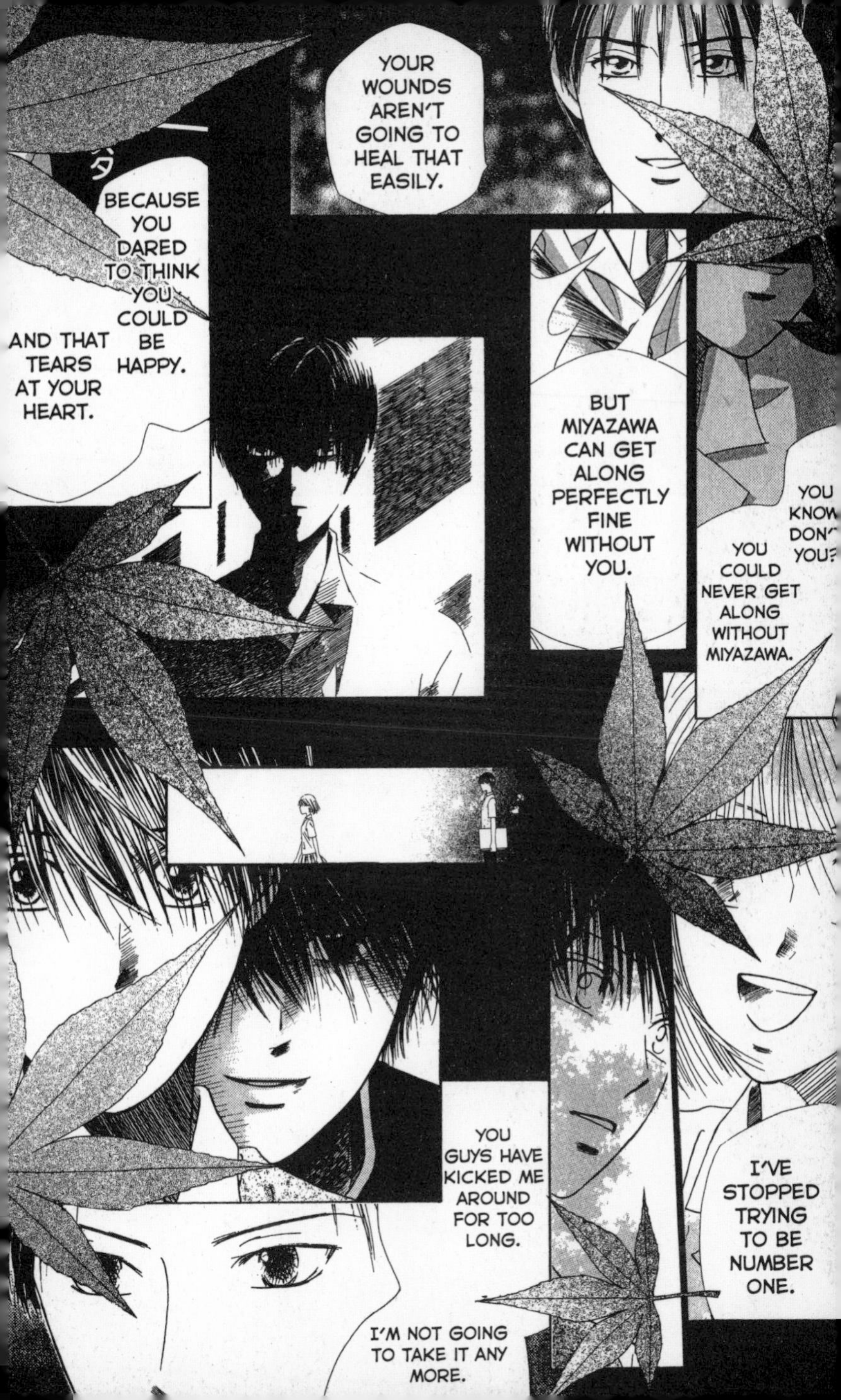
YOUR WOUNDS AREN'T GOING TO HEAL THAT EASILY.
BECAUSE YOU DARED TO THINK YOU COULD BE HAPPY.
AND THAT TEARS AT YOUR HEART.
YOU KNOW DON'T YOU?
YOU COULD NEVER GET ALONG WITHOUT MIYAZAWA.
BUT MIYAZAWA CAN GET ALONG PERFECTLY FINE WITHOUT YOU.
I'VE STOPPED TRYING TO BE NUMBER ONE.
YOU GUYS HAVE KICKED ME AROUND FOR TOO LONG.
I'M NOT GOING TO TAKE IT ANY MORE.

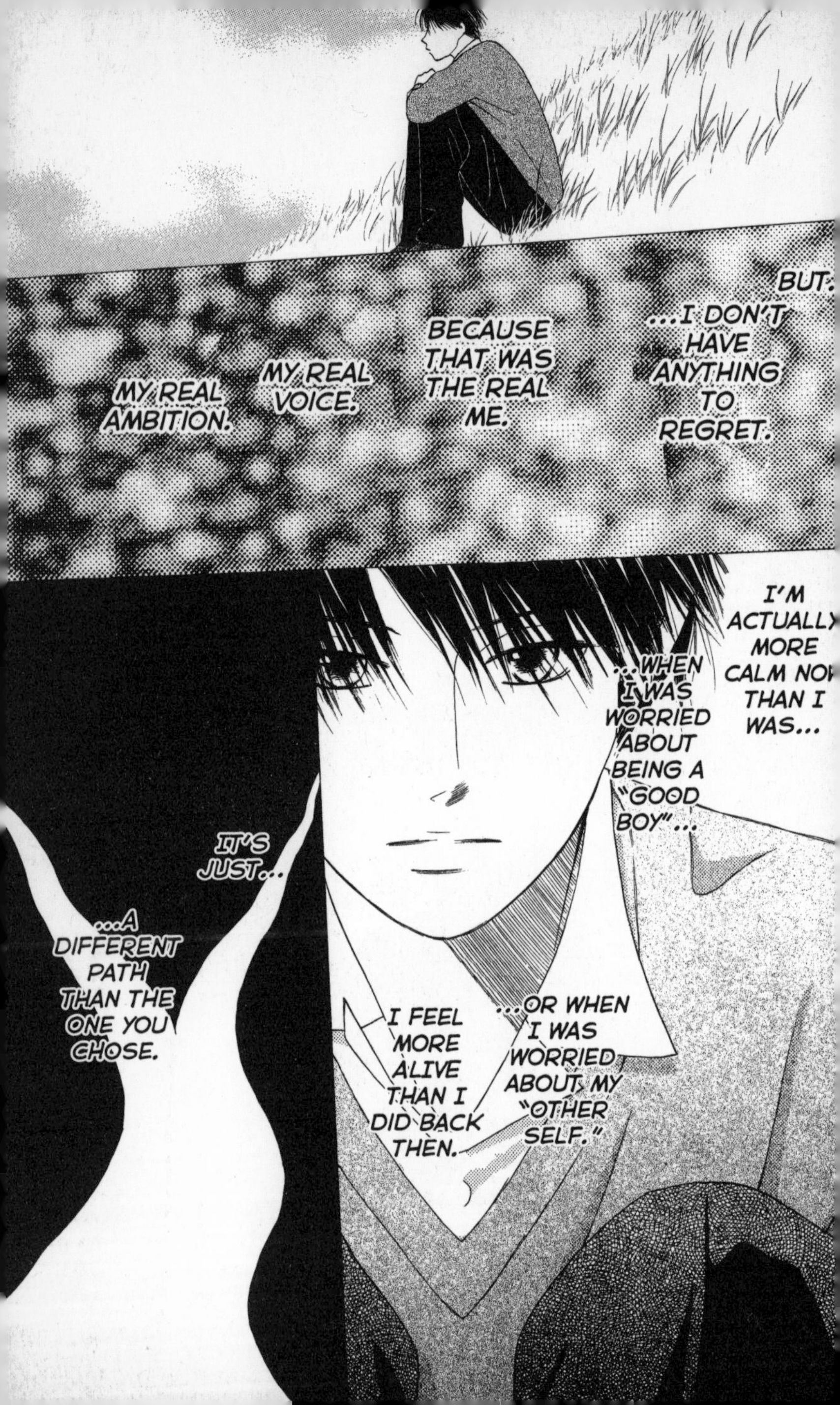
BUT...
...I DON'T HAVE ANYTHING TO REGRET.
BECAUSE THAT WAS THE REAL ME.
MY REAL VOICE.
MY REAL AMBITION.
I'M ACTUALLY MORE CALM NOW THAN I WAS...
...WHEN I WAS WORRIED ABOUT BEING A "GOOD BOY"...
...OR WHEN I WAS WORRIED ABOUT MY "OTHER SELF."
I FEEL MORE ALIVE THAN I DID BACK THEN.
IT'S JUST...
...A DIFFERENT PATH THAN THE ONE YOU CHOSE.

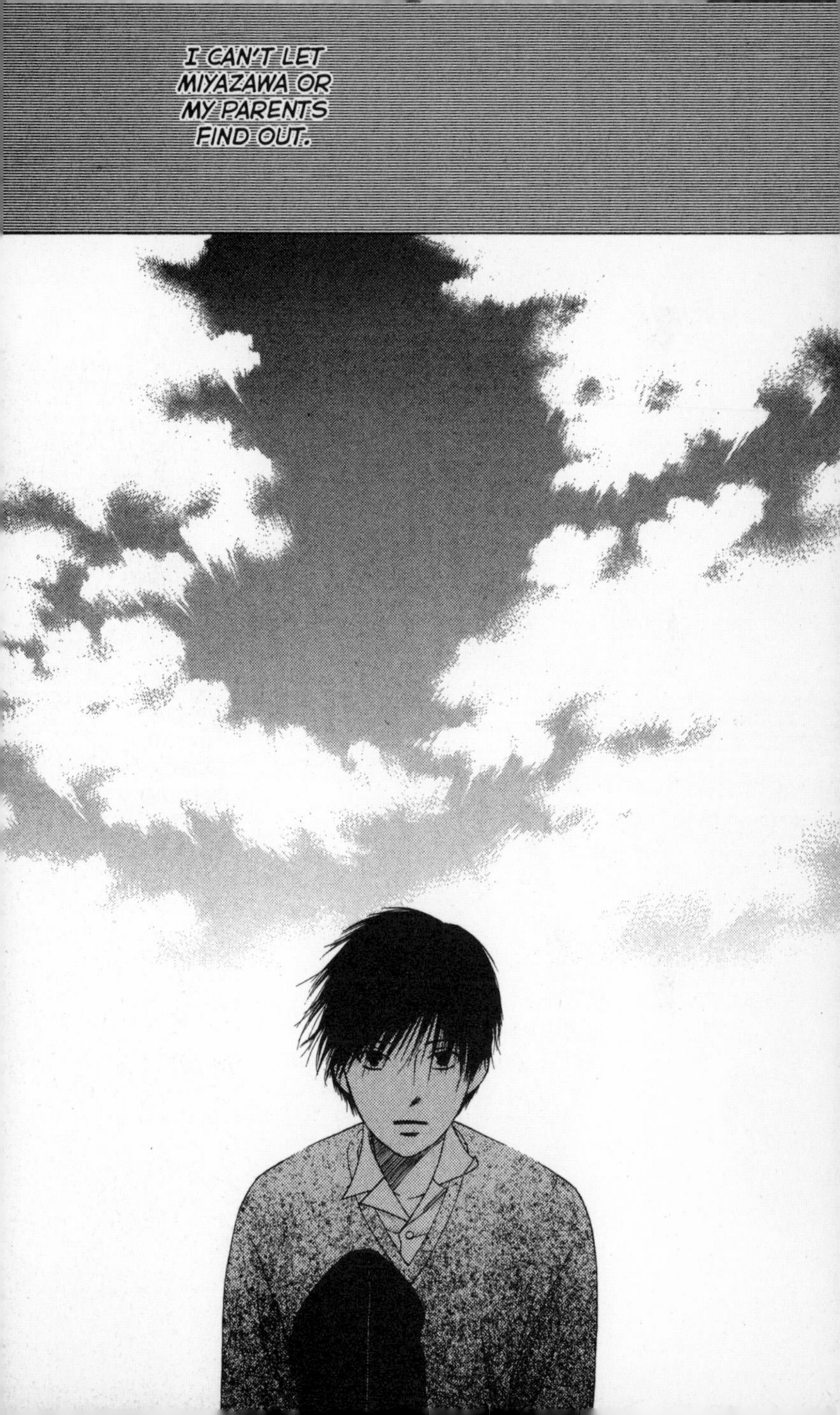
I CAN'T LET MIYAZAWA OR MY PARENTS FIND OUT.

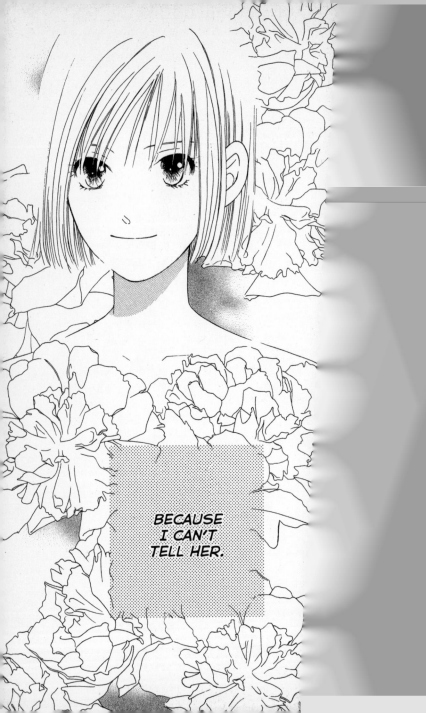

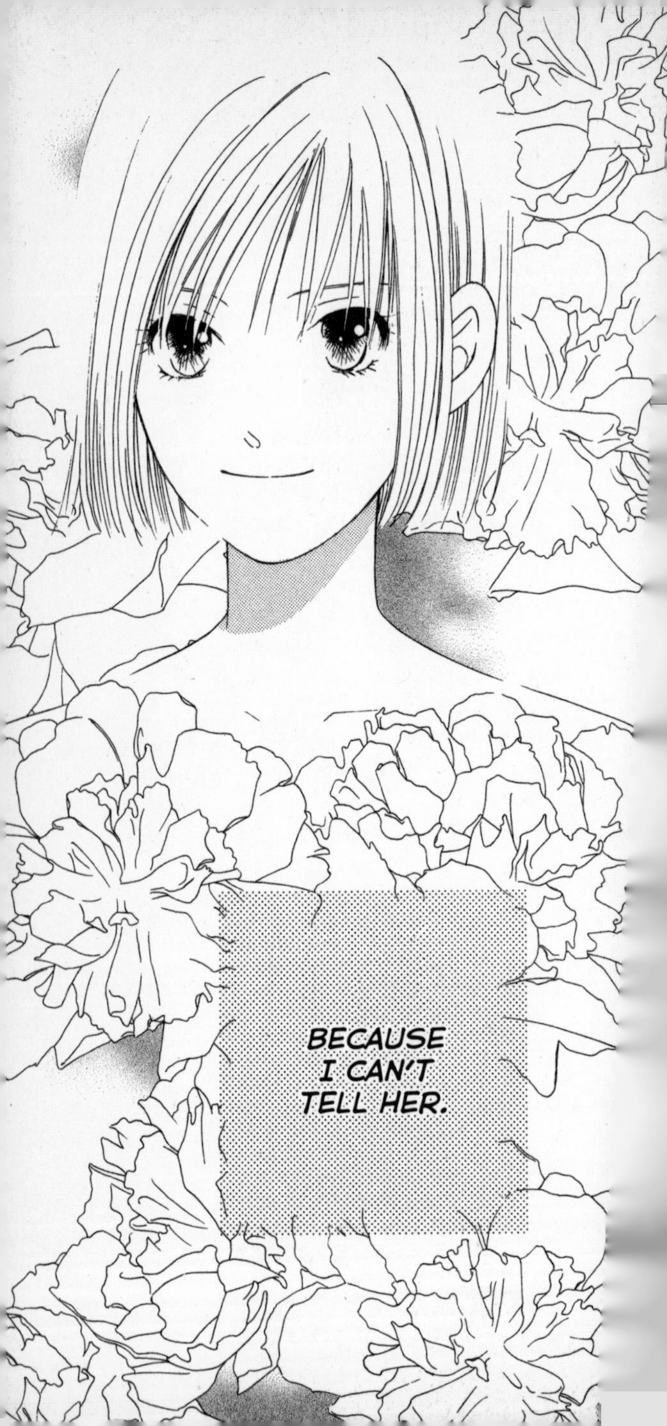
BECAUSE I CAN'T TELL HER.

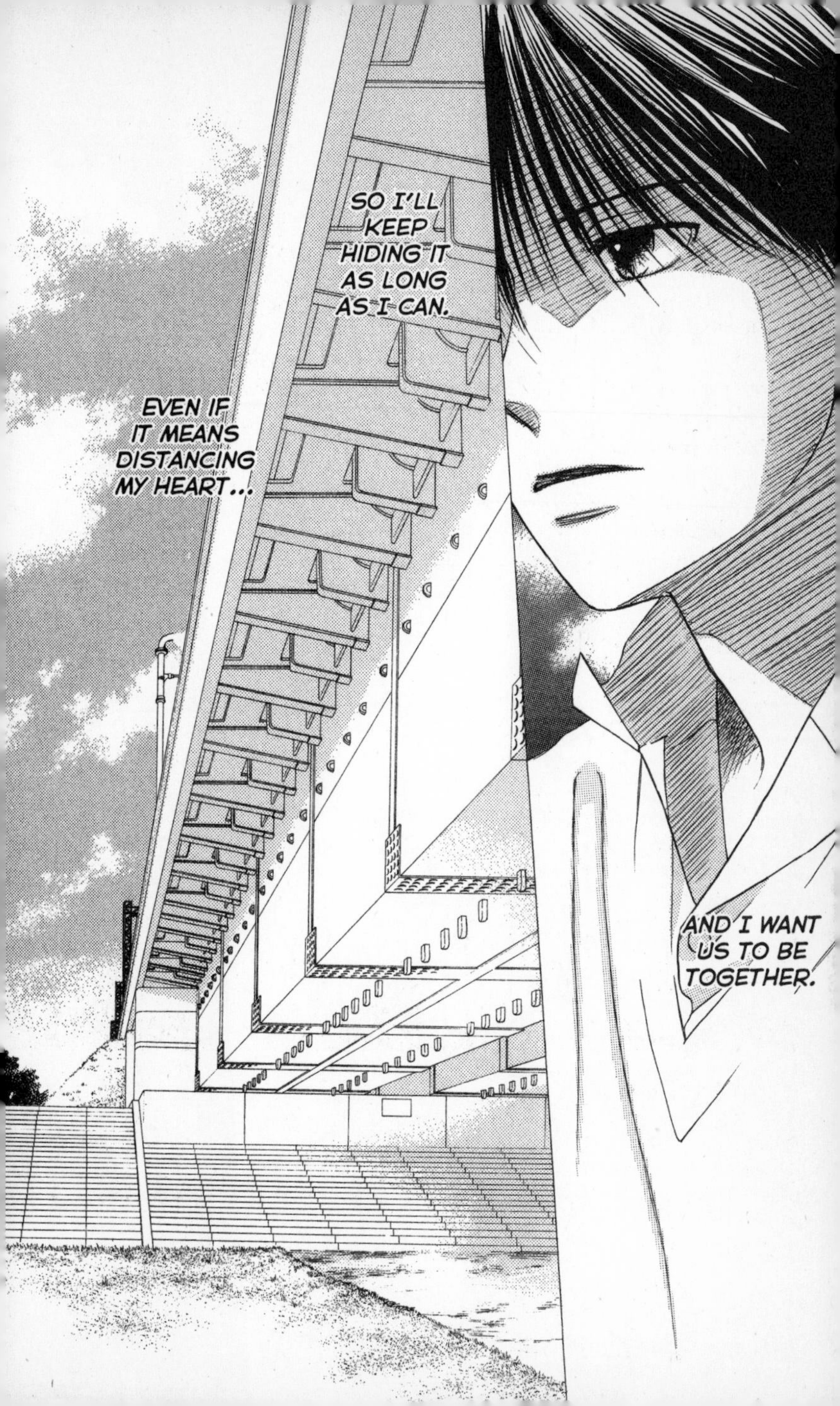
SO I'LL KEEP HIDING IT AS LONG AS I CAN.
EVEN IF IT MEANS DISTANCING MY HEART...
AND I WANT US TO BE TOGETHER.

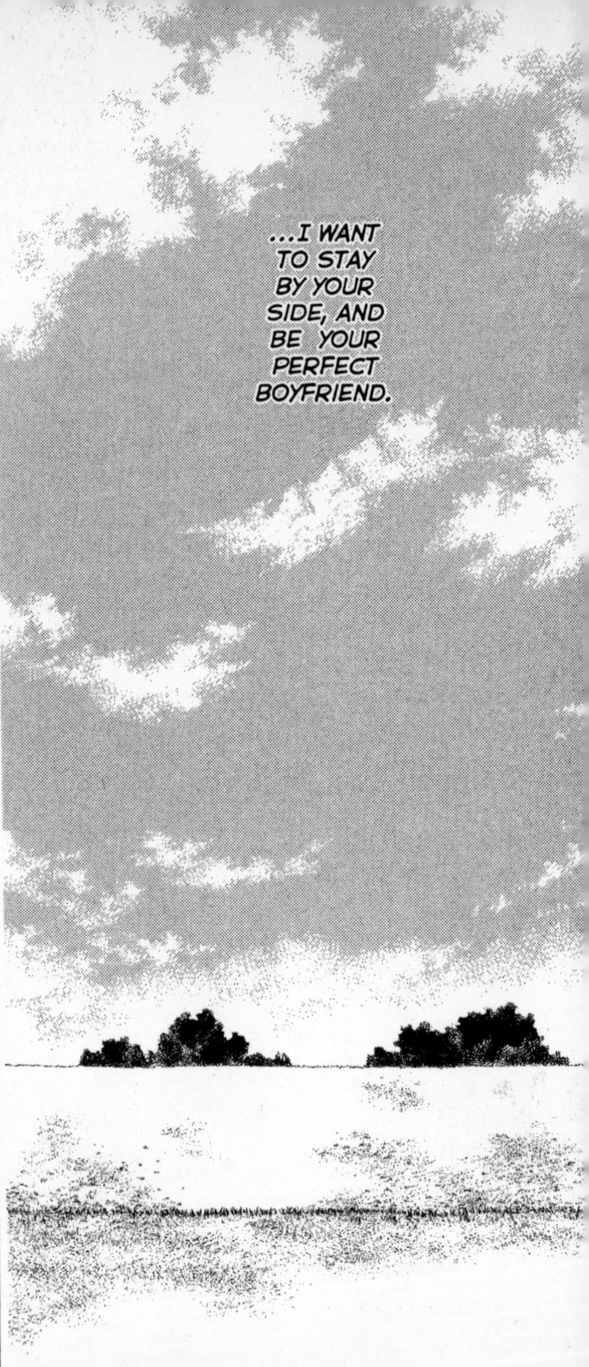
...I WANT TO STAY BY YOUR SIDE, AND BE YOUR PERFECT BOYFRIEND.

5

This is my last free space.

I feel like things are starting to develop now.

I've given up on taking a trip overseas. Hawaii...

I've decided to take better care of myself.

Well then, I hope to see you in the next volume!

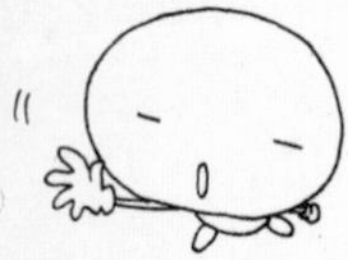

Masami Tsuda

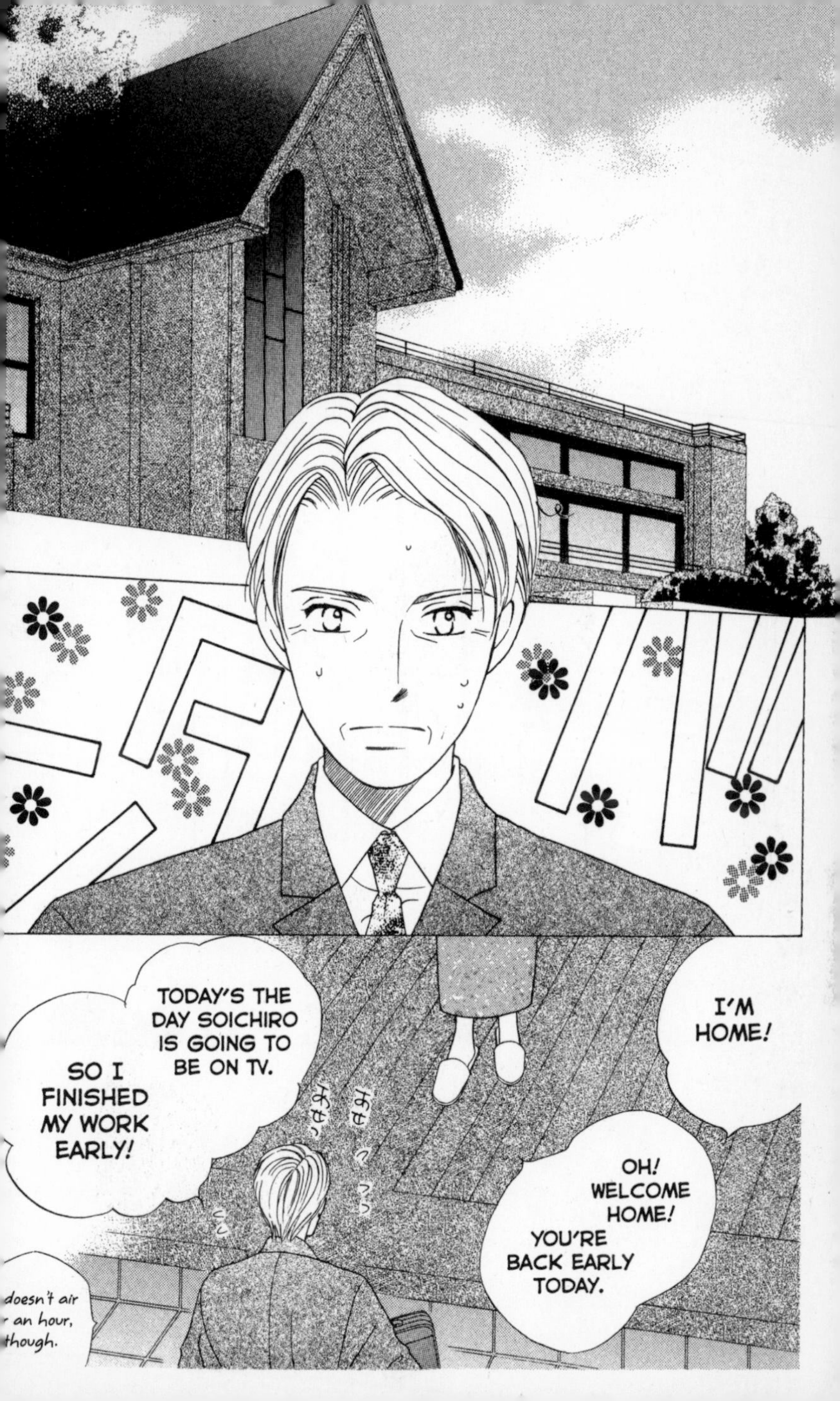
I'M HOME!
OH! WELCOME HOME! YOU'RE BACK EARLY TODAY.
TODAY'S THE DAY SOICHIRO IS GOING TO BE ON TV.
SO I FINISHED MY WORK EARLY!
doesn't air an hour, though.

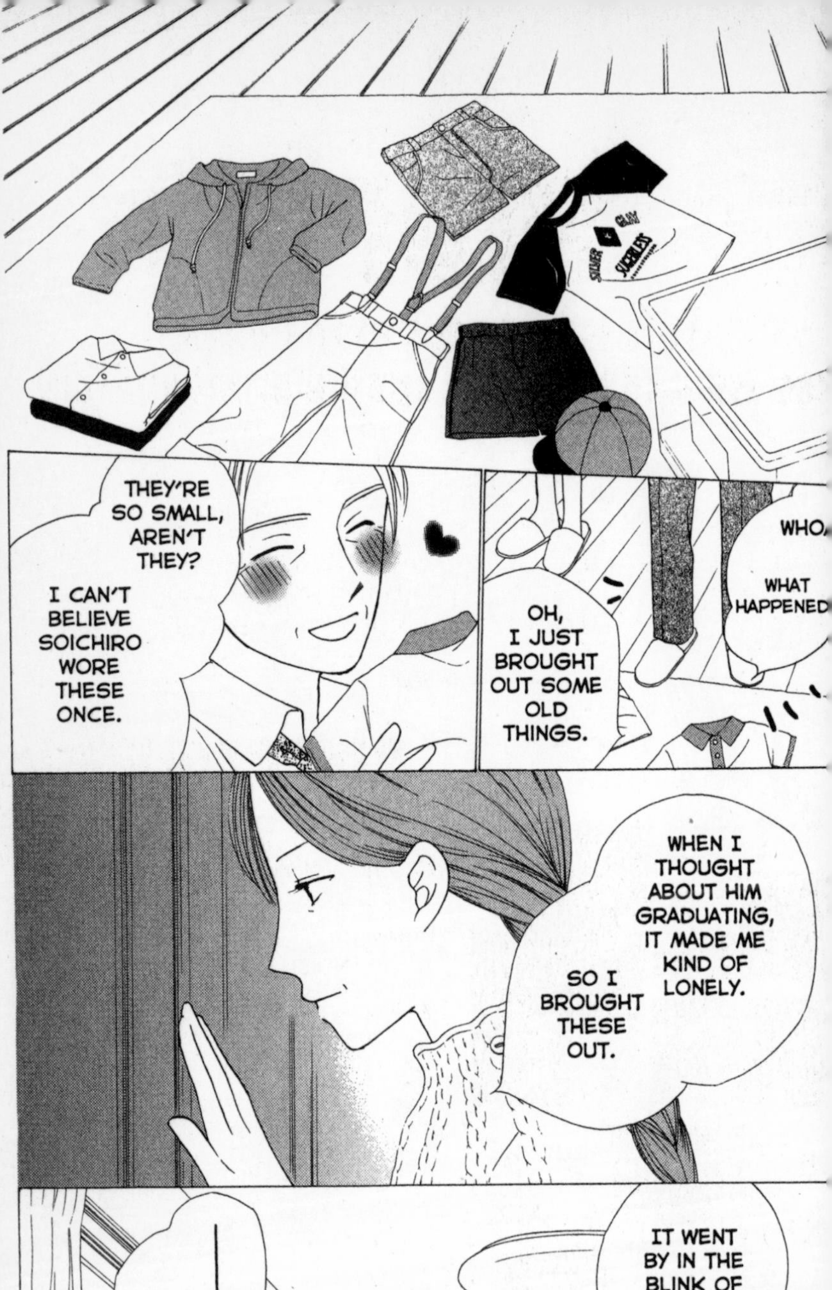
WHO,
WHAT HAPPENED
OH, I JUST BROUGHT OUT SOME OLD THINGS.
THEY'RE SO SMALL, AREN'T THEY?
I CAN'T BELIEVE SOICHIRO WORE THESE ONCE.
WHEN I THOUGHT ABOUT HIM GRADUATING, IT MADE ME KIND OF LONELY.
SO I BROUGHT THESE OUT.
IT WENT BY IN THE BLINK OF AN EYE.
YEAH...

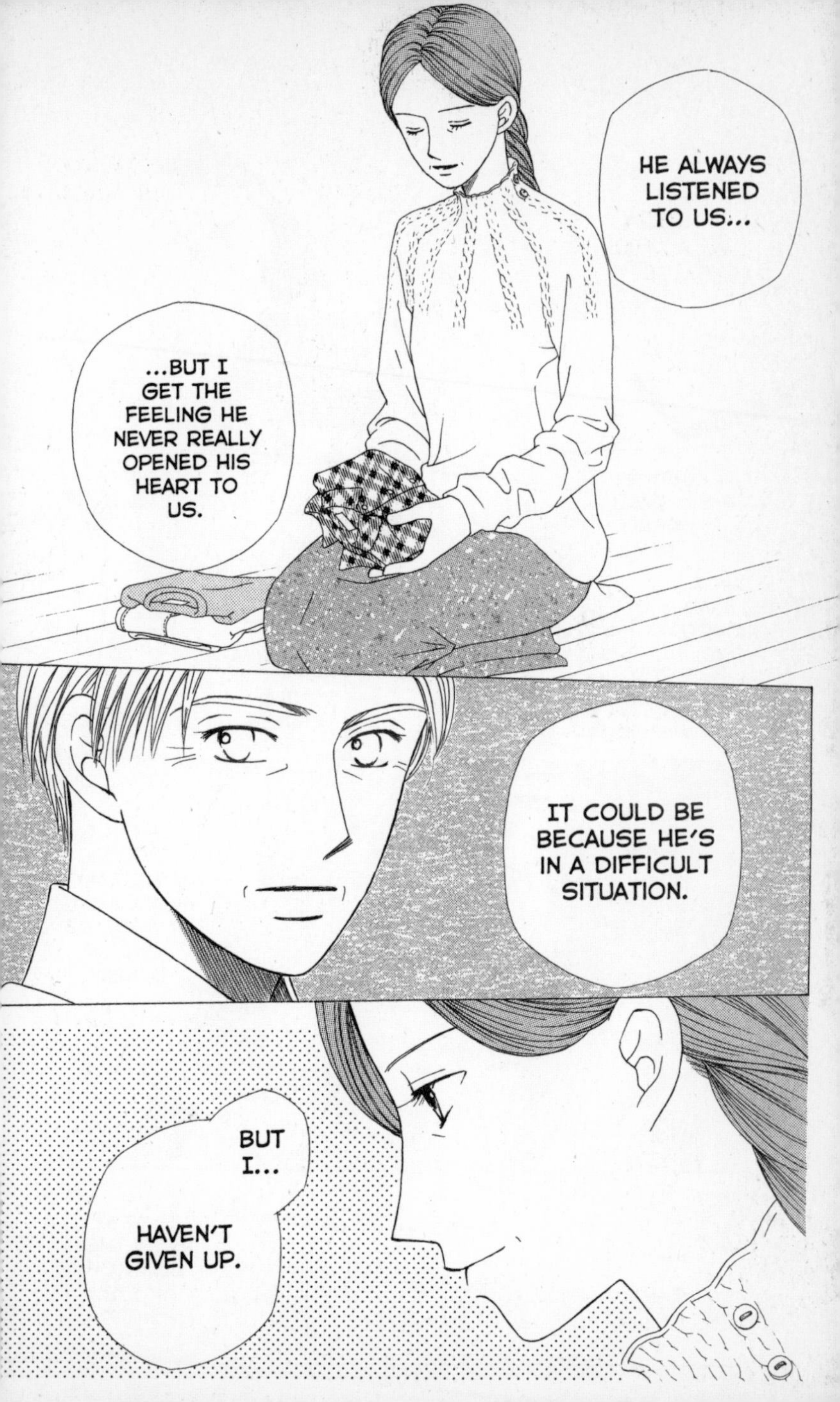
HE ALWAYS LISTENED TO US...
...BUT I GET THE FEELING HE NEVER REALLY OPENED HIS HEART TO US.
IT COULD BE BECAUSE HE'S IN A DIFFICULT SITUATION.
BUT I...
HAVEN'T GIVEN UP.

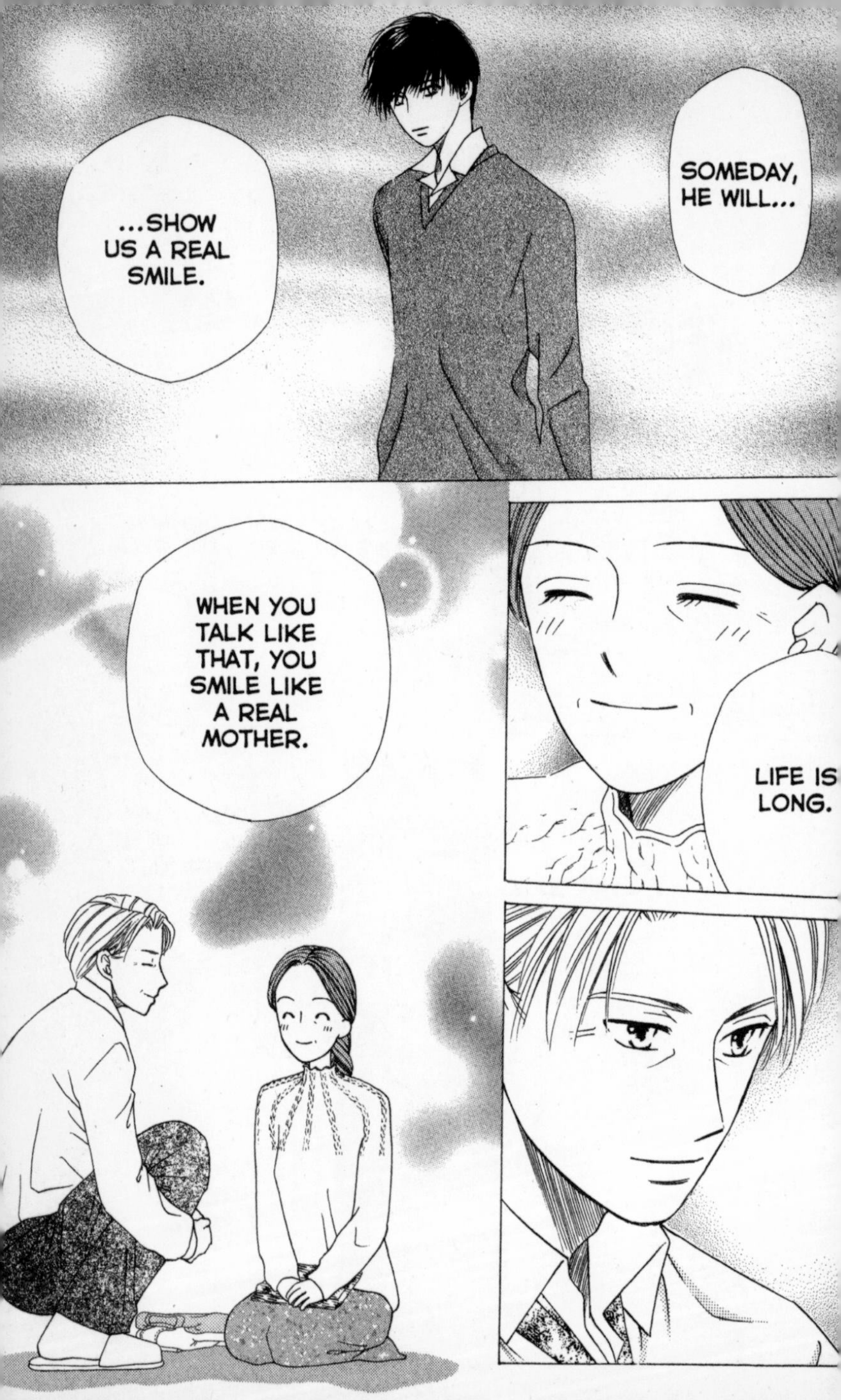
SOMEDAY, HE WILL...
...SHOW US A REAL SMILE.
LIFE IS LONG.
WHEN YOU TALK LIKE THAT, YOU SMILE LIKE A REAL MOTHER.

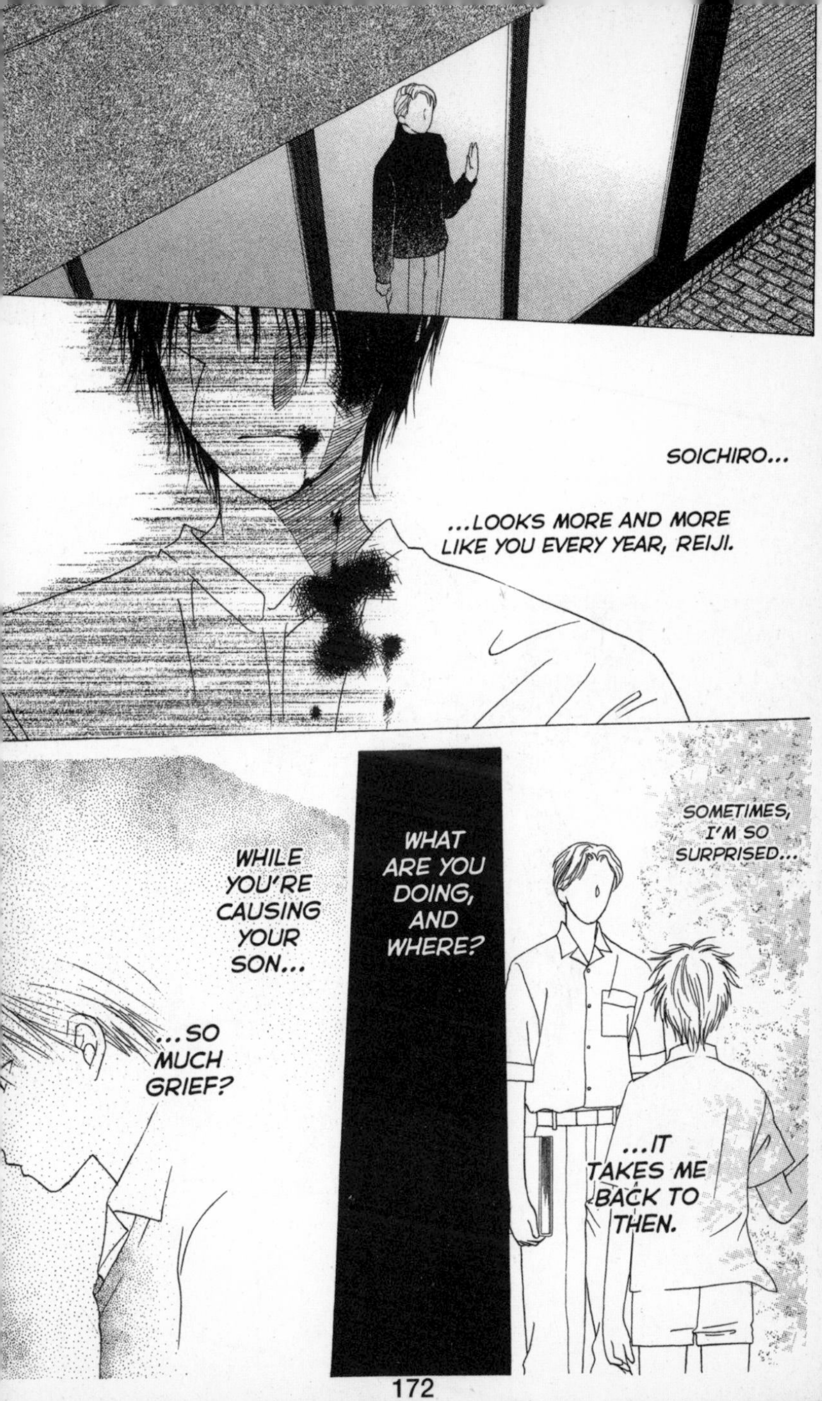
SOICHIRO...
...LOOKS MORE AND MORE LIKE YOU EVERY YEAR, REIJI.
SOMETIMES, I'M SO SURPRISED...
...IT TAKES ME BACK TO THEN.
WHAT ARE YOU DOING, AND WHERE?
WHILE YOU'RE CAUSING YOUR SON...
...SO MUCH GRIEF?

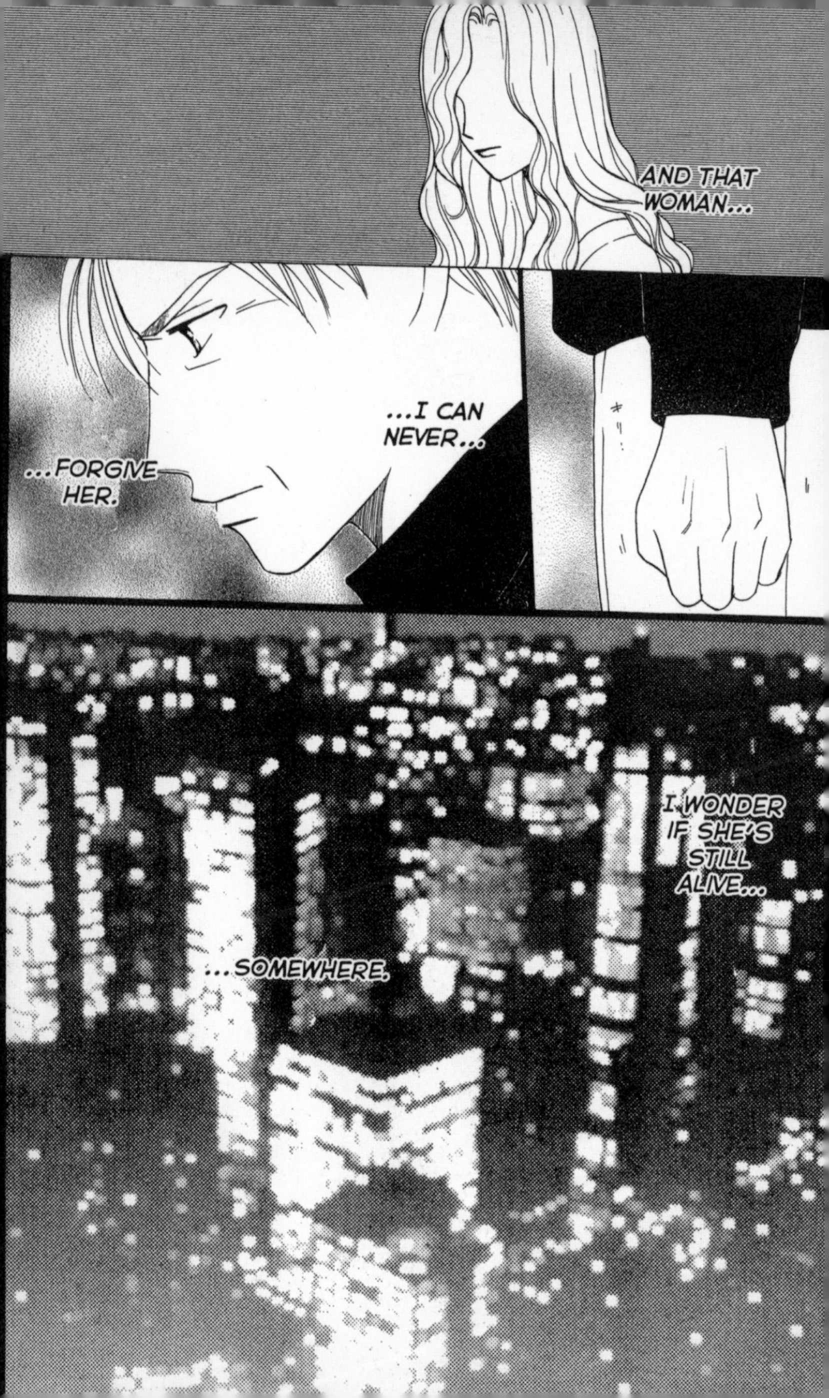
AND THAT WOMAN...
...I CAN NEVER...
...FORGIVE HER.
I WONDER IF SHE'S STILL ALIVE...
...SOMEWHERE.

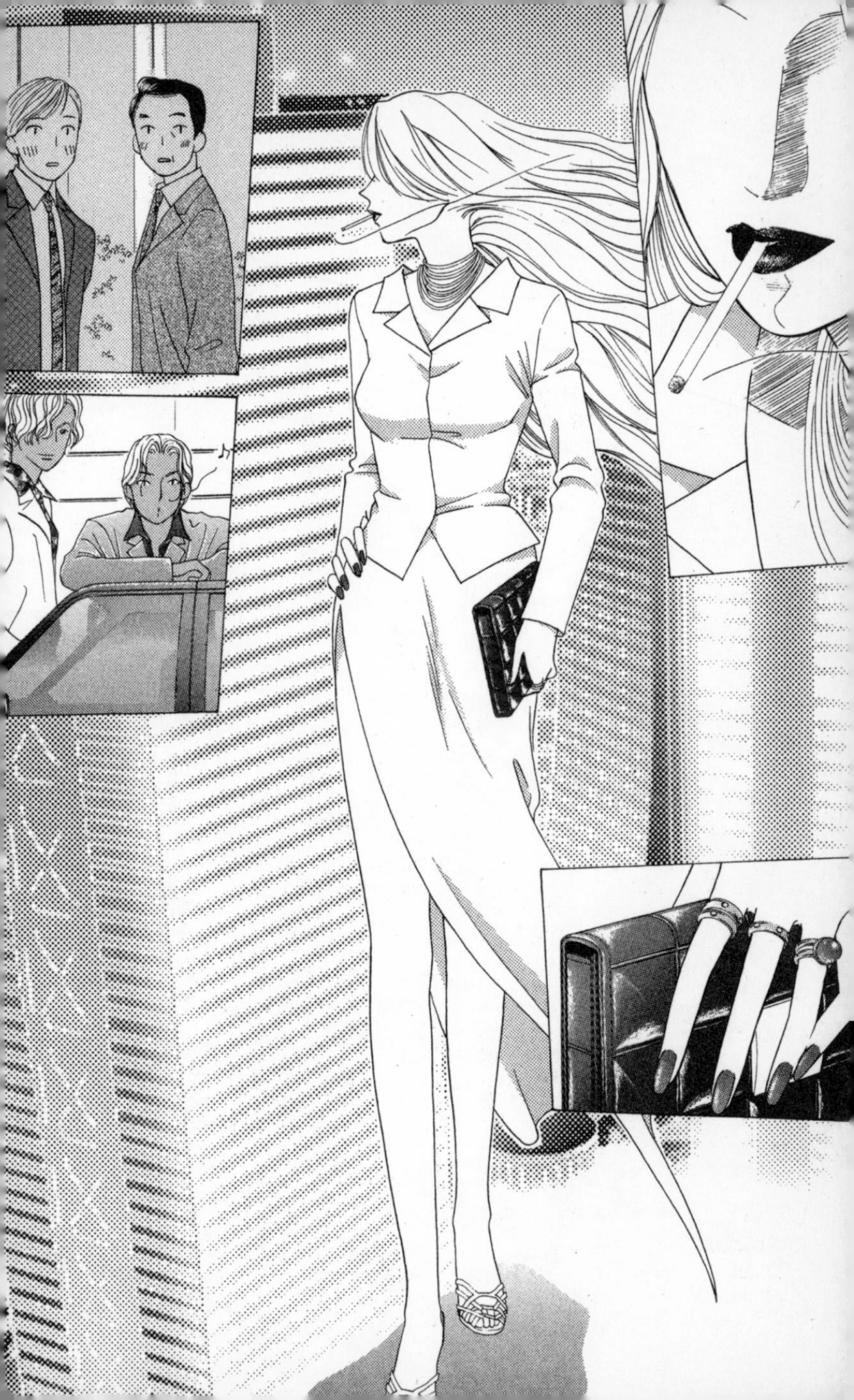

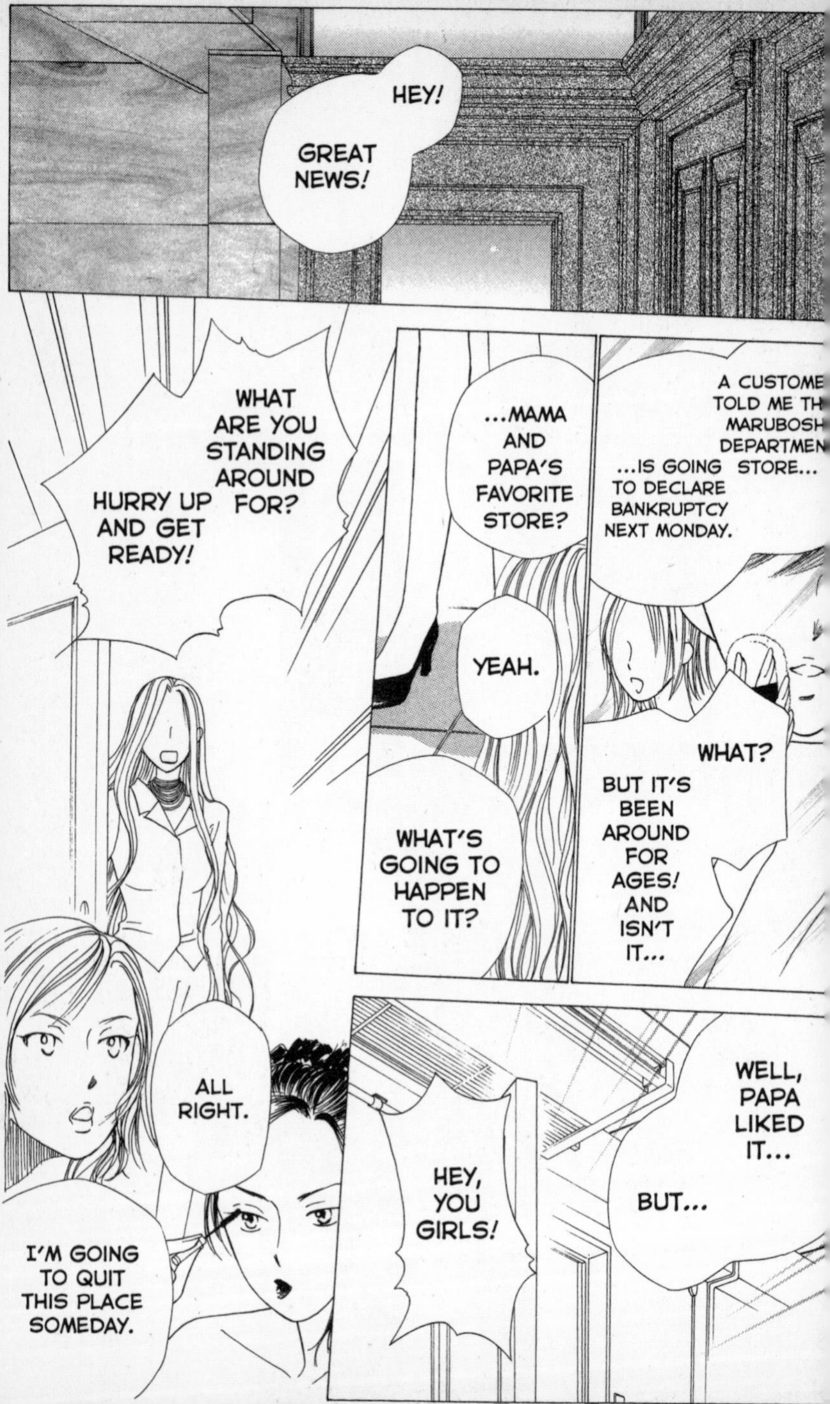
HEY!
GREAT NEWS!
A CUSTOME TOLD ME TH MARUBOSH DEPARTMEN STORE...
...IS GOING TO DECLARE BANKRUPTCY NEXT MONDAY.
WHAT?
BUT IT'S BEEN AROUND FOR AGES! AND ISN'T IT...
...MAMA AND PAPA'S FAVORITE STORE?
YEAH.
WHAT'S GOING TO HAPPEN TO IT?
WELL, PAPA LIKED IT...
BUT...
HEY, YOU GIRLS!
WHAT ARE YOU STANDING AROUND FOR?
HURRY UP AND GET READY!
ALL RIGHT.
I'M GOING TO QUIT THIS PLACE SOMEDAY.

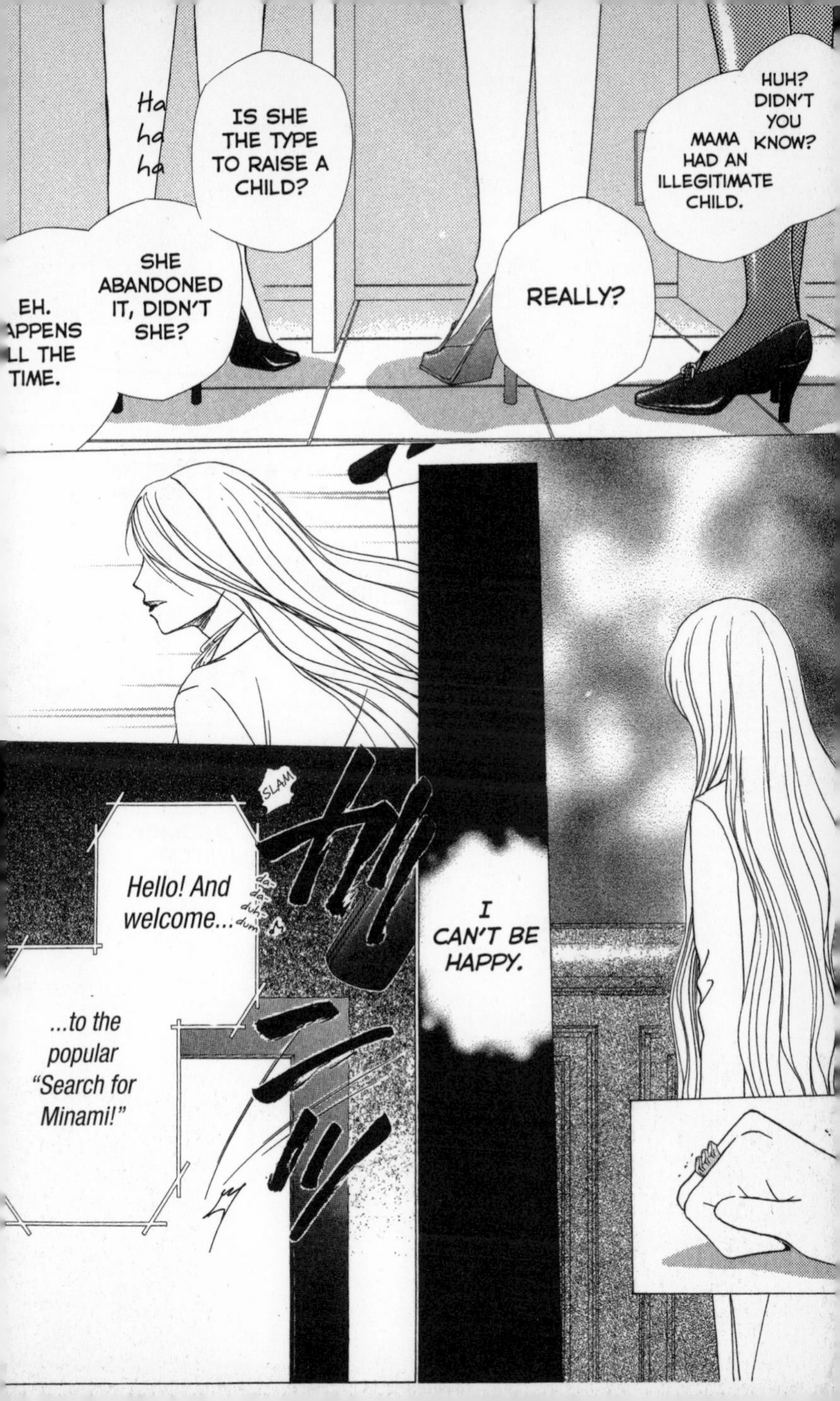
HUH? DIDN'T YOU KNOW?
MAMA HAD AN ILLEGITIMATE CHILD.
REALLY?
IS SHE THE TYPE TO RAISE A CHILD?
Ha ha ha
SHE ABANDONED IT, DIDN'T SHE?
EH. APPENS LL THE TIME.
I CAN'T BE HAPPY.
SLAM
Hello! And welcome...
da-da-duh-dum
...to the popular "Search for Minami!"

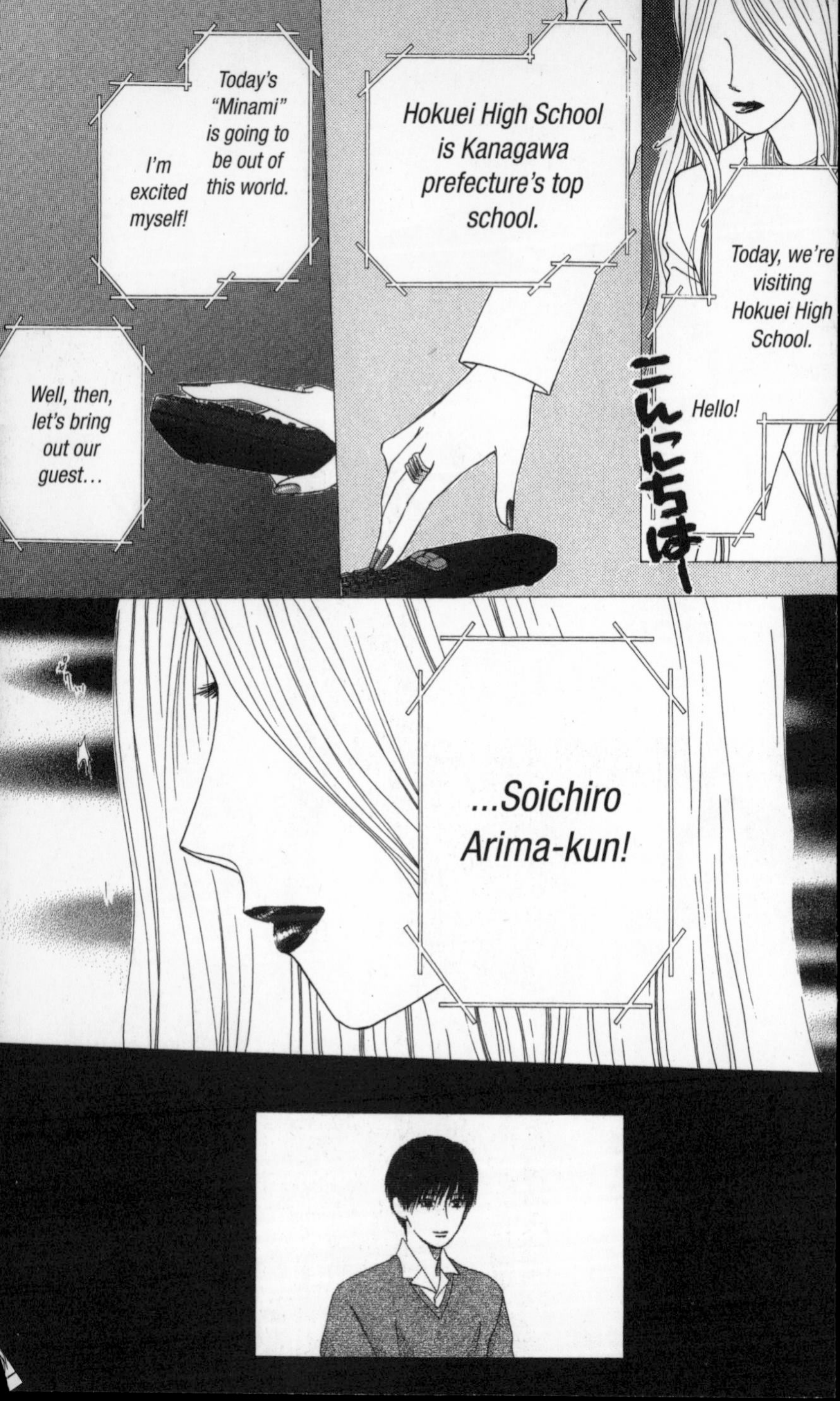
Today, we're visiting Hokuei High School.
こんにちはー
Hello!
Hokuei High School is Kanagawa prefecture's top school.
Today's "Minami" is going to be out of this world.
I'm excited myself!
Well, then, let's bring out our guest...
...Soichiro Arima-kun!

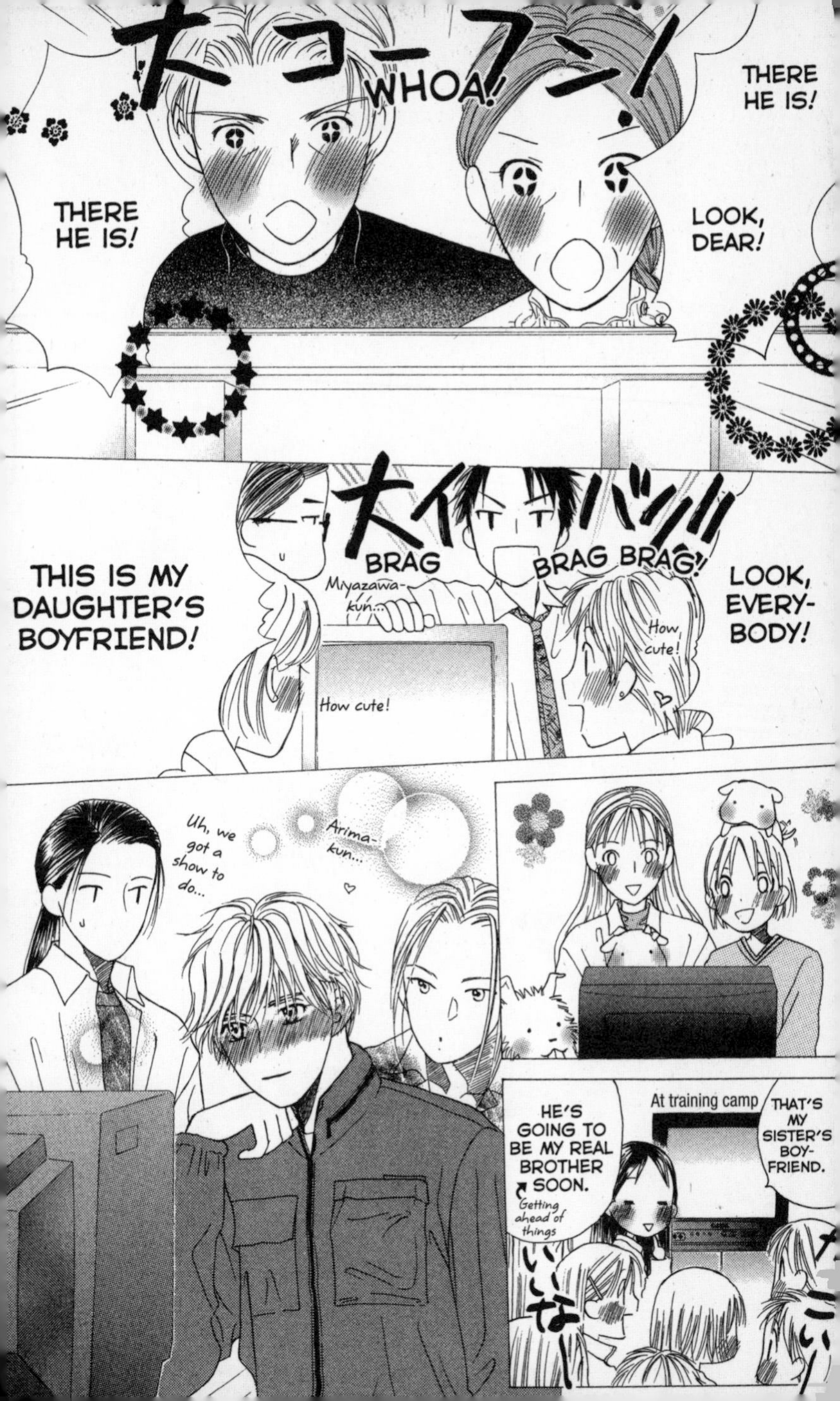
THERE HE IS!
LOOK, DEAR!
WHOA!
THERE HE IS!
LOOK, EVERY-BODY!
BRAG BRAG BRAG!
How cute!
Miyazawa-kun...
How cute!
THIS IS MY DAUGHTER'S BOYFRIEND!
THAT'S MY SISTER'S BOY-FRIEND.
At training camp
HE'S GOING TO BE MY REAL BROTHER SOON.
Getting ahead of things
Arima-kun...
Uh, we got a show to do...

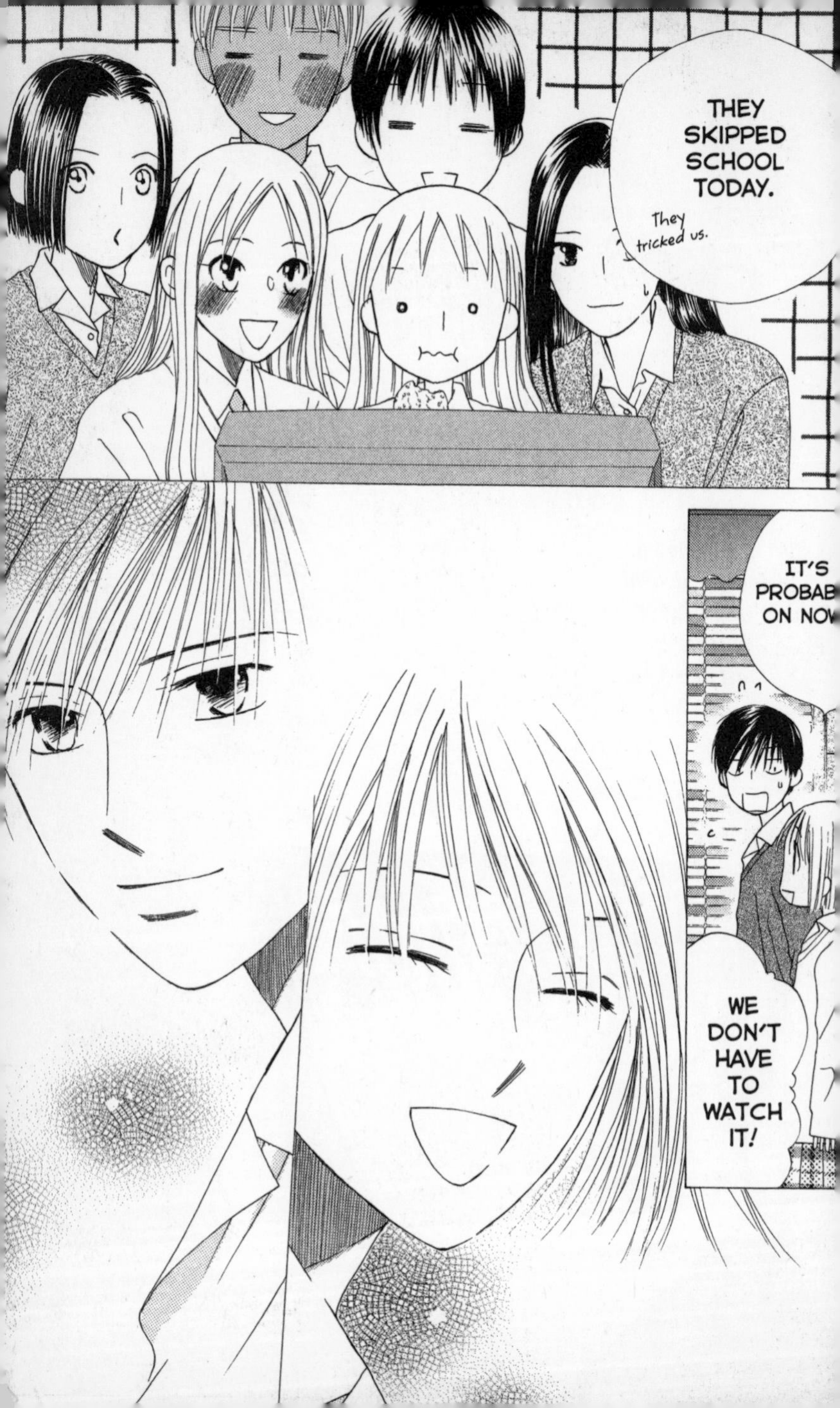
THEY SKIPPED SCHOOL TODAY.
They tricked us.
IT'S PROBAB ON NOW
WE DON'T HAVE TO WATCH IT!

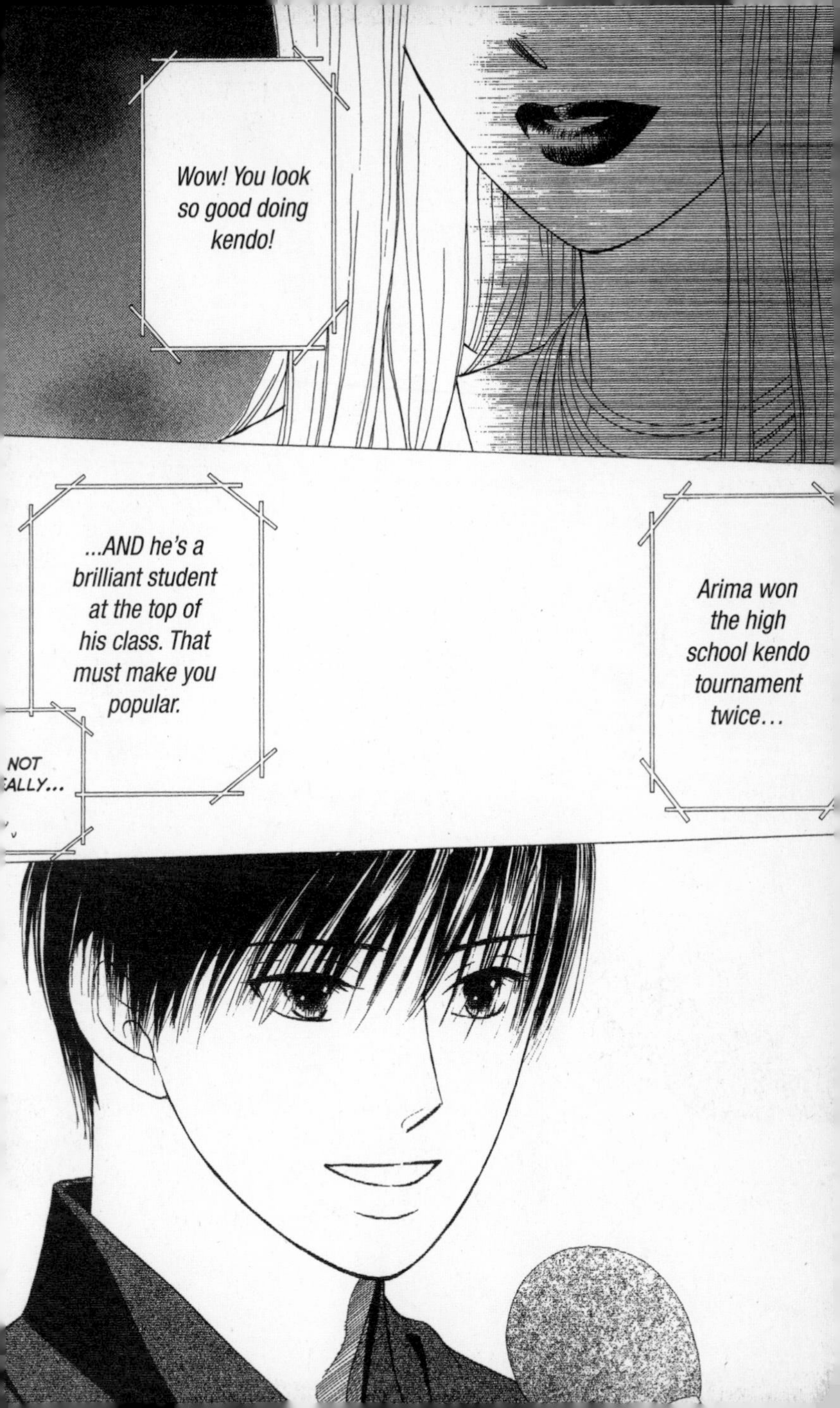
Wow! You look so good doing kendo!
Arima won the high school kendo tournament twice…
...AND he's a brilliant student at the top of his class. That must make you popular.
NOT
ALLY...

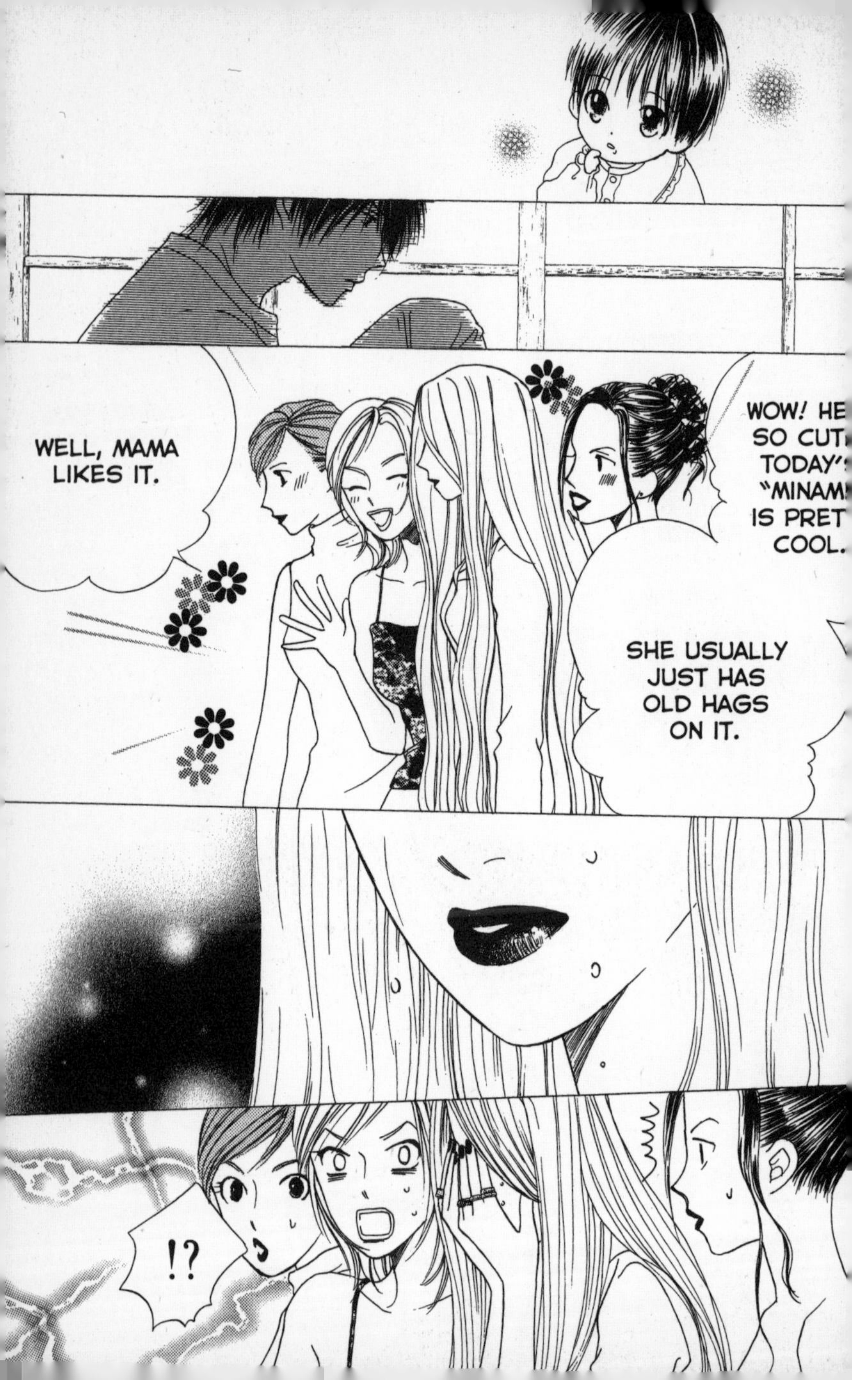
WOW! HE SO CUT TODAY" "MINAM IS PRET COOL.
SHE USUALLY JUST HAS OLD HAGS ON IT.
WELL, MAMA LIKES IT.
!?

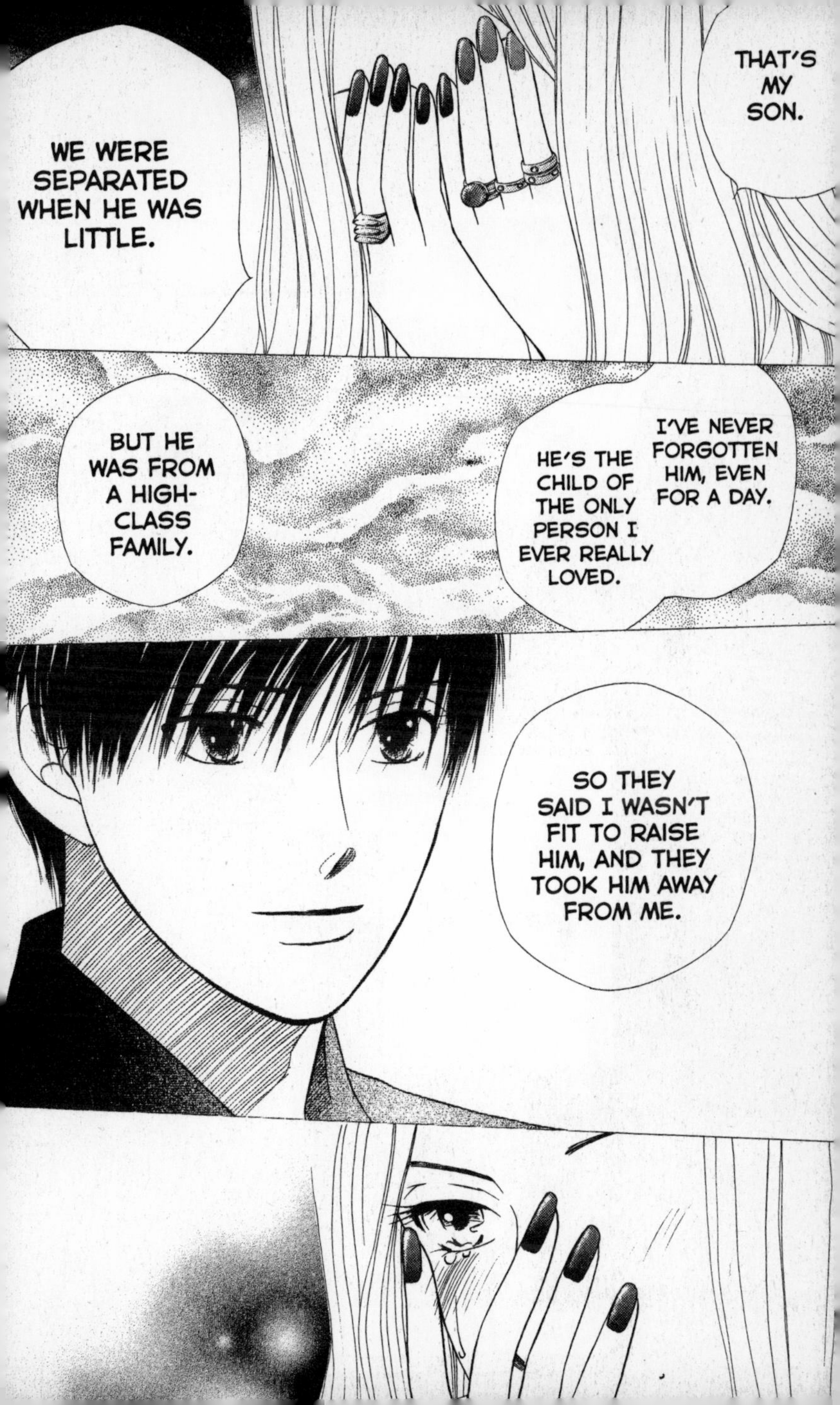
THAT'S MY SON.
WE WERE SEPARATED WHEN HE WAS LITTLE.
I'VE NEVER FORGOTTEN HIM, EVEN FOR A DAY.
HE'S THE CHILD OF THE ONLY PERSON I EVER REALLY LOVED.
BUT HE WAS FROM A HIGH-CLASS FAMILY.
SO THEY SAID I WASN'T FIT TO RAISE HIM, AND THEY TOOK HIM AWAY FROM ME.

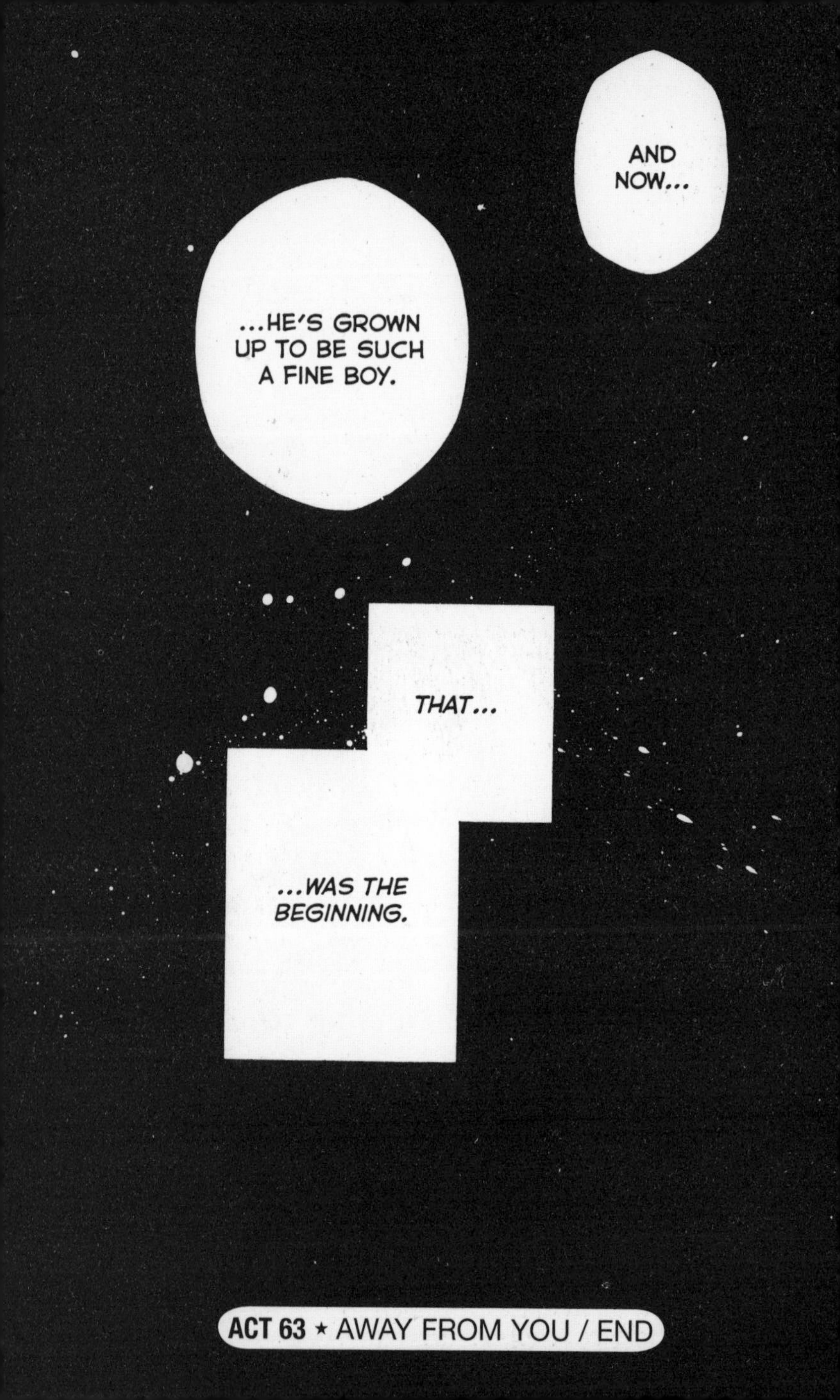
AND NOW...
...HE'S GROWN UP TO BE SUCH A FINE BOY.
THAT...
...WAS THE BEGINNING.
ACT 63 ★ AWAY FROM YOU / END

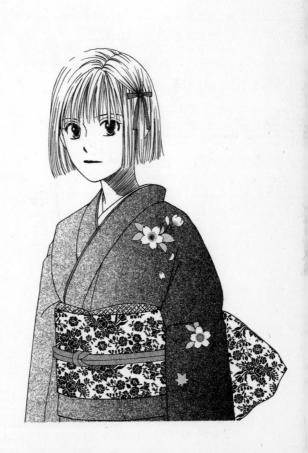

Tsuda Diary

Of all the children's literature I've read lately, Hiroshi Saito's "Story of the White Fox" was one of the best! That smart fox Shirakomaru is SO cute! And it's wonderful how he gets along so well with his master. For some reason, I couldn't help but think of the anime "Night on the Galaxy Express," and I fell in love with it. At any rate, as practice, I tried drawing it, but it turned out completely wrong. But I have such a great image in my head... sob...After Volume 11, I got letters telling me that children's literature is a treasure trove of good stories. So I'll be sure to keep my eye out for more!

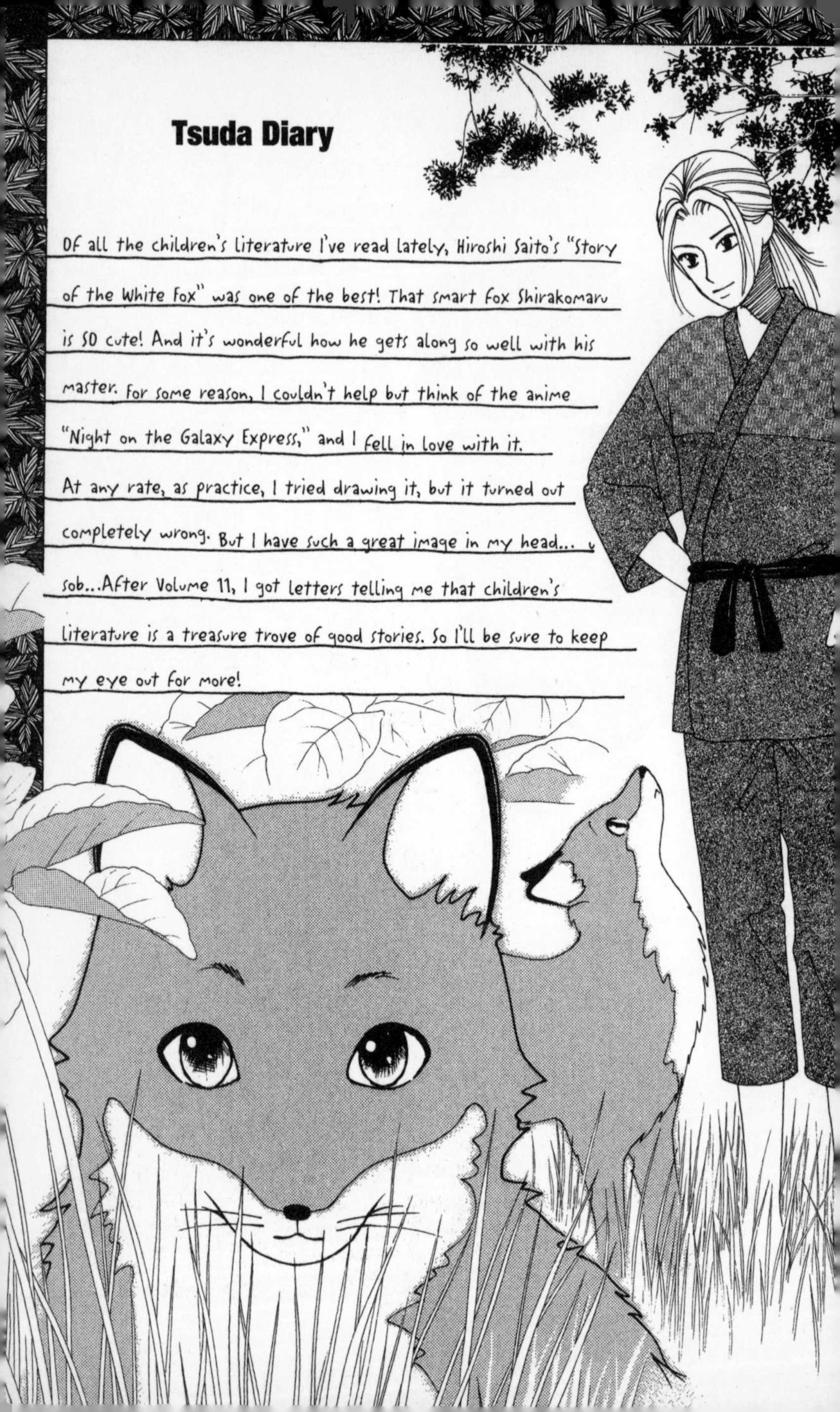

源氏物語 THE TALE OF GENJI

ve been studying a lot lately. I read "The Tale of Genji." The more interesting he book is to you, the more you'll understand it. I also read "The life of ady Rokujo in the Tale of Genji" and "Seiko Tanabe's translation of the Tale of Genji." And I ended up getting really into the story. Of course, to a lot of people who don't know or understand the details, it seems like a simple story about a playboy, which is REALLY unfortunate. The last half is so deep, it's amazing to think it was written so long ago.

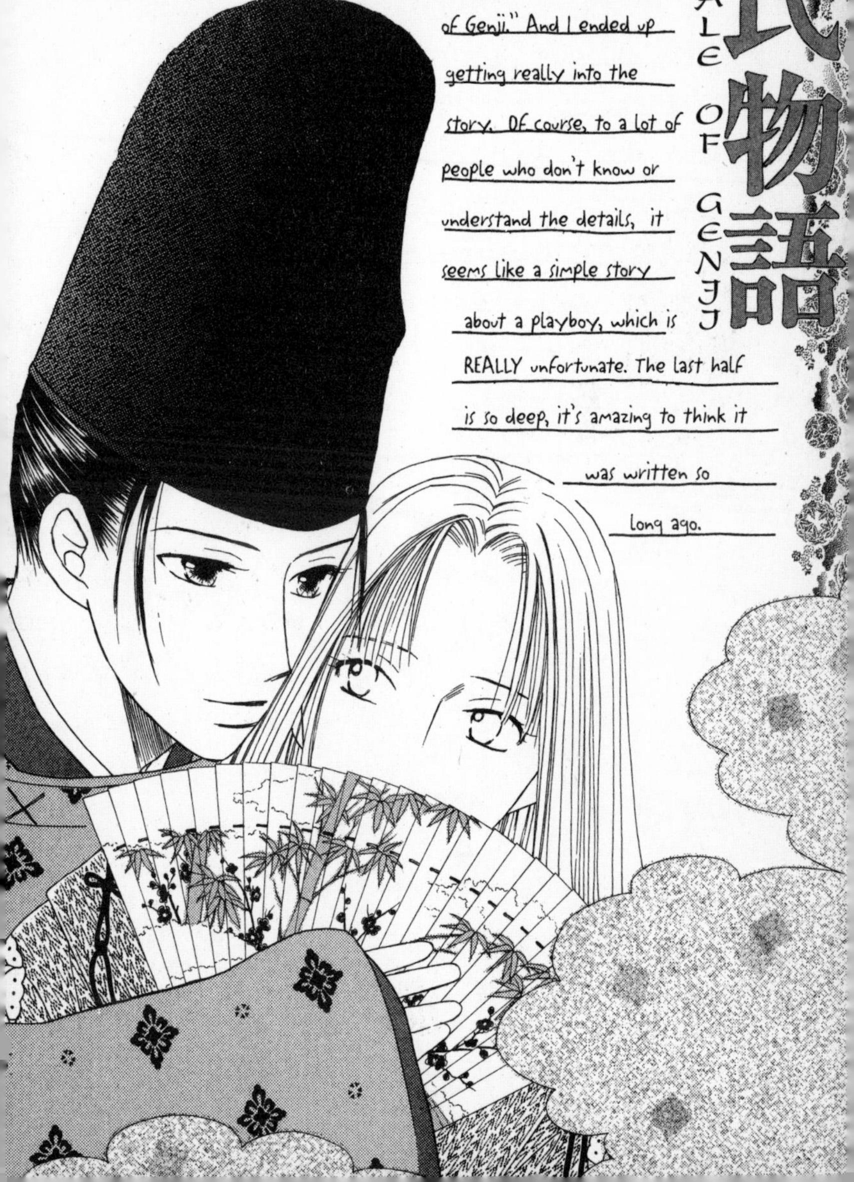

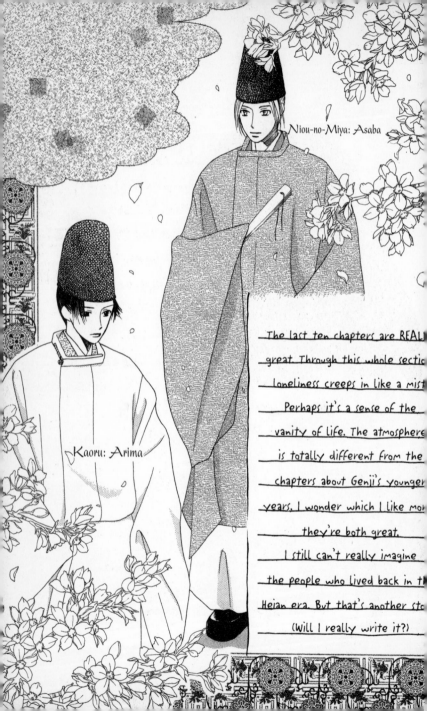

Niou-no-Miya: Asaba

Kaoru: Arima

The last ten chapters are REAL[
great. Through this whole sectic
loneliness creeps in like a mist
   Perhaps it's a sense of the
   vanity of life. The atmosphere
   is totally different from the
   chapters about Genji's younger
years. I wonder which I like mor
       they're both great.
    I still can't really imagine
   the people who lived back in t[
   Heian era. But that's another sto
      (Will I really write it?)

 THANKS

Editor   S. Taneoka

Staff   N. Shimizu
            R. Ogawa
            Y. Etō
            R. Takahashi

     AND K. U
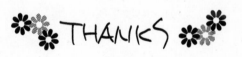

coming soon

kare kano

his and her circumstances

volume fourteen

Ever since Arima appeared on TV, everyone has taken notice. But Arima never counted on his birth mother taking notice! Arima wonders why, after so long, she has finally decided to come back into his life. Slowly, the inner demons of his past begin to surface, and Arima begins to learn just how much he is like his real mother. Will Arima follow his mother down the path of darkness…or will Yukino save him?

SHOP TOKYOPOP
WE NEVER CLOSE!

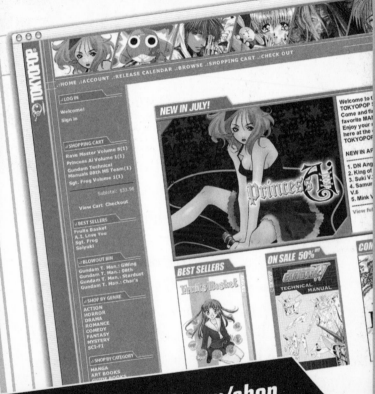

www.TOKYOPOP.com/shop

Manga · Cine-Manga · Novels

- Look for special offers!
- Pre-order upcoming releases!
- Complete your collections!

She crash-landed on earth...

now she
has a
thing or
two to
get off
her chest.

Dear S

ディアーズ

The hit series that inspired the anime and video games!

www.TOKYOPOP.com / dears

T
TEEN
AGE 13+

www.TOKYOPOP.com

© Sumiko Amakawa. ©2004 TOKYOPOP Inc. All Rights Reser

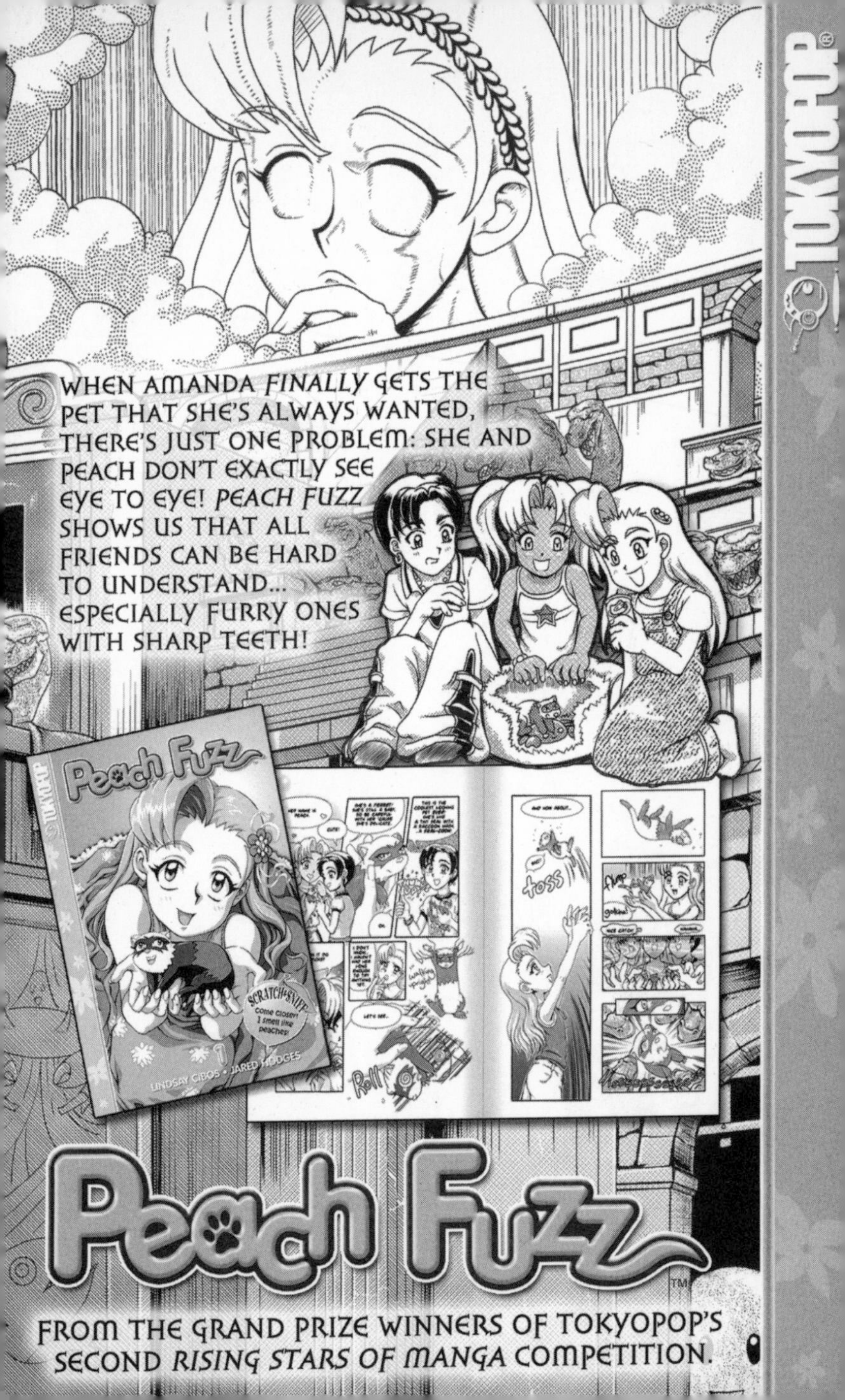
TOKYOPOP
WHEN AMANDA FINALLY GETS THE PET THAT SHE'S ALWAYS WANTED, THERE'S JUST ONE PROBLEM: SHE AND PEACH DON'T EXACTLY SEE EYE TO EYE! PEACH FUZZ SHOWS US THAT ALL FRIENDS CAN BE HARD TO UNDERSTAND... ESPECIALLY FURRY ONES WITH SHARP TEETH!
Peach Fuzz
SCRATCH'N SNIFF Come closer! I smell like peaches!
1
LINDSAY CIBOS • JARED HODGES
toss
Roll
Peach Fuzz™
FROM THE GRAND PRIZE WINNERS OF TOKYOPOP'S SECOND RISING STARS OF MANGA COMPETITION.

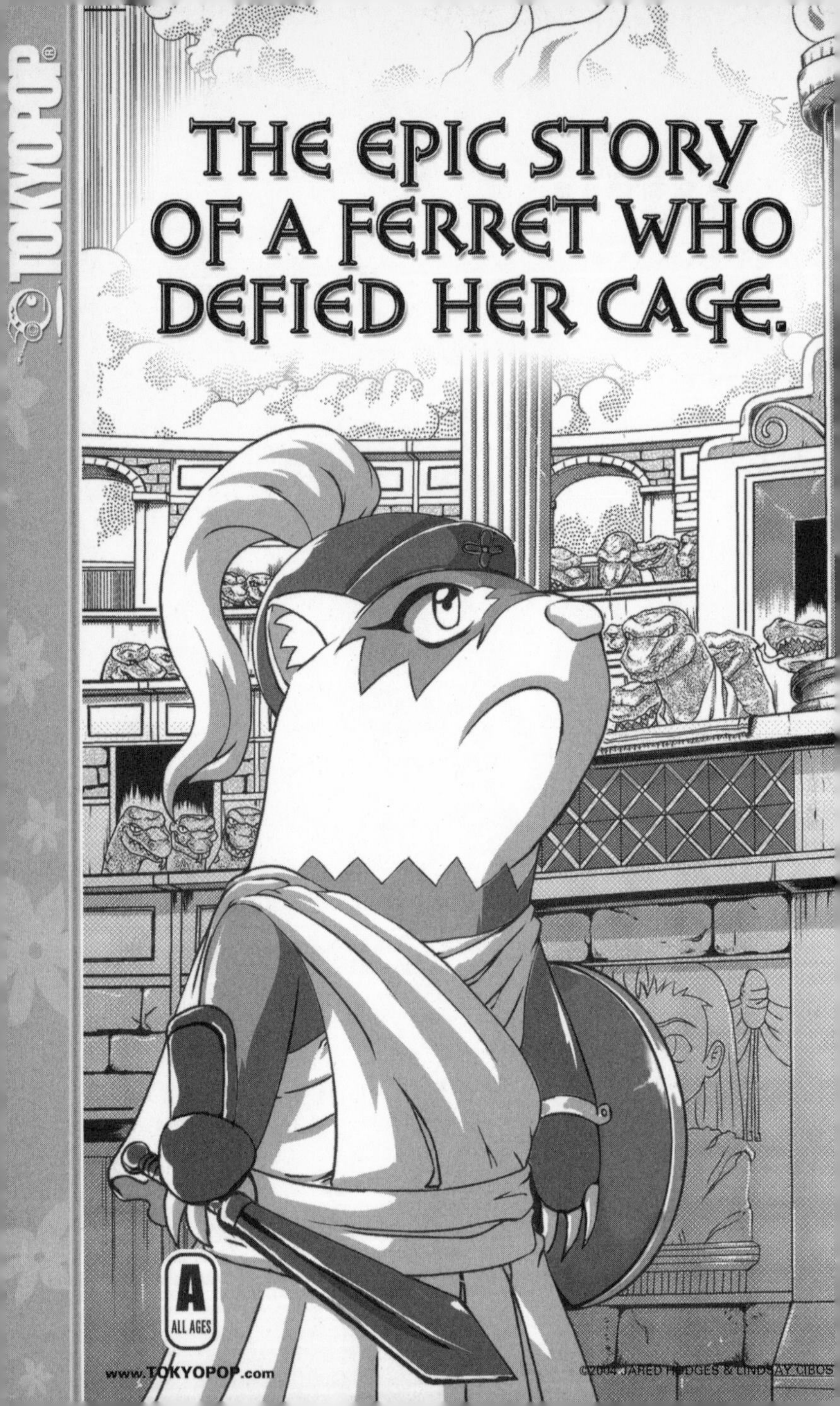

TOKYOPOP®
THE EPIC STORY OF A FERRET WHO DEFIED HER CAGE.
A
ALL AGES
www.TOKYOPOP.com
©2004 JARED HODGES & LINDSAY CIBOS

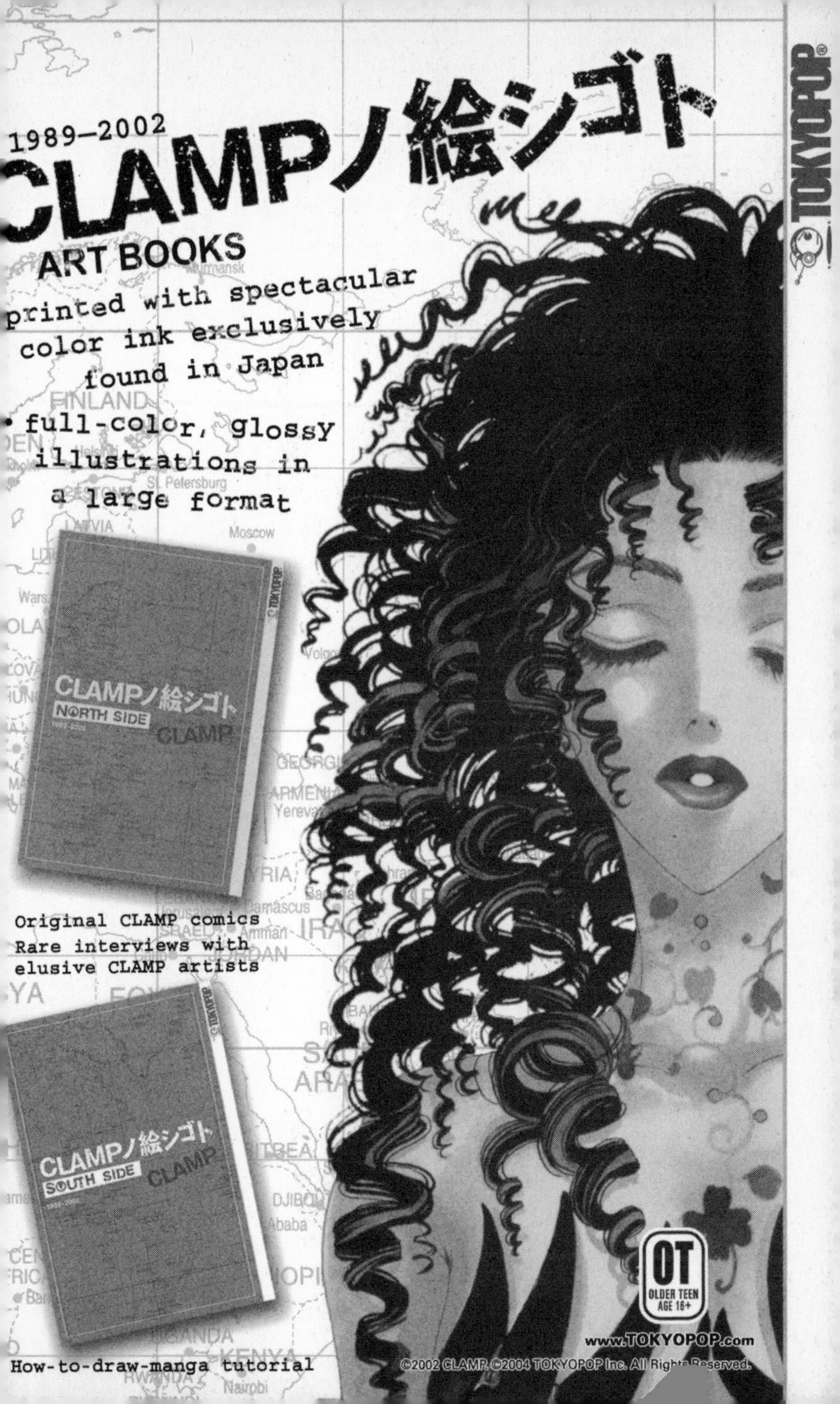
1989–2002
CLAMPノ絵シゴト
ART BOOKS
printed with spectacular color ink exclusively found in Japan
• full-color, glossy illustrations in a large format
CLAMPノ絵シゴト
NORTH SIDE
CLAMP
Original CLAMP comics
Rare interviews with elusive CLAMP artists
CLAMPノ絵シゴト
SOUTH SIDE
CLAMP
How-to-draw-manga tutorial
TOKYOPOP
OT
OLDER TEEN
AGE 16+
www.TOKYOPOP.com
©2002 CLAMP. ©2004 TOKYOPOP Inc. All Rights Reserved.

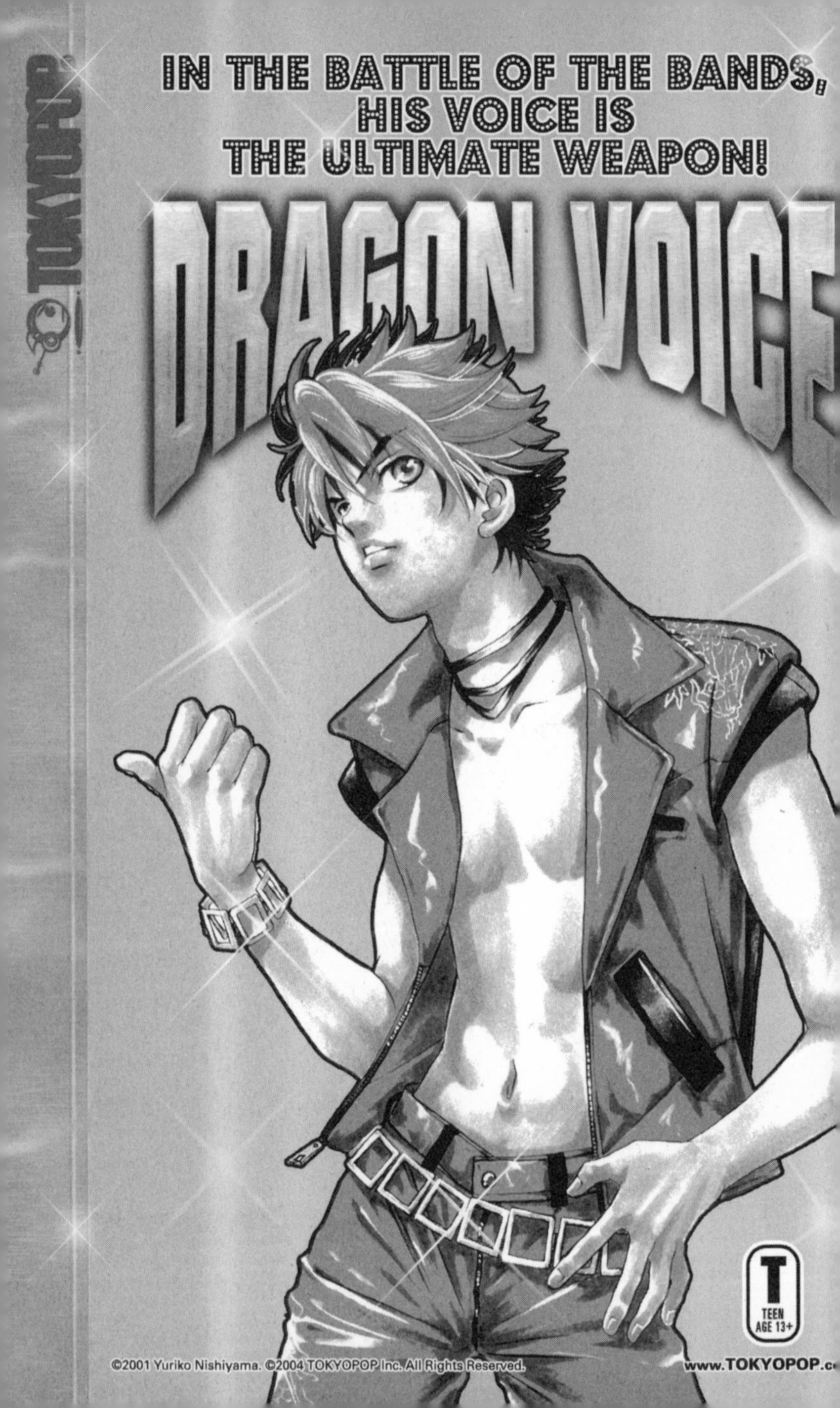
TOKYOPOP
IN THE BATTLE OF THE BANDS,
HIS VOICE IS
THE ULTIMATE WEAPON!
DRAGON VOICE
T
TEEN
AGE 13+
©2001 Yuriko Nishiyama. ©2004 TOKYOPOP Inc. All Rights Reserved.
www.TOKYOPOP.c

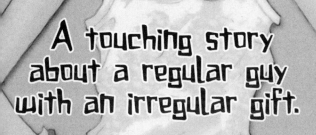

A touching story
about a regular guy
with an irregular gift.

HANDS OFF!

TM

T
TEEN
AGE 13+

Kasane Katsumoto. ©2004 TOKYOPOP Inc. All Rights Reserved.

www.TOKYOPOP.com

"I can honestly say that the da I got the call was the best day of my life."

—Nathan Maurer, Grand Prize winner, *Rising Stars of Manga* volum Maurer's series *Atomic King Daidogan* will be published by TOKYOPOP in 20

"Want to be a manga artist? No one makes it easier than TOKYOPC
—*WIZARD*

Enter TOKYOPOP's

Competition

★*Cash prizes! Get published!*★

"Thanks to TOKYOPOP for reading between the lir
—Felipe Smith, Second Place winner, *Rising Stars of Manga* volume 3.
Smith's series *MBQ* will be published by TOKYOPOP in Summer 2005.

"TOKYOPOP is also stepping up its efforts to develop American manga creators."—*Publishers Weekly*

Don't miss out! For details, vis
www.TOKYOPOP.com/rso

© TOKYOPOP Inc. All Rights Reserved.

ALSO AVAILABLE FROM ⦿TOKYOPOP®

PLANETES
PRESIDENT DAD
PRIEST
PRINCESS AI
PSYCHIC ACADEMY
QUEEN'S KNIGHT, THE
RAGNAROK
RAVE MASTER
REALITY CHECK
REBIRTH
REBOUND
REMOTE
RISING STARS OF MANGA™, THE
SABER MARIONETTE J
SAILOR MOON
SAINT TAIL
SAIYUKI
SAMURAI DEEPER KYO
SAMURAI GIRL™ REAL BOUT HIGH SCHOOL
SCRYED
SEIKAI TRILOGY, THE
SGT. FROG
SHAOLIN SISTERS
SHIRAHIME-SYO: SNOW GODDESS TALES
SHUTTERBOX
SKULL MAN, THE
SNOW DROP
SORCERER HUNTERS
SOUL TO SEOUL
STONE
SUIKODEN III
SUKI
TAROT CAFÉ, THE
THREADS OF TIME
TOKYO BABYLON
TOKYO MEW MEW
TOKYO TRIBES
TRAMPS LIKE US
UNDER THE GLASS MOON
VAMPIRE GAME
VISION OF ESCAFLOWNE, THE
WARCRAFT
WARRIORS OF TAO
WILD ACT
WISH
WORLD OF HARTZ
X-DAY
ZODIAC P.I.

NOVELS

CLAMP SCHOOL PARANORMAL INVESTIGATORS
SAILOR MOON
SLAYERS

ART BOOKS

ART OF CARDCAPTOR SAKURA
ART OF MAGIC KNIGHT RAYEARTH, THE
PEACH: MIWA UEDA ILLUSTRATIONS
CLAMP NORTH SIDE
CLAMP SOUTH SIDE

ANIME GUIDES

COWBOY BEBOP
GUNDAM TECHNICAL MANUALS
SAILOR MOON SCOUT GUIDES

TOKYOPOP KIDS

STRAY SHEEP

CINE-MANGA®

ALADDIN
CARDCAPTORS
DUEL MASTERS
FAIRLY ODDPARENTS, THE
FAMILY GUY
FINDING NEMO
G.I. JOE SPY TROOPS
GREATEST STARS OF THE NBA
JACKIE CHAN ADVENTURES
JIMMY NEUTRON: BOY GENIUS, THE ADVENTURES OF
KIM POSSIBLE
LILO & STITCH: THE SERIES
LIZZIE MCGUIRE
LIZZIE MCGUIRE MOVIE, THE
MALCOLM IN THE MIDDLE
POWER RANGERS: DINO THUNDER
POWER RANGERS: NINJA STORM
PRINCESS DIARIES 2, THE
RAVE MASTER
SHREK 2
SIMPLE LIFE, THE
SPONGEBOB SQUAREPANTS
SPY KIDS 2
SPY KIDS 3-D: GAME OVER
TEENAGE MUTANT NINJA TURTLES
THAT'S SO RAVEN
TOTALLY SPIES
TRANSFORMERS: ARMADA
TRANSFORMERS: ENERGON

You want it? We got it!
A full range of TOKYOPOP
products are available now at:
www.TOKYOPOP.com/shop

10.19.04T

ALSO AVAILABLE FROM TOKYOPOP®

MANGA

.HACK//LEGEND OF THE TWILIGHT
@LARGE
ABENOBASHI: MAGICAL SHOPPING ARCADE
A.I. LOVE YOU
AI YORI AOSHI
ALICHINO
ANGELIC LAYER
ARM OF KANNON
BABY BIRTH
BATTLE ROYALE
BATTLE VIXENS
BOYS BE...
BRAIN POWERED
BRIGADOON
B'TX
CANDIDATE FOR GODDESS, THE
CARDCAPTOR SAKURA
CARDCAPTOR SAKURA - MASTER OF THE CLOW
CHOBITS
CHRONICLES OF THE CURSED SWORD
CLAMP SCHOOL DETECTIVES
CLOVER
COMIC PARTY
CONFIDENTIAL CONFESSIONS
CORRECTOR YUI
COWBOY BEBOP
COWBOY BEBOP: SHOOTING STAR
CRAZY LOVE STORY
CRESCENT MOON
CROSS
CULDCEPT
CYBORG 009
D•N•ANGEL
DEARS
DEMON DIARY
DEMON ORORON, THE
DEUS VITAE
DIABOLO
DIGIMON
DIGIMON TAMERS
DIGIMON ZERO TWO
DOLL
DRAGON HUNTER
DRAGON KNIGHTS
DRAGON VOICE
DREAM SAGA
DUKLYON: CLAMP SCHOOL DEFENDERS
EERIE QUEERIE!
ERICA SAKURAZAWA: COLLECTED WORKS
ET CETERA
ETERNITY
EVIL'S RETURN
FAERIES' LANDING
FAKE
FLCL
FLOWER OF THE DEEP SLEEP
FORBIDDEN DANCE
FRUITS BASKET
G GUNDAM
GATEKEEPERS
GETBACKERS

GIRL GOT GAME
GRAVITATION
GTO
GUNDAM SEED ASTRAY
GUNDAM SEED ASTRAY R
GUNDAM WING
GUNDAM WING: BATTLEFIELD OF PACIFISTS
GUNDAM WING: ENDLESS WALTZ
GUNDAM WING: THE LAST OUTPOST (G-UNIT)
HANDS OFF!
HAPPY MANIA
HARLEM BEAT
HYPER POLICE
HYPER RUNE
I.N.V.U.
IMMORTAL RAIN
INITIAL D
INSTANT TEEN: JUST ADD NUTS
ISLAND
JING: KING OF BANDITS
JING: KING OF BANDITS - TWILIGHT TALES
JULINE
KARE KANO
KILL ME, KISS ME
KINDAICHI CASE FILES, THE
KING OF HELL
KODOCHA: SANA'S STAGE
LAGOON ENGINE
LAMENT OF THE LAMB
LEGAL DRUG
LEGEND OF CHUN HYANG, THE
LES BIJOUX
LILING-PO
LOVE HINA
LOVE OR MONEY
LUPIN III
LUPIN III: WORLD'S MOST WANTED
MAGIC KNIGHT RAYEARTH I
MAGIC KNIGHT RAYEARTH II
MAHOROMATIC: AUTOMATIC MAIDEN
MAN OF MANY FACES
MARMALADE BOY
MARS
MARS: HORSE WITH NO NAME
MINK
MIRACLE GIRLS
MIYUKI-CHAN IN WONDERLAND
MODEL
MOURYOU KIDEN: LEGEND OF THE NYMPH
NECK AND NECK
ONE
ONE I LOVE, THE
PARADISE KISS
PARASYTE
PASSION FRUIT
PEACH FUZZ
PEACH GIRL
PEACH GIRL: CHANGE OF HEART
PET SHOP OF HORRORS
PHD: PHANTASY DEGREE
PITA-TEN
PLANET BLOOD
PLANET LADDER

S0-BHX-323

STOP!

This is the back of the book.
You wouldn't want to spoil a great ending!

This book is printed "manga-style," in the authentic Japanese right-to-left format. Since none of the artwork has been flipped or altered, readers get to experience the story just as the creator intended. You've been asking for it, so TOKYOPOP® delivered: authentic, hot-off-the-press, and far more fun!

DIRECTIONS

If this is your first time reading manga-style, here's a quick guide to help you understand how it works.

It's easy... just start in the top right panel and follow the numbers. Have fun, and look for more 100% authentic manga from TOKYOPOP®!